Allez 2

Teacher Handbook

Melissa Weir

With answers, transcripts
and additional material by
Corinne Dzuilka-Heywood
Yvonne Kennedy

OXFORD
UNIVERSITY PRESS

Great Clarendon Street, Oxford, OX2 6DP, United Kingdom

Oxford University Press is a department of the University of Oxford.
It furthers the University's objective of excellence in research,
scholarship, and education by publishing worldwide. Oxford is a
registered trade mark of Oxford University Press in the UK and in
certain other countries

© Oxford University Press 2015

The moral rights of the authors have been asserted

First published in 2015

All rights reserved. No part of this publication may be reproduced,
stored in a retrieval system, or transmitted, in any form or by any
means, without the prior permission in writing of Oxford University
Press, or as expressly permitted by law, by licence or under terms
agreed with the appropriate reprographics rights organization.
Enquiries concerning reproduction outside the scope of the above
should be sent to the Rights Department, Oxford University Press,
at the address above.

You must not circulate this work in any other form and you must
impose this same condition on any acquirer

British Library Cataloguing in Publication Data
Data available

978-0-19-839507-2

3 5 7 9 10 8 6 4 2

Paper used in the production of this book is a natural, recyclable
product made from wood grown in sustainable forests.
The manufacturing process conforms to the environmental
regulations of the country of origin.

Printed in Great Britain by Bell and Bain Ltd, Glasgow

Acknowledgements
The authors and publisher would like to thank the following people
for their help and advice: Pat Dunn (Student Book editor); Geneviève
Talon (author of the Lire, Vidéo and Grammaire pages); Karine Couly
(language consultant); Liz Black (author of plenaries in Planner
sections), Vee Harris and Kate Scappaticci (authors of 'Language
learning strategies', page 9); Katie Smith and Christoph Largen
(course consultants).

Cover illustration by: Claire Rollet

Although we have made every effort to trace and contact all
copyright holders before publication this has not been possible in all
cases. If notified, the publisher will rectify any errors or omissions at
the earliest opportunity.

Links to third party websites are provided by Oxford in good faith
and for information only. Oxford disclaims any responsibility for
the materials contained in any third party website referenced in
this work.

Contents

Summary of Unit Contents	4	Kerboodle	10
Introduction	6	Lessons, Resources and Assessment	10
The course	6	Kerboodle Book	13
The components of *Allez 2*	6	Teaching notes for *Allez 2*	
Student Book	6	Unit 1 C'est quoi, la France?	14
Teacher Handbook	6	Unit 2 Le monde des médias	30
Audio CDs	7	Unit 3 Accro à la technologie?	50
Worksheets	7	Unit 4 Être ado, c'est quoi?	69
Grammar and Skills Workbook	7	Unit 5 En pleine forme!	87
Kerboodle	7	Unit 6 Rendez-vous	106
Video	7	Unit 7 Autour du monde	126
Teaching with *Allez*	7	Unit 8 Chez moi, ça veut dire quoi?	145
Course progression	7	Unit 9 Un métier, un rêve!	165
Personal, Learning and Thinking Skills (PLTS)	8	Grammar and Skills Workbook Answers	186
Differentiation	8		
Language learning strategies	8		
Use of plenaries	8		
Spontaneous speech	9		
The National Curriculum from 2014	9		

Symbols used in this Teacher Handbook:

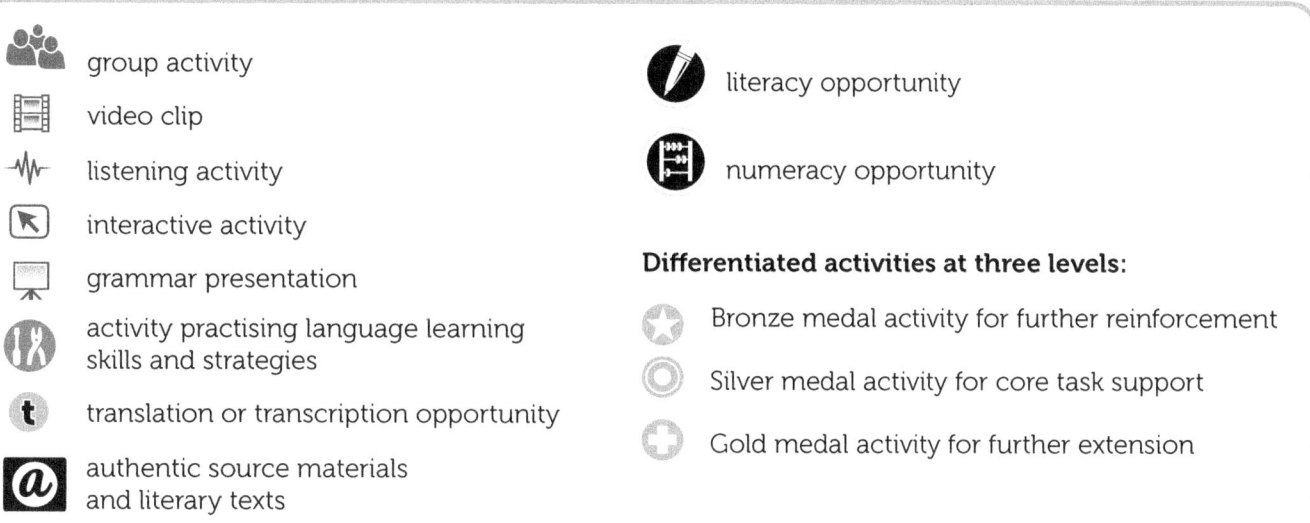

- group activity
- video clip
- listening activity
- interactive activity
- grammar presentation
- activity practising language learning skills and strategies
- translation or transcription opportunity
- authentic source materials and literary texts
- literacy opportunity
- numeracy opportunity

Differentiated activities at three levels:
- Bronze medal activity for further reinforcement
- Silver medal activity for core task support
- Gold medal activity for further extension

Summary of Unit Contents

Unit	Contexts and objectives	Grammar	Strategies and skills	Pronunciation	Culture
Unit 1 C'est quoi, la France?	• Compare France and Britain • Describe a country • Talk about French people • Talk about transport and new technology • Discuss Francophone cartoon characters	• Present tense • Using *on* • Comparatives and superlatives • Perfect tense (revision) • Asking questions • Use *qui* to link sentences	• Motivation strategies • Agree and disagree • Develop geographical knowledge • Develop cultural awareness • Say dates • Intonation when asking questions • Extend sentences • Understand longer texts	• Intonation	• Aspects of life in France • Rivers and mountains of French-speaking countries • Famous French people • Technology and transport in France • French cartoon characters
Unit 2 Le monde des médias	• Talk about types of television programmes • Talk about musical genres and express detailed opinions of music • Talk about film genres and review a film • Talk about reading preferences • Understand and use the language of advertising	• Direct object pronouns: *le, la, les* • *Faire* + infinitive and *rendre* + adjective • *Ce que* • Opinions using the perfect and imperfect tenses • 'Verb + infinitive' structures	• Reading strategies • Listening and writing strategies • Translation strategies • Identify, express and justify opinions • Apply knowledge of phonics • Recognise persuasive and informative language	• *qu*	• TV, music, films and books from French-speaking countries • French poetry
Unit 3 Accro à la technologie?	• Describe old and new technology • Talk about using technology for leisure activities • Identify the potential dangers of social networking sites • Talk about the pros and cons of new technologies • Talk about favourite technology and gadgets	• Adjectives (agreement and position) • Verb + preposition + infinitive • Impersonal structures • Structure an argument • *À* + definite article	• Speaking strategies • Memorisation strategies • Use reading strategies to work out meaning • Use connectives to justify opinions • Extend sentences • Spoken and written register • Debate a point	• *eu*	• Experiences and perspectives of French teenager's
Unit 4 Être ado, c'est quoi?	• Discuss relationships with parents • Talk about pocket money and what you do to help at home • Talk about the pressures faced by teenagers and understand advice • Discuss what life used to be like for teenagers • Describe the life of homeless children	• Pronouns *me, te* and *se* in positive and negative sentences • Modal verbs: *devoir, pouvoir* and *vouloir* • *Tu* form of the imperative • Imperfect tense • Present and imperfect tenses (revision)	• Listening strategies • Cultural awareness strategies • Express opinions with confidence • Agree and disagree • Ask and answer questions • Understand longer reading passages	• Silent verb endings	• Experiences, perspectives and concerns of French teenagers
Unit 5 En pleine forme!	• Talk about healthy eating • Discuss healthy lifestyles • Talk about how diet affects health • Talk about resolutions to be healthier • Talk about what life will be like in the future	• Impersonal structures • The pronoun *en* • Perfect tense (revision) • Expressions of quantity • Future tense	• Evaluate your performance • Strategies for checking written work • Dictionary skills • Use context to work out meaning • Build confidence in asking questions • Use connectives to extend sentences • Translate into French	• The French *r* sound	• French food and drink

Unit	Contexts and objectives	Grammar	Strategies and skills	Pronunciation	Culture
Unit 6 **Rendez-vous**	• Organise a party • Suggest activities and make excuses • Talk about a festival or special event that you've been to • Communicate with people in formal situations • Talk about traditions and festivals	• Near future • Conditional: *on pourrait* + infinitive • Perfect tense with *être* • Imperfect tense • *Vous* form (present tense) • Use past and present tenses	• Strategies to improve speaking • Cultural awareness strategies • Evaluate your own and others' performance • Conversation skills • Formal and informal language	• The perfect tense and the imperfect	• French festivals, celebrations and special events
Unit 7 **Autour du monde**	• Talk about how you travel and compare means of transport • Buy tickets and talk about travel plans • Plan a holiday • Describe a past holiday • Talk about transport in books and films	• *Ne …jamais/ni … ni …* • Present tense of *choisir* and *partir* • Correct tenses with *si* and *quand* • Perfect and imperfect tenses • Use different tenses	• Super Strategies • Grammar memorisation strategies • Use comparisons to develop writing and speaking • 24-hour clock • Translation skills • Understand more complex reading texts	• *u* and *ou*	• French transport preferences • Holiday destinations • 24-hour clock • French train tickets • French books and films
Unit 8 **Chez moi, ça veut dire quoi?**	• Describe what type of home you live in • Describe rooms in a house • Describe a bedroom, items in it and their location • Describe the type of home you would like to have • Describe places in detail and express how you feel about them	• *Y* • *Depuis* + present tense • Regular *-re* verbs in the present tense • Prepositions • *Si* clauses + imperfect tense and conditional	• Super Strategies • Translation strategies • Memorisation strategies • Recognise and compare writing styles • Extend vocabulary • Debate a point • Develop knowledge of connectives to extend sentences	• *i* and *y*	• Different types of homes in French-speaking countries around the world • Types of homes and areas to live in France • French artists and paintings
Unit 9 **Un métier, un rêve!**	• Talk about jobs and the qualities needed for certain jobs • Talk about ideal jobs • Talk about ambitions • Talk about part-time jobs • Talk about success and failure	• Masculine and feminine forms of jobs • Imperfect tense and the conditional (revision) • Use different tenses together • *Si* clauses + imperfect tense and conditional (revision) • *Quand* with different tenses	• Super Strategies • Translation strategies • Motivation strategies • Ask and answer questions • Improve speaking and writing • Combine tenses to improve speaking and writing	• Tongue-twisters	• French charitable organisations

Introduction

The course

Welcome to **Allez 2**.

Inspire all your students with **Allez**, whatever their starting point at Key Stage 3. **Allez** is an exciting two-part French course offering fresh, engaging material to motivate every learner, and is fully tailored to the 2014 Programme of Study.

Allez offers:

- full flexibility with a clear route through for students following a two- or three-year course
- an emphasis on independent learning and progression for all, giving students the best chance of success
- graded activities in the Student Book and a wealth of differentiated interactive resources, including Record and Playback activities to boost confidence in speaking
- inspiring video clips, making the language relevant to students and providing a real insight into life in the French-speaking world
- clear structure and layout
- a full suite of accompanying resources, including Grammar and Skills Workbooks, innovative ideas for starters and plenaries, editable schemes of work and much more
- reliable and effective assessment resources
- a comprehensive transition module.

The components of Allez 2

Student Book

The 176-page Student Book consists of nine main units. Two clear routes through the book are suggested: one for students following a two-year course, and one for students following a three-year course. Depending on the route followed, one unit represents either four or six weeks' work.

The Student Book contains the following sections:

Units 1–9

There are nine 18-page units set in different contexts. Each unit has been planned to be interesting and motivating, as well as to provide a coherent and systematic approach to language development in terms of grammar, pronunciation, and study skills. An outline of the content of each unit is given on pages 4–5 of this Handbook.

Each unit consists of:

- four core spreads, offering activities in all four skills, language learning tips and grammar explanations
- a fifth spread offering more in-depth coverage of the topic areas, specifically intended for students following a three-year Key Stage 3
- a *Labo-langue* spread, divided into three sections: grammar (focusing on the key grammar points from the core spreads), language strategies and pronunciation
- two pages of reinforcement and extension material, one for lower- and one for higher-ability students (*Extra Star* and *Extra Plus*) – these are ideal for independent work, either during lesson time or for homework
- a page of extra reading material (*Lire*) focusing on aspects of lifestyle and culture in the French-speaking world, designed to encourage independent reading and help students develop reading strategies
- a page of activities focusing on the video drama (*Vidéo*)
- a *Test* page, which revises the language and structures of the unit and can also be used as a quick formative test of all four skills
- a list of key language from the unit (*Vocabulaire*), which students can use as a reference tool or as an aid to learning
- an end-of-unit grammar and skills checklist (*I can ...*), enabling students to review what they've learnt and reflect on areas for improvement.

Grammaire

The key grammar points are taught in each unit and a detailed grammar reference with verb tables is provided at the back of the Student Book. Further grammar practice is provided in the Grammar and Skills Workbook, on the Worksheets and via the grammar presentations on Kerboodle.

Glossaire

A French–English glossary contains the words in the Student Book for students' reference.

Teacher Handbook

Each unit contains the following detailed teaching notes:

- a unit overview grid, providing a summary of the unit: contexts and objectives, grammar, strategies and skills (including pronunciation), key language, range of AT levels for each spread
- a week-by-week overview grid, providing details of the two- and three-year routes through each unit
- a Planner section for each core teaching spread for ease of lesson planning, including cross-references to other course components, opportunities to develop Personal, Learning and Thinking Skills (PLTS), and suggestions for starter, plenary and homework/self-study activities
- detailed notes on all the Student Book material, including answers to all activities
- transcripts for all listening material and video clips.

Answers for the Grammar and Skills Workbook activities are provided at the back of the Teacher Handbook.

Audio CDs

The Audio CD Pack provides listening material to accompany the Student Book. Sound files for the Student Book material, including additional audio for the *Vocabulaire* pages, are also available on Kerboodle and can be launched from the Kerboodle Book.

Worksheet and assessment audio is provided on Kerboodle.

All listening material was recorded by native French speakers.

Worksheets

The Worksheets provide opportunities for further practice and extension of the language of the Student Book units. All the Worksheets, together with answers and transcripts, are provided on Kerboodle. There are nine Worksheets per unit, as follows:

1 *Vocabulaire*: a list of key vocabulary from the unit, for reference or as an aid to learning
2 *Checklist*: an opportunity for students to review their progress and reflect on areas for improvement
3 *Écouter*: listening activities at *Star* and *Plus* level
4 *Parler*: speaking activities at *Star* and *Plus* level
5 *Lire*: reading activities at *Star* and *Plus* level
6 *Écrire*: writing activities at *Star* and *Plus* level
7 *Grammaire*: reinforcement of key grammar points from the unit, accessible to all levels
8 *Stratégies*: more detailed coverage of learning strategies from the unit, accessible to all levels
9 *Un jeu*: a game.

Grammar and Skills Workbook

The Grammar and Skills Workbook provides activities to reinforce grammar and learning skills.

Grammar is covered thematically. Each page of grammar activities suggests a cross-reference to a double-page spread in the Student Book where the activities may be used. However, these cross-references are just our suggestions and you may choose to use the grammar activities at other points, depending on the needs of your students.

The skills section of the Workbook provides further practice of language learning strategies and skills. There are two pages per unit, each focusing on at least one particular strategy or skill from the corresponding unit.

The final two pages of the Workbook focus on dictionary skills and pronunciation.

The Workbook is designed for students to write in, with rubrics in English throughout, so is ideal for homework and self-study. Answers to all Workbook activities are provided at the back of this Handbook.

Kerboodle

Allez is accompanied by Kerboodle, which consists of:

- a Kerboodle Book – a fully electronic version of the printed Student Book, with digital tools and audio/video hotspots to launch straight from the page for ease of use
- Kerboodle: Lessons, Resources and Assessment – with digital lessons, a suite of interactive activities and assessments, and paper-based worksheets and tests.

See pages 10–13 of this Handbook for further information.

Video

Video drama

A key feature of **Allez** is the video drama available on Kerboodle. The video drama:

- provides an insight into French culture and life in a French-speaking country
- introduces seven aspirational French-speaking teenagers, providing students with additional motivation for learning French
- provides examples of key language in use, making the language relevant to students and translating language learning from theory into practice.

There are nine episodes of the video drama, one per unit. Activities focusing on each video episode are provided on the *Vidéo* page in each unit of the Student Book. Although the level of language in the video drama can be challenging, it is made accessible for all via the activities and support on the *Vidéo* page. This allows students of all abilities to experience authentic material at a higher level.

The *Phrases clés* section at the end of each video episode is a useful tool for highlighting and clarifying key language. Captions are shown on-screen to facilitate oral practice.

A full transcript of each episode, together with an English synopsis, is provided in the corresponding teaching notes. A transcript is also available on-screen when the video is played.

Phonics video

Also provided on Kerboodle is a phonics video, enabling students to access key phonic sounds used in the course.

Teaching with *Allez*

Course progression

Allez is a two-part course, consisting of two Student Books of nine units each. It caters both for schools following a two-year Key Stage 3, and for those

Introduction

following a three-year Key Stage 3, by offering different 'routes' through each unit:

- For the three-year Key Stage 3, we suggest that you cover each unit in its entirety, including core spreads 1–4, the optional spread 5 (which provides more in-depth coverage of the unit themes) and spread 6 (grammar and skills), selecting additional material from the *Extra*, *Lire* and *Vidéo* pages as appropriate. This provides sufficient material for a half-term's teaching per unit. Following this route, two units are covered per term.
- For the two-year Key Stage 3, we suggest that your main focus should be core spreads 1–4 and spread 6 (grammar and skills), but that you may wish to use additional material selectively if time permits. On the core spreads themselves, certain activities may be used selectively too. Following this 'accelerated' route, three units are covered per term.

	Test	Suggested 2-year pathway	Suggested 3-year pathway
1st year	End of term 1	Book 1 Units 1–3	Book 1 Units 1–2
	End of term 2	Book 1 Units 4–6	Book 1 Units 3–4
	End of year 1	Book 1 Units 7–9	Book 1 Units 5–6
2nd year	End of term 1	Book 2 Units 1–3	Book 1 Units 7–8
	End of term 2	Book 2 Units 4–6	Book 1 Unit 9, Book 2 Unit 1
	End of year 2	Book 2 Units 7–9	Book 2 Units 2–3
3rd year	End of term 1		Book 2 Units 4–5
	End of term 2		Book 2 Units 6–7
	End of year 3		Book 2 Units 8–9

For an indication of which activities and spreads to cover each week according to the route you are following, see the week-by-week overview grid at the beginning of each unit in this Handbook.

Personal, Learning and Thinking Skills (PLTS)

A key aim of **Allez** is that students should be able to learn in a meaningful way, thinking flexibly, analysing language, problem-solving, justifying answers and making predictions based on previous knowledge. The Planner sections throughout this book show activities from each spread that promote the six PLTS: Independent enquirers; Creative thinkers; Reflective learners; Team workers; Self-managers; Effective participators.

Differentiation

With emphasis on independent learning and progression for all, **Allez** is designed to provide for learners of all abilities, offering graded activities in the Student Book together with differentiated interactive resources via Kerboodle. Key features include:

- Activities at three levels (Bronze – for further reinforcement, Silver – for core task support, and Gold – for further extension) on the core spreads of the Student Book provide clear differentiation and make it easier to manage different abilities.
- Differentiated plenary activities (again Bronze, Silver and Gold) are provided on spreads 1–5 of each unit of the Student Book, enabling all students to review what they've learnt and set their own targets for improvement.
- Each double-page spread of the Student Book is supported by differentiated interactive activities on Kerboodle and by differentiated (*Star* and *Plus*) activities on the Worksheets.
- The *Extra Star* and *Extra Plus* spread at the end of each unit in the Student Book provides additional differentiated material.
- The *Test* pages in the Student Book provide students with guidance on Bronze, Silver and Gold medal criteria in speaking and writing, encouraging students to take responsibility for their learning.
- Differentiated assessment via Kerboodle – formative and summative assessments are differentiated into *Star* and *Plus*.

Language learning strategies

The strategy boxes are designed to foster independent learning by teaching students how to manage their learning. We know from research that one of the reasons some students find language learning difficult and boring is because, unlike their more successful peers, they don't know how to tackle the tasks. For example, they may not realise that a text is much less daunting if you begin by looking out for cognates and familiar words and skip what you don't know.

In **Allez 2**, strategies are initially introduced through the four skill areas and in memorising vocabulary and checking written work, so that students see their relevance. These boxes help students reflect on the strategies they already use and then introduce new ones. Towards the end of the units, strategies are presented more generically as **Super Strategies**, as a form of revision, to encourage transfer, and to encourage independence.

Care is taken to provide plenty of practice in using all strategies so that students experience for themselves how they can make learning French easier, more effective and more fun.

Use of plenaries

The plenaries in **Allez** can be used for a range of purposes and at different times during the lesson, for example at a strategic moment in the teaching

sequence but more often at the end of the lesson to review the lesson objectives diagnostically. The flexibility of the course materials enables teachers to alter their planning based on how well students are progressing and grasping new grammar and vocabulary. Rapid and sustained progress can be made as students deepen and extend their learning in each unit.

The plenaries throughout the Student Book assess both individual and collective learning. Students need to actively process their new learning in French and should be given ample time during the plenary to reflect on comments and respond to feedback from both the teacher and their peers. Increasingly, as their confidence grows, students should be encouraged to use the target language to discuss their progress. Plenaries to facilitate student–teacher and student–student talk feature towards the end of the book.

There are additional plenaries in the Planner sections of this Teacher Handbook, as well as a bank of plenaries available on Kerboodle. They are designed to help students develop the habit of reflection, crystallise their thoughts on what has been learnt and how, and increase students' anticipation about the next stage of their learning.

Spontaneous speech

There are many opportunities throughout the course to encourage the development of spontaneous speech in and out of the classroom.

From the outset, students carry out simple conversations spontaneously, which helps to develop a good level of confidence and fluency. **Allez** sets out to greatly increase the use of the target language in lessons and meet Ofsted criteria in this area. Students listen regularly to young native speakers and communicate frequently in the target language. They are taught how to ask questions and respond to everyday requests. The video materials and other visual resources inspire spontaneous speech.

Planned use of the target language over time using the speaking activities and in plenaries ensures that all groups of learners become confident speakers with good intonation and pronunciation. Teaching that encourages 'exploitation' of core structures in the wealth of listening and reading material provided by **Allez** leads to fluent speakers who are also culturally aware.

The National Curriculum from 2014

Allez has been planned to ensure full coverage of the 2014 National Curriculum and Key Stage 3 Programme of Study for Modern Foreign Languages. In line with the higher profile given to the following key areas in the 2014 Curriculum, **Allez** offers:

- **Grammar**: a wealth of features and resources to support students' needs: see **The components of Allez 2** on pages 6–7 and **Kerboodle Resources** on page 11

- **Translation and transcription**: opportunities throughout (in the Student Book and other student materials, as well as via suggestions in the Teacher Handbook), enabling students to develop these skills progressively through the course
- **Authentic source materials and literary texts**: a range of inspiring authentic material of different types throughout, particularly via the *Lire* pages in the Student Book, the mini-readers with podcasts on Kerboodle, and the video drama
- **Literacy**: opportunities to help students develop key literacy skills across the curriculum
- **Numeracy**: opportunities to help students develop numeracy skills and recognise the relevance of mathematics in everyday contexts.

Activities practising literacy and numeracy skills are highlighted in the Student Book and extra practice is provided on Kerboodle.

Assessment

The former National Curriculum Attainment Target level descriptors no longer apply. However, the following features of **Allez** provide a guide to the level of activities:

- In the unit overview grid at the beginning of each unit's teaching notes, the range of AT levels in listening, speaking, reading and writing is shown for each core spread and for the *Test* page.
- In the Planner section for each *Test* page, approximate guidelines are provided to help equate the Bronze, Silver and Gold medal activities with the former AT levels.
- In the summative assessments on Kerboodle, which are differentiated into *Star* and *Plus*, National Curriculum levels are offered, together with Bronze, Silver and Gold medals and Foundation, Core and Higher alternatives.

Please note that the Bronze, Silver and Gold medals are intended only for guidance on a specific task, so a Bronze medal that might be an approximate level 2 in Unit 1 is not the same as a Bronze medal in Unit 9.

The following table gives an approximate indication of how the Bronze, Silver and Gold medals correspond to the former AT levels in Key Stage 3:

	Year 7 AT levels	Year 8 AT levels	Year 9 AT levels
Bronze/ Foundation	1–4 +	2–4 +	3–5
Silver/Core	2–4/5	3–5/6	4–6/7
Gold/Higher	3–5	4–6	5–7/8

9

Kerboodle

Allez Kerboodle is packed full of guided support and ideas for running and creating effective Key Stage 3 French lessons, and assessing and facilitating students' progress. It's intuitive to use, customisable, and can be accessed online.

Allez Kerboodle consists of:

- *Allez* Lessons, Resources and Assessment (includes teacher access to the accompanying Kerboodle Book)
- *Allez* Kerboodle Books.

Lessons, Resources and Assessment

Allez Kerboodle – **Lessons, Resources and Assessment** provides hundreds of engaging lesson resources as well as a comprehensive assessment package. Kerboodle offers flexibility and comprehensive support for both *Allez* and your own scheme of work.

You can **adapt** many of the resources to suit your students' needs, with many non-interactive activities available as editable Word documents. You can also **upload** your existing resources so that everything can be accessed from one location.

Kerboodle is online, allowing you and your students to access the course anytime, anywhere. Set homework and assessments through the Assessment system, and **track** progress using the Markbook.

Lessons, Resources and Assessment provides:

- Lessons
- Resources
- Assessment and Markbook
- Teacher access to the Kerboodle Book.

Lessons

Click on the **Lessons tab** to access the *Allez* lesson players and notes.

Ready-to-play lesson players complement every spread 1–5 in the Student Book and the Teacher Handbook. Each lesson player is easy to launch and features spread objectives, activity guidance and a plenary. You can further **personalise** the lessons by adding in your own resources and notes. This means that the lesson players and accompanying notes sections are 100% customisable. Your lessons and notes can be accessed by your whole department and they are ideal for use in cover lessons.

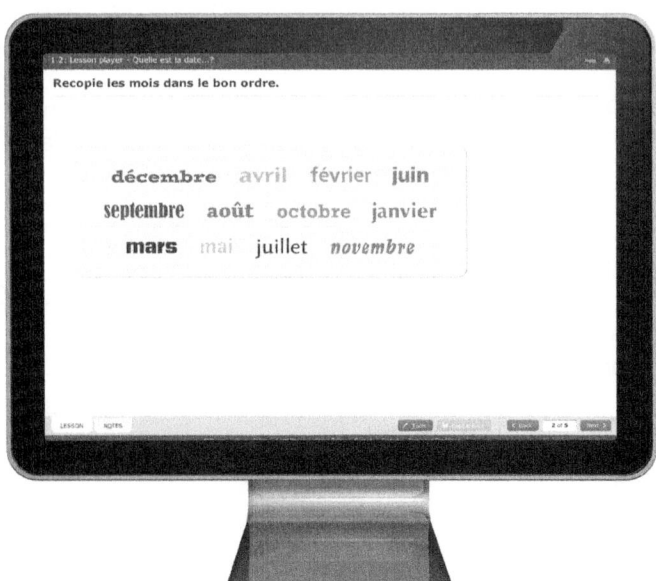

Lessons include:

 Ready-made, editable lesson players

 Lesson plans for each double-page spread of the Student Book

 Editable schemes of work

 'How To' guides with tips on using new technologies in your lessons

 Answers for all activities and transcripts for all audio and video

Resources

Click on the **Resources tab** at the top of the screen to access the full list of *Allez* lesson resources.

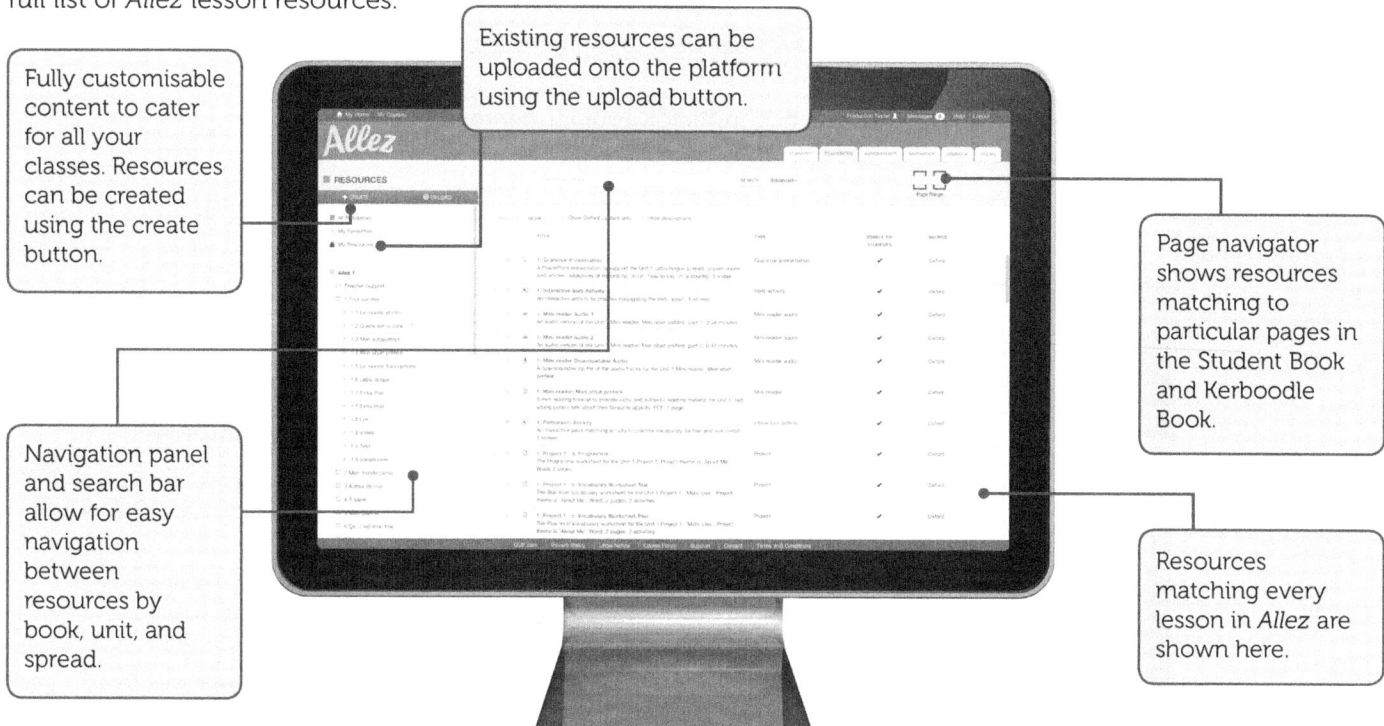

- Fully customisable content to cater for all your classes. Resources can be created using the create button.
- Existing resources can be uploaded onto the platform using the upload button.
- Page navigator shows resources matching to particular pages in the Student Book and Kerboodle Book.
- Navigation panel and search bar allow for easy navigation between resources by book, unit, and spread.
- Resources matching every lesson in *Allez* are shown here.

Resources include:

Free KS2–3 transition module, featuring an e-book story, worksheets and interactive activities

Kerboodle Books

- Video dramas
- Phonics video
- Differentiated interactive activities
- Mini-readers with podcasts using authentic texts for extra reading and listening
- Projects to take language further and to give it a real purpose
- Record and Playback activities*
- Pronunciation practice
- Worksheets
- Grammar presentations
- Interactive vocabulary-learning activities
- Bank of starters and plenaries
- Audio for the Student Book and Worksheets
- Answers for all activities and transcripts for all audio and video

*Please note: the Record and Playback function uses Adobe Flash, and will not be available on devices that do not support the Adobe Flash plug-in.

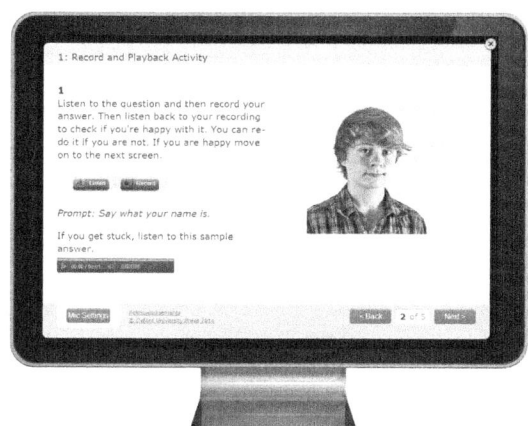
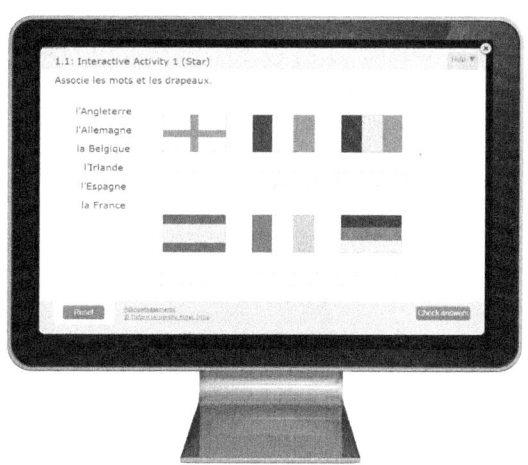

Kerboodle

Assessment and Markbook

Click on the **Assessment tab** to find a wide range of assessment materials to help you deliver a varied, motivating, and effective assessment programme.

The Assessment section provides ample opportunity for student assessment before, during, and after studying a unit.

It's easy to import class registers and create user accounts for your students. Once your classes are set up, you can assign them assessments to do at home, individually, or as a group.

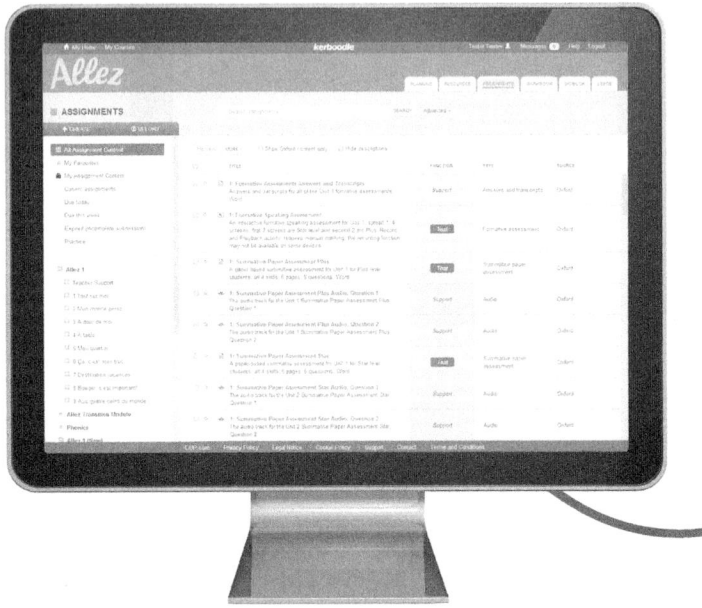

Assessment includes:

 Interactive formative assessments in all four skills

 Interactive and paper summative assessments in all four skills

 Audio material for use with the paper summative assessments in listening and speaking

 Self-assessment checklists

 Diagnostic test

 Answer files and transcripts as well as levelling guidance and mark schemes

A Markbook with reporting function helps you to keep track of your students' results. This includes both automarked assessments and work that needs to be marked by you.

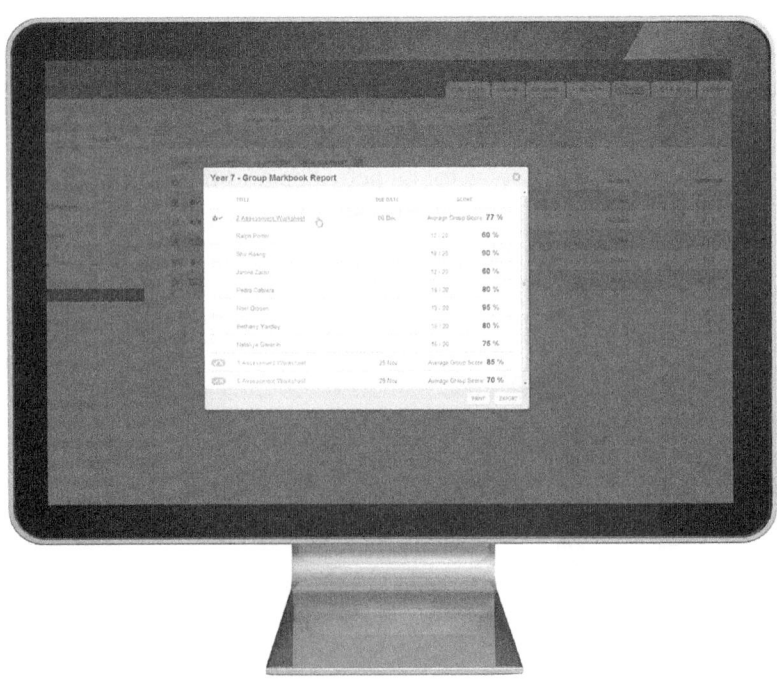

Formative and summative assessment

The **Allez** assessment package offers both formative and summative automarked tests. There are also paper summative assessments.

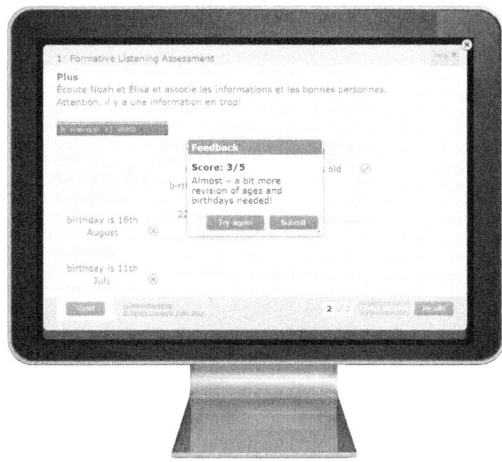

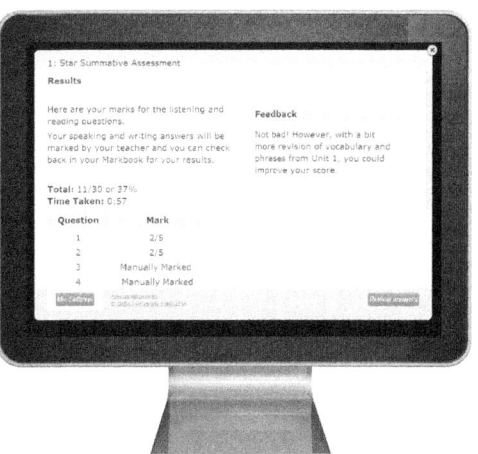

Formative assessments provide screen-by-screen feedback. Students are given the opportunity to try again. Marks are reported to the Markbook.

Summative assessments provide feedback on performance at the end of the test. Students are only given one attempt at each screen but can review them and see which answers they got wrong after completing the activity. Marks are reported to the Markbook.

Kerboodle Book

The **Allez** Kerboodle Book provides a digital version of the Student Book for you to use with your students at the front of the classroom.

Teacher access to the Kerboodle Book is automatically available as part of the Lessons, Resources and Assessment package. You can also purchase additional access for your students.

A set of tools is available with the Kerboodle Book so you can personalise your book and make notes.

Like all other resources offered on Kerboodle, the Kerboodle Book can also be accessed using a range of devices.

Every teacher and student has their own digital notebook for use within their Kerboodle Book. You can even choose to share some of your notes with your students, or hide them from view – all student notes are accessible to themselves only.

Use different tools such as sticky notes, bookmarks, and pen features to personalise each page.

Zoom in and spotlight any part of the text.

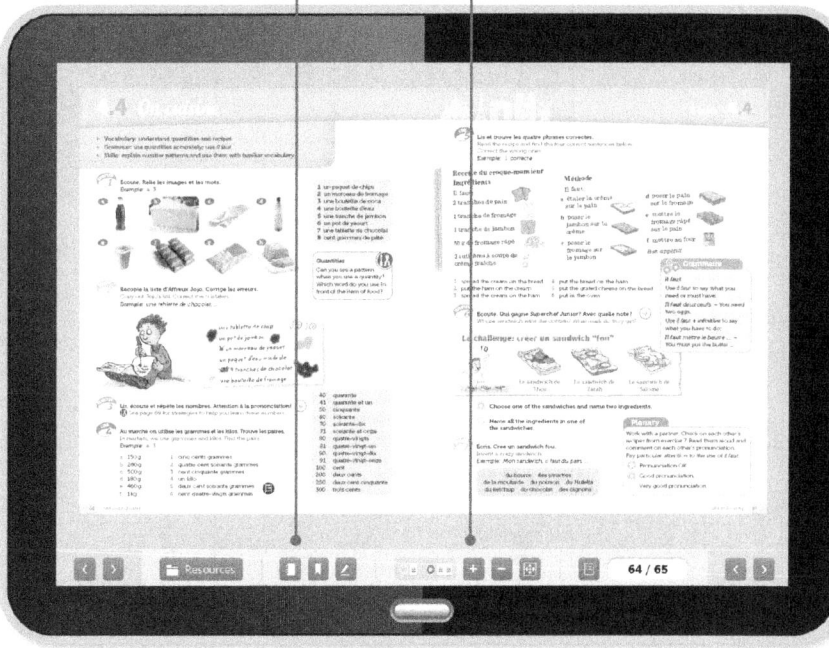

13

1 C'est quoi, la France?

Unit 1: C'est quoi, la France? Overview grid

Page reference	Contexts and objectives	Grammar	Strategies and skills	Key language	AT levels*
4–5 **1.1 On est différents?**	Compare France and Britain	Present tense Use *on*	Agreeing and disagreeing Motivation strategies	En France/En Grande-Bretagne … on a un président de la république/une monarchie, on utilise l'euro/la livre sterling, on porte un uniforme (à l'école), il y a le tournoi de tennis de Roland-Garros, il y a des volets aux fenêtres, les gendarmes portent un képi, c'est une île, on roule à droite/gauche C'est super/intéressant/top/une bonne idée/une mauvaise idée/différent/bizarre.	L: 2–3 S: 2–4 R: 2–4 W: 2–4
6–7 **1.2 La géo, tu aimes?**	Describe a country	Comparatives and superlatives	Motivation strategies Develop geographical knowledge	Les pays: l'Italie, l'Espagne, la Belgique, l'Allemagne, la Suisse Les fleuves: la Seine, la Loire, le Rhône, la Garonne Les montagnes: les Pyrénées, les Alpes, le Jura, le Massif central Londres/La Seine/Le Ben Nevis/La France est plus/moins/aussi … que Lille/la Tamise/le mont Blanc/la Grande-Bretagne. long(ue), haut(e), petit(e), grand(e), peuplé(e) La France fait 674 843 km² (kilomètres carrés). Le mont Blanc/La Seine mesure … mètres/kilomètres.	L: 3–4 S: 3–4 R: 3–4 W: 3–4
8–9 **1.3 Quelques Français célèbres**	Talk about French people	Perfect tense (revision)	Develop cultural awareness Say dates Motivation strategies	Large numbers (years) Il/Elle est acteur/actrice/artiste/auteur/chanteur/chanteuse/couturier/couturière. Il/Elle a créé des personnages/écrit des livres/dessiné des vêtements/fait un film/album. Il/Elle a travaillé avec/sur … Il/Elle est créatif/créative. Il/Elle est né(e)/mort(e) en …	L: 4–5 S: 4–5 R: 2–5 W: 4–5
10–11 **1.4 En France, on innove!**	Talk about transport and new technology	Asking questions	Intonation when asking questions	Je suis pilote (dans l'armée)/physicien/physicienne/chercheur/chercheuse/conducteur/conductrice. Je travaille pour/dans/à … depuis un/deux an(s). Je parle anglais/espagnol couramment. J'ai fait/suivi deux/trois ans d'études/de formation.J'aime/J'adore/Je n'aime pas mon travail … parce que c'est intéressant/difficile/passionnant … parce qu'il y a des risques.	L: 4–5 S: 4–5 F: 4–5 W: 4–5
12–13 **1.5 La BD, culture française?**	Discuss Francophone cartoon characters	Use *qui* to link sentences	Extend sentences Understand longer texts	C'est un personnage historique/imaginaire qui est journaliste/détective. Il/Elle est très/assez/un peu … malin(e), déterminé(e), téméraire, paresseux(-euse), gourmand(e), courageux(-euse), intelligent(e), astucieux(-euse), jaloux(-ouse), amoureux(-euse), intelligent(e), nul(le), populaire, tenace, bête Il/Elle a un chien/des copains/des copines/beaucoup de/d'… Il/Elle aime/n'aime pas le collège/les filles/les vêtements/le sport. Sa passion, c'est sortir avec ses copains/manger.	L: 4–5 S: 3–4 R: 4–5 W: 3–4
14–15 **1.6 Labo-langue**	Grammar, language strategies and pronunciation	Present tense The comparative Asking questions Perfect tense	Motivation strategies Pronunciation: intonation		
16–21 **1.7 Extra Star, Extra Plus 1.8 Lire, Vidéo 1.9 Test, Vocabulaire**	Reinforcement and extension; reading material; activities based on the video material; revision and assessment		**Lire:** understanding rhyme, R: 5–6 **Vidéo:** L: 4–6; S: 3–4		**Test** L: 4 S: 4–5 R: 4–5 W: 4

*See teacher notes for alternative assessment options. Guidelines for the various assessment criteria are provided in the introduction of this Teacher Handbook.

Unit 1: Week-by-week overview

(Three-year KS3 route: assuming six weeks' work or approximately 10–12.5 hours)
(Two-year KS3 route: assuming four weeks' work or approximately 6.5–8.5 hours)

About Unit 1, *C'est quoi, la France?*: In this unit, students work in the context of France: they compare France and Britain, describe a country (country names, rivers, mountains), talk about famous French people, discuss French transport and technology, and describe and give their opinion of Francophone cartoon characters.

Students continue to use the present tense and reinforce their use of *on*. They extend their knowledge of comparatives and learn how to use superlatives. They revise the perfect tense, consolidate their knowledge of asking and answering questions and learn to use *qui* to link sentences.

Throughout the unit, students are encouraged to use motivation strategies when learning new vocabulary and verb forms. They are given an opprtunity to make their language more interesting when expressing agreement and disagreement and there is a focus on expressing dates correctly. The unit allows students to develop geographical knowledge and cultural awareness, as well as practising extending their sentences and understanding longer texts. The pronunciation point focuses on using correct intonation in questions.

Three-year KS3 route

Week	Resources
	*Material from the end-of-unit pages (**1.7 Extra Star/Plus**, **1.8 Lire** and **Vidéo**) may be used during week 6 or selectively during weeks 1–5 as time permits.*
1	1.1 On est différents? 1.6 Labo-langue, activity 1 1.6 Labo-langue, Motivation strategies
2	1.2 La géo, tu aimes? 1.6 Labo-langue, activity 2 1.6 Labo-langue, Motivation strategies
3	1.3 Quelques Français célèbres 1.6 Labo-langue, activity 4 1.6 Labo-langue, Motivation strategies
4	1.4 En France, on innove! 1.6 Labo-langue, activity 3 1.6 Labo-langue, Pronunciation: intonation
5	1.5 La BD, culture française?
6	1.7 Extra Star, Extra Plus 1.8 Lire 1.8 Vidéo 1.9 Test 1.9 Vocabulaire

Two-year KS3 route

Week	Resources
	*Material from the end-of-unit pages (**1.7 Extra Star/Plus**, **1.8 Lire** and **Vidéo**) may be used selectively during weeks 1–4 as time permits.*
1	1.1 On est différents? 1.6 Labo-langue, activity 1 1.6 Labo-langue, Motivation strategies
2	1.2 La géo, tu aimes? 1.6 Labo-langue, activity 2 1.6 Labo-langue, Motivation strategies
3	1.3 Quelques Français célèbres (Omit activities 4 and 6) 1.6 Labo-langue, activity 4 1.6 Labo-langue, Motivation strategies
4	1.4 En France, on innove! 1.6 Labo-langue, activity 3 1.6 Labo-langue, Pronunciation: intonation 1.9 Test 1.9 Vocabulaire

1 C'est quoi, la France?

1.1 On est différents?
pages 4–5

Planner

Objectives
- Vocabulary: compare France and Britain
- Grammar: use the present tense; use *on*
- Skills: agree and disagree; use motivation strategies

Resources
- Student Book, pages 4–5
- CD 1, track 2
- Grammar and Skills Workbook, pages 4, 25 and 28
- Kerboodle, Unit 1

Key language

En France/En Grande-Bretagne ...

on a un président de la république/une monarchie, on utilise l'euro/la livre sterling, on porte un uniforme (à l'école), il y a le tournoi de tennis de Roland-Garros, il y a des volets aux fenêtres, les gendarmes portent un képi, c'est une île, on roule à droite/gauche

C'est super/intéressant/top/une bonne idée/une mauvaise idée/différent/bizarre.

Grammar
- The present tense of *-er* verbs
- Use *on*

PLTS
- Activity 3: Self-managers
- Activity 6: Effective participators
- Plenary: Reflective learners

Homework and self-study
- Student Book, page 5, activity 4
- Student Book, page 5, activity 5
- Grammar and Skills Workbook, pages 4, 25 and 28

Starters
- In preparation for activity 1, hold a **Class discussion** about what students already know about France and Britain. Encourage them to draw on their own experiences in France and on their learning from *Allez 1*. Draw up a list on the board of things that students identify as being peculiar to France and to Britain.
- Revise with the class different ways of **Agreeing and disagreeing**. Ask students to work in pairs to note down as many different expressions as they can think of which express agreement and disagreement. Make two lists on the board and encourage students to refer to them when carrying out activity 3.

Plenaries
- **Reflecting on differences**. Students should be reminded that they have been looking at factual, concrete differences between Britain and France. During the time they will be using *Allez 2* they will be starting to consider differences that are not always easy to see and understand. In this short plenary students should work in small groups discussing cultural differences that they have noticed (or heard about) at home or on holiday and should note down any questions arising in their minds that they would like to put forward for whole class discussion later in the year. If time permits ask for brief feedback from the class. (When marking, copy down the questions raised to inform planning at a later date.)

1 Lis (1–10). C'est en France ou en Grande-Bretagne?
Before students embark on this activity, do the **Class discussion** starter activity. Students then read the ten descriptions and decide whether each one is something that applies to Britain or to France. They copy the grid and tick the correct column for each item. As a follow-up activity, compare the items in activity 1 with those the class identified in the starter activity.

Draw students' attention to *Les gendarmes portent un képi* and elicit which form of the verb *porter* is used here (*ils/elles* (they) form). Explain that although *gendarme* has been used here, *agent(e) de police* and *policier(-ière)* are also used to mean 'police officer' in French.

Answers: **France:** 2, 4, 5, 6, 7, 10; **Grande-Bretagne:** 1, 3, 8, 9

2 Écoute (1–10) et vérifie.
Students listen to the recording and check their answers to activity 1.

CD 1, track 2   page 4, activité 2

1. En Grande-Bretagne, on a une monarchie.
2. On utilise l'euro en France.
3. En Grande-Bretagne, on porte un uniforme à l'école.
4. En France, on a un président de la République.
5. En France, il y a le tournoi de tennis de Roland-Garros.
6. En France, il y a des volets aux fenêtres.
7. En France, les gendarmes portent un képi.
8. La Grande-Bretagne, c'est une île.
9. En Grande-Bretagne, on roule à gauche.
10. En France, on roule à droite.

 3   À deux. Vrai ou faux? A ↔ B.

Before students attempt this activity, do the **Agreeing and disagreeing** starter activity and run through the **Agreeing and disagreeing** skills box. Encourage students to use the various phrases in their dialogues. Encourage students to refer also to the more in-depth lists of expressions compiled in the starter activity.

➕ Students use a connective to make a comparison. Encourage them to use a range of different connectives.

t   4   Lis le blog de Sacha et traduis les expressions soulignées.

Students read the blog and translate the underlined phrases. Refer them back to the key language in activity 1 and also ask them to look out for cognates and near-cognates to help them. Remind students that there are, of course, a lot of similarities between France and Britain too, as well as the differences Sacha describes.

Answers: it's a bit different; we drive on the right; the traffic lights don't change to orange; there are shutters on the windows, not just curtains; they use the pound sterling; we don't wear a uniform

5   Écris un blog sur la Grande-Bretagne. Donne tes opinions. 🖱

Before students begin this activity, run through the grammar box on **The present tense of -er verbs**.

Remind students of where *on* is used in French, and direct them to the **Motivation strategies** on page 15 for help with learning verb patterns.

Students then write a blog describing things that they consider apply to Britain. They use the pictures as prompts and should draw on the key language presented in activity 1. Refer them also to the blog in activity 4 as a model. Encourage students to include their opinions and refer them to the key language box for support.

➕ Students extend their sentences by comparing Britain with France.

6   Fais une présentation sur les différences entre ton pays et un pays francophone pour une émission de radio. Utilise *on*.

Students prepare a short presentation about differences between where they live and a French-speaking country for a radio programme. Encourage them to research a French-speaking country other than France.

⭐ Students give two differences.

◯ Students add an opinion.

➕ Students create longer sentences using connectives to compare the two countries.

Plenary

Students work in pairs to assess each other's presentations and make suggestions for improvement.

⭐ Students assess their partner's use of simple sentences.

◯ Students assess how their partners use simple sentences and express opinions.

➕ Students assess how their partners use connectives to make longer sentences and express opinions.

1.2   La géo, tu aimes?

pages 6–7

Planner

Objectives

- Vocabulary: describe a country
- Grammar: use comparatives and superlatives
- Skills: use motivation strategies; develop geographical knowledge

Resources

- Student Book, pages 6–7
- CD 1, track 3
- Grammar and Skills Workbook, page 18
- Kerboodle, Unit 1
- Unit 1 Worksheet 6 (ex. 3)

1 C'est quoi, la France?

Key language

Les pays: l'Italie, l'Espagne, la Belgique, l'Allemagne, la Suisse

Les fleuves: la Seine, la Loire, le Rhône, la Garonne

Les montagnes: les Pyrénées, les Alpes, le Jura, le Massif central

Londres/La Seine/Le Ben Nevis/La France est plus/moins/aussi ... que Lille/la Tamise/le mont Blanc/la Grande-Bretagne.

long(ue), haut(e), petit(e), grand(e), peuplé(e)

La France fait 674 843 km² (kilomètres carrés).

Le mont Blanc/La Seine mesure ... mètres/kilomètres.

Grammar

- Comparatives and superlatives

PLTS and Numeracy

- Activity 4: Independent enquirers
- Activity 6: Creative thinkers
- Plenary: Reflective learners
- Numeracy: Activity 5: understanding statistics

Homework and self-study

- Student Book, page 6, activity 2
- Student Book, page 6, activity 3
- Student Book, page 7, activity 6
- Grammar and Skills Workbook, page 18

Starters

- Hold a **Class discussion** and invite students to share what they know about France. Encourage them to think about where they have been, and to call out the names of any towns, cities, rivers or mountains that they have heard of. Ask them then to look at the map in activity 1 and to try to locate where they think these places or features might be.
- Before students begin using comparatives and superlatives, recap on the **Comparisons** covered in *Allez 1*, Unit 9. Ask students, *C'est plus tranquille en ville ou à la campagne?* Try to elicit full-sentence answers: *C'est plus tranquille à la campagne. C'est moins tranquille en ville.* Write a list of adjectives (e.g. *grand, petit, haut, bruyant*) on the board and ask students to work in pairs to think up more comparisons using these adjectives.

Plenaries

- **Learning how to express disagreement politely.** Demonstrate (or ask a confident lead learner in the class to demonstrate) a phrase from the skills box on **Agreeing and disagreeing** on page 4, by miming or drawing, but without speaking. Students have to guess the correct phrase. Remind students how useful mime, facial expression and body language can be, and give them time to discuss in pairs how gestures facilitate dialogue and ensure greater tolerance and understanding, or can have the opposite effect. They should also reflect on how important the comparison vocabulary on page 7 will be.

 1 Écoute et regarde 1–13 sur la carte. C'est où?

Refer students first to the list of countries, rivers and mountains in the key language box and recap on the compass points. Before playing the recording, ask students to make a list of the numbers 1–13, representing the numbers on the map, and explain that the features are mentioned on the recording in the same sequence as in the key language box. Students then listen to two teenagers labelling the features on a map of France. As each place is mentioned, students locate the number on the map and write down the name beside the corresponding number on their list. Refer students to page 15 for motivation strategies to help them learn the vocabulary.

t As a follow-up task, ask students to translate the French names into English.

Answers: **1** l'Italie; **2** la Suisse; **3** l'Espagne; **4** l'Allemagne; **5** la Belgique; **6** le Rhône; **7** la Loire; **8** la Garonne; **9** la Seine; **10** les Alpes; **11** le Jura; **12** les Pyrénées; **13** le Massif central

---

⌁⋀⋁⌁ **CD 1, track 3**   **page 6, activité 1**

- Alors, regarde ... quels pays ont une frontière commune avec la France?
- Alors, l'Italie, c'est au sud-est ... l'Espagne, au sud-ouest ... au nord, c'est la Belgique ... puis au nord-est, il y a l'Allemagne ... puis au centre-est, il y a la Suisse.
- Et les fleuves?
- Il y a quatre grands fleuves: la Seine au nord ... la Loire à l'ouest ... le Rhône au sud-est ... et la Garonne au sud-ouest.

18

– Pour finir, les montagnes?
– Alors ... au sud-ouest, ce sont les Pyrénées ... les Alpes sont au sud-est ... le Jura est à l'est ... et le Massif central est au centre. Voilà, notre carte est bien remplie!

2 Lis et trouve les réponses dans le texte.
Students read the text comparing France and Britain, and find the correct answer for each statement.
Answers: **1** la France; **2** Paris; **3** Lyon; **4** la Grande-Bretagne/la France; **5** les Alpes; **6** le mont Blanc

3 Relis le texte et trouve le français pour a–f.
Students read the text in activity 2 again and find the French equivalents for the English phrases.
Answers: **a** deux fois plus grande; **b** la deuxième plus grande ville; **c** il y a environ; **d** habitants; **e** se trouvent; **f** le plus haut

 4 Traduis ces phrases en anglais. Vrai ou faux?

Before students attempt this activity, run through the grammar box on **Making comparisons**. Revise comparatives using the **Comparisons** starter activity and then ensure that students have grasped how to form the superlative before they translate the French comparative and superlative sentences. Once translated, they decide whether each sentence is true (V) or false (F).
Answers: **a** France is bigger than Great Britain. (V) **b** Lyon is the biggest city in France. (F) **c** Nice is less big (smaller) than Lyon. (V) **d** Mont Blanc is the highest peak/point in the world. (F) **e** Dunkirk is more (further) south than Nice. (F) **f** Great Britain is less big (smaller) than France. (V)

5 Regarde les informations et compare.
In pairs, students use the information from the box to put together comparative statements. Refer students to the key language box for support.

○ Students take this further and put together superlative statements

6 Écris un article pour comparer la France et la Grande-Bretagne. Utilise les activités 2–5.
Students draw on the key language from the spread and write their own article comparing France and Britain. Encourage the use of comparatives and superlatives and suggest that students research and add two new facts to their articles.

Plenary

Pupils reflect on how much they know about the geography of France and how they are able to express what they know.

 Students make a statement using *plus*, *moins* or *aussi* to compare France and Britain.

 Students make three statements comparing France and Britain.

 Students add some superlatives.

1.3 Quelques Français célèbres
pages 8–9

Planner

Objectives
- Vocabulary: talk about famous French people
- Grammar: revise the perfect tense
- Skills: develop cultural awareness; say dates; use motivation strategies

Resources
- Student Book, pages 8–9
- CD 1, tracks 4–5
- Grammar and Skills Workbook, pages 35, 38 and 44
- Kerboodle, Unit 1
- Unit 1 Worksheets 3, 4 (ex. 1), 5 (ex. 1, 3), 6 (ex. 2)

Key language
Large numbers (years)

Il/Elle est acteur/actrice/artiste/auteur/chanteur/chanteuse/couturier/couturière.

Il/Elle a créé des personnages/écrit des livres/dessiné des vêtements/fait un film/album.

Il/Elle a travaillé avec/sur ... Il/Elle est créatif/créatiive. Il/Elle est né(e)/mort(e) en ...

Grammar
- The perfect tense

19

1 C'est quoi, la France?

PLTS and Numeracy
- Activity 5: Team workers
- Activity 7: Creative thinkers
- Numeracy: Activity 3: recognising dates in words and digits

Homework and self-study
- Student Book, page 8, activity 2
- Student Book, page 9, activity 6
- Student Book, page 9, activity 7
- Grammar and Skills Workbook, pages 35, 38 and 44, activities 1 and 2

Starters
See Kerboodle Starters bank for further details of **Noughts and crosses**.
- Run through the famous people in the pictures in activity 1 and ask students if they recognise any of the names or know what they did/are famous for.
- Play **Noughts and crosses** with large numbers in year formation, in preparation for covering dates. Play as a class first, and then encourage students to draw their own grids and to play this game in pairs.

Plenaries
- **Learning pyramids**. Students reflect individually on their progress in speaking in recent months. Explain that this information will not be shared with the class – it is private to them. They then draw a pyramid to illustrate their progress: they note down at the base of the pyramid three things they can say really well, then above, two things they still need to practise and, finally, one aspect of this vital skill that they know they need to work on with determination: for example, pronunciation, intonation, presenting new information clearly, etc.

1 Écoute et lis. Relie les descriptions et les personnalités.

Before playing the recording, do the starter activity to see if any of the famous French people are familiar to students. They then read and listen to the descriptions and match them to the correct photos.

CD 1, track 4   page 8, activity 1

1 Il est né en 1802, il est écrivain et il a écrit *Les Misérables*.
2 Il est homme politique et empereur. Il est né en 1769 et il est mort en 1821.
3 Il est auteur et a écrit *Les Trois Mousquetaires*.
4 Il est scientifique. Il a inventé le vaccin contre la rage.
5 Ils ont inventé le cinématographe et ils ont fait le premier film.
6 Il est ingénieur et il a construit une tour célèbre à Paris.
7 Elle est née en 1883, elle est couturière et elle a créé des robes haute-couture et du parfum. Elle est morte en 1971.
8 Elle est physicienne et a travaillé sur la radioactivité. Elle est morte en 1934.

Answers: **1** b; **2** a; **3** f; **4** c; **5** g; **6** h; **7** d; **8** e

2 Relis 1–8 et trouve les expressions en français.

Before students begin this activity, refer them to the grammar box on **The perfect tense** and revise the perfect tense with *avoir* with them. Students then read texts 1–8 in activity 1 again and find the correct French phrases for the English expressions (a–h).

Answers: **a** il est écrivain; **b** il a inventé; **c** il est ingénieur; **d** une tour célèbre; **e** elle a créé; **f** elle a travaillé sur; **g** il est né; **h** il a écrit

 **3 Trouve les dates dans l'activité 1.**

Do the **Noughts and crosses** starter activity and run through the **Dates in French** skills box with students, to ensure that they understand how they are formed. Students then look back at the texts in activity 1 and find the numerical versions of the years given in words (a–f).

Answers: **a** 1934; **b** 1769; **c** 1971; **d** 1883; **e** 1821; **f** 1802

4 Écoute et trouve les dates.

Students listen and identify when each of the famous people mentioned was born. They match the names to the dates (a–e).

Answers: **Marie Curie:** d; **Louis Pasteur:** a; **Coco Chanel:** e; **Victor Hugo:** b; **Napoléon:** c

CD 1, track 5   page 9, activité 4

Alors, Marie Curie est née en 1867 en Pologne. Elle a obtenu le Prix Nobel de physique.

Pasteur est né en 1822. Il a inventé la pasteurisation.

Coco Chanel est née en 1883. Elle a créé des robes et des parfums.

Victor Hugo est né en 1802, à Besançon. Il a écrit *Les Misérables* qui raconte l'histoire de Cosette et de Jean Valjean.

Napoléon est né en 1769 à Ajaccio en Corse, une île en Méditerranée.

20

 Students note down any further details they can from the recording.

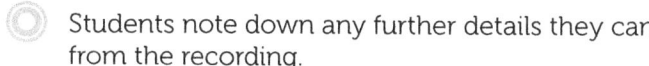 **Cultural awareness strategies**

Ask students to read through the **Cultural awareness strategies** and to answer the question on the pronunciation of *Les Misérables*. Encourage students to look back at the names in activity 1 and to compare their pronunciation in both English and French.

 5 Pose ces questions à cinq personnes.

Before students attempt this activity, run through the perfect tense verbs given in the examples and refer students back to the grammar box on **The perfect tense**. Students then ask five other people questions a–d and elicit responses. Encourage students to note down the information for use in activity 7 and the Plenary medal activities.

6 Lis ce reportage. Vrai ou faux?
Students read the article about Jean-Paul Gaultier and decide whether each of the statements (a–f) is true or false.

Answers: **Vrai:** c, f; **Faux:** a, b, d, e

 Students correct the false statements.

Answers: **a** *Jean-Paul Gaultier est un styliste et un grand couturier.* **b** *Il est français.* **d** *Il a dessiné les costumes de Madonna pour un concert.* **e** *Il a travaillé avec Lady Gaga.*

 Students translate the underlined sentences into English.

Answers: He is quite eccentric and often wears a kilt and a striped T-shirt. He has often dressed men as women! He is considered to be one of the symbols of French haute-couture and fashion.

7 Fais des recherches. Écris un article sur une personnalité française.
Students draw on the language covered in the spread to write an article about a famous French person. Encourage them to research someone who has not been covered in the spread. Alternatively, students could use the information from activities 1, 3, 5 and 6 as the basis of their texts. Refer students to the key language box for support.

> **Plenary**
>
> In pairs, students choose and talk about one person they have learnt about on pages 8–9.
>
> Students say what their chosen person is famous for.
>
> Students add when their chosen person was born and give one detail about what he/she did.
>
> Students add two details and give their opinion of the person.

1.4 En France, on innove!
pages 10–11

Planner

Objectives
- Vocabulary: talk about transport and new technology
- Grammar: ask and answer questions
- Skills: use correct intonation when asking questions

Resources
- Student Book, pages 10–11
- CD 1, tracks 6–7
- Grammar and Skills Workbook, page 10
- Kerboodle, Unit 1

Key language
Je suis pilote (dans l'armée)/physicien/physicienne/ chercheur/chercheuse/conducteur/conductrice.

Je travaille pour/dans/à … depuis un/deux an(s).

Je parle anglais/espagnol couramment.

J'ai fait/suivi deux/trois ans d'études/de formation.

J'ai étudié la chimie/la physique.

J'aime/J'adore/Je n'aime pas mon travail …

parce que c'est intéressant/difficile/passionnant.

… parce qu'il y a des risques.

Grammar
- Asking questions

PLTS
- Activity 5: Creative thinkers
- Activity 6: Team workers
- Plenary: Reflective learners

Homework and self-study
- Student Book, page 10, activity 3
- Student Book, page 11, activity 5
- Grammar and Skills Workbook, page 10

1 C'est quoi, la France?

Starters
- Hold a **Class discussion** about different modes of transport. Elicit the French for each mode and write a list on the board. Ask students to identify which relate particularly to France (TGV, Eurostar, etc.)
- Revise **Question words**: ask the class to call out as many question words as they can think of and write a list of them on the board. Then call out each question word in turn and challenge students to think up topic-based questions using each word: Teacher: *Qui!* Student: *Qui est la reine de Grande-Bretagne?*

Plenaries
- **The working world of the 21st century.** Ask students to reflect on the value of learning foreign languages. (Try to relate this to their options evening if at all possible.) Draw students' attention to the interview with Sylvie on page 10, and to other jobs in which languages are used, particularly unusual jobs that they might not have thought of. Older students (for example, sixth formers who study languages at A Level) could be asked to attend this part of the lesson, as this can be very motivating for students. In addition, you could play short recorded clips of students who have been on school trips/exchanges, expressing the benefits of learning languages. There may be people working at the school from other countries who have mastered English well and are therefore good role models, or you may be able to display photos/details of famous people who can speak foreign languages well. Finally, ask students if their minds have been changed during the lesson and to consider what has influenced their opinions.

1 Lis et trouve les paires.
Before students start reading, do the **Class discussion** starter activity to familiarise them with the French modes of transport. Students then read the facts about French transport inventions and match them with the correct pictures and cities.
Answers: **1** d; **2** b; **3** a; **4** c

2 Écoute (1–3). On parle de quoi?
Students listen and identify which of the transport inventions from activity 1 is being described.
Answers: **1** c; **2** a; **3** b

~~~ CD 1, track 6   page 10, activité 2

1 Le 27 avril 2005, Jacques Rosay a piloté le nouvel avion de la compagnie Airbus, l'A380. Il est parti de l'aéroport de Toulouse, au sud-ouest de la France. L'A380 est le plus gros avion de la compagnie.
2 C'est le maire de Paris, Bertrand Delanoë, qui a eu l'idée des « Autolib' » en 2011. C'est un service de voitures électriques en libre-service. Les voitures ne sont pas polluantes parce qu'elles sont électriques.
3 C'est une compagnie franco-britannique qui a construit ce tunnel entre la France et la Grande-Bretagne. Le tunnel fait plus de 50 kilomètres et ce sont la Reine Elizabeth II et le Président François Mitterrand qui ont inauguré le tunnel en 1994.

○ Students pick out the three dates.
Answers: 2005, 2011, 1994

✚ Students note down any further details they can.

3 Lis l'interview de Sylvie. Vrai, faux ou pas mentionné?
Students read the interview with a Eurostar train driver and decide whether the English statements (a–g) are true, false or not mentioned. As a follow-up task, ask students to correct the false statements.
Answers: **Vrai:** d, e, f; **Faux:** a (Sylvie is a train driver), c (She did a training course for six months); **Pas mentionné:** b, g

4 Écoute. Recopie et remplis la grille.
Students listen to two young people being interviewed about their jobs at CERN and the Salon-de-Provence military base. They complete the grid with the correct details for each speaker. As a follow-up task, students note down where each person works (Marc: CERN; Audrey: Salon-de-Provence military base).

✚ t Students transcribe Marc's answers.
Answers:

	Job	Studies	Languages	Opinion
Marc	physicist/researcher	physics for 6 years	French, English	loves it, fascinating job
Audrey	army pilot	flying school for 3 years	French, English	loves it, it's difficult, exciting

~~~ CD 1, track 7   page 11, activité 4

– Bonjour, Marc. Tu travailles où?
– Je travaille au CERN (le Centre Européen pour la Recherche Nucléaire) à Genève en Suisse. Je suis physicien-chercheur.

– Quelles études as-tu faites?
– J'ai étudié la physique pendant six ans.
– Quelles langues parles-tu?
– Quand on travaille au CERN, il est important de parler français et anglais couramment.
– Est-ce que tu aimes ton travail?
– Oui, j'adore mon travail parce que je fais de la recherche et c'est passionnant.
– Merci, Marc. Et toi, Audrey, tu fais quel travail?
– Je suis pilote dans l'armée.
– Où travailles-tu?
– Je travaille à la base militaire de Salon-de-Provence.
– Quelles études as-tu faites?
– Je suis allée à l'école de l'air pendant trois ans. J'ai fait une formation militaire et scientifique.
– Quelles langues parles-tu?
– C'est important de parler français et anglais.
– Tu aimes ton travail?
– Oui, je l'adore. C'est un travail difficile mais très excitant parce qu'il y a toujours des risques. C'est un peu dangereux!

5 Imagine que tu es Sylvie, Marc ou Audrey. Écris un article et décris ton travail. Utilise les activités 3 et 4.
Students take on the role of one of the people interviewed in activities 3 and 4, and write an article describing their job. Refer students to the key language box for support and encourage them to use their answers from activities 3 and 4.

 6 Imagine que tu es un(e) scientifique ou une(e) innovateur/innovatrice. Invente une interview. Utilise les questions de l'activité 3.
Students work in pairs and interview each other about an imaginary job in the field of science and invention. They may need to do some research to gather/prepare material for their interviews. Before they start, do the **Question words** starter activity, and run through the grammar box on **Asking questions** and the skills box on **Intonation when asking questions**. Encourage students to use a variety of different questions words and to practise using question intonation in their interview.

Plenary

Students listen to their partner's interview, make up some extra interview questions and assess their partner's answers.

They decide whether their partner's interview:

 uses simple questions and sentences

 includes a perfect tense and at least one connective

 includes more than one tense and different kinds of questions.

1.5 La BD, culture française?

pages 12–13

Planner

Objectives
- Vocabulary: discuss Francophone cartoon characters
- Grammar: use *qui* to link sentences
- Skills: extend sentences; understand longer texts

Resources
- Student Book, pages 12–13
- CD 1, track 8
- Grammar and Skills Workbook, page 9
- Kerboodle, Unit 1
- Unit 1 Worksheets 4 (ex. 2–3), 5 (ex. 2), 6 (ex. 1)

Key language
C'est un personnage historique/imaginaire qui est journaliste/détective.

Il/Elle est très/assez/un peu ...

malin(e), déterminé(e), téméraire, paresseux(-euse), gourmand(e), courageux(-euse), intelligent(e), *astucieux(-euse), jaloux(-ouse), amoureux(-euse), intelligent(e), nul(le), populaire, tenace, bête*

Il/Elle a un chien/des copains/des copines/beaucoup de/d'...

Il/Elle aime/n'aime pas le collège/les filles/les vêtements/le sport.

Sa passion, c'est sortir avec ses copains/manger.

Grammar
- *qui* (who/which)

PLTS
- Activity 1: Independent enquirers
- Activity 6: Self-managers
- Plenary: Reflective learners

Homework and self-study
- Student Book, page 13, activity 4
- Student Book, page 13, activity 6
- Grammar and Skills Workbook, page 9, activity 1

1 C'est quoi, la France?

Starters
See Kerboodle Starters bank for further details of **Dominoes**

- Invite students to share anything they already know about Francophone cartoons: names, authors, characters, etc. Write a list of character names mentioned on the board and ask students to list adjectives that might be appropriate to describe each character. They should draw on previously-learned language to do this.
- Play **Dominoes** with the adjectives covered on the spread (see **Key language** above).

Plenaries
- **Cartoon strips**. Ask students to think of their favourite childhood cartoon character (preferably one that has not already been mentioned on the spread) and to make notes in French to help them describe their chosen character to their group. Remind them to justify their choice. Students then create a short cartoon strip with dialogue, using an online comic strip creator such as makebeliefscomix.com.
- Ask students to reflect on the time capsule task from *Allez 1* and imagine themselves in 2050. Will they still be reading cartoons? Which characters do they think will still be appealing? Why? This section may need to be conducted in English, but there should be a strong emphasis on linking it to literacy, persuasive language, etc.

---

1 Lis et réponds aux questions.
Begin with a class discussion to find out what students may already know about French or Belgian cartoons (see **Starters**). Students then read the text about Francophone cartoon characters and answer the questions in English. Suggest to them that that they read it through for gist first and then go back and look for the details that will enable them to answer the questions. Note that the French names of the characters have been used in questions a–h, to match the reading text. As a follow-up task, students could research the characters' French names to find out which have the same names in English and which have different names (in English, the *Schtroumpfs* are the Smurfs, the cat *Azraël* is the same (but spelt Azrael in English); Tintin's dog *Milou* is Snowy, and *les Dupondt* are Thomson and Thompson; *le capitaine Haddock* is the same in English (Captain Haddock)).

Run through the grammar box on **qui (who/which)** and ask students to look back at the text and spot the examples of this structure. (*qui l'accompagne partout; qui a créé ces personnages; qui habitent dans un village champignon; qui a inventé cette bande dessinée*).

Answers: **a** Obélix; **b** more than 110; **c** to make fun of French society; **d** journalist; **e** Tintin's dog; **f** Belgian; **g** blue; **h** in a mushroom village

t Students translate the underlined expressions.

Answers: true international stars; They have sold more than; the best known in the world; who accompanies him everywhere; who created these characters; who live in a mushroom village; it is the Belgian cartoonist/illustrator, Peyo, who invented this cartoon

2 Relie le français et l'anglais.
Students match the French and English adjectives. Encourage students to draw on their strategies for working out the meaning of words when completing this activity.

Answers: **a** devious; **b** determined; **c** daring; **d** lazy; **e** greedy; **f** brave; **g** intelligent; **h** ingenious

3 Écoute Adrien, Caroline, Luca, Maeva et Aziz. Qui aime quoi?
Students listen to five teenagers being interviewed about their favourite cartoon characters. They complete the grid by ticking which character each person likes.

Students also note down each speaker's reasons.

Answers: **Adrien:** Astérix (likes historical characters); **Caroline:** les Schtroumpfs (make her laugh/white hat); **Luca:** les Schtroumpfs (likes imaginary characters/they are funny); **Maeva:** Tintin (likes to solve puzzles); **Aziz:** Astérix (likes Obélix because he's kind but a bit silly/loves eating)

CD 1, track 8   page 12, activité 3

- Adrien, tu aimes quels personnages de BD?
- J'adore les personnages historiques donc j'aime beaucoup Astérix. J'ai lu tous les albums et j'ai vu les films aussi. Je suis fan.
- Et toi, Caroline?
- Moi, j'adore les Schtroumpfs! Ils me font rire parce qu'ils portent un chapeau blanc!
- Et toi, Luca?
- Moi, j'aime les personnages imaginaires comme les Schtroumpfs parce qu'ils sont amusants.
- Maeva, tu aimes quoi?
- Moi, j'ai lu toutes les histoires de Tintin parce que j'adore résoudre des énigmes. Tintin est un super détective! J'ai vu deux films.
- Et toi, Aziz?
- Mon personnage préféré, c'est Obélix parce qu'il est gentil et un peu bête. Il adore manger aussi, comme moi! J'ai vu le film *Astérix aux Jeux olympiques* au cinéma.

4 Lis et trouve les adjectifs. C'est Ducobu (D), Titeuf (T) ou Nadia (N)?

Before students do this activity, do the **Dominoes** starter activity to consolidate students' knowledge of the adjectives. Students then read the two texts about cartoon characters. They find the French equivalents for the English adjectives and decide whether they are used in relation to Ducobu (D), Titeuf (T) or Nadia (N).

Answers: lazy: paresseux – D; funny: comique – D; jealous: jalouse – N; unruly: turbulent – T; popular: populaire – D; pretentious: prétentieuse – N; rubbish at school: nul à l'école – D; in love: amoureuse – N

5 A choisit un personnage de BD de l'activité 1 et prépare une courte présentation. B devine: c'est qui? A ↔ B.

In pairs, students take turns to choose one of the cartoon characters from activity 1 and prepare a brief presentation about them. Their partner has to guess who it is. Refer students back to the grammar box on *qui* (who/which). Remind them that *qui* is usually followed by a verb and encourage them to use these structures in their mini-presentations.

6 Invente deux personnages de BD. Décris-les. Qu'est-ce qu'ils aiment faire?

Students invent two cartoon characters and write a short description of them and what they like doing. Before they attempt this activity, direct students to the **Extending sentences** strategies box and encourage them to use connectives and qualifiers in their writing.

- Students give the names of their invented characters and describe their personalities.
- Students make their writing more complex by linking two sentences using *qui*.
- Students extend their writing further by using a range of connectives and some qualifiers.

Plenary

Working in groups of three, students create a description of a cartoon character. They assess each other's fluency, accent and use of tenses.

- Students say a simple sentence about their chosen character.
- Students say two sentences, including a perfect tense.
- Students say three sentences, including a perfect tense and the connective *qui*.

1.6 Labo-langue

pages 14–15

Planner

Objectives
- Grammar: the present tense; the comparative; asking questions; the perfect tense
- Skills: motivation strategies
- Pronunciation: intonation

Resources
- Student Book, pages 14–15
- CD 1, track 9
- Grammar and Skills Workbook, page 45
- Kerboodle, Unit 1
- Unit 1 Worksheets 7, 8

PLTS
- Creative thinkers, Reflective learners, Self-managers

Present tense

1 Choose the correct verb.

If appropriate for the ability of the class, point out that some regular verbs change very slightly in the present tense. For example, *manger*: an extra 'e' is added in the *nous* form (*nous mangeons*); *acheter*: an accent is added in the *je, tu, il/elle/on* and *ils/elles* forms (*j'achète, tu achètes, il/elle/on achète, ils/elles achètent*).

Answers: a roule; b porte; c travaillez; d parlons; e Aimes; f roulent

The comparative

2 Complete these comparative expressions.

Answers: a plus haut; b plus grande; c moins intelligent; d plus longue; e aussi peuplée; f plus petite

Asking questions

3 Put the words in the correct order to make four questions.

 As a follow-up task, ask students to translate the questions into English.

Answers: a La Seine est plus longue que la Tamise? b Qui a inventé le cinéma? c Où as-tu fait tes études? d Est-ce que tu aimes l'Eurotunnel?

1 C'est quoi, la France?

Translations: **a** Is the Seine longer than the Thames? **b** Who invented cinema? **c** Where did you study? **d** Do you like Eurotunnel?

Perfect tense

4 Complete the sentences using the verbs from the box.

Answers: **a** sont nés; **b** ont travaillé; **c** ont joué; **d** ont inventé; **e** ont fait

Motivation strategies

This section encourages students to think about strategies for learning by heart. Ask students to work in pairs and talk about any strategies they might already have tried and any that they feel would be helpful for them in their everyday learning.

Students are encouraged to try out the new strategies with the vocabulary on page 6 and the verb patterns on pages 5 and 8.

Pronunciation: intonation

5 Listen (1–6). Decide whether each sentence is a statement (S) or a question (Q).

Answers: **Statement:** 3, 5; **Question:** 1, 2, 4, 6

-⋀- CD 1, track 9   page 15, activité 5

1 Tu travailles où?
2 Qui a inventé la pasteurisation?
3 Pasteur a inventé la pasteurisation.
4 Tu aimes lire des BD?
5 Les voitures électriques sont moins polluantes.
6 Est-ce que tu as pris le nouvel Airbus A380?

1.7 Extra Star page 16

1 Read the sentences. Decide whether each one describes France or Britain.

Answers: **France:** a, b, e; **GB:** c, d, f

2 Complete the sentences.

Students create complete sentences by matching the sentence beginnings (a–e) to the correct endings (1–5).

Answers: **a** 3; **b** 2; **c** 1; **d** 5; **e** 4

3 Unjumble the sentences.

Answers: **a** Il a écrit Les Trois Mousquetaires. **b** À Paris il y a des voitures électriques. **c** Napoléon est né en Corse en 1769. **d** En France, on a un président de la République. **e** En Grande-Bretagne, on utilise la livre sterling. **f** Victor Hugo a écrit Notre-Dame de Paris en 1831.

t 4 Translate the sentences from activity 3 into English.

Answers: **1** He wrote The Three Musketeers. **2** In Paris there are electric cars. **3** Napoleon was born in Corsica in 1769. **4** In France they have a President of the Republic. **5** In Britain we use the pound sterling. **6** Victor Hugo wrote Notre-Dame of Paris in 1831.

5 Read the text and answer the questions.
Students answer the questions in English.

Answers: **a** he's a pilot; **b** Montpellier airport; **c** in the south of France; **d** went to flying school for three years; **e** English, French and a bit of Spanish; **f** it's exciting/he's passionate about it and it's very interesting

1.7 Extra Plus page 17

1 Relie les verbes et les photos. Complète les phrases.
Students match the photos to the correct verbs and complete the sentences with appropriate information about each famous person.

Answers: **1** b; **2** d; **3** a; **4** c

** 2 Traduis les phrases de l'activité 1 en anglais.**

Students translate into English the sentences they wrote in activity 1.

3 Lis les blogs. Vrai ou faux?
Students read the blogs about life in Brittany and in Guadeloupe, and decide whether the statements (a–f) are true or false. As a follow-up task, ask students to correct the false sentences.

Answers: **Vrai:** c, g; **Faux:** a, b, d, e, f

Corrected sentences: **a** Gwenaël lives in Brittany. **b** Where Gwenaël lives, some people speak Breton. **d** Kenavo means 'Goodbye' in Breton. **e** Margaux went to Guadeloupe when she was four. **f** She can say a few words in Creole.

4 Traduis les phrases soulignées de l'activité 3.

Students translate the underlined sentences in the blogs.

Answers: In the towns, the signs are written in French and Breton. I was born in the mainland of France but at the age of four I went to Guadeloupe in the West Indies with my family/I left France and went to Guadeloupe in the West Indies with my family. The best thing here is the sun, the beach and the sea.

1.8 Lire

page 18

Resources
- Student Book, page 18
- Kerboodle, Unit 1

PLTS
- Independent enquirers

1 Read the words of the song. Match these phrases about rail travel (a–i) to the highlighted phrases in the song.

Students read the song lyrics and match the English words and phrases to the highlighted French terms in the text. Encourage students to include the articles where appropriate: for example, *le wagon* instead of *wagon*. Draw students' attention to the skills box and elicit that the word *aimerais* has been hyphenated in this way to aid the rhyming of the lines. Encourage students to read the cultural information provided and, as a follow-up task, to find out more about Angoulême.

Answers: a (le) wagon; b rentre en gare; c (la) correspondance; d je descends; e en gare; f en chemin de fer; g trois minutes d'arrêt; h jusqu'au prochain coup de sifflet; i tu continues

2 In films and songs, train journeys are often used as a background to romantic meetings. Find in the song three more phrases that suggest romance.

Answers: Any three: Rendez-vous, qui du hasard du destin nous a mis dans le même train, correspondance entre deux inconnus, croiser l'amour, Nous reverrons-nous?

3 Find these phrases in French in the song.

Answers: a Je ne sais pas si vous mais moi j'aimerais savoir; b Je suis beaucoup plus doué que j'en ai l'air pour me perdre en chemin de fer; c le plus pur des hasards; d dans un jour ou une semaine;

4 Imagine what happened after the chance encounter in the song. Write two to four lines.

Encourage students to use their imagination and to include both the perfect and imperfect tenses.

1.8 Vidéo

page 19

Resources
- Student Book, page 19
- Kerboodle, Unit 1 Video clip

PLTS
- Independent enquirers

Épisode 1: Au Musée de l'Histoire de Montpellier

This clip reintroduces the group of teenagers from the video drama in *Allez 1*, including some new friends. They will feature throughout the video drama in Units 1–9. Zaied, Basile, Clarisse, Jémilie, Thouraya, Maxime and Jules are outside, discussing what they are going to do during the holidays. The girls are keen to spend their time using social media, but the boys would prefer to find a more active pastime.

Jules finds the solution online: a competition in their home town of Montpellier, testing their knowledge of France, Montpellier and young people. The competition will offer a series of challenges for them to undertake.

They begin by going to the history museum, where they attempt the first challenge based on history. They take turns to dress up as historical figures, whilst the others ask questions to try to guess who they are.

Episodes 2–9 will follow the friends as they attempt the other challenges in the competition.

1 C'est quoi, la France?

Video clip, Unit 1   page 19

Zaied:	Qu'est-ce qu'on va faire pendant les vacances?
Basile:	Trop de temps libre, c'est ennuyeux!
Clarisse:	Ah non, c'est super!
Jémilie:	On a plein de temps pour aller sur les réseaux sociaux ou …
Thouraya:	… envoyer des textos.
Maxime:	Moi, je suis quelqu'un de très actif. Je ne veux pas rester devant un ordi toute la journée.
Jules:	Ca y est. J'ai trouvé la solution. La ville de Montpellier organise un concours pour les jeunes. « La France, Montpellier et les Jeunes. Venez tester vos connaissances! » Il y a toute une série de défis à faire.

(At the history museum)

Jules:	Vous avez apporté vos costumes?
Thouraya:	Oui, mais qu'est-ce qu'on fait ici?
Jules:	Le premier défi du concours, c'est l'histoire. Nous allons deviner qui sont les personnages historiques.
Jules:	Je suis né en 1802 à Paris.
Clarisse:	Monsieur, est-ce que vous êtes un ingénieur?
Jules :	Non, mademoiselle, je suis un écrivain.
Zaied:	Qu'est-ce qu'il a écrit?
Jules:	J'ai écrit beaucoup de livres très importants. Par exemple *Le Comte de Monte Cristo* et *Les Trois Mousquetaires*.
Maxime:	J'adore *Les Trois Mousquetaires*.
Les trois garçons:	Un pour tous et tous pour un!
Jules:	Mais qui je suis?
Jémilie:	Facile. Vous êtes Alexandre Dumas.
Jules:	Oui, mademoiselle. Je suis Alexandre Dumas, père. Auteur célèbre.
Jémilie:	Je suis née en 1883 dans la Loire.
Thouraya:	Est-ce que vous êtes chanteuse?
Jémilie:	Quand j'étais jeune, j'ai chanté dans les cafés.
Zaied:	Vanessa Paradis. Elle est Vanessa Paradis.
Basile:	Zaied. Vanessa Paradis est née en 1972, pas en 1883!
Jémilie:	Je suis célèbre pour mon style élégant et mes colliers de perles.
Clarisse:	C'est facile. Vous êtes Coco Chanel. Vous avez créé de robes de haute couture et des parfums.
Jémilie:	Je suis Gabrielle Bonheur Chanel. Je suis la plus célèbre couturière du monde.
Clarisse:	Je suis née en 1867, en Pologne.
Maxime:	Vous êtes née en Pologne? Vous n'êtes pas française?
Clarisse:	Je suis française par le mariage.
Basile:	Vous êtes scientifique?
Clarisse:	Pas exactement. Je suis plutôt physicienne.
Maxime:	Avez-vous reçu des prix Nobel pour votre travail?
Clarisse:	J'ai gagné deux prix Nobel pour mon travail.
Zaied:	Ah oui – vous êtes Marie-Curie. Vous avez inventé la radioactivité!
Clarisse:	Oui, je suis Marie Curie et j'ai travaillé sur la radioactivité.
Zaied:	Je suis né en 1769 en Corse.
Thouraya:	Vous portez un uniforme, Monsieur. Vous êtes soldat?
Zaied:	Je suis plus important qu'un soldat. Je suis un général.
Clarisse:	Est-ce que vous êtes un empereur aussi?
Zaied:	Je suis un homme politique et Empereur de la France.
Jémilie:	Ben oui, vous êtes Napoléon.
Jules:	Super. L'histoire est très importante.
Maxime:	Et il y a des personnages très intéressants dans l'histoire de France.
Thouraya:	On est forts. On va gagner le concours.
Boys:	Un pour tous et tous pour un!

1 Regarde l'épisode 1. Réponds aux questions en anglais.

Students watch the video and answer the questions in English.

Answers: **a** *going to social networking sites, sending texts;* **b** *being in front of a computer all day;* **c** *a competition about 'France, Montpellier and young people', with questions and challenges;* **d** *the first challenge of the competition is history*

2 Relie les personnages historiques et les caractéristiques.

Students match the historical figures to their characteristics. Encourage students to note down the details about each of the historical figures as they watch the video.

Answers: Le personnage de Jules: g, j, b; Le personnage de Jémilie: i, e, a; Le personnage de Clarisse: h, k, c; Le personnage de Zaied: f, l, d

3 Comment s'appellent les quatre personnages historiques?

Students note down the names of each of the historical characters.

Answers: Le personnage de Jules s'appelle Alexandre Dumas. Le personnage de Jémilie s'appelle Coco Chanel/Gabrielle Bonheur Chanel. Le personnage de Clarisse s'appelle Marie Curie. Le personnage de Zaied s'appelle Napoléon.

4 Regarde encore l'épisode. Comment dit-on en français ...?

Students watch the video again and note down the French equivalents for the English words.

Answers: a défi; b costumes; c collier; d célèbre; e soldat

5 Choisis un personnage célèbre (français, britannique ou autre). Décris ses caractéristiques. Le groupe devine.

In groups, students take turns to describe the famous person of their choice. The rest of the group asks questions to help them guess who it is.

1.9 Test

page 20

Resources
- Student Book, page 20
- CD 1, track 10

PLTS
- Creative thinkers, Reflective learners, Effective participators

AT levels
Approximate medal guidelines:

⭐ (Foundation) L: 3; S: 3–4; R: 3–4; W: 3–4

⊙ (Core) L: 3–4; S: 4; R: 4; W: 4

✚ (Higher) L: 4; S: 5; R: 5; W: 5

1 Listen to Daniel and Thomas talking about their countries. Copy out and tick the grid to show who says what. (See pages 4–5.)

Answers: **Daniel:** *lives on an island, wears a school uniform, has a monarchy;* **Thomas:** *the cars drive on the right, uses the euro, has a president*

🎵 **CD 1, track 10   page 20, activité 1**

- Bonjour, Daniel. Tu es anglais ... Parle-moi de ton pays.
- Moi, j'habite sur une île. C'est un pays où on n'utilise pas l'euro mais la livre sterling. On a une monarchie. Dans les écoles, on porte un uniforme.
- D'accord, merci. Et toi, tu es français, Thomas. Parle-moi de ton pays.
- Ici en France, on roule à droite. On a un président de la République et on utilise l'euro. Il y a des volets aux fenêtres et les gendarmes portent un képi.
- Merci à tous les deux.

2 Prepare a short talk about a famous French person. (See pages 8–9.)

Students prepare a presentation, drawing on the key language covered in spread 1.3. They will use the perfect tense, and possibly also the imperfect.

3 Read Paul's text and answer the questions in English. (See pages 6–9.)

Students read the text about France and answer the questions in English.

Answers: **a** *it's a fascinating country;* **b** *no, bigger;* **c** *in the east of France near Switzerland;* **d** *the Alps;* **e** *high-speed train;* **f** *Lyon;* **g** *the Lumière Brothers museum;* **h** *because he loves cinema*

4 Imagine that a French family is coming to visit your town for the first time. Send an email or fact file to give them some information about the differences between France and where you live. (See pages 4–7.)

Students produce a written text comparing France with where they live. Refer them to the bullet points for inspiration and remind them to develop their answers as much as possible. Encourage more able students also to include a fact about a famous person from their area and what this person did/has done.

2 Le monde des médias

Unit 2: Le monde des médias — Overview grid

Page reference	Contexts and objectives	Grammar	Strategies and skills	Key language	AT levels*
22–23 **2.1 La télé, ma réalité!**	Talk about types of television programmes	Direct object pronouns: *le, la, les*	Reading strategies Identify and express opinions	les comédies, les émissions musicales, les émissions de télé-réalité, les émissions de sport, les séries, les dessins animés, les jeux télévisés, les documentaires J'adore/J'aime (bien/beaucoup) … Je n'aime pas (du tout)/Je déteste … parce que/car … Je les trouve très/un peu/assez … amusant(e)s, intéressant(e)s, divertissant(e)s, enfantin(e)s, ennuyeux(-euses), éducatifs(-ives), nuls/nulles mais, pourtant, cependant, par contre, en revanche	L: 3–4 S: 3–4 R: 3–4 W: 3–4
24–25 **2.2 La musique, ma muse!**	Talk about musical genres and express detailed opinions of music	*Faire + infinitive* and *rendre + adjective* *Ce que*	Justify opinions	déprimant, ennuyeux, entraînant, gai, moderne, original, rapide, relaxant, vif le rock, le reggae, le hip-hop, le jazz, la country, le heavy metal, le rap, le classique, la pop, la musique folklorique J'aime/Je n'aime pas/Je déteste/J'ai aimé/Je n'ai pas aimé/J'ai détesté la chanson/l'album … … parce que le rythme/la mélodie/la voix (du chanteur/de la chanteuse) est/était … … car les paroles/les sentiments sont/étaient … Ça me fait danser/dormir/rêver. Ça me rend heureux(-euse)/triste. Ça me calme.	L: 3–4 S: 3–4 R: 4–5 W: 4–5
26–27 **2.3 Le ciné, ma passion!**	Talk about film genres and review a film	Give opinions using the perfect and imperfect tenses	Express and justify opinions Listening and writing strategies	un film d'horreur, un film d'action, un film de science-fiction, un film d'arts martiaux, un film romantique, un film à suspense, un western, un film comique à la télé, au cinéma, en DVD, en streaming J'ai vu … qui s'appelait … L'action se déroule … Il y a un/deux personnage(s) principal/principaux. Je l'ai aimé/adoré/détesté parce que c'était … Je ne l'ai pas aimé parce que c'était … Je (ne) le recommande (pas).	L: 3–5 S: 3–5 R: 4–5 W: 4–5
28–29 **2.4 Lire, ça me fait plaisir!**	Talk about reading preferences	'Verb + infinitive' structures	Apply knowledge of phonics Translation strategies	les romans historiques/comiques/d'aventure/d'amour/d'horreur/de science-fiction, les (auto)biographies, la littérature non-romanesque J'ai lu (un livre qui s'appelle) … écrit par … Un de mes livres préférés est … écrit par … C'est un roman d'horreur. Je (ne) l'ai (pas) aimé parce que c'était … Ensuite, je vais lire (un livre qui s'appelle) … écrit par … C'est …	L: 4 S: 3–5 R: 4–6 W: 4–6
30–31 **2.5 Publicité ou duplicité?**	Understand and use the language of advertising	*Faire + infinitive*	Recognise persuasive and informative language	le cynisme, le marketing, l'information, la protection, la persuasion J'adore/J'aime (bien/beaucoup) cette publicité parce que … Je n'aime pas/ Je déteste cette publicité car … j'aime/je n'aime pas les images/couleurs. … c'est beau/intéressant/amusant. … ça me fait rire/sourire/rêver. … ça me rend triste/heureux/heureuse. J'ai lu un livre/J'ai vu/regardé un film qui s'appelle … Je (ne) l'ai (pas) aimé/adoré/détesté parce que/car c'était …	L: 4 S: 4 R: 4 W: 4–5
32–33 **2.6 Labo-langue**	Grammar, language strategies and pronunciation	Direct object pronouns *Ce que* ('what') Verbs + infinitive Imperfect tense	Writing strategies Pronunciation: *qu*		
34–39 **2.7 Extra Star, Extra Plus 2.8 Lire, Vidéo 2.9 Test, Vocabulaire**	Reinforcement and extension: reading material; activities based on the video material; revision and assessment			**Lire:** R: 5–6 **Vidéo:** L: 4–6; S: 4–5	**Test:** L: 4–5 S: 4–5 R: 4–5 W: 4–5

*See teacher notes for alternative assessment options. Guidelines for the various assessment options are provided in the introduction of this Teacher Handbook.

Unit 2: Week-by-week overview

(Three-year KS3 route: assuming six weeks' work or approximately 10–12.5 hours)
(Two-year KS3 route: assuming four weeks' work or approximately 6.5–8.5 hours)

About Unit 2, *Le monde des médias*: In this unit, students work in the context of the media: they talk about types of television programmes, musical genres, film genres and reading preferences. They express detailed opinions of music and review a film, as well as understanding and using the language of advertising.

Students revise and consolidate their use of direct object pronouns. They use *faire* + infinitive to say that something makes something happen and revise the use of other verbs + infinitive. They use *rendre* + adjective to describe how something makes them feel and also learn to give opinions using the perfect and imperfect tenses.

Reading, writing, listening and translation strategies are provided to give students opportunities to focus on improving these skill areas. Students learn to identify, express and justify opinions. They also apply their knowledge of phonics when analysing a poem and learn to recognise the difference between persuasive and informative language in advertising material. The pronunciation point focuses on the correct pronunciation of *qu*.

Three-year KS3 route

Week	Resources
	*Material from the end-of-unit pages (**2.7 Extra Star/Plus**, **2.8 Lire** and **Vidéo**) may be used during week 6 or selectively during weeks 1–5 as time permits.*
1	2.1 La télé, ma réalité! 2.6 Labo-langue, activity 1
2	2.2 La musique, ma muse! 2.6 Labo-langue, activity 2 2.6 Labo-langue, Pronunciation: *qu*
3	2.3 Le ciné, ma passion! 2.6 Labo-langue, activity 4 2.6 Labo-langue, Writing strategies
4	2.4 Lire, ça me fait plaisir! 2.6 Labo-langue, activity 3
5	2.5 Publicité ou duplicité?
6	2.7 Extra Star, Extra Plus 2.8 Lire 2.8 Vidéo 2.9 Test 2.9 Vocabulaire

Two-year KS3 route

Week	Resources
	*Material from the end-of-unit pages (**2.7 Extra Star/Plus**, **2.8 Lire** and **Vidéo**) may be used selectively during weeks 1–4 as time permits.*
1	2.1 La télé, ma réalité! (Omit activity 4) 2.6 Labo-langue, activity 1
2	2.2 La musique, ma muse! 2.6 Labo-langue, activity 2 2.6 Labo-langue, Pronunciation: *qu*
3	2.3 Le ciné, ma passion! (Omit activities 4 and 5) 2.6 Labo-langue, activity 4 2.6 Labo-langue, Writing strategies
4	2.4 Lire, ça me fait plaisir! (Omit activities 3 and 6) 2.6 Labo-langue, activity 3 2.9 Test 2.9 Vocabulaire

2 Le monde des médias

2.1 La télé, ma réalité!

pages 22–23

Planner

Objectives
- Vocabulary: talk about types of television programmes
- Grammar: use direct object pronouns: *le, la, les*
- Skills: use reading strategies; identify and express opinions

Resources
- Student Book, pages 22–23
- CD 1, tracks 11–12
- Grammar and Skills Workbook, pages 11 and 46
- Kerboodle, Unit 2
- Unit 2 Worksheet 3 (ex. 1)

Key language

les comédies, les émissions musicales, les émissions de télé-réalité, les émissions de sport, les séries, les dessins animés, les jeux télévisés, les documentaires

J'adore/J'aime (bien/beaucoup) …
Je n'aime pas (du tout)/Je déteste … parce que/car …
Je les trouve très/un peu/assez …
amusant(e)s, intéressant(e)s, divertissant(e)s, enfantin(e)s, ennuyeux(-euses), éducatifs(-ives), nuls/nulles
mais, pourtant, cependant, par contre, en revanche

Grammar
- Direct object pronouns: *le, la, les*

PLTS
- Activity 2: Team workers
- Activity 3: Self-managers
- Plenary: Reflective learners

Homework and self-study
- Student Book, page 23, activity 3
- Student Book, page 23, activity 5
- Grammar and Skills Workbook, pages 11 and 46

Starters

- In preparation for activity 1, introduce the TV programme types. Ask students to look at each of the pictures and captions in turn and to try to identify what each programme type would be in English. Remind them to think about cognates and to use the pictures to help them.
- Revise phrases to express likes and dislikes: hold a brainstorming session with the class and write on the board a list of possible expressions, ranging from the most negative to the most positive. Students can refer to these when undertaking activity 1.

Plenaries

- **Freeze Frames**. Students work in small groups on a short sketch based on a chance encounter between two people (see page 18 (Unit 1, *Lire*) for an example of a chance encounter on a train). They act out their sketch, freezing at the point of encounter or just after; other students in the class describe the possible feelings of the people in the frame. Spontaneous talk should be encouraged: for example, what might the two people say to each other? Students should then be given a minute to reflect on their progress in speaking in recent weeks.

1 Écoute (1–8) et décide. Ils aiment ou ils n'aiment pas?

Before playing the recording, do the starter activities to introduce the TV programme types and revise phrases to express likes and dislikes. Students then listen to the recording and decide what each speaker's opinion is of the type of TV programme mentioned. They note down the relevant emoticon for each speaker. Before starting this activity, run through the various opinion phrases and ensure that pupils understand their meaning. Note that the recording is in the same order as the photos and captions.

Answers: **1** ☺☺; **2** ☺; **3** ☹☹; **4** ☺; **5** ☹; **6** ☺; **7** ☹; **8** ☺

➕ Students note down any extra details they can from the recording.

🎵 CD 1, track 11   page 22, activité 1

1. Les comédies? Ben ... je les adore, bien sûr!
2. Les émissions musicales? Ça dépend. Pas toutes.
3. Les émissions de télé-réalité? Non, non ... Je les déteste.
4. Les émissions de sport? Je les aime, oui ... Et ma mère aussi.
5. Les séries? Ça dépend. Les séries policières, je les aime, mais les séries médicales, je ne les aime pas.
6. Les dessins animés. Je les aime bien ... surtout *Les Simpson*.
7. Les jeux télévisés? Je ne les aime pas. Pas du tout. J'ai horreur de ça.
8. Les documentaires? Ça dépend ... si c'est un sujet qui m'intéresse.

👥 2 En groupe: « Qu'est-ce que tu aimes regarder à la télé? Qu'est-ce que tu n'aimes pas regarder à la télé? »

Before students attempt this activity, run through the grammar box on **Direct object pronouns**, recapping on position and agreement of the pronouns. Students then work in small groups to discuss the various TV programme types presented in activity 1.

➕ Encourage students to use the listed expressions to make their conversations more interesting.

3 Lis. Qu'est-ce que Samuel et Ellen aiment et n'aiment pas regarder?

Before students read the texts, take them through the **Reading strategies** box. Check that students remember what cognates are: these were covered in *Allez 1*. Ask them to read the texts and then, working in pairs, to pick out examples of cognates (e.g. *magazines, intéressant, séries, comédies, sport*), and any language that helps them make predictions. Remind them, though, to look out for 'false friends' (e.g. *magazines* = 'chat shows' in this context, not magazines). They also pick out examples of set phrases that indicate positive or negative opinions (e.g. *en revanche, par contre*), and examples of punctuation which give them clues about meaning. Students then note down in English what Samuel and Ellen like and dislike watching.

Answers:

Samuel: *hates cartoons and game shows (a bit childish), doesn't like chat shows, likes reality TV, unsure about music programmes – 'it depends', loves the news and documentaries (very interesting)*

Ellen: *loves series (American, medical, detective/police), likes game shows (entertaining), not a fan of cartoons, loves comedies and documentaries, hates sports programmes (quite boring)*

⭕ Students note down why Samuel and Ellen like or dislike the programmes they mention.

➕ Students identify how many direct object pronouns there are in each text.

Answers: four in each text

4 Écoute (1–4) et note les opinions en anglais.

The recording is an example of *micro-trottoir*, a journalistic technique whereby a reporter stops passers-by in the street to ask for their spontaneous opinion about a specified subject or question. Students listen and note down each speaker's opinion of the programme types he/she mentions.

⭕ Students note down any extra details they can identify from the recording.

Answers: **1** *loves comedies (funny), hates documentaries (rubbish);* **2** *finds some documentaries interesting, loves detective series (e.g. 'Special Investigation' on Saturday evening, which her parents don't like so she watches it on her tablet in her bedroom);* **3** *likes sports programmes (all sports), doesn't like chat shows (not his sort of thing);* **4** *likes music programmes and reality TV, doesn't like/hates cartoons, hates the news (boring)*

🎵 CD 1, track 12   page 23, activité 4

– Je suis reporter pour Télé-France. Je peux te parler? On fait un micro-trottoir pour notre émission de ce soir. Qu'est-ce que tu aimes regarder et qu'est-ce que tu n'aimes pas regarder à la télé?

1. – Je commence? Alors moi, j'adore les comédies parce qu'elles sont amusantes, mais les documentaires, je déteste. Je les trouve nuls.
2. – Pas tous, quand même! Moi, les documentaires ... ça dépend. Certains m'intéressent beaucoup. Mais les séries policières comme *Investigation Spéciale* qui passent le samedi soir, je les adore. Par contre, mes parents n'aiment pas ça. Alors, je les regarde en streaming sur ma tablette, dans ma chambre.
3. – J'aime les émissions de sport. J'aime tous les sports. N'importe quel sport! Par contre, les magazines ... je ne les aime pas parce que ... ce n'est pas mon truc.

33

2 Le monde des médias

4 – Euh … C'est à moi, là? … OK. Voyons … les émissions musicales … je les aime bien, et les émissions de télé-réalité aussi. Mais je n'aime pas les dessins animés. Je les déteste en fait. Et les infos! Qu'est-ce que je déteste les infos! Je déteste ça parce que c'est ennuyeux.
   – C'est pour quelle émission, votre interview, au fait, madame?
   – Alors, c'est … c'est pour le journal télévisé de vingt heures. Merci, tout le monde et au revoir.

5 Qu'est-ce que tu aimes et n'aimes pas regarder à la télé? Écris un paragraphe.
Students write a paragraph about their own TV likes and dislikes. Encourage them to draw on the language covered in the spread and to use the key language box for support. Remind students to include opinions. More able students should be able to justify their opinions and also extend their sentences by giving a contrasting opinion.

Plenary

Elicit from the class why it is important to know the gender of nouns and what effect this has on other words in a sentence (agreement of direct object pronouns, adjectives, etc.).

★ Students name at least five types of TV programmes.

◎ Students name a type of programme they like or dislike and explain why.

✚ Students talk about two types of programmes: one that they like and one that they dislike, giving reasons for their opinions.

2.2 La musique, ma muse!

pages 24–25

Planner

Objectives
- Vocabulary: talk about musical genres and express detailed opinions of music
- Grammar: use *faire* + infinitive and *rendre* + adjective; use *ce que*
- Skills: justify opinions

Resources
- Student Book, pages 24–25
- CD 1, tracks 13–15
- Grammar and Skills Workbook, pages 9 and 15
- Kerboodle, Unit 2

Key language

déprimant, ennuyeux, entraînant, gai, moderne, original, rapide, relaxant, vif

le rock, le reggae, le hip-hop, le jazz, la country, le heavy metal, le rap, le classique, la pop, la musique folklorique

J'aime/Je n'aime pas/Je déteste … le rock/ le hip-hop …

J'ai aimé/Je n'ai pas aimé/J'ai détesté la chanson/ l'album …

… parce que le rythme/la mélodie/la voix (du chanteur/de la chanteuse) est/était …

… car les paroles/les sentiments sont/étaient …

Ça me fait danser/dormir/rêver. Ça me rend heureux(-euse)/triste. Ça me calme.

Grammar
- *Faire* + infinitive and *rendre* + adjective
- *Ce que*

PLTS
- Activity 5: Team workers
- Activity 7: Creative thinkers
- Plenary: Reflective learners

Homework and self-study
- Student Book, page 25, activity 6
- Student Book, page 25, activity 7
- Grammar and Skills Workbook, page 9, activity 2, and page 15

Starters

See Kerboodle Starters bank for further details of **Word tennis**.

- Hold a class **Brainstorming** session to think of possible adjectives to describe music. Students call out the adjectives in English and say whether they are positive or negative adjectives. Write a list of both categories on the board, to which students can refer when completing activity 2.
- In preparation for activity 4, play **Word tennis** using the musical genres introduced in activity 3.

Plenaries

- **Exploiting music**. Working in a computer room or using mobile phones or tablets, students search online for a French song they have never heard before, listen to it carefully and find the lyrics. In pairs, they read the lyrics and decide on five new words that they think would be useful for the others in the class to learn. They should give a reason for their choice, i.e. why they think it would be useful for their study of the language. They must be able to tell their peers whether the words selected are nouns, adjectives, verbs, etc. (Dictionaries should be available.) They then teach another pair the words.
  At the end of the session, hold a whole-class session using 'snowballing': words are shared across the class on small pieces of scrap paper, screwed up like a snowball. If time allows, follow up with a brief discussion of which new vocabulary the class thinks could be particularly important or useful.

1 Écoute (1–6) et note les réactions à la musique.
Students listen to six short excerpts of music and various speakers' reactions to them, and match the reactions to the pictures and captions. Suggest to students that they use the feel of the music and tone of voice to try to deduce meaning.

Once students have completed the listening task, refer them to the grammar box on **Faire + infinitive, rendre + adjective** and practise forming these constructions with familiar verbs and adjectives. Then elicit from the class the English equivalent for each of the phrases.

Answers: **1** f; **2** e; **3** a; **4** d; **5** c; **6** b

---

 **CD 1, track 13**   **page 24, activités 1 et 2**

1 Ça me calme parce que c'est relaxant.
2 Ça me rend triste parce que c'est déprimant.
3 Ça me fait danser parce que c'est entraînant et rapide.
4 – Ça me rend heureux.
   – Oui, ça me rend heureuse aussi parce que c'est gai et vif.
5 Ça me fait rêver parce que c'est original et moderne.
6 Ça me fait … dormir parce que c'est ennuyeux.

---

t 2 Réécoute et note les adjectifs. C'est quoi en anglais?
Students listen again to the recording from activity 1, this time noting down the adjectives given as the speakers' reasons, drawing from the words given in the box. Students then translate the adjectives into English. They can work out the meanings of the adjectives through a combination of the followng strategies: recognising language they know, identifying cognates, speakers' tone of voice, and clues from the music itself. Refer students also to the list of English adjectives created during the **Brainstorming** starter activity.

Answers: **1** relaxant (relaxing); **2** déprimant (depressing); **3** entraînant/rapide (lively/fast); **4** gai/vif (happy/lively); **5** original/moderne (original/modern); **6** ennuyeux (boring)

3 Écoute et lis les genres (a–j).
Students listen to the recording and read the graffiti wall-art displaying the different music genres.

One of the purposes of this activity is to focus on the difference between the French and English pronunciation of similar terms. Once students have listened for the first time, discuss with them the concept of 'loan words': words which are 'borrowed' from another language. An example of a loan word in English is 'genre' (meaning 'type'), which is borrowed from French. Ask students to identify how many of the French musical genres in activity 3 are loan words from English. Can they find out the French for other musical genres, for example punk? How many of these are loan words? What gender (masculine or feminine) are they usually?

Answer: Most loan words tend to be masculine in gender.

 **CD 1, track 14**   **page 24, activité 3**

a Le rock.
b Le reggae.
c Le hip-hop.
d Le jazz.
e La country.

2 Le monde des médias

f Le heavy metal.
g Le rap.
h Le classique.
i La pop.
j La musique folklorique.

4 Écoute (1–10). Note le genre (a–j de l'activité 3) et l'opinion.
Before playing the recording, do the **Word tennis** starter activity to reinforce the music genres. Students then listen and note down the correct letter for the musical genre (from activity 3) and the speaker's opinion of it. This activity consolidates students' learning from this spread and spread 2.1.
Answers: **1** c ☹; **2** e ☹☹; **3** a ☺☺; **4** h ☺; **5** i ☺; **6** b ☺☺; **7** j ☺; **8** d ☹☹; **9** f ☹; **10** g ☺☺

CD 1, track 15   page 24, activité 4

– Je m'ennuie vraiment. J'en ai marre de réviser. Tu veux écouter un peu de musique?
– J'ai une idée … révision musicale! Attends … je vais allumer mon lecteur MP4 … OK? Moi, je vais appuyer sur le bouton Shuffle et toi, tu vas deviner le genre de musique. D'accord?
– D'accord … vas-y alors.
1 C'est du hip-hop, non? Je n'aime pas, le hip-hop.
2 C'est de la country, hein? Je déteste!
3 Ah ouais … c'est du rock … j'adore la musique rock.
4 C'est du classique, hein? J'aime bien la musique classique.
5 C'est de la musique populaire, non? Oui, j'aime la pop parce que les paroles sont souvent originales.
6 C'est du reggae! Ce que j'adore, c'est le reggae … c'est cool.
7 C'est de la musique folklorique, non? J'aime bien. C'est traditionnel et le rythme est vif.
8 C'est du jazz … Ce que je déteste, c'est le jazz. J'ai horreur de ça. La mélodie est démodée.
9 C'est du heavy metal, non? J'aime ça. C'est trop cool.
10 Eh oui. C'est du rap! J'adore le rap.

---

5 En groupe: « Qu'est-ce que tu aimes comme musique? »

In groups, students ask each other about their musical tastes. Before they begin this activity, play the recording from activity 4 again and draw students' attention to some of the informal expressions: for example, *puais*, and adding *non?* or *hein?* at the end of a question: *C'est du hip-hop, non? C'est du classique, hein?* Encourage students to use these expressions in their own speaking, but make sure they realise that they should only speak like this in informal contexts: for example, with their friends and family. Remind them that they can also use *Et toi?* instead of repeating a question. Encourage more able students to use a variety of expressions from the spread, including some informal language.

6 Lis le texte de Thomas. C'est vrai, faux ou pas mentionné?
Students read the text and decide whether statements a–g are true, false or not mentioned in the text. As a follow-up task, ask students to correct the false statements. Draw students' attention to the grammar box on **Ce que**, and ask them to spot all the instances of this construction in Thomas's text. They could then work in pairs to make up their own sentences using *Ce que …*

Answers: **a** vrai; **b** faux (hates it because it's fast/complicated); **c** vrai; **d** faux (he finds it lively); **e** faux (he does listen to music on his phone and on the computer but it isn't expensive); **f** pas mentionné; **g** faux (he did this yesterday)

7 Imagine que tu es journaliste pour une revue musicale. Écris la critique (positive ou négative) d'un extrait ou d'un genre musical.
Students imagine they are a music journalist and write a review (positive or negative) of a piece of music or of a musical genre. Run through the strategy box on **Justifying opinions**, and encourage students to extend their writing by including reasons for their opinions. Remind them to draw on the vocabulary and structures they have covered in this spread and in spread 2.1, and direct them to the key language box for support.

Plenary

Students reflect on what they have learnt and achieved through their work on this spread. Encourage students to work in pairs to think about what they need to work on and how they can improve.

⭐ Students say what genre(s) of music they like, naming a favourite singer or group.

⭕ Students add why they like this music, singer or group.

➕ Students talk with their partners about genres of music, justifying their opinions and using a variety of language, including the past tense.

2.3 Le ciné, ma passion!

pages 26–27

Planner

Objectives
- Vocabulary: talk about film genres and review a film
- Grammar: give opinions using the perfect and imperfect tenses
- Skills: express and justify opinions; use listening and writing strategies

Resources
- Student Book, pages 26–27
- CD 1, tracks 16–17
- Grammar and Skills Workbook, page 14
- Kerboodle, Unit 2
- Unit 2 Worksheets 3 (ex. 2), 4 (ex. 1), 5 (ex. 3), 6 (ex. 1)

Key language
un film d'horreur, un film d'action, un film de science-fiction, un film d'arts martiaux, un film romantique, un film à suspense, un western, un film comique

à la télé, au cinéma, en DVD, en streaming
J'ai vu ... qui s'appelait ...
L'action se déroule ...
Il y a un/deux personnage(s) principal/principaux.
Je l'ai aimé/adoré/détesté parce que c'était ...
Je ne l'ai pas aimé parce que c'était ...
Je (ne) le recommande (pas).

Grammar
- Give opinons using the perfect and imperfect tenses

PLTS
- Activity 1: Independent enquirers
- Activity 5: Effective participators
- Activity 6: Self-managers

Homework and self-study
- Student Book, page 27, activity 3
- Student Book, page 27, activity 6
- Grammar and Skills Workbook, page 14, activity 1

Starters
See Kerboodle Starters bank for further details of **Odd one out** and **Categorise**.

- Play **Odd one out** to revise the perfect and imperfect tenses. Use sets of phrases in the two tenses; students identify which is the odd one out and say why (description in the past (imperfect), or completed action in the past (perfect)).
- Before students begin activity 1, ask them to work in pairs to identify what each of the film types is in English. Remind them to draw on their knowledge of cognates, but also to think about appropriate translations (particularly for *un film à suspense* ('a thriller'), which is not translated literally in English).
- Play **Categorise** to brainstorm positive and negative adjectives for use in activity 2.

Plenaries
- **Exploiting films and film reviews**. Project on the board an online local cinema guide, a French cinema web page or a screen shot of current films. Provide photocopies of short film reviews too. Students analyse their progress in reading by first looking at the film titles, then at the short description, and then finally at a short review. Encourage them to look ahead to GCSE study and to reflect on how useful their developing skills will be. Students discuss in pairs how to improve their reading skills, particularly decoding and working out meaning in context. To encourage students to increase their exposure to the foreign language outside class, discuss the options that are available when watching films on DVD: for example, changing the language, turning subtitles on or off, etc.

2 Le monde des médias

1 Écoute (1–8). C'est quel genre? Quel format? Et quelle opinion?

Before playing the recording, do the starter activity to present the film types. Students then listen and identify for each speaker the correct film genre, format (TV, cinema, DVD or Internet) and the speaker's opinion. It might be helpful if students tackle this activity in stages: on the first listening, they focus on identifying the pictures/genres; on the second listening they identify the format, and then finally the opinion.

Answers: **1** = b 1 ☺; **2** = a 3 ☹; **3** = e 2 ☹; **4** = d 4 ☺; **5** = g 4 ☹☹; **6** = c 2 ☺☺; **7** = h 2 ☺☺; **8** = f 3 ☺

〜 CD 1, track 16   page 26, activité 1

1 J'ai regardé un film d'action à la télé. Je l'ai aimé. C'était bien.
2 J'ai vu un film d'horreur en DVD. Je ne l'ai pas aimé. C'était horrible.
3 Le film? Je ne l'ai pas aimé. C'était un film romantique. Je l'ai vu au cinéma.
4 J'ai regardé un film d'arts martiaux en streaming. Je l'ai beaucoup aimé. C'était passionnant.
5 J'ai vu un western en streaming. Je l'ai détesté. C'était trop long et ennuyeux.
6 J'ai vu un film de science-fiction au cinéma. Je l'ai adoré. C'était extra.
7 J'ai vu un film comique au ciné. Je l'ai adoré. C'était trop rigolo!
8 J'ai regardé un film à suspense en DVD. C'était captivant. Je l'ai beaucoup aimé.

---

2 À deux: « Quel dernier film as-tu vu? Tu l'as aimé? » A ↔ B.

In pairs, students practise using the language introduced in activity 1.

Before they start, run through the grammar box on **Opinions in the past**. Begin by reinforcing opinions in the present tense (*J'aime/J'adore/Je déteste le film*), and then go on to opinions using direct object pronouns (recapped on in spread 2.1): *J'aime/Je l'adore/Je le déteste*. Transfer this then to the perfect tense and elicit from students the various opinion phrases from activity 1, using the emoticons as prompts. Draw students' attention to the use of the imperfect tense for giving reasons for their opinions: *C'était fantastique*, etc. Do the **Odd one out** starter activity, to emphasise the difference in usage between the two tenses.

3 Lis. Réponds aux questions sur chaque film en anglais.

Students read the two texts describing films and answer the questions in English. As a follow-up activity, ask students to make a list of some of the phrases from activity 3 that can be used for describing a film: *Il y deux personnages principaux … L'action se déroule …*

Answers: **Jémilie: a** martial arts film; **b** Internet/iPlayer; **c** the hero and his worst enemy; **d** China; **e** yes, loved it because it was exciting/thrilling; **f** yes; **Jules: a** thriller/suspense film; **b** cinema; **c** a duke; **d** a castle; **e** no, didn't like it much because it was boring; **f** no

⊕ Students translate the two highlighted expressions into English.

Answers: It was well written and well acted. / It was neither well written nor well acted.

4 Écoute ce podcast. Recopie et remplis la grille en anglais.

Students listen to a podcast reviewing the latest films for young people and note down the genre for each film mentioned. Before playing the recording, refer students to the **Listening strategies** box. Encourage them to try to work out the film titles and to use this knowledge to help predict the answers: it seems fairly obvious that *Mission sur Mars* must be science fiction, and *Lié par le sang* is a horror film, as shown in the example answer; so, by a process of elimination, *Les Sonnets perdus* must be historical.

◎ Students identify the film critic's opinion (with reasons) of each film, and whether or not he recommends the film.

⊕ Students also note down extra details about the plot of each film.

Answers:

Film title	Genre	◎ Opinion?	⊕ Extra details
Lié par le sang	horror	Hated it because it was boring and childish. Neither well written nor well acted. Doesn't recommend it.	Takes place in old castle. A young man discovers that Count Dracula is his great-great-grandfather.
Mission sur Mars	science fiction	Liked it a lot because it was exciting/thrilling. Recommends it.	Takes place in space shuttle. 20 volunteers want to colonise the red planet. Disaster strikes and the dramatic tension begins.
Les Sonnets perdus	war film and historical film	Loved it because it was interesting and charming. Well written and well acted. Recommends it.	Takes place in London in the 1960s. Two elderly people (a French man and German man – veterans of the First World War) become friends.

CD 1, track 17   page 27, activité 4

Salut, mes chers spectateurs. Je vais vous parler des films que j'ai vus au cinéma cette semaine. D'abord, j'ai regardé un film d'horreur qui s'appelle *Lié par le sang*. L'action se déroule dans un vieux château. Quel cliché! Un jeune homme découvre que le fameux comte Dracula est son arrière-arrière-grand-père. Je l'ai détesté, ce film, parce que c'était ennuyeux et enfantin. Ce n'était ni bien écrit, ni bien joué. Je ne le recommande pas. Restez chez vous et attendez la sortie de ce film en DVD!

J'ai aussi regardé un film de science-fiction qui s'appelle *Mission sur Mars*. La science-fiction, c'est un genre que j'adore. L'action se déroule dans une navette spatiale. Vingt volontaires veulent coloniser la planète rouge. Mais, en chemin, un désastre les frappe et le drame commence. J'ai beaucoup aimé ce film parce qu'il était passionnant. Ce film, je le recommande. Achetez votre billet de cinéma immédiatement!

Et pour finir, parlons d'un film qui s'appelle *Les Sonnets perdus*. C'est à la fois un film de guerre et un film historique. L'action se déroule à Londres, pendant les années soixante. Deux personnes âgées, un français et un allemand (deux vétérans de la Première Guerre mondiale), deviennent amis. J'ai adoré ce film parce qu'il était intéressant et charmant. C'était bien écrit et bien joué. Ce film, je le recommande. N'oubliez pas vos mouchoirs!

Voilà, c'est tout pour aujourd'hui ... à la semaine prochaine, chers spectateurs!

5 Parle d'un film que tu as vu récemment.
Students use the language covered in the spread to talk about a film they have seen recently. They could do this as a conversation with a partner, or could make it into a more formal presentation to the class. Refer them to the key language box for support. Students could also listen again to the recording from activity 4 and note down some phrases that they could use for their presentation/conversation.

6 Écris la critique d'un film que tu as vu récemment.
Students write a review of a film they have seen recently. Refer students to the **Writing strategies** on page 33 and encourage them to use these tips to help them plan their writing. More able students could also draw on the phrases they found in activities 3 and 4 to make their writing more detailed and interesting.

Plenary

Students review their learning, focusing on their pronunciation and fluency.

- Students name a genre of film they have seen recently and say how they watched it (cinema, TV, Internet).
- Students add their opinion.
- Students go further and add extra details about the film, such as the setting and characters.

2.4 Lire, ça me fait plaisir!

pages 28–29

Planner

Objectives
- Vocabulary: talk about reading preferences
- Grammar: use 'verb + infinitive' structures
- Skills: apply knowledge of phonics; use translation strategies

Resources
- Student Book, pages 28–29
- CD 1, tracks 18–19
- Grammar and Skills Workbook, page 13
- Kerboodle, Unit 2
- Unit 2 Worksheets 3 (ex. 3), 4 (ex. 2–3), 5 (ex. 1), 6 (ex. 2–3)

Key language
les romans d'horreur, les romans d'amour, les romans historiques, les romans de science-fiction, les romans comiques, les romans d'aventure, les (auto)biographies, la littérature non-romanesque

J'ai lu (un livre qui s'appelle) ... écrit par ...
Un de mes livres préférés est ... écrit par ...
C'est un roman d'horreur.
Je (ne) l'ai (pas) aimé parce que c'était ...
Ensuite, je vais lire (un livre qui s'appelle) ... écrit par ... C'est ...

Grammar
- 'Verb + infinitive' structures

PLTS
- Activity 2: Self-managers
- Activity 4: Team workers
- Activity 7: Creative thinkers

Homework and self-study
- Student Book, page 28, activity 2
- Student Book, page 29, activity 6
- Student Book, page 29, activity 7
- Grammar and Skills Workbook, page 13

2 Le monde des médias

Starters

See Kerboodle Starters bank for further details of **Dominoes** and **Pictionary**.

- Play **Dominoes** to prepare students for activity 2. Use the many nouns cited in the poem in activity 1 for the dominoes.

- Before students attempt activity 5, present the book genres. Write on the board a list of the English translations and ask students to work in pairs and to match up the English translations to the French pictures and captions on page 29. Remind them to draw on their knowledge of cognates and to use the pictures as clues. Once students are sure of the book genres, they could play **Pictionary** in groups to reinforce the vocabulary.

Plenaries

- **Using technology to support the development of reading.** Discuss briefly with the class the role of online translators such as babelfish.com or Google Translate. Ask students to reflect on the advantages and disadvantages of online translators and take feedback. Continue by comparing wordreference.com and linguee.com as examples of web-based dictionaries. Give students a range of online tools, for example quizlet.com, vocabexpress.com and memrise.com, and ask them to think of ways of using them. Encourage students to think about apps on their mobile phones and to share ways of saving vocabulary for learning with their peers.

1 Écoute et lis le poème.
What rhymes can you spot by:
- listening to the poem?
- reading the poem?

Students listen and read the poem. They draw on their knowledge of phonics to spot rhymes in the poem.

Answers: odeurs/couleurs, pomme/gomme, orange/mange, nougat/pas*, mandarine/marine, or/port*, mère/lumière, papa/chocolat*

* final silent consonants, so do not affect the rhyme

CD 1, track 18   page 28, activité 1

Mon cartable a mille odeurs.
Mon cartable sent la pomme,
Le livre, l'encre, la gomme,
Et les crayons de couleurs.
Mon cartable sent l'orange,
Le buisson et le nougat.
Il sent tout ce que l'on mange
Et ce qu'on ne mange pas.
La figue et la mandarine,
Le papier d'argent ou d'or,
Et la coquille marine,
Les bateaux sortant du port. (...)
Les longs cheveux de ma mère
Et les joues de mon papa,
Les matins dans la lumière,
La rose et le chocolat.

---

2 Fais l'analyse du poème.

Before students attempt this activity, refer them to the box on **Translation strategies** and encourage them to think carefully about meaning and what sounds best when transferring the words to English. It would also be worth doing the **Dominoes** starter activity at this point, to ensure students know the meanings of the nouns in the poem. As an additional Gold medal activity, students could decide which 'smells' might be real and which ones might be imaginary.

Students note down which things the poet can 'smell' in his school bag.

Answers: a thousand smells, e.g. apple, school books, ink, rubber, coloured pencils, oranges, shrubbery/bushes, nougat, figs, mandarins, silver or gold paper, sea shells, boats leaving port, my mother's long hair, my father's cheeks, sunny mornings, roses, chocolate

Students pick their favourite three lines and translate them into English.

Translation of poem:

My school bag contains a thousand smells.
My school bag smells of apples,
Books, ink, rubbers,
And coloured pencils.
My school bag smells of oranges,
Shrubbery/Bushes and nougat.
It smells of what can be eaten
And what can't.
Figs and mandarins,
Silver paper or gold,
And seashells,
Ships leaving port. (...)

My mother's long hair
My daddy's cheeks,
Sunny mornings,
Roses and chocolate.

3 Lis le poème à haute voix.

Students read the poem out loud, using their knowledge of phonics to accentuate the rhyme. This could be done in pairs or as a whole-class activity in which each line is read out by a different student in turn.

4 En groupe: « Tu as aimé le poème? Pourquoi? »

Students discuss the poem in groups, expressing their opinions in the past tense and using direct object pronouns, as covered in spread 2.3. Encourage them to use a range of adjectives.

As a follow-up task to encourage students to come up with more unusual adjectives, write on the board a list of banned (common) adjectives (*Les adjectifs interdits!: intéressant, ennuyeux, nul, amusant, stupide, fantastique, cool, horrible, super*). This time, students have to repeat the conversation using adjectives other than the banned ones on the board. If students need support with this, have a class brainstorming session first and write on the board a list of more interesting adjectives that could be used.

5 Écoute Alice et Milo. Qu'est-ce qu'ils préfèrent lire? Recopie et remplis la grille en anglais.

Before students attempt this activity, use the **Pictionary** starter activity to present the book genres (displayed as a web page at the top of page 29). Once students are sure of the genres, they listen to Alice and Milo talking about their reading preferences and copy and complete the table. They note down which genres each speaker likes and dislikes.

Answers: **Alice:** *likes: horror stories, adventure novels, historical novels, comic novels; dislikes: science fiction novels, romantic fiction;* **Milo:** *likes: non-fiction, biographies, autobiographies (sometimes a historical novel if based on a true story); dislikes: novels*

t Students transcribe what either Alice or Milo says. Challenge more able students to do both.

Once students have completed the activity, run through the grammar box on **Verbs followed by an infinitive**. Elicit from the class other 'verb + infinitive' constructions with which they are already familiar (*vouloir/pouvoir/aller* + infinitive) and ask students to think up examples of each type. Then play the recording again and ask students to note down all instances of the 'verb + infinitive' construction (*je préfère lire, j'aime lire, j'adore rire, j'aime bien lire, je déteste lire, j'aime lire*). Students could then write sentences using each of these constructions in turn, drawing on the language of the spread.

CD 1, track 19   page 29, activité 5

– Moi, je préfère lire les romans d'horreur. C'est mon genre préféré. Mais j'aime lire les romans d'aventure et les romans historiques aussi. Je n'aime pas les romans de science-fiction. J'ai toujours aimé les romans comiques parce que j'adore rire. Les romans d'amour, je ne suis pas fan.
– Moi, je préfère la littérature non-romanesque donc j'aime bien lire les biographies et les autobiographies. Je déteste lire les romans mais parfois, j'aime lire un roman historique s'il est tiré d'une histoire vraie.

6 Lis le texte de Léo. Réponds aux questions en anglais.

Students read the text and answer the questions in English.

Answers: **a** *He likes it a lot.* **b** *Cheval de Guerre (War Horse), Michael Morpurgo;* **c** *last year, on holiday, on an e-reader;* **d** *very moving, a war/historical novel;* **e** *He is going to watch the film, because he wants to compare it with the book.* **f** *Soldat Peaceful (Private Peaceful), Michael Morpurgo*

7 Écris la critique de ton livre préféré ou d'un livre que tu as lu. Utilise les expressions soulignées de l'activité 6.

Students write a review of their favourite book or a book that they have read, using the underlined phrases in activity 6 to provide the framework for their writing.

Students also mention what they are going to read next.

Plenary

- Students name seven literary genres.
- Students say which genres they like and don't like to read.
- Working in pairs, students talk about a book they have read and one that they are going to read next, using the perfect tense and the future.

2 Le monde des médias

2.5 Publicité ou duplicité?

pages 30–31

Planner

Objectives
- Vocabulary: understand and use the language of advertising
- Grammar: use *faire* + infinitive
- Skills: recognise persuasive and informative language

Resources
- Student Book, pages 30–31
- CD 1, track 20
- Kerboodle, Unit 2
- Unit 2 Worksheet 5 (ex. 2)

Key language

le cynisme, le marketing, l'information, la protection, la persuasion

J'adore/J'aime (bien/beaucoup) cette publicité parce que …
Je n'aime pas/Je déteste cette publicité car …
… j'aime/je n'aime pas les images/couleurs.
… c'est beau/intéressant/amusant.
… ça me fait rire/sourire/rêver.
… ça me rend triste/heureux/heureuse.
J'ai lu un livre/J'ai vu/regardé un film qui s'appelle …
Je (ne) l'ai (pas) aimé/adoré/détesté parce que/car c'était …

Grammar
- *Faire* + infinitive

PLTS
- Activity 3: Independent enquirers
- Activity 4: Team workers
- Activity 5: Creative thinkers

Homework and self-study
- Student Book, page 30, activity 2
- Student Book, page 30, activity 3
- Student Book, page 31, activity 5

Starters
- Before embarking on this spread, it would be useful to hold a **Class discussion** of the spread title (*Publicité ou duplicité*) and all that it implies. Ask students to think of the positive and negative aspects of advertising and write their ideas about the two categories on the board. Students can refer back to these ideas when working on activities 2 and 3.
- Before students embark on activities 4 and 5, revise the constructions *Ça me fait* + verb and *Ça me rend* + adjective, covered in spread 2.2. Use a variety of printed adverts: hold up each in turn and call out *Ça me fait …* or *Ça me rend …* and ask students to complete the sentence. Then go on to elicit full setences from students.

Plenaries
- **Advantages and disadvantages of advertising.** This plenary needs to be planned in advance and should ideally be mentioned a couple of weeks before the lesson, to give students enough time to find an advert to discuss and to ask older members of their family for information. Students interview an older relative and then discuss in small groups the influences of advertising past and present. They should be encouraged to bring an old and a new magazine to school, or a photo of an old and current advert, old or new packaging, etc. This is also an ideal opportunity to include and reflect on cultural differences if there are members of the class who originally come from other continents.

1 Écoute et lis cette analyse de la publicité.
Students listen to the recording of a radio programme and follow the text. Before students begin this activity, it would be useful to do the **Class discussion** starter activity, which explores the meaning of the spread title (*Publicité ou duplicité*). This will help students anticipate the type of language and themes that they might expect to hear in the recording and see in the text.

🎵 **CD 1, track 20   page 30, activité 1**

– Bonjour, chers auditeurs et chères auditrices. Aujourd'hui, on parle de la publicité. La question, c'est: la pub, est-elle bonne ou mauvaise pour nous? Exerce-t-elle une influence positive ou négative dans notre vie de tous les jours? J'ai avec moi une experte pour nous en parler.
Bonjour, Madame Bazin. Quels sont, pour vous, les objectifs principaux de la publicité?

– Je dirais que l'objectif numéro un de la publicité, c'est d'informer le public ... au sujet d'un nouveau produit ou d'un nouveau service. L'objectif numéro deux, c'est de persuader le public que ce produit ou ce service est nécessaire ou même essentiel. Et, pour finir, l'objectif numéro trois, c'est de vendre ce produit ou ce service au public pour gagner de l'argent. Si mon évaluation de la publicité est un peu cynique, c'est parce que l'objectif principal de la publicité est souvent un peu cynique aussi. Il y a, bien sûr, des exceptions. La publicité peut aider à protéger le public. Je pense à des campagnes de santé publique, par exemple.

2 Relis et note les thèmes (a–e) dans l'ordre où ils sont mentionnés.

Students read Madame Bazin's analysis of advertising again and list a–e in the order in which she mentions them. Explain to students that the terms are not used in the text exactly as listed, but that they will need to look for a description or synonym of the concept, or the stem of the word used in a different form (i.e. used as a verb or adjective, rather than as a noun). Remind students to draw on their knowledge of language when looking for the terms: can they find the stem used in a different form (e.g. *l'information – informer; la persuasion – persuader; le cynisme – cynique; la protection – protéger*)? For term b, *le marketing*, students will need to look for a description of marketing: *vendre ce produit ou ce service au public pour gagner de l'argent.*

Answers: c, e, b, a, d

3 Lis les deux publicités (page 31). Recopie et remplis la grille en anglais.

Before students begin this activity, run through the box on **Persuasive or informative language?** with them. Refer students back to the ideas compiled in the **Class discussion** starter activity. Once students are happy with the difference between persuasive and informative language, they read the two adverts on page 31, and copy and complete the table in English, listing examples of persuasive and informative language.

Students translate one of the posters into English.

Answers:

	Ceci n'est pas une Comédie 2	La Noce des Vampires
Les éléments persuasifs	By the same makers as *This is not a Comedy*, which was a big hit in 2014. Quotes: 'a hilarious film, gags galore' (Paris-Max) 'the best comedy of all time' (Le Figarolo) 'a funny film, not to be missed' (Le Mondial) 'five stars' (Mon Ciné)	The bestseller of the summer. The sequel to the 2014 cult novel, *Vampires in Love*. 'an exciting and romantic film' (Revue Romanesque) 'the best book of the year' (Les Bibliophiles) 'a film to make you dream and cry' (Le Mondial) 'ten out of ten' (Revue Fiction)
Les éléments informatifs	In cinemas in April. Certificate U (suitable for all).	Written by Suzanne Solane. On sale in bookshops or to download for your e-reader.

4 À deux: parlez d'une publicité de votre choix.

Before students embark on this activity, revise the constructions *Ça me fait* + verb and *Ça me rend* + adjective (see **Starters**). Provide a selection of adverts for students to choose from for this activity, ensuring they are appropriate in terms of prompting discussion of persuasive/informative language, and for generating opinions.

In pairs, students discuss an advert of their own choice, giving their opinions with reasons. Encourage them to use a variety of expressions for agreeing and disagreeing. Refer them back to the skills box on **Agreeing and disagreeing** on page 4, and to the key language box for support.

5 Fais une publicité pour ton film/livre préféré.

Students design a poster to advertise their favourite book or film.

Students write a paragraph advertising their favourite book or film, using a variety of informative and persuasive language.

Encourage students to draw on the language covered in the spread, and particularly on their work on persuasive and informative language in activity 3. Refer them also to the key language box for support.

2 Le monde des médias

Plenary

- Students name (in English) the three main aims of advertising.
- Students explain (in English) how advertising can be both good and bad.
- Students give (in French) an example of a persuasive element and an informative element from the adverts they have been working on.

2.6 Labo-langue
pages 32–33

Planner

Objectives
- Grammar: direct object pronouns; *ce que* ('what'); verbs followed by an infinitive; the imperfect tense
- Skills: writing strategies
- Pronunciation: *qu*

Resources
- Student Book, pages 32–33
- CD 1, track 21
- Grammar and Skills Workbook, page 47
- Kerboodle, Unit 2
- Unit 2 Worksheets 7, 8

PLTS
- Creative thinkers, Reflective learners, Self-managers

Direct object pronouns

1 Rewrite these sentences. Replace each noun with a direct object pronoun.

Answers: **a** *Je les aime.* **b** *Je la déteste.* **c** *Je l'aime.* **d** *Je les adore.* **e** *Je l'aime.* **f** *Je ne les aime pas.* **g** *Je ne les regarde pas.* **h** *Je ne l'aime pas.*

Ce que ('what')

2 Rewrite these sentences. Use *Ce que ..., c'est ...* in each sentence.

Answers: **a** *Ce que j'aime, c'est la techno.* **b** *Ce que je déteste, c'est la country.* **c** *Ce que j'adore, c'est la littérature non-romanesque.* **d** *Ce que je n'aime pas, c'est écouter le jazz.* **e** *Ce que je n'aime pas, c'est regarder les séries.* **f** *Ce que j'aime, c'est lire.*

Verbs followed by an infinitive

3 Rewrite these sentences with a second verb in the infinitive. Use: *écouter*, *lire* or *regarder*.

Answers: **a** *J'aime écouter les infos à la radio.* **b** *J'adore écouter la musique punk.* **c** *Je déteste lire les biographies.* **d** *J'aime regarder le film.* **e** *Je n'aime pas lire le livre.* **f** *J'adore regarder les comédies et les jeux télévisés.*

The imperfect tense

4 Read this film review.

Students change the examples of the present tense in red to the imperfect tense, choosing from the imperfect tense verbs in the box. Then, elicit from the class the difference between the perfect and imperfect tenses (the imperfect is used for showing a continuous state in the past, whereas the perfect is used for a one-off action that has finished).

Answers: *Samedi dernier, je suis allé au cinéma. J'ai regardé un film qui s'appelait Le Règne de la Haine. C'était un film à suspense. L'action se déroulait dans une cité de banlieue. Il y avait trois personnages principaux: le héros, sa petite-amie et son meilleur ami. Ce film était choquant, émouvant et tragique. Je l'ai beaucoup aimé. Un film à ne pas rater!*

Writing strategies

This section encourages students to create a detailed plan before they begin writing. Remind students to follow these stages when completing activity 6 on page 27, and to employ them in future when planning detailed pieces of writing.

Pronunciation: *qu*

5 Read this passage aloud, then listen and compare. How many times do you hear 'qu' pronounced 'kuh'?

Answers: 8 times: *Qu'est-ce que tu aimes comme musique? Moi, ce que j'aime, c'est la musique folklorique et le classique, mais ce que j'adore, c'est le rock.*

CD 1, track 21   page 33, activité 5

– Qu'est-ce que tu aimes comme musique?
– Moi, ce que j'aime, c'est la musique folklorique et le classique, mais ce que j'adore, c'est le rock.

2.7 Extra Star

page 34

1 Match up the sentence halves.
Students create complete sentences by matching the sentence beginnings (1–6) to the correct endings (a–f).
Answers: **1** c; **2** a; **3** b; **4** f; **5** d; **6** e

2 Read the film review and answer the questions in English.
Answers: **a** One, two, YOU!; **b** in a school in the suburbs of a big town; **c** two; **d** Albert is 13 and doesn't see his father, Delphine is Albert's stepmother; **e** Albert gets a surprise when he sees that his stepmother is a new teacher at his school; **f** funny, charming and moving

3 The lines of this film review are all mixed up! Rewrite them in the correct order.
Remind students to add capital letters and full stops.
Answers: Le studio ELSAM présente un film qui s'appelle Cœur de Beurre. L'action se déroule dans un petit village de campagne. Il y a trois personnages principaux: un boulanger, son apprenti et une jeune fille (une cliente de la boulangerie). Ce film est charmant, émouvant et amusant.

2.7 Extra Plus

page 35

1 Lis les opinions. Recopie les phrases dans le bon ordre.
Students read the texts (a–c) and reorder the words in each sentence. Remind students to add capital letters and any necessary punctuation. Note that in text b, a different word order is possible: students might choose *Je n'aime pas la country ou le heavy metal* instead of the answer shown below. This will affect their translation in the follow-up activity below.

Answers:
a J'ai vu un film en DVD qui s'appelle All is Lost. C'est un film d'aventure. Il y a un personnage principal. L'action se déroule dans un bateau dans l'océan Indien. Je l'ai aimé et je le recommande.
b Ce que j'aime, c'est la pop. Ça me fait danser. Je n'aime pas le heavy metal ou la country. J'aime le jazz aussi. Ça me fait rêver. Mon groupe préféré est Union J. Mon artiste préférée est Lady Gaga.

t As a follow-up task, ask students to translate the texts into English.

Answers:
a I saw a film on DVD called All is Lost. It was an adventure film. There is one main character. The action takes place in a boat on the Indian Ocean. I liked it and I recommend it.
b What I like is pop (music). It makes me dance. I don't like heavy metal or country. I like jazz too. It makes me dream. My favourite group is Union J. My favourite artiste is Lady Gaga.

2 Lis l'opinion de Noah. Vrai ou faux?
Students read Noah's text and decide whether the English statements are true or false.
Answers: **Vrai:** c, e; **Faux:** a, b, d, f, g

3 Écris un résumé d'un film.
Students write a synopsis of a film. More able students will be able to make up their own review, but for those needing a little more support or inspiration, provide the director's notes below as a set of prompts on which they can base their review.

Notes du directeur: concept du film	
Titre:	Petit Oiseau
Action:	une grande ville pendant la Seconde Guerre mondiale
Personnages principaux:	2 un petit garçon son papa (sa maman est morte)
Opinion de l'histoire:	adoré!
Raison(s):	charmant, émouvant

45

2 Le monde des médias

2.8 Lire
page 36

Resources
- Student Book, page 36
- Kerboodle, Unit 2

PLTS
- Independent enquirers

1 Read the interview given by the writer Silène Edgar to the newspaper *Sud Ouest*. Find these words and phrases in French in the interview.

Students read the newspaper interview and find in the text the French equivalents for the English words and phrases. Refer students to the cultural information box about the French daily newspaper, *Sud Ouest*. Ask students to translate its title into English ('South West'). Explain that Silène Edgar is a young people's author and draw students' attention to an extract from her novel *14–14* on page 162 (Unit 9 *Lire*).

Answers: **a** *(la) mémoire;* **b** *(les) livres;* **c** *(la) dictature;* **d** *(l')écologie;* **e** *la société de consommation*

2 Read Silène's first response again. Choose words from the box to fill in the gaps in this summary of *La Saveur des figues*.

Refer students to the glossed vocabulary when reading the text.

Answers: **a** *future;* **b** *dictature;* **c** *regarder;* **d** *vieux;* **e** *principal;* **f** *passé;* **g** *agée;* **h** *vivre*

3 Read the rest of the interview again. Answer these questions in English.

Answers: **a** *science fiction;* **b** *literature;* **c** *French teacher in a secondary school;* **d** *passing on the pleasure of reading;* **e** *she provides material for a website on teenage literature;* **f** *end of the year: the third volume of her trilogy will be published; next year: she will publish a collection of short stories for adults*

2.8 Vidéo
page 37

Resources
- Student Book, page 37
- Kerboodle, Unit 2 Video clip

PLTS
- Independent enquirers

Épisode 2: De la pub pour Montpellier
The friends have gone to the town hall to undertake the second challenge of the competition: this time, they must create an advertising poster to encourage young people to visit Montpellier.

They decide to work in teams, boys versus girls. Each team takes a different approach, both with pleasing results!

Video clip, Unit 2   page 37

Clarisse: C'est quoi, le nouveau défi du concours?

Jules: « Faire de la pub. Créer une affiche pour encourager les jeunes à visiter Montpellier. »

Clarisse: Faire de la pub? Super, j'adore faire de la pub!

Basile: Excellent. Et on va travailler en équipe?

Jémilie: Les filles contre les garçons.

Maxime: Si tu veux.

Jules: Attention. Nous avons une heure et puis un représentant de la Mairie va venir nous juger.

Thouraya: À vos marques, 3, 2, 1. *(Blows whistle)*

Clarisse: Je dirais que l'objectif numéro un serait d'informer les jeunes que Montpellier est une ville qui organise beaucoup de choses pour eux.

Thouraya: Puis l'objectif numéro deux est de persuader les jeunes de visiter Montpellier.

Zaied: Je pense qu'il faut mettre beaucoup d'images.

Basile:	Quoi comme images?	Jules:	Je les trouve nuls!
Zaied:	Des images d'endroits intéressants pour les jeunes.	Clarisse:	La Fête de la Musique, Montpellier Danse, le Printemps des Comédiens, les Estivales, le Festival International des Sports Extrêmes ...
Jules:	Comme par exemple?		
Zaied:	Le stade, mon club de boxe, le bowling et le karting ...		
Jules:	Je ne les visite jamais. Ça fait dormir! Par contre, je sais qu'il faut montrer quelque chose sur la technologie.	Thouraya:	Venez faire la fête à Montpellier!
		Clarisse:	Objectif numéro un: « informer les jeunes que Montpellier est une ville qui propose beaucoup de choses pour eux ».
Maxime:	Ah oui, Montpellier est un peu « la silicon valley » de la France.	Jémilie:	Fait.
Basile:	C'est ennuyeux, ça. Qu'est-ce qu'on met comme image alors?	Thouraya:	Objectif numéro deux: « persuader les jeunes de visiter Montpellier ».
Thouraya:	Regardez, on peut commencer avec cette image.	Jémilie:	Fait!
		Jules:	Dépêchez-vous, le représentant de la Mairie arrive.
Clarisse:	Super, Thouraya, c'est très vivant. Ça me rend heureuse.	Jérôme:	Bon. D'abord les filles. Je trouve l'affiche très intéressante. J'aime beaucoup les images et le message. En disant « Venez faire la fête à Montpellier », vous invitez beaucoup de gens. Et maintenant les garçons. Ça me fait rêver aux vacances. Je dirais que c'est une annonce très personnelle car vous dites « Viens vivre des aventures ». C'est une décision très difficile. Je pense que les filles ont gagné avec leur publicité pour la ville de Montpellier. Mais l'équipe des garçons gagne aussi pour leur publicité sur la région de Montpellier.
Jémilie:	Et qu'est-ce qu'on va mettre comme texte?		
Clarisse:	Venez à Montpellier?		
Jémilie:	Ce n'est pas très original.		
Basile:	Regarde, il y a beaucoup d'images de paysages de Montpellier.		
Zaied:	Des paysages? Les jeunes ne viendront pas pour « des paysages ».		
Basile:	Oui, mais ils viendront pour vivre des aventures ou faire des sports extrêmes.		
Maxime:	Là, tu as raison, Basile. Viens vivre des aventures!		
Zaied:	Excellent. C'est ce que je disais – les endroits sportifs, je les trouve divertissants.	Jules:	J'ai toujours dit que le sport, c'était une excellente idée.

1 Regarde l'épisode 2. Quel est le nouveau défi? Choisis les quatre bonnes réponses.
Students watch the video and choose the four statements which best describe the next challenge.
Answers: b, c, f, h

2 Les garçons parlent de quoi pour illustrer l'affiche? Choisis trois thèmes et quatre endroits sportifs.
Students notes down three themes/topic areas that the boys talk about putting on their poster, and four sporting venues. Refer them to the prompts boxes for support.
Answers: **Themes:** *les paysages, les sports extrêmes, la technologie;* **Venues:** *le stade, le club de boxe, le karting, le bowling*

3 Quel est le slogan des filles? Et le slogan des garçons? Traduis les slogans en anglais.
Answers: **Boys' slogan:** *Viens vivre des aventures! (Come and have adventures!)* **Girls' slogan:** *Venez faire la fête à Montpellier! (Come and celebrate/Come and have fun/Come and party in Montpellier!)*

4 Regarde encore l'épisode 2. Trouve et note l'équivalent français de ces adjectifs.
Students watch the video again and note down the French equivalents for the English adjectives.
Answers: excellent – excellent; interesting – intéressant; boring – ennuyeux; lively – vivant; original – original; entertaining – divertissant; rubbish – nul; personal – personnel

47

2 Le monde des médias

5 Tu préfères l'affiche des filles ou l'affiche des garçons? Pourquoi?

In groups, students discuss the girls' and the boys' posters, giving their opinions with reasons.

6 Imagine que ton groupe crée une affiche pour ta ville ou ta région.

In groups, students discuss what to put on a poster to advertise their home town or region, and what their slogan will be.

2.9 Test

page 38

Resources
- Student Book, page 38
- CD 1, track 22

PLTS
- Reflective learners, Self-managers

AT levels

Approximate medal guidelines:

- (Foundation) L: 3–4; S: 3–4; R: 3–4; W: 3–4
- (Core) L: 4; S: 4; R: 4; W: 4
- (Higher) L: 5; S: 5; R: 5; W: 5

1 Listen to these opinions (1–5). Which media is each person talking about (a–d)? Copy and complete the grid. (See pages 22–29.)

Make students aware that one of the media is mentioned by <u>two</u> people.

Answers:

	Media	Favourite genres	Example	Extra details
1 Malika	d	Music and sports programmes; sometimes watches documentaries	Watched a medical drama yesterday evening.	Prefers to watch programmes on her tablet instead of on TV. Mum loves medical dramas.
2 Siméon	b	Romantic, historical, comedy, war, science fiction	Read a book last weekend called *Toro! Toro!* by Michael Morpurgo.	Likes everything except horror. Likes a wide variety of literary genres.
3 Magali	a	Folk and classical; sometimes listens to rock and pop too	Listened to Beethoven's Fifth Symphony yesterday after school.	Likes to listen to music on her phone on the school bus. Beethoven's Fifth is wonderful/magnificent.
4 Enzo	d	Cartoons	Favourite cartoon is the one with the dancing dog; watched it three times last week.	Silly/stupid but makes him laugh. The dog is so cute.
5 Alizée	c	Biopics and historical period films	Saw a film about the life of Yves Saint Laurent last Saturday. Liked it a lot.	Film is showing at the cinema at the moment. She is going to buy the DVD.

◾ CD 1, track 22   page 38, activitié 1

1 – Alors, Malika, qu'est-ce que tu aimes regarder à la télé?
 – À la télé, pas grand-chose. Je préfère ma tablette parce que je peux regarder ce que je veux où je veux. J'adore les émissions musicales et les émissions de sport. Je regarde même les documentaires parfois. Hier soir, j'ai regardé une série médicale parce que ma mère adore ça.
2 – Et toi, Siméon, qu'est-ce que tu aimes lire?
 – J'adore les romans. À part les livres d'horreur, j'aime tout: les livres romantiques, les livres historiques et comiques, les histoires de guerre et de science-fiction. J'aime une grande variété de genres littéraires. Le week-end dernier, j'ai lu un livre de Michael Morpurgo qui s'appelle Toro! Toro!
3 – Magali, qu'est-ce que tu aimes?
 – J'aime écouter de la musique sur mon portable dans le bus, quand je vais à l'école. Ce que j'aime, c'est la musique folklorique et la musique classique, mais j'écoute parfois du rock et de la pop aussi. Hier, après l'école, j'ai écouté la cinquième symphonie de Beethoven. C'est magnifique!
4 – Tu as décidé, Enzo?
 – Laisse-moi réfléchir un instant … ça y est, j'ai décidé! J'adore regarder les dessins animés à la télévision. Mon préféré, c'est le dessin animé avec le chien qui danse. C'est nul, mais ça me fait rire. Le chien est trop mignon. Je l'ai vu trois fois la semaine dernière.
5 – Et pour finir, Alizée?
 – Je préfère surtout les films biographiques et historiques. Il y a un film sur la vie d'Yves Saint Laurent qui passe au cinéma en ce moment. Je l'ai vu samedi dernier et je l'ai beaucoup aimé. Je vais acheter le DVD.

2 Give a short presentation about your favourite types of TV programmes and music. (See pages 22–25.)
Encourage more able students to extend their presentations and to include more detail, justifying their opinions and reasons wherever possible.

3 Read Manon's text and answer the questions in English. (See pages 22–27.)
Answers: **a** punk and techno; **b** game shows and series for young people; **c** she watched her favourite programme (Feedback) in her room; **d** it's quite expensive; **e** she can watch it on her tablet at home; **f** she watched War Horse; **g** she loved it; **h** she cried, because it's very moving

4 Write about your favourite films and books. (See pages 26–29.)
Remind students to cover all the bullet points and to develop their answers as much as possible, drawing on the language they have learned throughout the unit.

3 Accro à la technologie?

Unit 3: Accro à la technologie? Overview grid

Page reference	Contexts and objectives	Grammar	Strategies and skills	Key language	AT levels*
40–41 **3.1 Alors, quoi de neuf?**	Describe old and new technology	Adjectives (agreement and position)	Use connectives to justify opinions	les écouteurs, les touches, l'appareil photo, l'écran tactile, les applis Je préfère/J'aime/J'adore mon nouveau portable/mon nouvel ordinateur/ma nouvelle console (de jeux)/ma nouvelle tablette parce que/qu'… Je n'aime pas/Je déteste mon vieux portable/mon vieil ordinateur/ma vieille console (de jeux)/ma vieille tablette car … c'est/il/elle est super/petit(e)/grand(e)/ léger/légère/moderne/démodé(e)… il y a un appareil photo/un écran tactile/ des touches. Comme c'est/il est/elle est/il y a …, je préfère …	L: 3–4 S: 3–4 R: 3–4 W: 3–4
42–43 **3.2 La technologie: juste pour s'amuser?**	Talk about using technology for leisure activities	Verb + preposition + infinitive	Extend sentences Speaking strategies	regardes des émissions en streaming, écouter de la musique en ligne, jouer à des jeux en ligne, surfer et trouver des sites intéressants, aller sur les réseaux sociaux, passer des appels vidéo C'est divertissant, pas cher, éducatif, informatif, facile, pratique, rapide, simple En moyenne, je passe (environ) … à regarder/jouer/surfer … une heure/deux heures/trop de temps/peu de temps par jour/semaine/le soir/le week-end	L: 3–4 S: 3–4 R: 3–5 W 4–6
44–45 **3.3 Les ados et les réseaux sociaux**	Identify the potential dangers of social networking sites	Impersonal structures	Memorisation strategies Spoken and written register	la cyberintimidation, la cyberdépendance, la cyberpermanence, la cybersécurité Il est important/impossible/essentiel/obligatoire/nécessaire de/d'… comprendre/effacer/limiter/se protéger/en parler avec/traiter les autres … Il faut/Il ne faut pas/Il est important de ne pas mettre son nom complet.	L: 4–5 S 4 R 4–5 W: 4
46–47 **3.4 Pour ou contre la technologie?**	Talk about the pros and cons of new technologies	Structure an argument	Debate a point	Les nouvelles technologies sont excellentes mais chères/rendent la vie plus simple. Cela décourage l'activité physique. On peut en devenir dépendant. On risque de devenir antisocial Il y a un risque de/d'… Il est facile de rester en contact … Internet est une source d'information très riche.	L: 4–5 S: 4–5 R: 4–6 W: 4–5
48–49 **3.5 Le meilleur gadget?**	Talk about favourite technology and gadgets	À + definite article	Speaking strategies Use reading strategies to work out meaning	un smartphone, un baladeur numérique, une tablette, un ultra-portable Je préfère … au/à la/à l'/aux … parce que/car … … c'est/il est/elle est léger/légère, compact(e), pratique, moderne … … on peut prendre des photos, écouter de la musique, lire des mails, faire/ regarder des vidéos, envoyer des textos, téléphoner. Comme c'est/il est/elle est …, je préfère …	L: 4–5 S: 3–4 R: 4–5 W: 3–5
50–51 **3.6 Labo-langue**	Grammar, language strategies and pronunciation	Position and agreement of adjectives Impersonal structures Verb + preposition + infinitive	Speaking strategies Pronunciation: eu		
52–57 **3.7 Extra Star, Extra Plus 3.8 Lire, Vidéo 3.9 Test, Vocabulaire**	Reinforcement and extension; reading material; activities based on the video material; revision and assessment		**Lire:** R 4–5 **Vidéo:** L 4–5; S 3–4		Test: L: 3–4 S: 4 R: 4–5 W:3–4

*See teacher notes for alternative assessment criteria. Guidelines for the various assessment options are provided in the introduction of this Teacher Handbook.

Unit 3: Week-by-week overview

(Three-year KS3 route: assuming six weeks' work or approximately 10–12.5 hours)
(Two-year KS3 route: assuming four weeks' work or approximately 6.5–8.5 hours)

About Unit 3, *Accro à la technologie?*: In this unit, students work in the context of new technology: they describe old and new technological devices, talk about using technology for leisure activities, identify the potential dangers of social networking sites, discuss the pros and cons of new technologies, and talk about their favourite technology and gadgets.

Students learn to use correct word order with adjectives, and to turn adjectives into nouns by adding the definite article. They use verb + preposition + infinitive constructions and learn to use impersonal structures in both the spoken and written register. Students also learn to structure an argument using appropriate phrases, and to use à + definite article when expressing preferences.

There is a focus on speaking strategies, giving students the opportunity to think carefully about planning their spoken work and to participate effectively in a debate. Students learn to use connectives to justify their opinions, and tips are also given on extending sentences. There is the opportunity to apply memorisation strategies when learning longer items of vocabulary, and the difference between spoken and written registers is addressed in the context of impersonal structures. In addition, students learn to use reading strategies to work out meaning. The pronunciation point focuses on the correct pronunciation of *eu*.

Three-year KS3 route

Week	Resources
	*Material from the end-of-unit pages (**3.7 Extra Star/Plus**, **3.8 Lire** and **Vidéo**) may be used during week 6 or selectively during weeks 1–5 as time permits.*
1	3.1 Alors, quoi de neuf? 3.6 Labo-langue, activity 1
2	3.2 La technologie: juste pour s'amuser? 3.6 Labo-langue, activity 3 3.6 Labo-langue, Speaking strategies 3.6 Labo-langue, Pronunciation: *eu*
3	3.3 Les ados et les réseaux sociaux 3.6 Labo-langue, activity 2
4	3.4 Pour ou contre la technologie?
5	3.5 Le meilleur gadget? 3.6 Labo-langue, Speaking strategies
6	3.7 Extra Star, Extra Plus 3.8 Lire 3.8 Vidéo 3.9 Test 3.9 Vocabulaire

Two-year KS3 route

Week	Resources
	*Material from the end-of-unit pages (**3.7 Extra Star/Plus**, **3.8 Lire** and **Vidéo**) may be used selectively during weeks 1–4 as time permits.*
1	3.1 Alors, quoi de neuf? (Omit activity 5) 3.6 Labo-langue, activity 1
2	3.2 La technologie: juste pour s'amuser? (Omit activity 4) 3.6 Labo-langue, activity 3 3.6 Labo-langue, Speaking strategies 3.6 Labo-langue, Pronunciation: *eu*
3	3.3 Les ados et les réseaux sociaux (Omit activities 3 and 6) 3.6 Labo-langue, activity 2
4	3.4 Pour ou contre la technologie? (Omit activity 4) 3.9 Test 3.9 Vocabulaire

3 Accro à la technologie?

3.1 Alors, quoi de neuf?
pages 40–41

Planner

Objectives
- Vocabulary: describe old and new technology
- Grammar: use adjectives (agreement and position)
- Skills: use connectives to justify opinions

Resources
- Student Book, pages 40–41
- CD 1, track 23
- Grammar and Skills Workbook, pages 16–17
- Kerboodle, Unit 3
- Unit 3 Worksheet 5 (ex. 1)

Key language

les écouteurs, les touches, l'appareil photo, l'écran, l'écran tactile, les applis

Je préfère/J'aime/J'adore mon nouveau portable/ mon nouvel ordinateur/ma nouvelle console (de jeux)/ma nouvelle tablette parce que/qu'…

Je n'aime pas/Je déteste mon vieux portable/mon vieil ordinateur/ma vieille console (de jeux)/ma vieille tablette car …

… c'est super/petit/grand/léger/moderne/démodé.

… il/elle est super/petit(e)/grand(e)/léger/légère/ moderne/démodé(e).

… il y a un appareil photo/un écran tactile/ des touches.

Comme c'est/il est/elle est/il y a …, je préfère …

Grammar
- Adjectives (agreement and position)

PLTS
- Activity 2: Independent enquirers
- Activity 6: Team workers
- Activity 7: Creative thinkers

Homework and self-study
- Student Book, page 40, activity 2
- Student Book, page 40, activity 4
- Student Book, page 41, activity 7
- Grammar and Skills Workbook, pages 16–17

Starters

See Kerboodle Starters bank for further details of **Word tennis**.

- As a class, compile a list of the features of a mobile phone. Ask students to categorise these into old and new technology and write a list of the features in English on the board, to provide support for less able students when completing activity 1.
- Play **Word tennis** to reinforce using adjectives in the standard position (i.e. after the noun), in preparation for activity 4. Students take it in turns to think of a 'noun + adjective' construction (e.g. *un chien féroce, des yeux bleus*).

Plenaries

- **Design**. Following on from the advert that students designed in activity 7 on page 41, ask students to write three phrases or full sentences (using a conjunction and two clauses if possible) to say how they would use the new gadget/ app on their phones: *Mon nouveau portable est super, parce qu'il est très moderne! Il y a des applications gratuites – mon magazine préféré, par example!* Students then take turns to dictate one of their sentences to their partner, who transcribes it. Students should assess each other's sentences and correct their own incorrect spellings.

1 Relie les mots (1–6) et les images (a–f).

Students match the technical terms to the relevant features labelled on the photos of the mobile phones. Encourage more able students to do this without a dictionary and then to explain to a partner how they worked out their answers. Less able students might benefit from a list of the features in English on the board (see **Starters**).

Answers: 1 f; 2 b; 3 e; 4 a; 5 c; 6 d

2 Lis. On parle de quoi? Choisis les mots (1–6) de l'activité 1.

Students read the texts (a–f) and match each one with the most appropriate term (1–6) from activity 1. Once they have done this, refer them to the skills box on **Justifying opinions**. Elicit from students which familiar connectives used for justifying opinions they can spot in the texts (*parce que, car*) and ask them to find the third that they won't yet know (*comme*). To give them a clue, tell them that it is at the beginning of the sentence, not in the middle. As a follow-up task, students could make up their own sentences as in a–f, using the three connectives they found in activity 2.

Answers: a 1; b 4; c 3; d 6; e 5; f 2

3 Écoute les clients dans un magasin de téléphones (1–6). Écris la transcription.

Students listen and transcribe what the customers say.

Answers: see audio script

Students identify whether each customer is talking about their old phone, new phone or both. Students could also be challenged to note down each customer's opinion/reason.

Answers: 1 old one (doesn't like it because it's black and quite small); 2 new one (prefers it because there's a big touchscreen); 3 both (prefers new one because the old one had a small screen and buttons); 4 old one (hates it because there's no camera); 5 new one (prefers it because there's a camera, it's electric blue, it's pretty); 6 new one (loves it because there are lots of apps)

CD 1, track 23   page 40, activité 3

– Pour la première fois, les ventes de smartphones dépassent celles des portables ordinaires. Me voilà dans un magasin de téléphones portables pour Radio Allez. Je vais demander aux clients pourquoi ils ont acheté un smartphone.
1 – Bonjour, mademoiselle. Pourquoi avez-vous acheté un nouveau portable aujourd'hui?
 – Je n'aime pas mon vieux portable parce qu'il est noir et assez petit.
2 – Et vous, monsieur?
 – Je préfère mon nouveau smartphone parce qu'il y a un grand écran tactile.
3 – Et vous, madame?
 – Comme le vieux a un petit écran avec des touches, je préfère mon nouveau portable.
4 – Et vous, monsieur? Pourquoi un smartphone?
 – Je déteste mon vieux portable car il n'y a pas d'appareil photo.
5 – Madame?
 – Moi aussi, je préfère mon nouveau portable parce qu'il y a un appareil photo. Le nouveau est bleu électrique aussi. C'est joli.
6 – Et finalement, vous, madame. Vous êtes contente de votre nouveau portable?
 – Ah oui, j'adore mon nouveau portable car il y a beaucoup d'applis.

4 Et toi? Fais des phrases comme dans les activités 2 et 3.

Students write sentences using those in activities 2 and 3 as a model. Refer them to the skills box on other technology terms and encourage them to use these in their sentences.

Before students attempt this written task, refer them to the grammar box on **Adjectives**. Do the **Word tennis** starter activity to revise the standard position of adjectives (after the noun), and then go on to highlight the difference of position when using *vieux/vieille* and *nouvel/nouvelle* and practise this with the class. Explain also that there is an easy way to turn an adjective into a noun (by putting a definite article in front of it) and practise this too: write on the board a list of adjectives and have students call out in turn the noun equivalent.

5 Lis et réponds aux questions en anglais.

Students read the text about smartphones and answer the questions in English.

Answers: a ordiphone; b because you can do more than make/receive telephone calls with it (read emails, listen to music, surf the Internet, watch films); c a computer; d free apps and apps that you pay for; e games, tube/metro maps, recipes, newspapers, magazines; f getting addicted to it

Students note down extra details from the text.

As a follow-up task, remind students about 'loan words' (see page 35). Explain that many of these appear in French as new technology is produced and marketed, but that eventually a new word will be coined. These new words are called 'neologisms'. For example, *un smartphone* was adopted in French to accompany the new telephone technology, but there is now a new French word: *un ordiphone*. Can students work out what two words this new word is composed of? Why were those words chosen?

Answers: ordinateur + téléphone – chosen because the phone is like a mini-computer

3 Accro à la technologie?

6 À deux: parlez d'un vieux gadget et d'un nouveau.
In pairs, students compare old and new versions of a gadget. Refer them to the key language box for support, but encourage more able students to use their own words as well.

7 Dessine une pub pour un nouveau gadget.
Students design an advertising poster for a new gadget.

⭐ Students draw their gadget and label the features.

◯ Students use verbs when labelling the features: *C'est ... Il y a ...*

➕ Students add opinions and justify them: *J'adore mon nouveau portable car ...*

Plenary

⭐ Students name five features of a phone and say what gender they are.

◯ Students choose a favourite gadget and explain why they like it.

➕ Students make up a sentence about modern technology, using the words 'new' and 'old'.

3.2 La technologie: juste pour s'amuser?
pages 42–43

Planner

Objectives
- Vocabulary: talk about using technology for leisure activities
- Grammar: use 'verb + preposition + infinitive'
- Skills: extend sentences; use speaking strategies

Resources
- Student Book, pages 42–43
- CD 1, tracks 24–25
- Grammar and Skills Workbook, page 21
- Kerboodle, Unit 3
- Unit 3 Worksheets 3 (ex. 2), 4 (ex. 1), 6

Key language
regarder des émissions en streaming, écouter de la musique en ligne, jouer à des jeux en ligne, surfer et trouver des sites intéressants, se connecter à des sites sociaux, passer des appels vidéo

C'est divertissant, pas cher, éducatif, informatif, facile, pratique, rapide, simple.

En moyenne, je passe (environ) ... à regarder/jouer/surfer ...

une heure/deux heures/trop de temps/peu de temps par jour/semaine/le soir/le week-end

Grammar
- Verb + preposition + infinitive

PLTS and Numeracy
- Activity 2: Self-managers
- Activity 5: Team workers
- Plenary: Reflective learners
- Numeracy: Activity 5, Follow-up: working out averages

Homework and self-study
- Student Book, page 42, activity 2
- Student Book, page 42, activity 4
- Student Book, page 43, activity 6
- Grammar and Skills Workbook, page 21

Starters
See Kerboodle Starters bank for further details of **Odd one out** and **Pictionary**.

- In preparation for the grammar point on verb + preposition + infinitive, play **Odd one out** using conjugated verbs and infinitives instead of nouns.

- Before students start on activity 5, play **Pictionary** to consolidate familiarity with the technology activities presented in activity 1.

> **Plenaries**
>
> - **The advantages and disadvantages of surfing the Internet.** Ask students to read through any statements made about the Internet on the spread and to assemble their own thoughts and opinions on the pros and cons of Internet usage: *Surfer sur Internet? C'est éducatif et informatif! Mais il faut limiter le temps qu'on passe en mode « connecté ».* They should then attribute one of the statements they have found to a member of the class, starting with their name and a simple statement: *À mon avis, c'est James. Je pense que c'est James./Je pense que ce n'est pas ...* Ask the class: *C'est vrai ou faux?* Finally, explain that this method of discussion is the start of debating techniques and skills, which will lead to greater fluency. Discuss briefly with the class the type of language that is used in TV debates and ask students if they can predict what they will be covering later in the unit to enable them to debate in French.

1 Écoute (1–5) et lis. On parle de quelle activité?
Students listen and note down which of the activities pictured are referred to by each speaker.
Answers: **1** c; **2** b; **3** e and f; **4** a; **5** d

Students note down what opinion each person has of the activity mentioned.
Answers: **1** entertaining; **2** simple and not expensive; **3** quick and practical, can stay in touch with people; **4** you can watch what you want, when and where you want; **5** educational and informative

---

CD 1, track 24   page 42, activité 1

1 J'adore jouer à des jeux en ligne parce que c'est divertissant.
2 J'aime bien écouter de la musique en ligne parce que c'est simple et pas cher.
3 Aller sur les réseaux sociaux, c'est rapide et pratique. J'adore ça parce qu'on peut rester en contact avec des gens. J'aime bien passer des appels vidéo aussi.
4 Je préfère regarder des émissions en streaming parce qu'on peut regarder ce qu'on veut, où on veut et quand on veut.
5 J'aime surfer sur Internet et trouver des sites intéressants ... parce que c'est éducatif et informatif.

---

2 Traduis les phrases a–e en anglais.
Students translate the sentences into English. Before they do this, run through the skills box on **Extending sentences** and draw their attention to the use of these connectives in the sentences they are about to translate. Check they can remember what *on peut* and *on veut* mean (both taught in *Allez 1*).

Answers: **a** I like to watch streamed programmes because you can watch what you want, where you want and when you want. **b** I love listening to music online because you can listen to it on your favourite gadget. **c** I love playing games online because it's entertaining. **d** Because/As you can easily stay in touch with people all over the world, I love going on social networking sites. **e** I like surfing (the Internet) because it's educational and informative.

3 Écoute l'interview de deux jeunes. Recopie et remplis la grille en anglais.
Students listen to two young people being interviewed about what technology they use for leisure activities. They copy the grid and note down what activities each person does, their reasons and any other details.
Answers:

	Activities	Why?	Other details
1	Going on the Internet and using social networking sites Surfing the Internet and finding interesting websites	To stay in contact with friends. It's easy and practical. To find useful sites to help her with homework because it's very informative.	Likes to use social networking sites if she has lots of homework and can't go out.
2	Playing online games Downloading music	It's cool, also entertaining and relaxing. It's simple and not very expensive.	Has an enormous collection of music.

CD 1, track 25   page 42, activité 3

– Excusez-moi, les jeunes, on fait un sondage. Vous voulez bien nous aider?
– Bon, ben ... d'accord. Allez-y, madame.
– Qu'aimez-vous faire à l'aide des nouvelles technologies?
– Moi ... j'aime me connecter à Internet et aller sur les réseaux sociaux ... pour rester en contact

3 Accro à la technologie?

avec mes amis ... parce que c'est facile et pratique. J'aime faire ça quand j'ai beaucoup de devoirs, par exemple, et que je ne peux pas sortir. Mais j'aime aussi surfer et trouver des sites intéressants ... pour m'aider à faire mes devoirs. C'est très informatif.
- OK. Merci. Et ton copain?
- J'adore jouer à des jeux en ligne, c'est cool. J'aime ça parce que c'est très divertissant et ça me relaxe. J'aime télécharger de la musique aussi parce que c'est simple et peu cher. J'ai une collection énorme.
- Je vous remercie, tous les deux, et au revoir ... Excusez-moi, les jeunes, on fait un sondage. Vous voulez bien nous aider? ...

4 Lis. C'est vrai ou faux?
Students read the texts and decide whether the English statements are true or false. Encourage them to draw on their reading strategies when working out meanings in the text. Point out also that *accro* (listed in the glossary box) is short for *accroché*.
Answers: **Vrai:** d, e; **Faux:** a, b, c, f

Students translate Lola's paragraph into English. Before they do so, run through the grammar box on **Verb + preposition + infinitive** and ask students to look back through both Mathis's and Lola's texts to find examples of this construction. This would also be a good moment to do the **Odd one out** starter activity.

Answer: I'm hooked/addicted. From morning to night, I'm online/connected to the Internet. Going on social networking sites, watching funny videos, listening to streamed music, chatting online – you can do everything, where and when you want. In the evening, I love reading my friends' blogs (I write a blog too) and I like playing online games until midnight because it's entertaining. But now I think I'm addicted to/hooked on technology. So I'm going to try to limit the time that I'm 'connected', because at the moment, I'm spending 10 hours a day on the Internet!

5 Sondage. Interviewe dix personnes dans la classe. Utilise les expressions de l'activité 1.
Before students attempt this activity, refer them to the **Speaking strategies** on page 51, which will help them plan what they want to say. Encourage them to try out these strategies when carrying out their surveys. This would also be a good point at which to reinforce students' knowledge of the technology activities, by doing the **Pictionary** starter activity.

Working in groups, students then survey 10 students about their use of technology. They should use the key expressions from activity 1 as the basis for their enquiries.

As a follow-up task, students work out the average number of hours that the students surveyed spend on each activity.

6 Écris un article: « La technologie: tu es accro? »
Students write an article about technology and addiction. They use the underlined phrases from activity 4 as a basis for their writing. Refer students also to the key language box for support.

Students also include an example of both the past tense and the future tense.

Plenary

Students work in pairs and give feedback to their partner on his/her pronunciation.

Students tell their partner five or more ways to use technology for leisure activities.

Students say which activity they like and explain why.

Students describe how much time they spend online, whether they feel it to be too much and whether they think they are addicted..

3.3 Les ados et les réseaux sociaux
pages 44–45

Planner

Objectives
- Vocabulary: identify the potential dangers of social networking sites
- Grammar: use impersonal structures
- Skills: use memorisation strategies; use spoken and written register

Resources
- Student Book, pages 44–45
- CD 1, tracks 26–27
- Grammar and Skills Workbook, pages 20 and 48
- Kerboodle, Unit 3

Key language

la cyberintimidation, la cyberdépendance, la cyberpermanence, la cybersécurité

Il est important/impossible/essentiel/obligatoire/ nécessaire de/d'... comprendre/effacer/limiter/se protéger/en parler avec/traiter les autres ...

Il faut/Il ne faut pas/Il est important de ne pas mettre son nom complet.

Grammar
- Impersonal structures

PLTS
- Activity 1: Self-managers
- Activity 7: Creative thinkers
- Plenary: Reflective learners

Homework and self-study
- Student Book, page 44, activity 3
- Student Book, page 45, activity 6
- Student Book, page 45, activity 7
- Grammar and Skills Workbook, page 20, activity 1, and page 48

Starters

See Kerboodle Starters bank for further details of **Up, down**.

- In preparation for the work on **Memorisation strategies**, ask students to work in pairs and discuss the techniques they use when learning long words. Pool the ideas as a class and write a list on the board.
- Play **Up, down** to practise recognition of impersonal structures. Read out the text from activity 2 and ask students to stand up whenever they hear an impersonal structure.

Plenaries

- **Spoken and written register**. Working in the same groups as for the Plenary on page 45, students check their understanding of the formal *Il est important de ...* and the informal *C'est important de ...* Give the groups two minutes to discuss this and to relate these phrases to examples in English. Then give the groups three minutes to note down on pieces of paper examples in French. The examples should be passed on to the next group, who check their understanding again by stating whether the language used is formal or informal.

1 Lis et relie. C'est toi, le détective!

Students match the English words to their French equivalents.

As a follow-up task, ask students to analyse how they worked out the answers: what clues did they use (cognates, synonyms, etc.)? They then talk about it with their partner.

Do the **Memorisation strategies** starter activity and then run through the **Memorisation strategies** box with students and encourage them to use the tips when learning vocabulary. Two examples of online 'word cloud' creators are www.tagxedo.com and www.wordle.net.

Answers: **1** c; **2** a; **3** d; **4** b

2 Écoute et lis (1–4). On parle de quel risque (a–d)?

Students listen and read the text about the dangers of social networking sites. They match each paragraph to the correct potential danger from activity 1. Explain to students that they need to read the text for gist and decide which potential danger is described (rather than being actually named).

Answers: **1** c; **2** b; **3** d; **4** a

CD 1, track 26   page 44, activité 2

Quels risques présentent les réseaux sociaux?

1. Il est important de comprendre que vos commentaires, photos et vidéos sont accessibles par d'autres. Une fois postés, il est impossible d'effacer toute trace d'images et de messages. Internet a une mémoire illimitée.
2. Il est nécessaire de limiter l'utilisation des réseaux sociaux si on ne veut pas risquer d'aimer un peu trop la vie « virtuelle ». Si on commence à préférer la vie virtuelle à la vie réelle, on risque de devenir dépendant des réseaux sociaux.
3. Il est essentiel de se protéger sur Internet. Partager trop d'informations peut rendre vulnérable aux contacts indésirables et aux prédateurs du Net. Il est important de ne pas mettre son nom complet et d'ajouter à sa liste d'amis uniquement des personnes que l'on connaît.
4. Si on est victime d'une cyberintimidation, il est absolument essentiel d'en parler avec un adulte. En ligne, il faut traiter les autres de la même façon qu'on aimerait être traité.

Point final: l'âge recommandé pour l'inscription sur les réseaux sociaux est de treize ans d'habitude.

3 Accro à la technologie?

3 Relis le texte et trouve le français pour les phrases a–f.
Students read the text again and find the French equivalents for the English sentences.
Answers: **a** Partager trop d'informations peut rendre vulnérable. **b** Il faut traiter les autres de la même façon qu'on aimerait être traité. **c** Il est nécessaire de limiter l'utilisation de réseaux sociaux. **d** Il est impossible d'effacer toute trace d'images et de messages. **e** Il est important de comprendre que vos commentaires, photos et vidéos sont accessibles par d'autres. **f** Si on est victime d'une cyberintimidation, il est absolument essentiel d'en parler avec un adulte.

Students choose a paragraph and translate it into English.

As a follow-up task, ask students to read the text again and answer the following questions in English:
a List two things that are impossible to delete once posted online.
b How can you tell if you're becoming addicted to social media?
c To protect yourself on social networking sites, what is it important not to give?
d Who should you have on your 'friends' list?

Answers: **a** pictures, messages; **b** you start to prefer social media to real life; **c** your full name; **d** only people that you know

4 Écoute (1–4). Recopie et remplis la grille.

Students listen and note down the letter of the risk from activity 1 that is being discussed.

Students note down in English what advice is given.

Students transcribe the advice.

Answers:

	Risk	Advice
1	a	It's essential to talk about it with an adult if you're a victim of cyber-bullying.
2	c	It's important to understand that the Internet has a long memory. (It's impossible to wipe out all traces of a picture or message that has been posted online.)
3	d	You must protect yourself online.
4	b	It is necessary to/You have to limit your use of social networking sites.

CD 1, track 27   page 45, activité 4

1 Si on est victime d'une cyberintimidation, c'est essentiel d'en parler avec un adulte.
2 C'est important de comprendre qu'Internet a une mémoire illimitée. C'est impossible d'effacer toute trace d'images et de messages postés.
3 Partager trop d'informations peut rendre vulnérable. Il faut se protéger sur Internet.
4 Si on préfère la vie virtuelle, il est nécessaire de limiter l'utilisation des réseaux sociaux.

Once students have completed activity 4, run through the grammar box on **Impersonal structures**. Use the **Up, down** starter activity, or ask them to listen again to the recording from activity 4 and to note down all the instances of impersonal expressions. On a third listening, they could also identify register (*Il est .../C'est ...*).

5 À deux. Parlez des risques. Que faire?
In pairs, students discuss the four risks (a–d in activity 1) and what they can do about them. They should use impersonal structures and spoken register in their conversations. Refer students to the key language box for support.

6 Lis « En ligne, protège-toi! ». Traduis en anglais.
Students read and translate the set of guidelines (a–e) giving advice about how to stay safe online. Remind students to draw on their reading strategies when decoding meaning and to refresh their memory of the **Translation strategies** covered in Unit 2 (page 28).

Answers: Protect yourself online! **a** It is important never to give your name, address or phone number. **b** It is essential never to share information that would allow someone to find out where you live. **c** It is absolutely essential never to agree to meet someone. **d** It is important never to send a photo or video of yourself or someone else. **e** If a message or a picture shocks you, it is important to talk about it to an adult.

7 Dessine une page web.
Students design a web page to promote safe use of social media. Encourage them to use the full range of language covered in the spread and, where appropriate, to include impersonal expressions and correct register in their writing.

Students name the four key areas of risk.

Students name three areas of risk and give a piece of advice for each one, using impersonal structures.

Students name four areas of risk, give advice for each one using impersonal structures and add some extra advice and information.

Key language

la cyberintimidation, la cyberdépendance, la cyberpermanence, la cybersécurité

Il est important/impossible/essentiel/obligatoire/ nécessaire de/d'... comprendre/effacer/limiter/se protéger/en parler avec/traiter les autres ...

Il faut/Il ne faut pas/Il est important de ne pas mettre son nom complet.

Grammar
- Impersonal structures

PLTS
- Activity 1: Self-managers
- Activity 7: Creative thinkers
- Plenary: Reflective learners

Homework and self-study
- Student Book, page 44, activity 3
- Student Book, page 45, activity 6
- Student Book, page 45, activity 7
- Grammar and Skills Workbook, page 20, activity 1, and page 48

Starters
See Kerboodle Starters bank for further details of **Up, down**.

- In preparation for the work on **Memorisation strategies**, ask students to work in pairs and discuss the techniques they use when learning long words. Pool the ideas as a class and write a list on the board.
- Play **Up, down** to practise recognition of impersonal structures. Read out the text from activity 2 and ask students to stand up whenever they hear an impersonal structure.

Plenaries
- **Spoken and written register**. Working in the same groups as for the Plenary on page 45, students check their understanding of the formal *Il est important de ...* and the informal *C'est important de ...* Give the groups two minutes to discuss this and to relate these phrases to examples in English. Then give the groups three minutes to note down on pieces of paper examples in French. The examples should be passed on to the next group, who check their understanding again by stating whether the language used is formal or informal.

1 Lis et relie. C'est toi, le détective!

Students match the English words to their French equivalents.

As a follow-up task, ask students to analyse how they worked out the answers: what clues did they use (cognates, synonyms, etc.)? They then talk about it with their partner.

Do the **Memorisation strategies** starter activity and then run through the **Memorisation strategies** box with students and encourage them to use the tips when learning vocabulary. Two examples of online 'word cloud' creators are www.tagxedo.com and www.wordle.net.

Answers: **1** c; **2** a; **3** d; **4** b

2 Écoute et lis (1–4). On parle de quel risque (a–d)?

Students listen and read the text about the dangers of social networking sites. They match each paragraph to the correct potential danger from activity 1. Explain to students that they need to read the text for gist and decide which potential danger is described (rather than being actually named).

Answers: **1** c; **2** b; **3** d; **4** a

CD 1, track 26   page 44, activité 2

Quels risques présentent les réseaux sociaux?

1 Il est important de comprendre que vos commentaires, photos et vidéos sont accessibles par d'autres. Une fois postés, il est impossible d'effacer toute trace d'images et de messages. Internet a une mémoire illimitée.

2 Il est nécessaire de limiter l'utilisation des réseaux sociaux si on ne veut pas risquer d'aimer un peu trop la vie « virtuelle ». Si on commence à préférer la vie virtuelle à la vie réelle, on risque de devenir dépendant des réseaux sociaux.

3 Il est essentiel de se protéger sur Internet. Partager trop d'informations peut rendre vulnérable aux contacts indésirables et aux prédateurs du Net. Il est important de ne pas mettre son nom complet et d'ajouter à sa liste d'amis uniquement des personnes que l'on connaît.

4 Si on est victime d'une cyberintimidation, il est absolument essentiel d'en parler avec un adulte. En ligne, il faut traiter les autres de la même façon qu'on aimerait être traité.

Point final: l'âge recommandé pour l'inscription sur les réseaux sociaux est de treize ans d'habitude.

3 Accro à la technologie?

3 Relis le texte et trouve le français pour les phrases a–f.
Students read the text again and find the French equivalents for the English sentences.

Answers: **a** *Partager trop d'informations peut rendre vulnérable.* **b** *Il faut traiter les autres de la même façon qu'on aimerait être traité.* **c** *Il est nécessaire de limiter l'utilisation de réseaux sociaux.* **d** *Il est impossible d'effacer toute trace d'images et de messages.* **e** *Il est important de comprendre que vos commentaires, photos et vidéos sont accessibles par d'autres.* **f** *Si on est victime d'une cyberintimidation, il est absolument essential d'en parler avec un adulte.*

Students choose a paragraph and translate it into English.

As a follow-up task, ask students to read the text again and answer the following questions in English:

a List two things that are impossible to delete once posted online.
b How can you tell if you're becoming addicted to social media?
c To protect yourself on social networking sites, what is it important not to give?
d Who should you have on your 'friends' list?

Answers: **a** *pictures, messages;* **b** *you start to prefer social media to real life;* **c** *your full name;* **d** *only people that you know*

4 Écoute (1–4). Recopie et remplis la grille.

Students listen and note down the letter of the risk from activity 1 that is being discussed.

Students note down in English what advice is given.

Students transcribe the advice.

Answers:

	Risk	Advice
1	a	It's essential to talk about it with an adult if you're a victim of cyber-bullying.
2	c	It's important to understand that the Internet has a long memory. (It's impossible to wipe out all traces of a picture or message that has been posted online.)
3	d	You must protect yourself online.
4	b	It is necessary to/You have to limit your use of social networking sites.

CD 1, track 27   page 45, activité 4

1 Si on est victime d'une cyberintimidation, c'est essentiel d'en parler avec un adulte.
2 C'est important de comprendre qu'Internet a une mémoire illimitée. C'est impossible d'effacer toute trace d'images et de messages postés.
3 Partager trop d'informations peut rendre vulnérable. Il faut se protéger sur Internet.
4 Si on préfère la vie virtuelle, il est nécessaire de limiter l'utilisation des réseaux sociaux.

Once students have completed activity 4, run through the grammar box on **Impersonal structures**. Use the **Up, down** starter activity, or ask them to listen again to the recording from activity 4 and to note down all the instances of impersonal expressions. On a third listening, they could also identify register (*Il est …/C'est …*).

5 À deux. Parlez des risques. Que faire?
In pairs, students discuss the four risks (a–d in activity 1) and what they can do about them. They should use impersonal structures and spoken register in their conversations. Refer students to the key language box for support.

6 Lis « En ligne, protège-toi! ». Traduis en anglais.
Students read and translate the set of guidelines (a–e) giving advice about how to stay safe online. Remind students to draw on their reading strategies when decoding meaning and to refresh their memory of the **Translation strategies** covered in Unit 2 (page 28).

Answers: Protect yourself online! **a** *It is important never to give your name, address or phone number.* **b** *It is essential never to share information that would allow someone to find out where you live.* **c** *It is absolutely essential never to agree to meet someone.* **d** *It is important never to send a photo or video of yourself or someone else.* **e** *If a message or a picture shocks you, it is important to talk about it to an adult.*

7 Dessine une page web.
Students design a web page to promote safe use of social media. Encourage them to use the full range of language covered in the spread and, where appropriate, to include impersonal expressions and correct register in their writing.

Students name the four key areas of risk.

Students name three areas of risk and give a piece of advice for each one, using impersonal structures.

Students name four areas of risk, give advice for each one using impersonal structures and add some extra advice and information.

58

> **Plenary**
>
> 👥 Working in groups, students present their web page in turn. The groups look carefully at the specification for activity 7 and assess each web page, giving two positive comments about each and suggesting how to improve it.
>
> ⭐ Students provide simple information in their web page.
>
> ◎ Students provide information and advice.
>
> ⊕ Students provide more detailed information and advice.

3.4 Pour ou contre la technologie?

pages 46–47

Planner

Objectives
- Vocabulary: talk about the pros and cons of new technologies
- Grammar: structure an argument
- Skills: debate a point

Resources
- Student Book, pages 46–47
- CD 1, tracks 28–29
- Grammar and Skills Workbook, page 49
- Kerboodle, Unit 3
- Unit 3 Worksheets 5 (ex. 2–3)

Key language

Les nouvelles technologies sont excellentes mais chères/rendent la vie plus simple. Cela décourage l'activité physique. On peut en devenir dépendant. On risque de devenir antisocial. Il y a un risque de/d'… Il est facile de rester en contact … Internet est une source d'information très riche.

Grammar
- Structure an argument

PLTS
- Activity 3: Independent enquirers
- Activity 6: Effective participators
- Activity 7: Creative thinkers

Homework and self-study
- Student Book, page 46, activity 3
- Student Book, page 46, activity 4
- Student Book, page 47, activity 7
- Grammar and Skills Workbook, page 49

Starters

See Kerboodle Starters bank for further details of **Categorise**.

- Hold a **Class discussion** on the pros and cons of new technologies, in preparation for activity 1. Can students think of any that are not covered in the activity?
- Before students embark on activity 6, play **Categorise** with the phrases for structuring arguments. Put the three categories ('Start', 'Develop', 'Finish') on the board and ask students to work in pairs to note down as many examples as they can for each category.

Plenaries

- **Preparing a debate**. There are strong links to citizenship teaching on this spread and students should be given time to structure their thoughts and relate where possible what they are learning to real-life situations they have come across in school, in their town or village, or at home. Students work in pairs, noting down their thoughts and opinions, using dictionaries as necessary. To help students develop the skill of substitution, encourage them to substitute key vocabulary from the spread into phrases from other spreads and units in *Allez 2*, to make these relevant to the learning context of the spread.

Allow time for a whole-class discussion of any questions or opinions that arise during this activity, or come back to this at a later date to allow for confidence in speaking to grow. Students will be working again on substitution on page 48.

1 Lis et relie les phrases 1–8 aux phrases a–h.
Students read the texts about the pros and cons of new technology and match the English sentences to the correct French equivalents. As a follow-up activity, look back at the pros and cons that students came up with in the **Class discussion** starter activity, and identify whether there were any that were not mentioned in the texts. Can students work out how they would say these in French?

Answers: **1** c; **2** a; **3** f; **4** e; **5** h; **6** g; **7** d; **8** b

3 Accro à la technologie?

2 Écoute (1–8) et vérifie tes réponses.
Students listen and check their answers.

CD 1, track 28 — page 46, activité 2

1. Les nouvelles technologies sont excellentes mais chères. Elles ne sont donc pas accessibles à tous.
2. Cela décourage l'activité physique.
3. On peut en devenir dépendant.
4. Il y a un risque d'être victime de prédateurs du Net ou de cyberintimidation.
5. Internet est une source d'information très riche mais ce n'est pas toujours fiable ou crédible.
6. Les nouvelles technologies rendent la vie plus simple.
7. On risque de devenir antisocial.
8. Il est facile de rester en contact avec des gens.

3 Lis les phrases de l'activité 1. C'est un argument pour (P), contre (C) ou pour et contre (P + C) les nouvelles technologies?
Students read the French sentences from activity 1 again and decide whether each is a pro or con (or both) of new technology. As an extension task, students could give their answers in French: *a, c'est un argument contre,* etc.
Answers: **a** C; **b** P; **c** P + C; **d** C; **e** C; **f** C; **g** P; **h** P + C

⭐ Students look back at the sentences in activity 1 and spot the cognates and near-cognates.

◎ They look again to spot examples of the infinitive structures covered earlier in the unit.

4 Lis le blog de Clarisse. C'est vrai ou faux?
Students read the text and decide whether the English statements are true or false. Draw students' attention to the glossed term (*la toile* – 'the Web'), and explain that *la toile d'araignée* is a spider's web. As a follow-up extension task, ask students to correct the false statements in French.
Answers: **a** faux (*j'avais un ami qui s'appelle Marc*); **b** vrai; **c** faux (*il a passé vingt heures à jouer à des jeux en ligne le week-end dernier*); **d** faux (*j'aime aller sur les réseaux sociaux*); **e** faux (*je ne veux pas devenir quelqu'un d'antisocial*); **f** vrai

5 Écoute le débat et réponds aux questions en anglais.
Students listen and answer the questions in English. Before playing the recording, run through the grammar box on **Structuring arguments**. Ask students to look back at the text in activity 4 to see which of the terms listed were used there (*pour commencer, en plus, finalement*) and to note their use in structuring the line of argument. As a follow-up task, students listen again and note down the phrases each speaker uses to structure his/her arguments.
Answers: **a** New technologies make life easier, e.g. online shopping. **b** It's easy (and quick) to stay in touch with people, e.g. friends and family. **c** New technologies provide a rich source of information, e.g. you can surf the Internet and consult wikis. **d** It discourages young people from doing physical activity and if you spend too much time online you can become antisocial. **e** The risk of predators and cyber-bullying. He agrees that it is easy to stay in contact with people. **f** Information online isn't always reliable or credible. The Internet is a rich source of information.

CD 1, track 29 — page 47, activité 5

– Je vais vous expliquer pourquoi je suis pour les nouvelles technologies.
Pour commencer, les nouvelles technologies rendent la vie plus simple. Je pense à la possibilité de faire du shopping en ligne, par exemple.
En outre, il est facile de rester en contact avec des gens, avec ses amis ou sa famille, par exemple, et c'est plus rapide aussi.
Pour terminer, avec les nouvelles technologies, on a accès à une source d'information très riche. On peut surfer et consulter des wikis, par exemple.

– Moi, je vais vous expliquer pourquoi je suis contre les nouvelles technologies.
Premièrement, cela décourage les jeunes de faire de l'activité physique et si on passe trop de temps en ligne, on risque de devenir antisocial.
Deuxièmemement, je suis d'accord qu'il est facile de rester en contact avec les gens, mais il y a un risque d'être victime de prédateurs du Net ou de cyberintimidation.
Finalement, Internet est une source d'information très riche mais ce n'est pas toujours fiable ou crédible.

6 Débat en groupe: « Pour ou contre les nouvelles technologies? »
Working in pairs, students take a standpoint for or against new technologies and then have a debate with another pair who take the opposite standpoint. Before students embark on this task, refer them to the skills box on **Debating a point** and encourage them to use a range of these phrases in their debate. This would also be a good point at which to do the **Categorise** starter activity.

7 Écris un mail à ton/ta député(e).
Students write an email to their MP, outlining their arguments for and/or against new technologies. Refer them to the sample email as a model, and remind them to structure their arguments using the phrases from the grammar and skills boxes.

⭐ Students give three arguments for <u>or</u> against new technologies.

◎ They give three arguments for <u>and</u> against.

✚ Students make their opening statement using the future tense, as in the example. They use and adapt other language from pages 46–47 and develop their arguments as much as possible.

60

Plenary

⭐ Students give three reasons why they are for new technologies.

⭕ Students add three reasons why someone might be against them.

➕ Students give three reasons for and against them, using connectives such as *mais* and *par contre* to contrast the positive and negative points of each argument.

3.5 Le meilleur gadget? pages 48–49

Planner

Objectives
- Vocabulary: talk about favourite technology and gadgets
- Grammar: use the preposition *à* + definite article
- Skills: use speaking strategies; use reading strategies to work out meaning

Resources
- Student Book, pages 48–49
- CD 1, track 30
- Grammar and Skills Workbook, page 21
- Kerboodle, Unit 3
- Unit 3 Worksheets 3 (ex. 1), 4 (ex. 2)

Key language

un smartphone, un baladeur numérique, une tablette, un ultra-portable

Je préfère ... au/à la/à l'/aux ... parce que/car ...

... c'est/il est/elle est léger/légère, compact(e), pratique, moderne.

... on peut prendre des photos, écouter de la musique, lire des mails, faire/regarder des vidéos, envoyer des textos, téléphoner.

Comme c'est/il est/elle est ..., je préfère ...

Grammar
- *à* + definite article

PLTS
- Activity 1: Independent enquirers
- Activity 5: Team workers, Self-managers
- Plenary: Reflective learners

Homework and self-study
- Student Book, page 48, activity 2
- Student Book, page 49, activity 4
- Student Book, page 49, activity 6
- Grammar and Skills Workbook, page 21

Starters

See Kerboodle Starters bank for further details of **Pictionary**.

- Play **Pictionary** to help students learn the French for the four devices presented in activity 1.
- Revise *à* + definite article in preparation for activity 2. This construction was first covered in *Allez 1*, Unit 5, in the context of places in town. Call out a series of phrases and ask students to say whether the *à* + definite article construction is correct and to correct the incorrect versions: Teacher: *Je vais à la patinoire*. Student: *Correcte!* Teacher: *Je vais à le cinéma*. Student: *Incorrecte! Je vais au cinéma*. Teacher: *Je vais à les États-Unis*. Student: *Incorrecte! Je vais aux États-Unis*. Tell students that the gender will be correct each time, and that they simply need to focus on whether the *à* + definite article construction is correct.

Plenaries

- **A walking plenary**. This plenary should be used after students have watched the Unit 3 video clip (see page 55). Students should be given time in advance to prepare for this activity: ask them to set up a simple grid to log their Internet usage for a week, including how long they spent on various websites and social media sites, what they were doing, and the ways in which they use their gadgets. More confident learners could also note down activities with friends, so that the *il/elle* forms of the verbs can be practised too. This could be started in class, with students walking around the class, interviewing three other members of the class with whom they don't normally work: *Quel est ton gadget préféré? Est-ce que tu écoutes de la musique/joues à des jeux en ligne? C'est important d'essayer de limiter le temps qu'on passe sur Internet?*

3 Accro à la technologie?

1 Lis. C'est quelle image?
Students read the texts and match them to the correct photos. Point out that the names of the devices are in bold and that the rest of the text describes the device and its features. As a follow-up task, students could list the features of each of the devices.

After students have completed the activity, ask them how they worked out the answers (and if they've done the Gold medal activity, ask them what helped them with the translation). Encourage them to share any strategies they've used: for example, they will have been helped by the photos, cognates in the texts, and their own knowledge of the context/what they know about modern technology.

Answers: **1** d; **2** a; **3** c; **4** b

➕ ⓣ Students choose one of the descriptions and translate it into English.

Translations: **1** With a smartphone you can do much more than just make phonecalls. It's a true pocket computer. **2** It's a digital music player with a touchscreen, which looks like a smartphone but without the phone functions. **3** It's a tablet with a touchscreen. It's half-way between a laptop and a smartphone. **4** A netbook is a laptop which is very light and reduced in size, and can be transported and used anywhere.

2 Qu'est-ce qu'on préfère? 🔍
Before students attempt this activity, run through the grammar box on **The preposition à**. Draw their attention to the contraction with the definite articles *le* and *les* (but not with *la* or *l'*) and explain that they will be using this construction in activity 2. Remind them that they have come across this construction before (with places in *Allez 1*, Unit 5) and do the starter activity to reinforce this.

Students then complete the sentences by adding in the correct definite article of the first device in brackets, and the correct form of à + definite article before the second device. Point out to students that the nouns are colour-coded so they do not need to look up genders.

Answers: **a** *Je préfère la tablette au smartphone …* **b** *Je préfère la tablette à l'ultra-portable …* **c** *Je préfère le baladeur numérique à la tablette …* **d** *Je préfère le smartphone au portable traditionnel …* **e** *Je préfère l'ultra-portable à la tablette …* **f** *… je préfère les livres numériques aux livres traditionnels.*

➕ Students rewrite the sentences, giving different reasons for the opinions. They use activity 1 for support.

3 Écoute l'émission de radio. Anne Formatik parle de ses gadgets préférés. Recopie et remplis la grille en anglais.

Answers:

	Gadget	Description/Opinion
3	smart glasses	very exciting innovation; doesn't know if it is going to be a serious rival for more traditional gadgets; has potential but remains to be seen
2	tablet	a device with a touchscreen; prefers it to traditional portable computers because it's lighter and more compact
1	smartphone	the ultimate/top gadget; prefers it to all the other gadgets mentioned; it's a computer and a mobile phone at the same time; the most portable gadget of all; the success of the smartphone is surely going to continue for a long time

◎ Students listen again and spot examples of the past and/or future tenses.

Answers: **Past:** *a été sélectionnée, j'ai choisi, J'ai décidé*; **Near-future:** *va rivaliser, va continuer*

〰️ **CD 1, track 30   page 49, activité 3**

— Bonsoir, chers auditeurs et chères auditrices. L'émission *Le Top du Gadget* vous souhaite la bienvenue. Ce mois-ci, notre liste de top gadgets a été sélectionnée par Anne Formatik, de la revue mensuelle *Le Monde Virtuel*. Alors, Anne, selon vous, quels sont les gadgets en tête du top trois en ce moment?

— En troisième place, j'ai choisi … les lunettes intelligentes. C'est une innovation très excitante mais je ne sais pas si cette invention va rivaliser sérieusement avec les gadgets plus traditionnels. Il y a du potentiel mais cela reste à voir.
J'ai décidé de donner la deuxième place à … la tablette numérique. Une tablette, c'est un appareil à écran tactile. Je la préfère aux ordinateurs portables traditionnels parce qu'elle est plus légère et plus compacte aussi. C'est du sérieux, tout ça.
Mais pour moi, le top gadget, c'est … le smartphone. Je le préfère à tous les autres gadgets mentionnés. Il fait à la fois ordinateur et téléphone portable. C'est le gadget le plus facile à porter. Le succès du smartphone va sûrement continuer longtemps. Et pour moi, ça, c'est top!

— Merci d'être venue, Anne, et d'avoir partagé vos top gadgets avec nous ce soir. Et maintenant, chers auditeurs et chères auditrices …

4 Lis et réponds aux questions en anglais.
Students read the text and answer the questions in English.

⭐ Students answer the main part of the question.

⭕ Students answer the part in brackets.

➕ **t** Students translate the underlined phrases.

Answers: **a** smartphone and tablet; **b** telephone, send texts, watch videos, listen to music, read books; **c** It's more practical for things like reading, watching things or typing long documents. **d** laptops (even smaller ones like netbooks/mini-laptops); **e** smartphone; **f** a smartphone (It would be the same size as his tablet.)

Translations: It's the ultimate gadget in my opinion. You can do everything with it. when I want ...
If I were ... The gadget of my dreams/My ideal gadget

5 En groupe: « Quel gadget préfères-tu? » Le groupe est d'accord?
In groups, students discuss their opinions of the various devices. Refer them to the section on **Speaking strategies** on page 51 and encourage them to use these tips to plan what they want to say.

Refer them also to the key language box on page 49 for support and back to page 4 for expressions of agreement and disagreement.

6 Fais la description de ton gadget préféré. Donne ton opinion.
Students write a review of their favourite gadget. Remind them to include a range of opinion phrases and to justify their opinions with reasons. The key language box provides support. More able students could write in more detail, reviewing two or three gadgets and using connectives such as *mais* to compare them.

Plenary

Students give written answers to the medal activities, checking their work for accuracy of spelling. They then swap with a partner and give each other feedback.

⭐ Students list three gadgets in French.

⭕ Students name a gadget and say what one can do with it.

➕ Students name the gadget they prefer. They give a reason and say what they have used it for.

3.6 Labo-langue
pages 50–51

Planner

Objectives
- Grammar: position and agreement of adjectives; impersonal structures; verb + preposition + infinitive
- Skills: speaking strategies
- Pronunciation: *eu*

Resources
- Student Book, pages 50–51
- CD 1, track 31
- Grammar and Skills Workbook, page 49
- Kerboodle, Unit 3
- Unit 3 Worksheets 7, 8

PLTS
- Creative thinkers, Reflective learners, Self-managers

Position and agreement of adjectives

1 Copy and complete each sentence using the adjective provided.
Remind students that adjectives of size (e.g. *grand, petit*), as well as *nouveau* and *vieux*, go in front of the noun. Remind them also to ensure that each adjective agrees with the noun it is describing. (The nouns are colour-coded for support.)

Answers: **a** J'adore les <u>nouvelles</u> technologies. **b** Je n'aime pas mon <u>vieux</u> portable. **c** Je préfère la tablette <u>bleue</u>. **d** Je préfère mon <u>nouvel</u> ordinateur à mon vieil ordinateur. **e** Je déteste les <u>petits</u> portables. **f** Je n'aime pas la tablette <u>noire</u>.

Impersonal structures

2 Unscramble the sentences and rewrite them using correct word order.
As a follow-up task, students could read out the correct sentences to their partner, changing the register as appropriate.

Answers: **a** Il est essentiel de se protéger sur Internet. (Spoken: C'est ...) **b** Il est absolument essentiel d'en parler avec un adulte. (Spoken: C'est ...) **c** Il est impossible d'effacer toute trace d'une image ou d'un message. (Spoken: C'est ...) **d** Il est important de comprendre que vos messages, photos et vidéos sont accessibles par d'autres. (Spoken: C'est ...) **e** Il ne faut pas donner ton nom ou ton adresse. (Spoken: No need to change) **f** Il ne faut jamais accepter de rendez-vous. (Spoken: No need to change)

3 Accro à la technologie?

Verb + preposition + infinitive

t 3 Translate a–c into French and d–f into English.

Answers: **a** J'ai arrêté d'aller sur les réseaux sociaux. **b** Je passe du temps à jouer à des jeux en ligne. **c** J'ai arrêté d'écouter de la musique en ligne. **d** I have stopped making video calls. **e** I spend time using social networking sites. **f** I spend time watching streamed programmes.

Speaking strategies

This section encourages students to think about strategies for speaking. Ask them to work in pairs and discuss these and any other strategies they might have already tried and that they feel would be helpful for them.

Students are encouraged to try out the new strategies with activity 5 on page 43 and activity 5 on page 49.

Pronunciation: *eu*

4 Read aloud sentences 1–4. Then listen to check your pronunciation of the *eu* sounds.

CD 1, track 31   page 51, activité 4

1. Comme gadgets, j'ai un ordinateur, une liseuse et un baladeur numérique.
2. J'adore mon baladeur car je peux écouter de la musique où je veux et quand je veux.
3. En ligne, un interlocuteur peut être un prédateur alors fais attention!
4. Je passe des heures à jouer à des jeux en ligne mais mon ordinateur est vieux.

3.7 Extra Star   page 52

1 Match the words to the features (a–e).

Answers: **a** le smartphone; **b** l'écran tactile; **c** les applis; **d** les écouteurs; **e** l'appareil photo

2 Match up the sentence halves.

Answers: **1** e; **2** d; **3** c; **4** f; **5** b; **6** a

3 Read the article about the top three gadgets of the year. Copy and complete the grid in English.

Answers:

Place	Gadget	Reasons why ...
3rd	laptop	it's small and light; you have everything necessary for schoolwork; you can make video calls and listen to music online
2nd	tablet	you can watch streamed programmes, surf the Internet and read emails
1st	smartphone	it's a mobile phone and a mini-computer; you can make video calls, use social networking sites and play games online

4 What are your top three gadgets? Explain why you like them and what you can use them for.

Refer students to the key language box on page 49 if they need support.

3.7 Extra Plus
page 53

1 Mets les mots dans le bon ordre. Recopie les phrases.

Students re-order the sentences and write them out.

Answers: **a** *J'adore mon nouveau smartphone parce qu'il y a un écran tactile et beaucoup d'applis. Je préfère le smartphone au portable traditionnel.* **b** *Mon vieux portable est petit et démodé. J'aime le nouveau car c'est un portable et un ordinateur.* **c** *On peut aller sur les réseaux sociaux, surfer et trouver des sites intéressants. C'est le meilleur gadget.*

2 Lis l'article et réponds aux questions en anglais.

Students read the text and answer the questions in English.

Answers: **a** *in the USA;* **b** *more anxious than others;* **c** *schoolwork;* **d** *limiting the use of smartphones;* **e** *reduce anxiety, allow them to concentrate better on schoolwork*

3 Pour ou contre les smartphones? Dessine un poster ou une infographie.

Students design a poster or infographic on the pros and cons of smartphones. Encourage them to use ideas and vocabulary from activity 2 and from the whole of Unit 3, and to use the structures in the prompts box (opinion phrases, connectives, phrases to justify opinions, and phrases to structure arguments).

3.8 Lire
page 54

Resources
- Student Book, page 54
- Kerboodle, Unit 3

PLTS
- Independent enquirers

1 Read the text. Choose a title (below) for each paragraph (1–3). Careful: there are three titles that you will not need.

Tell students that the name *Biblio'Brousse* is a made-up name based on the word *bibliobus* ('library bus'/'mobile library bus'). Challenge them to come up with an appropriate English translation of *Biblio'Brousse*.

Answers: **1** *Pas assez d'enseignants;* **2** *Un bus qui sert d'école;* **3** *Initier les jeunes et les adultes*

2 True or false? For the false statements, find words from the text to justify your answer.

Answers: **a** *false (la plupart des écoles secondaires possèdent des salles d'informatique);* **b** *false (qui peut accueillir 20 personnes par cours);* **c** *true;* **d** *false (séances pour le public (employés de l'administration, autres services publics));* **e** *false (la formation dure quatre mois);* **f** *true*

3.8 Vidéo
page 55

Resources
- Student Book, page 55
- Kerboodle, Unit 3 Video clip

PLTS
- Independent enquirers

Épisode 3: Le gadget préféré
The friends are at the media library for the next challenge of the competition: what is the favourite technological device of young people in Montpellier?

The friends discuss and record their own preferences and then expand their survey by asking passers-by. Finally Jules, forever online, puts the question to a youth forum.

3 Accro à la technologie?

Video clip, Unit 3   page 55

(At the media library)

Jules: J'adore ce nouveau défi. C'est fait pour moi.

Clarisse: Oui, comme tu es accro à la technologie.

Jules: Bien sûr! « La technologie est très importante à Montpellier. Mais quel est le gadget préféré des jeunes et pourquoi? »

Basile: On est ici à la médiathèque pour faire un sondage et répondre à cette question.

Clarisse: J'adore les sondages. Moi, je vais commencer. J'adore mon nouveau portable – c'est un smartphone.

Jules: Tu as un ordiphone? J'adore les ordiphones parce qu'on peut tout faire – surfer et trouver des sites intéressants.

Clarisse: C'est à moi! Oui, je préfère mon nouveau smartphone à mon ancien portable car je peux lire des mails, écouter de la musique, aller sur les réseaux sociaux ... Tout est possible.

Zaied: Tu peux même envoyer des textos!

Basile: Maintenant à moi. Je déteste mon ancienne console car elle est démodée. Je préfère ma nouvelle tablette car il y a un écran tactile et je peux tout faire avec.

Thouraya: Attention. Le risque d'un gadget si intelligent, c'est l'addiction.

Basile: Tu as raison. Je ne veux plus me séparer de ma tablette.

Jules: Moi, j'aime mon vieil ordi car il est grand, il y a des touches ... C'est facile à utiliser.

Basile: Combien de temps passes-tu devant ton ordinateur, Thouraya?

Thouraya: En moyenne je passe deux heures par jour devant mon ordinateur parce que je fais mes devoirs en ligne. Mais le week-end, je passe environ trois heures à regarder des émissions en streaming.

Zaied: Alors ça, c'est super. Est-ce que je pourrais venir chez toi pour voir un film? C'est moins cher que d'aller au cinéma.

Thouraya: Quand tu veux, Zaied. Moi je préfère mon ordi ...

Jules: Et toi, Jémilie, c'est quoi, ton gadget préféré?

Jémilie: Moi, je déteste mon vieil ordinateur parce qu'il est trop grand et démodé. Je préfère ma nouvelle tablette, parce qu'elle est légère – je peux l'emmener partout. C'est très pratique.

Zaied: Est-ce qu'elle a un appareil photo?

Jémilie: Oui, bien sûr, regarde. *(Takes picture of him)* Moi, mon gadget préféré, c'est ma tablette.

Zaied: Moi, c'est ma console de jeux-vidéo. C'est très facile à utiliser et très divertissant. En moyenne je passe trois à quatre heures par jour à jouer sur ma console.

Basile: Moi aussi. Tu as vu le nouveau jeu de ...?

Clarisse: Mais on ne doit pas y passer trop de temps.

Jules: Moi, j'aime mon ordi mais j'aimerais avoir un smartphone aussi.

Clarisse: Voyons. Deux points pour les smartphones, deux points pour les tablettes, deux points pour les ordinateurs, un point pour la console de jeux.

Basile: Ça ne marche pas. On n'a pas un gadget qui gagne. Il faut demander à d'autres jeunes.

Jémilie: Pardon. Quel est ton gadget préféré et pourquoi?

Jeune 1: Je préfère mon vieux portable. Je n'aime pas aller en ligne parce que j'ai peur de la cyberintimidation. C'est important de se protéger en ligne, tu sais.

Zaied: Excuse-moi, quel est ton gadget préféré?

Jeune 2: Mon gadget préféré, c'est mon smartphone, bien sûr. J'adore mon nouveau smartphone parce qu'il est léger, moderne, il y a un écran tactile, c'est pratique et rapide.

Zaied: Tu es accro à la technologie donc?

Jeune 2: Je suis cyberdépendante!

Clarisse: Donc, quatre points pour les smartphones, deux points pour les tablettes, deux points pour les ordinateurs, un point pour la console de jeux. Ici à Montpellier on aime les gadgets les plus modernes.

Thouraya: Jules, qu'est-ce que tu fais?

Jules: Je suis connecté à un forum de jeunes. Je veux savoir ce que pensent les autres jeunes à Montpellier.

Jémilie: Vous voyez: surfer, c'est éducatif, informatif et addictif!

1 Regarde l'épisode 3. De quels gadgets parlent les jeunes?
Students watch the video and note down which gadgets the friends mention.
Answers: un portable, un smartphone/ordiphone, une console de jeux, une tablette, un ordi(nateur)

2 Lis les opinions a–e. Qui dit ça? C'est Clarisse, Jules, Zaied, Jémilie ou Basile?
Students read the opinions and decide which of the teenagers would be likely to say each one. In preparation for this task, check that students are sure of the names of the video characters.
Answers: a Zaied; b Clarisse; c Jémilie; d Jules; e Basile

3 Comment les jeunes utilisent-ils leurs gadgets? Qui parle de chaque activité a–d ?
Students identify which person from the video mentions using his/her gadget for each of the activities listed.
Answers: a Jules; b Clarisse; c Thouraya; d Thouraya

4 Parle de ton gadget préféré.
In groups, students discuss their favourite technological devices. Encourage them to refer to the prompts and example for support, and to draw on the language covered in the unit in their discussion.

3.9 Test

page 56

Resources
- Student Book, page 56
- CD 1, track 32

PLTS
- Creative thinkers, Reflective learners, Effective participators

AT levels
Approximate medal guidelines:
- (Foundation) L: 3; S: 3; R: 3–4; W: 3
- (Core) L: 3–4; S: 3–4; R: 4; W: 3–4
- (Higher) L: 4; S: 4; R: 5; W: 4

1 Listen to six young people talking about gadgets. Copy out and fill in the grid in English. (See pages 40–43.)
Make students aware that speaker 6 mentions two gadgets that they will need to note down.

Answers:

	Gadget	Opinion	Extra information
1	new mobile phone	☺	it's light and modern, she can listen to music where/whenever she wants
2	old mobile phone	☹	it's too big and has buttons
3	tablet	☺	loves making video calls on it because it's easy and cheap
4	computer	☺	spends two hours a day playing games online because it's entertaining
5	smartphone	☺	loves using social networking sites because you can easily stay in touch with people
6	old computer, new tablet	☹	hates computer because it's old-fashioned, prefers tablet because it's more modern

3 Accro à la technologie?

CD 1, track 32 — page 56, activitié 1

1 J'aime mon nouveau portable parce qu'il est léger et moderne. Je peux écouter de la musique où je veux et quand je veux.
2 Je n'aime pas mon vieux portable car il est trop grand et il y a des touches.
3 J'adore passer des appels vidéo sur ma tablette parce que c'est facile et pas cher.
4 J'aime bien mon ordinateur! Je passe deux heures par jour à jouer à des jeux en ligne parce que c'est divertissant.
5 Comme on peut rester facilement en contact avec les gens, j'adore aller sur les réseaux sociaux avec mon smartphone.
6 Je déteste mon vieil ordinateur parce qu'il est démodé. Je préfère ma nouvelle tablette parce qu'elle est plus moderne.

2 Give a presentation about new technologies. Are you for or against them? (See pages 40–47.)

Encourage students to cover all four bullet points in their presentations.

3 Read Noé's text and answer the questions in English. (See pages 42–47.)

Answers: **a** the computer in my pocket; **b** can download/listen to music; **c** can telephone them and can stay in touch using social networking sites; **d** can surf the Internet/find interesting websites; **e** limit the amount of time spent online; **f** with such a cool gadget, there's the danger of becoming addicted

4 Write an article for your school magazine about safe use of the Internet. (See pages 44–45.)

Encourage students to write as expansively as possible, drawing on language covered in the unit.

4 Être ado, c'est quoi?

Unit 4: Être ado, c'est quoi?   Overview grid

Page reference	Contexts and objectives	Grammar	Strategies and skills	Key language	AT levels*
58–59 **4.1 Ados–parents: c'est la guerre?**	Discuss relationships with parents	Use pronouns *me, te* and *se* in positive and negative sentences	Express opinions with confidence. Agree and disagree	*Mes parents me laissent sortir le week-end. Ma mère me fait confiance. Mon père me traite comme un bébé. Je ne peux pas sortir avec mes copains. Mes résultats scolaires sont très importants. J'ai de bonnes relations avec mes parents. Je parle beaucoup avec mes parents. Mes parents sont stricts, mais assez cool. Je (ne) peux/dois (pas) … sortir, jouer sur mon ordi, faire mes devoirs, rentrer*	L: 3–4 S: 3–4 R: 3–4 W: 3–4
60–61 **4.2 Les ados et l'argent**	Talk about pocket money and what you do to help at home	Identify and use modal verbs: *devoir, pouvoir* and *vouloir*	Ask and answer questions	Numbers 10–55 *Mes parents me donnent £10 par mois. Mon père me donne £10 par semaine. Mes parents m'achètent mes vêtements. Ma mère m'achète mes livres. Je dois … aider à la maison, faire la vaisselle, ranger ma chambre, tondre la pelouse, laver la voiture, faire les courses, garder mon petit frère/ma petite sœur, faire du baby-sitting. Je dois/Je veux/Je voudrais/Je peux/Je ne peux pas … acheter/payer mes places de ciné/mes CD/mes livres. … m'acheter une tablette/un jeu vidéo. … économiser/mettre de l'argent de côté.*	L: 3–4 S: 3–4 R: 4–6 W: 4–5
62–63 **4.3 Ados + pressions = problèmes?**	Talk about the pressures faced by teenagers and understand advice	*Tu* form of the imperative	Listening strategies	*Mon problème, c'est le collège/la presse parce que ça m'étouffe/me met trop de pression/me stresse. La plus grosse pression, ce sont les profs/les parents/les copains parce qu'ils m'étouffent/me mettent trop de pression/me stressent. La plus grosse pression, ce sont les profs/les parents/les copains parce que je veux leur ressembler/je veux réussir. J'ai/Je n'ai pas de bonnes relations avec les profs/mes parents/mes copains. Reste positif/positive. Ne t'inquiète pas. Garde confiance en toi. Parle avec tes amis/profs/parents. Discute de tes doutes/problèmes. Travaille régulièrement/tous les jours. Demande de l'aide à … Passe du temps avec …*	L: 4–5 S: ?–4 R: 4 W: 3–4
64–65 **4.4 La vie, c'était mieux avant?**	Discuss what life used to be like for teenagers	Imperfect tense	Express opinions. Identify lifestyle differences and develop cultural awareness	*Avant, on écoutait la musique sur un tourne-disque/les émissions étaient en noir et blanc/il y avait une ou deux chaînes/on faisait les courses avec des francs/on avait un téléphone fixe/la voiture « deux chevaux » de Citroën était populaire/on jouait aux jeux de société. Maintenant, il y a/on a/fait/joue/écoute …*	L: 4–5 S: 4–5 R: 3–5 W: 4–5
66–67 **4.5 Les enfants des rues**	Describe the life of homeless children	Present and imperfect tenses (revision)	Pronunciation of verb endings. Understand longer reading passages		L: 4–5 S: 4–5 F: 4–5 W: 4–5
68–69 **4.6 Labo-langue**	Grammar, language strategies and pronunciation	Modal verbs. Imperfect tense. Imperative	Cultural awareness strategies. Pronunciation: silent verb endings		
70–75 **4.7 Extra Star, Extra Plus** **4.8 Lire, Vidéo** **4.9 Test, Vocabulaire**	Reinforcement and extension; reading material; activities based on the video material; revision and assessment		**Lire:** R: 5–6 **Vidéo:** L: 4–6; S: 4–5		**Test:** L: 4–5 S: 4–5 R: 4–5 W: 4–5

*See teacher notes for alternative assessment options. Guidelines for the various assessment criteria are provided in the introduction of this Teacher Handbook.

4 Être ado, c'est quoi?

Unit 4: Week-by-week overview

(Three-year KS3 route: assuming six weeks' work or approximately 10–12.5 hours)
(Two-year KS3 route: assuming four weeks' work or approximately 6.5–8.5 hours)

About Unit 4, Être ado, c'est quoi?: In this unit, students work in the context of life as a teenager: they discuss relationships with parents, money and what they do to help at home, and the pressures faced by teenagers. They learn to understand advice given to teenagers, discuss what life used to be like for teenagers and describe the life of homeless children.

Students learn to use the pronouns *me, te* and *se* in positive and negative sentences, and identify and use modal verbs (*devoir, pouvoir* and *vouloir*). They revise the *tu* form of the imperative, and learn to use the imperfect tense.

There is a focus on expressing opinions, agreeing and disagreeing, and asking and answering questions, which students put into use in their spoken and written productive work. Listening strategies are also covered, and students are given the opportunity to develop cultural awareness strategies. They also work at understanding longer reading passages. The pronunciation point focuses on the correct pronunciation of silent verb endings.

Three-year KS3 route

Week	Resources
	*Material from the end-of-unit pages (**4.7 Extra Star/Plus**, **4.8 Lire** and **Vidéo**) may be used during week 6 or selectively during weeks 1–5 as time permits.*
1	4.1 Ados–parents: c'est la guerre?
2	4.2 Les ados et l'argent 4.6 Labo-langue, activity 1
3	4.3 Ados + pressions = problèmes? 4.6 Labo-langue, activity 3
4	4.4 La vie, c'était mieux avant? 4.6 Labo-langue, activity 2 4.6 Labo-langue, Cultural awareness strategies
5	4.5 Les enfants des rues 4.6 Labo-langue, Pronunciation: silent verb endings
6	4.7 Extra Star, Extra Plus 4.8 Lire 4.8 Vidéo 4.9 Test 4.9 Vocabulaire

Two-year KS3 route

Week	Resources
	*Material from the end-of-unit pages (**4.7 Extra Star/Plus**, **4.8 Lire** and **Vidéo**) may be used selectively during weeks 1–4 as time permits.*
1	4.1 Ados–parents: c'est la guerre? (Omit activity 5)
2	4.2 Les ados et l'argent (Omit activity 4) 4.6 Labo-langue, activity 1
3	4.3 Ados + pressions = problèmes? (Omit activity 6) 4.6 Labo-langue, activity 3
4	4.4 La vie, c'était mieux avant? (Omit activity 3) 4.6 Labo-langue, activity 2 4.6 Labo-langue, Cultural awareness strategies 4.9 Test 4.9 Vocabulaire

4.1 Ados–parents: c'est la guerre?

pages 58–59

Planner

Objectives
- Vocabulary: discuss relationships with parents
- Grammar: use pronouns *me*, *te* and *se* in positive and negative sentences
- Skills: express opinions with confidence; agree and disagree

Resources
- Student Book, pages 58–59
- CD 1, tracks 33–34
- Grammar and Skills Workbook, pages 11, 12 and 24
- Kerboodle, Unit 4
- Unit 4 Worksheet 5 (ex. 2–3)

Key language

Mes parents me laissent sortir le week-end. Ma mère me fait confiance. Mon père me traite comme un bébé. Je ne peux pas sortir avec mes copains. Mes résultats scolaires sont très importants. J'ai de bonnes relations avec mes parents. Je parle beaucoup avec mes parents. Mes parents sont stricts, mais assez cool.

Je (ne) peux (pas) ... Je (ne) dois (pas) ...
sortir, jouer sur mon ordi, faire mes devoirs, rentrer

Grammar
- Use pronouns *me*, *te* and *se* in positive and negative sentences

PLTS
- Activity 1: Independent enquirers
- Activity 4: Self-managers
- Plenary medal activities: Team workers

Homework and self-study
- Student Book, page 59, activity 5
- Student Book, page 59, activity 7
- Grammar and Skills Workbook, page 11, activity 4, page 12 and page 24

Starters

See Kerboodle Starters bank for further details of **Dominoes**.

- In preparation for activity 4, it would be useful for students to practise manipulating the key sentences from activity 1: i.e. substituting different forms of the verb, changing positives to negatives (and vice versa), etc. Give students some sentences to adapt, for example:

  My mum trusts me. – *Ma mère me fait confiance.*
  My parents trust me. – *... me ... confiance.*
  My dad treats me like a baby. – *Mon père me traite comme un bébé.*
  My parents treat me like a baby. – *... me ... comme un bébé.*
  I can't go out with my friends. – *Je ne peux pas sortir avec mes copains.*
  I can go out with my friends. – *...*

- Play a basic version of **Dominoes**, using just the three pronouns *me*, *te* and *se*, and their English equivalents for the texts. Play until students have mastered the pronouns and their meanings.

Plenaries

- **Golden Grammar Rules**. Students work independently to consolidate their learning. They note down in their own words what they consider to be important for them to understand and learn: for example, pronouns in positive and negative sentences, position and agreement of adjectives (as in *J'ai de bonnes relations avec mes parents*), etc. Students summarise these as 'golden rules' for their study of French and share them in small groups. Encourage them to ask questions of other students to help improve their understanding of any areas/grammar points about which they are unsure. This also provides an opportunity for planning future grammar-based lessons.

1 Lis et relie le français et l'anglais.
Students read the French sentences and match them to the correct English equivalents.
Answers: **1** d; **2** a; **3** f; **4** g; **5** b; **6** e; **7** h; **8** c

2 Écoute et vérifie.
Students listen and check their answers to activity 1.

─⋀─ **CD 1, track 33   page 58, activité 2**

1 – Mes parents me laissent sortir le week-end.
   – C'est d.
2 – Ma mère me fait confiance.
   – C'est a.

4 Être ado, c'est quoi?

3 – Mon père me traite comme un bébé.
   – C'est f.
4 – Je ne peux pas sortir avec mes copains.
   – C'est g.
5 – Mes résultats scolaires sont très importants.
   – C'est b.
6 – J'ai de bonnes relations avec mes parents.
   – C'est e.
7 – Je parle beaucoup avec mes parents.
   – C'est h.
8 – Mes parents sont stricts la semaine mais assez cool le week-end.
   – C'est c.

3 Regarde l'activité 1 avec ton/ta partenaire. C'est positif (P), négatif (N) ou les deux (P + N)?

In pairs, students discuss the statements in activity 1 and decide whether each one is positive, negative or both. Refer students to the skills box on **Expressing opinions, agreeing and disagreeing** and encourage them to use a range of these phrases in their conversations.

Students will not necessarily agree on these: some of the statements could be seen as positive or negative depending on the context or point of view. For example, *Mes parents me laissent sortir le week-end*: this could be seen as positive from a teenager's point of view in the short term (because they are able to enjoy themselves and do what they want); or it could be viewed as negative because this might not always be a good thing for the long term (i.e. if a teenager is always off having a good time at the expense of other responsibilities such as schoolwork, etc.).

4 Discute avec ton/ta partenaire: « Tu as de bonnes relations avec tes parents? » Utilise 1–8 de l'activité 1.

Before students complete this activity it would be useful to do the starter activity manipulating the key sentences from activity 1.

Students then use the statements from activity 1 as the basis of a discussion with their partner. They say how each statement applies to their own experience with their parents. Remind them to use some of the phrases from the **Expressing opinions, agreeing and disagreeing** skills box.

Students add opinions to their discussion: *Je pense que c'est important ...*

5 Lis. C'est Salomé (S), Florian (F) ou Lauren (L)?
Students read the texts and decide whether the statements relate to Lauren or Florian.
Answers: **a** *Florian;* **b** *Lauren;* **c** *Lauren;* **d** *Florian;* **e** *Florian;* **f** *Lauren*

t As a follow-up task, students translate **a–f** into English.

Answers: **a** *I can't go to the cinema during the week.* **b** *I talk a lot with my parents.* **c** *I can go out at the weekend.* **d** *My school results are important.* **e** *I can't use my computer for more than two hours in the evening.* **f** *I have to come home on time.*

6 Écoute Camille, Youssef, Olivier, Léa et Carlotta. Recopie et remplis la grille. Positif (P), négatif (N) ou les deux (P + N)?
Students listen and decide whether the speakers have a positive or negative (or both) relationship with their parents. They copy and complete the table.
Answers: **Camille:** *P;* **Youssef:** *N;* **Olivier:** *P;* **Léa:** *N;* **Carlotta:** *P + N*

Students name two speakers who have a good relationship with their parents.

Answers: Camille, Olivier, (Carlotta's relationship is positive/negative)

Students listen out for the French for three expressions.

Answers: J'ai une super relation avec mes parents. J'en ai marre! Ça m'énerve (un peu).

t Students transcribe what Camille says. As a follow-up task, ask students to translate what she says.

Answers: My parents respect me. My mother trusts me and we talk a lot. It's cool! I have a brilliant relationship with my parents.

CD 1, track 34   page 59, activité 6

– Bonjour! Quelle relation as-tu avec tes parents, Camille?
– Moi, mes parents me respectent. Ma mère me fait confiance et on parle beaucoup. C'est cool! J'ai une super relation avec mes parents.
– Et toi, Youssef?
– Mes parents sont très stricts. Je ne peux pas sortir avec mes copains, je dois rester à la maison et je dois travailler. C'est un peu nul!
– Olivier, et toi?
– Mes parents sont cool avec moi. Je peux sortir le samedi soir, je peux jouer sur mon ordi ... tout va bien. J'ai de bonnes relations avec mes parents.
– Et toi, Léa?
– Chez nous, c'est la guerre! Je ne peux rien faire et mon père me traite comme un bébé. Pour mon père, mes résultats scolaires sont très importants et je dois travailler ... travailler ... et en plus, ma mère lit mon journal intime! J'en ai marre!
– Carlotta?

– Moi, en général, tout va bien ... sauf quelquefois, quand ma mère me traite comme un bébé, ça m'énerve un peu. Mais en général, ça va!
– OK, merci à tous!

7 Écris un article: « Mes parents et moi ». Adapte les textes de l'activité 5. Invente si tu veux!

Before students embark on this written activity, introduce the **Pronouns: me, te, se** via the grammar box. Remind students that they have already come across the pronouns and elicit from the class in what context they remember using them in *Allez 1* (with reflexive verbs). Do the **Dominoes** starter activity to consolidate familiarity with the pronouns. Then ask students to look back at the texts in activities 1 and 5 and to spot all instances of these three pronouns. They could also be asked to translate the phrases or sentences in which they appear.

Once students are secure with using the pronouns, they write an article about their relationship with their parents. They use the texts from activity 5 as a model to adapt. Encourage them to use a wide range of the language covered in the spread and to include some examples of the prounouns. Reassure students that they can make up the content if they prefer.

Plenary

In groups of three, students make a list of expressions for discussing relationships with parents. Remind them to include opinions, connectives and time expressions (*toujours, jamais, toute la journée*).

⭐ Students describe their relationship with their parents in three simple sentences.

⚪ They add more information and use a connective.

➕ They add their opinion and use a variety of pronouns.

4.2 Les ados et l'argent
pages 60–61

Planner

Objectives
- Vocabulary: talk about pocket money and what you do to help at home
- Grammar: identify and use modal verbs: *devoir, pouvoir* and *vouloir*
- Skills: ask and answer questions

Resources
- Student Book, pages 60–61
- CD 1, track 35
- Grammar and Skills Workbook, page 31
- Kerboodle, Unit 4
- Unit 4 Worksheets 3, 4 (ex. 1), 5 (ex. 1), 6 (ex. 3)

Key language
Numbers 10–55

Mes parents me donnent £10 par mois. Mon père me donne £10 par semaine. Mes parents m'achètent mes vêtements. Ma mère m'achète mes livres.

Je dois ... aider à la maison, faire la vaisselle, ranger ma chambre, tondre la pelouse, laver la voiture, faire les courses, garder mon petit frère/ma petite sœur, faire du baby-sitting.

Je dois/Je veux/Je voudrais/Je peux/Je ne peux pas ... acheter/payer mes places de ciné/mes CD/mes livres. ... m'acheter une tablette/un jeu vidéo. ... économiser/mettre de l'argent de côté.

Grammar
- Identify and use modal verbs: *devoir, pouvoir* and *vouloir*

PLTS and Numeracy
- Activity 2: Team workers
- Activity 5: Creative thinkers
- Plenary medal activities: Reflective learners
- Numeracy: Activities 1–3: interpreting statistics, manipulating percentages, recognising numbers

Homework and self-study
- Student Book, page 61, activity 4
- Student Book, page 61, activity 5
- Grammar and Skills Workbook, page 31

Starters

See Kerboodle Starters bank for further details of **Loto**.

- To prepare for the group survey in activity 2, hold a **Class discussion** to brainstorm other expressions which are not listed in the survey grid but that students might wish to use: for example, *promener le chien, aider mes grands-parents, mettre le couvert,* etc. Write a list of these expressions on the board for students to refer to when carrying out the survey.

4 Être ado, c'est quoi?

- In preparation for activity 3, revise large numbers by playing **Loto** with the multiples of 5 from 10 to 55 (see key language box).

Plenaries
- **Pocket money and allowances**. This plenary needs to be planned in advance and researching the information needed could be set as prior homework. Students research the average income of teenagers of their age across Europe and the wider world, and then present their findings as a bar chart or other form of graph to a small group. Remind students to use target language phrases throughout and to express their opinions. At the end of the lesson, ask for information that has shocked or surprised students; the aim is to encourage the development of empathy for other people their own age.

1 Lis le sondage et réponds aux questions.
Students read and interpret the survey statistics, and answer the questions in English. Although only whole numbers have been used for the percentages in the survey, it might be worth pointing out to students that in French, decimal numbers use a comma rather than a point: 10,5% (dix virgule cinq pour cent), as opposed to 10.5% (ten point five per cent) in English.
Answers: **a** 80%; **b** 64%; **c** 23%; **d** 83%; **e** 61%; **f** 15%; **g** 24%; **h** 40%

2 Sondage. Recopie la grille de l'activité 1. Pose les deux questions à cinq personnes et note les réponses.
To prepare for the survey, do the **Class discussion** starter activity to extend the vocabulary students can use.

Students then copy the grid format from activity 1, ask five people the two questions and note down their responses using a tally system. Refer students to the skills box on **Asking questions** and encourage them to use verb–subject inversion and appropriate intonation when asking their questions. Once students have carried out the survey, combine the findings to give a whole-class picture using percentages as in activity 1.

- Students present their findings in a more detailed, written form.

3 Écoute (1–6). Recopie et remplis la grille. Ils ont combien d'argent? C'est assez?
Before playing the recording, do the **Loto** starter activity to revise large numbers. Students listen and note down how much money the speakers say they receive and whether or not they think it is sufficient. Draw students' attention to the glossed expressions of frequency (*par mois* and *par semaine*), which they will need to include in their answers.

Answers:

	Combien?	C'est assez?
1	30€ par mois	oui
2	10€ par semaine	non
3	40€ par mois	oui
4	15€ par semaine	oui
5	50€ par mois	oui
6	50€ par mois	oui

CD 1, track 35   page 60, activité 3

– Alors, aujourd'hui, je pose deux questions: combien d'argent de poche avez-vous? Est-ce que c'est assez?
1 – Moi, mes parents me donnent trente euros par mois. Ce n'est pas beaucoup, mais oui, c'est assez.
2 – Moi, j'ai dix euros par semaine et je trouve que ce n'est pas assez. C'est difficile parce que je dois gérer mon argent. Je voudrais avoir plus!
3 – Ma mamie me donne vingt euros et je dois tondre la pelouse pour mes parents donc j'ai aussi vingt euros. Quarante euros par mois en tout, ça va. C'est bien, j'ai assez!
4 – Moi, j'ai quinze euros par semaine. Oui, c'est pas mal. Ça va, j'ai assez.
5 – Je reçois cinquante euros tous les mois. C'est super, je peux économiser et acheter plein de choses!
6 – J'ai vingt-cinq euros de ma maman et vingt-cinq euros de mon papa par mois. Oui, c'est assez pour moi.

4 Lis les textes. Qui dit quoi?
Students read the emails and identify who says each English statement.
Answers: **a** Alex; **b** Alex; **c** Julie; **d** Julie; **e** Julie; **f** Alex

- Students note down the cognates in the texts. They should remember the term 'cognates' from *Allez 1*, but check this before students begin this task.
- Students find two sentences in the perfect tense.

Answers: mais la semaine dernière, j'ai acheté des places de ciné! / Hier, j'ai acheté deux robes et un sac!

- **t** Students translate the underlined expressions in the texts.

Answers: **Alex:** *I don't have pocket money; my parents buy me what I ask for; they give me; I would like to buy myself ...; I put money aside;* **Julie:** *my grandmother gives me ...; I can spend it all!; I want to go to the Beyoncé concert*

Run through the grammar box on **Modal verbs + infinitive**. Students are already familiar with *vouloir* and *pouvoir*. Revise the meanings of *je peux* and *je veux* and elicit from the class what they think *je dois* might mean. Ask them to look back through the texts in activity 4 and to pick out examples of these three modal verbs. Check students are secure with the three singular forms of these verbs and ask them to practise in pairs using the various forms from the grammar box, thinking of a different infinitive to add to the end of each (they could use the *sondage* phrases in activity 1 for support). Check students understand how to form the negative and encourage more able students to practise this structure in pairs too.

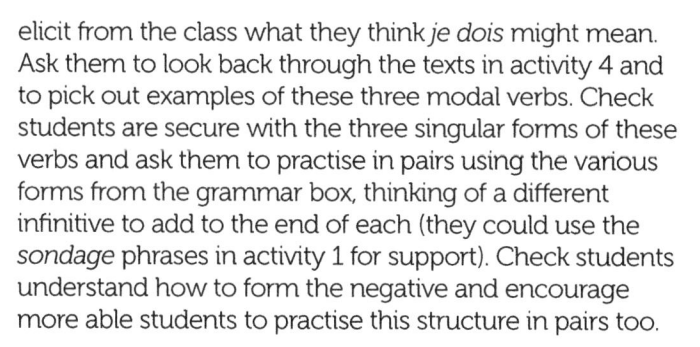

5 Écris un mail: « Mon argent de poche ».

Students write an email about the pocket money they receive and what they do to help at home. Students can use the emails in activity 4 as a model. Refer them also to the key language box for support and encourage them to include examples of modal verbs.

- Students add details of what they have bought recently.

Plenary

In pairs, students talk about pocket money. They give each other feedback on their pronunciation and intonation, then repeat the conversation, taking into account the feedback.

- Students say how much pocket money they get and how often they get it.
- Students add what they have to do and what they would like to buy.
- Students include three different connectives and a perfect tense.

4.3 Ados + pressions = problèmes?

pages 62–63

Planner

Objectives
- Vocabulary: talk about the pressures faced by teenagers and understand advice
- Grammar: use the *tu* form of the imperative
- Skills: use listening strategies

Resources
- Student Book, pages 62–63
- CD 1, tracks 36–37
- Grammar and Skills Workbook, pages 32 and 50
- Kerboodle, Unit 4
- Unit 4 Worksheets 4 (ex. 2), 6 (ex. 1–2)

Key language

Mon problème, c'est le collège/la presse parce que ça m'étouffe/me met trop de pression/me stresse.

La plus grosse pression, ce sont les profs/les parents/les copains parce qu'ils m'étouffent/me mettent trop de pression/me stressent.

La plus grosse pression, ce sont les profs/les parents/les copains parce que je veux leur ressembler/je veux réussir.

J'ai/Je n'ai pas de bonnes relations avec les profs/mes parents/mes copains.

Reste positif/positive. Ne t'inquiète pas. Garde confiance en toi. Parle avec tes amis/profs/parents. Discute de tes doutes/problèmes. Travaille régulièrement/tous les jours. Demande de l'aide à ... Passe du temps avec ...

Grammar
- *Tu* form of the imperative

PLTS and Numeracy
- Activity 3: Team workers
- Activity 6: Self-managers
- Plenary medal activities: Reflective learners
- Numeracy: Activity 3, Extension: presenting results as a bar chart

Homework and self-study
- Student Book, page 62, activity 2
- Student Book, page 62, activity 4
- Student Book, page 63, activity 7
- Grammar and Skills Workbook, page 32 and page 50, activity 1

Starters

See Kerboodle Starters bank for further details of **Pictionary**.

- Play **Pictionary** to consolidate the four types of pressure before students carry out the survey in activity 3.
- Revise the imperative in preparation for activity 5. Write on the board a list of infinitives (preferably relating to the spread topic, e.g. *demander, faire, rester, discuter*, etc.), avoiding *avoir* and *être* at this stage. Divide the class into groups of three. One group member says an infinitive, the second says the *tu* form, and the third states the *tu* imperative form.

Plenaries

- **Traffic lights**. Ask students to reflect on their progress with listening skills and to colour-code the various areas red, amber or green. They work in pairs to discuss their strengths

4 Être ado, c'est quoi?

and areas that they still need to improve on. Give them the following questions to help them with their evaluation: How do they approach contextualising (i.e. making use of clues in the title, subtitle or pictures)? Do they consider what they are listening to? Is it, for example, a review, an interview, an advert? Are they better at making inferences? Can they sustain their concentration? Do they listen with understanding? Do they take note of the tone of voice, or other clues, listening with empathy? How could these things help them during tests? What do they find difficult and why, and how can they work on overcoming any problems with listening?

1 Écoute, lis et trouve les titres.

Students listen and folllow the text. They match the titles (a–d) to the paragraphs (1–4). Encourage them to read for gist to work out what type of pressure each text is describing, and to draw on their reading strategies when trying to work out meaning.

Answers: **1** c; **2** b; **3** d; **4** a

CD 1, track 36   page 62, activité 1

1 – Alice, quelle est la plus grosse pression pour toi?
   – Pour moi, c'est le regard des autres qui est difficile. Je n'ai pas confiance en moi. Je trouve que mes copains sont plus intelligents, plus « fun » que moi mais j'ai besoin d'avoir beaucoup d'amis. Quelquefois, c'est difficile, au collège surtout.
2 – Et toi, Valentin?
   – Mes parents ne sont jamais contents! Ils m'étouffent, ils sont toujours sur mon dos: « travaille plus », « finis tes devoirs », « arrête avec ton portable ». J'en ai un peu marre!
3 – Camille?
   – Moi, je veux ressembler aux jeunes des magazines. Je voudrais être belle et mince! J'adore les stars alors je lis tous les magazines people.
4 – Et pour finir, Louis?
   – Moi, j'ai peur de ne pas réussir plus tard. Tous les profs disent « il faut travailler », « l'avenir est difficile pour les jeunes aujourd'hui », « fais des efforts » … et ça me stresse beaucoup. C'est l'école qui me met la pression.

Students translate the underlined phrases.

Answers: it is the view of others (what others think) which is difficult / they are always on my back / I want to look like / I am scared of not succeeding

2 Relis l'activité 1. Vrai, faux ou pas mentionné?

Students read the text in activity 1 again and decide whether each statement is true, false or not mentioned in the text. As a follow-up task, ask students to correct the false statements.

Answers: **Vrai:** a, c; **Faux:** b (elle n'a pas confiance en elle); d (il n'a pas de bonnes relations); e (il a un portable); **Pas mentionné:** f

3 Sondage: pose la question à cinq personnes.

Students ask five classmates what the greatest pressure is for them. In preparation for this activity, do the **Pictionary** starter activity to consolidate the four types of pressure. Then ask students to draw a grid with the four pressure types as headings. They tick the relevant column for each interiewee.

As a follow-up task, students talk about their findings in pairs: *Quatre personnes pensent que la plus grosse pression, c'est …*

As an extension activity, students could present their results in the form of a bar chart.

4 Quelles sont tes pressions? Écris des phrases.

Students write some sentences about the pressures (real or imaginary) that they feel they face. More able students could extend their writing to create an email, and could add a question (e.g. *Et toi, tu as quelles pressions?*). Refer students to the key language box and to the texts in activity 1 for support.

5 Lis et trouve les expressions en français.

Before students read the texts, run through the grammar box on **The imperative**, reminding students that to form the imperative they need to use the *tu* form of the present tense and take away *tu* (and the final *-s* for *-er* verbs and *aller*). Then do the starter activity to revise and consolidate this grammar point (first covered in *Allez 1*, Unit 5, in the context of giving directions). Once students have refamiliarised themselves with the imperative, they read the text and find the French equivalents for the English phrases. As a follow-up task, ask them how many imperative forms they can spot in the text (10) and to list them (*travaille, fais, révise, demande, ne t'inquiète pas, discute, demande, concentre-toi, garde, reste*).

Answers: **a** *fais tes devoirs*; **b** *révise pour tes contrôles*; **c** *demande à tes profs*; **d** *discute avec tes parents*; **e** *concentre-toi sur ton travail*; **f** *reste positif*

The following activities could be used to expolit the text further:

Ask students which teenager from activity 1 Agathe's advice might be for. *Answer: Louis*

Ask students to translate Agathe's text into English.

Translation: Work regularly, do your homework every day and revise for your tests because school results are important. Ask your teachers if you don't understand and don't worry about your future. Discuss it with your parents because they love you. Ask your friends for help too. You are young, so concentrate on your work and have confidence in yourself – that's the most important thing. Good luck and stay positive! Aunt Agathe

6 Écoute Tante Agathe et mets ses conseils dans l'ordre.

Students listen to the radio phone-in and put Agathe's pieces of advice into the order in which they are mentioned on the recording. Before playing the recording, run through the skills box on **Listening strategies** and ask students to work in pairs to predict which words they might expect to hear in the recording. Encourage students to put these strategies to use when completing the activity.

Answers: e, a, d, c, b, f

t Students transcribe Agathe's advice. As a follow-up task, ask students to translate Agathe's advice.

Answers: OK, but your parents love you very much, so talk to them. Explain your problems – that will help you. Don't stay alone in your room. For example, watch TV with your parents, do things with your mum, help your dad, go to the cinema with your family from time to time. Agree/Be willing to spend time with your parents because it is important to have a good relationship. But above all, talk about your problems – that's the most important thing. Good luck!

CD 1, track 37   page 63, activité 6

– Bonjour, Simon. Alors dis-moi, quel est ton problème?
– Mon problème, c'est mes parents! Mon père me traite comme un bébé et ma mère ne me fait pas confiance. En plus, elle lit mon journal intime. C'est horrible, c'est difficile à la maison!
– OK, mais tes parents t'aiment beaucoup alors discute avec eux. Explique tes problèmes, ça va t'aider. Ne reste pas seul dans ta chambre. Par exemple, regarde la télé avec tes parents, fais des choses avec ta mère, aide ton père, va au cinéma avec tes parents de temps en temps. Accepte de passer du temps avec tes parents parce que c'est important d'avoir de bonnes relations. Mais surtout parle de tes problèmes, c'est le plus important. Bon courage!

7 Choisis un problème dans l'activité 1 et écris une réponse.

Students choose one of the texts from activity 1 and write an 'agony-aunt' reply to it. Refer students to the text in activity 5 and to the key language box for support. Encourage students to include a range of imperatives and to develop and extend their writing as much as possible.

As an extra, end-of-spread online project, ask students to create a radio programme: *Les problèmes des jeunes*. In groups, students write two or three problems and answers, similar to those in activities 1 and 5, and then record them. Challenge them to be as creative as possible and to use as much of the language from the spread as they can.

Plenary

Students look back at the structures and vocabulary in the unit and reflect on how much they can remember and how they go about learning new language. They discuss memorisation strategies with a partner.

Students give two short pieces of advice using the imperative.

Students imagine they are a teenager with a problem and explain their problem.

Students give advice to a teenager on how to cope with their problem.

4.4 La vie, c'était mieux avant?

pages 64–65

Planner

Objectives

- Vocabulary: discuss what life used to be like for teenagers
- Grammar: use the imperfect tense
- Skills: express opinions; identify lifestyle differences and develop cultural awareness

Resources

- Student Book, pages 64–65
- CD 1, tracks 38–39
- Grammar and Skills Workbook, page 39
- Kerboodle, Unit 4

Key language

Avant, on écoutait la musique sur un tourne-disque/les émissions étaient en noir et blanc/

4 Être ado, c'est quoi?

il y avait une ou deux chaînes/on faisait les courses avec des francs/on avait un téléphone fixe/la voiture « deux chevaux » de Citroën était populaire/ on jouait aux jeux de société. Maintenant, il y a/ on a/fait/joue/écoute ...

Grammar
- Imperfect tense

PLTS
- Activity 1: Independent enquirers
- Activities 2, 3 and 4: Self-managers
- Activity 5: Creative thinkers

Homework and self-study
- Student Book, page 65, activity 3
- Student Book, page 65, activity 5
- Grammar and Skills Workbook, page 39

Starters
See Kerboodle Starters bank for further details of **Categorise**.
- Hold a **Class discussion** to compare the lists of phrases for expressing opinions that students put together in pairs when working on the **Expressing opinions** skills box. Write them on the board for students to refer to when working on activity 2.
- Play **Categorise** to consolidate the vocabulary items from the 'Avant' and 'Maintenant' key language boxes.

Plenaries
- **Cross curricular learning: history**. Comparing and contrasting aspects of life in the past and present in a foreign language is not easy, but this should help prepare students for the speaking test at the end of the unit. 'Setting the scene' or helping students to see the 'bigger picture' of their learning is very useful.

Ask students to reflect on why it is important to be able to understand and use the imperfect tense confidently. They then work in pairs to compare and contrast life in the past and present. Encourage them to draw on what they have discovered about life in their grandparents' generation for support, or simply to imagine life at school for two days without electricity. (If they have already watched the Unit 4 video clip (see page 73), they could also draw on what they have learnt from that.)

1 Écoute, lis et trouve les paires.
Students listen and read the statements and match them to the pictures. Remind students to draw on their reading strategies when doing this, and to use the pictures for clues.

Once students have done this, ask them to look at the verbs in the sentences in activity 1. Can they remember where they have seen this verb form before? (**Expressing opinions in the past**, Unit 2.3.) Explain that these are examples of the imperfect tense and run through the grammar box on **The imperfect tense** with them. Draw students' attention to when the imperfect tense is used (to say what used to be), as compared with the perfect tense. Explain that to form the imperfect, they need to take the *nous* form of the present tense, take off the *-ons* ending and add the imperfect endings (*-ais, -ais, -ait*). Ask students to look back at the text in activity 1 and to spot all the examples of the imperfect tense. More able students could also be asked to translate them, using the grammar box for support. Draw their attention to the 'used to' translation of the imperfect tense: 'We used to listen ...', 'There used to be ...', 'We used to go ...', etc.
Answers: **1** b; **2** d; **3** e; **4** a; **5** c; **6** f

CD 1, track 38   page 64, activité 1

1. On écoutait la musique sur un tourne-disque.
2. Les émissions étaient en noir et blanc et il y avait seulement une ou deux chaînes.
3. On faisait les courses avec des francs.
4. On avait un téléphone fixe.
5. La voiture « deux chevaux » de Citroën était populaire.
6. On jouait aux jeux de société, le jeu des « petits chevaux » par exemple.

2 Regarde les boîtes « Avant » et « Maintenant » et compare. Donne tes opinions. A ↔ B.

In pairs, students take turns to say a sentence about how things used to be and to compare this with how things are now. They use the 'Maintenant' texts and the 'Avant' texts from activity 1 as prompts. Remind them to add an opinion using *C'est* or *C'était* + adjective. Before they embark on this activity, refer them to the skills box on **Expressing opinions** and ask them to work in pairs to make a list of different phrases for expressing opinions. Can they categorise them into those which they use for showing surprise, agreement and disagreement? Do the **Class discussion** starter activity and encourage students to use some of these phrases in their dialogues.

3 Lis et réponds aux questions en anglais.

Before students do this, refer them to the **Cultural awareness strategies** on page 69. In pairs, students compile their own list of what has changed or stayed the same over the past 30–40 years. Encourage them to use this list when predicting what they might read in the text in activity 3. Students then read the text and answer the questions in English.

Answers: **1** *francs;* **2** *the euro arrived;* **3** *watched TV (one channel) or listened to the radio;* **4** *in her bedroom;* **5** *on Thursdays;* **6** *no, it was just different*

⭐ Students note down any cognates they can spot in the text, with their English equivalents. Check first that students remember what cognates are.

◯ Students find all the verbs in the imperfect tense in the text, and list them with their infinitives.

Answers: tu étais (être); c'était (être); n'existait pas (exister); on faisait (faire); coûtait (coûter); tu faisais (faire); on n'avait pas (avoir); on regardait (regarder); il y avait (avoir); on écoutait (écouter); j'écoutais (écouter); j'étais (être); on n'allait pas (aller); on ne téléphonait pas (téléphoner); c'était (être)

As a Gold medal activity, students could write a sentence about life in the past. For example: *C'était différent parce que/qu'...*

4 Écoute les quatre jeunes. Qu'est-ce qui a changé? Recopie la grille et note les réponses en anglais.

Before playing the recording, refer students again to the **Cultural awareness strategies** on page 69 and remind them to use their lists when predicting what they might hear. Students then copy out the grid, listen and and note down in English what each speaker says has changed.

Answers:

	Camille	**Florent**
Before	listened to music on a record player	TV programmes in black and white, just one or two channels
Now	can listen to music on computer, MP4 player, tablet, phone	lots of channels, can replay programmes, home cinema with big screen

	Robin	**Aïsha**
Before	telephone landline only	no computers
Now	phones are mobile, can send texts, take photos, make videos, listen to music, talk on Skype	uses computer for homework every day, watches DVDs, sends emails, listens to music, researches on the Internet

CD 1, track 39 page 65, activité 4

– Alors, Camille, quelles différences as-tu remarqué?
– Avant, on écoutait la musique sur un tourne-disque, mais maintenant, on peut utiliser un ordinateur, un MP4, une tablette, et même un portable! C'est facile!
– Et toi, Florent?
– Ma grand-mère avait la télé mais les émissions étaient en noir et blanc et il y avait seulement une ou deux chaînes, c'était tout. Aujourd'hui, il y a des dizaines de chaînes, des émissions en « replay » et même des home-cinémas avec des grands écrans comme au cinéma!
– C'est vrai! Et toi, Robin?
– C'est le téléphone le plus bizarre. Avant, on avait un téléphone, mais il était fixe. Maintenant, il est portable ... et avec mon portable, j'envoie des SMS, je prends des photos et je fais des vidéos. J'écoute de la musique et je parle à mes copains sur Skype – c'est génial!
– Et toi, Aïsha?
– Avant, il n'y avait pas d'ordinateur, c'est incroyable! Moi, j'utilise mon ordinateur tous les jours pour faire mes devoirs. Je regarde des DVD dans ma chambre, j'envoie des mails, j'écoute de la musique et je fais des recherches sur Internet. C'est indispensable.

5 Interview: « La vie avant et maintenant ».

Students write a short interview between an older person and a teenager, comparing life in the past and now. They use the underlined phrases from activity 3 to structure their writing, Encourage them also to draw on a variety of language from the spread.

Plenary

Working in pairs, students make a list of differences between life in the past and now. To prepare for this, ask students to talk (in English) to different generations of their own family about what life was like in the past and to use their ideas in the plenary tasks.

⭐ Students use one phrase in the imperfect tense.

◯ Students use a verb in the imperfect tense, plus an opinion.

➕ Students use the present tense and the imperfect tense.

4 Être ado, c'est quoi?

4.5 Les enfants des rues

pages 66–67

Planner

Objectives
- Vocabulary: describe the life of homeless children
- Grammar: revise the present and imperfect tenses
- Skills: develop good pronunciation of verb endings; understand longer reading passages

Resources
- Student Book, pages 66–67
- CD 1, tracks 40–42
- Kerboodle, Unit 4

Grammar
- Present and imperfect tenses (revision)

PLTS and Numeracy
- Activity 2: Team workers
- Activity 3: Independent enquirers
- Activity 5: Creative thinkers
- Numeracy: Activity 1: recognise large numbers

Homework and self-study
- Student Book, page 67, activity 4
- Student Book, page 67, activity 5

Starters

See Kerboodle Starters bank for further details of **Noughts and crosses** and **Up, down**.

- Revise large numbers by playing **Noughts and crosses**. Use numbers between 10 and 200 to prepare for activity 1.
- Play **Up, down** to revise the imperfect tense before students read the text in activity 4. Read out the text from activity 3 on page 65 and ask students to stand up whenever they hear an example of the imperfect tense.

Plenaries

- **Key thoughts**. In groups, students prepare a poster for a campaign to raise awareness of the plight of homeless children in another continent. They should reflect back on spread 3.5 on advertising (pages 30–31) and their thoughts on the use of persuasive language. Display the posters on the wall and ask one member of each group to stand next to their group's poster to explain the rationale for the comments and to answer any questions that might arise; the rest of the group moves around looking at the other posters. At the end of the session, gather students' key thoughts from the task and explain that these will be useful for learning how to express opinions on some deeper issues in future units.

1 Écoute et lis l'interview. Remplis les blancs a–g en anglais.

Students listen and follow the text. They complete the gaps in the English statements (a–g). Before they do this, draw students' attention to the photos and ask them to consider what the text might be about and the kind of language they might expect to hear/read. In addition, revise large numbers using the **Noughts and crosses** starter activity.

Answers: **a** 120 million; **b** (on the streets) in India; **c** 13; **d** (carpet) factory; **e** every day; **f** his parents; **g** four brothers

Students note down what Jasbir's brothers do, apart from working at the factory.

Answers: sell things on the streets, collect rubbish for recycling

t Students translate the first paragraph into English.

Answers: More than 120 million children in the world live on the streets without a family: 30 million in Africa, 30 million in Asia and 60 million in South America. We estimate that there are more than 11 million children who live on the streets in India.

CD 1, track 40   page 66, activité 1

– Plus de cent vingt millions d'enfants dans le monde vivent dans la rue, sans famille: trente millions en Afrique, trente millions en Asie et soixante millions en Amérique du Sud. On estime qu'il y a plus de onze millions d'enfants qui vivent dans les rues en Inde. Nous avons rencontré Jasbir:
Bonjour, Jasbir, quel âge as-tu?
– J'ai treize ans.
– Tu vas à l'école?
– Non, je n'ai pas le temps. Je travaille à l'usine de tapis toute la journée. Et le soir, je cire les chaussures dans les rues.
– Tu travailles quand?
– Tous les jours.
– Et tu habites avec ta famille?
– Non, mes parents sont morts. J'habite avec mes quatre frères.
– Tes frères travaillent aussi?
– Oui, ils travaillent à l'usine aussi, mais le soir, ils vendent des objets dans la rue ou ils collectent des déchets pour le recyclage.
– Merci, Jasbir.

Pronunciation of verb endings

Play the recording and ask students to repeat each verb. They could work in pairs and provide feedback on each other's pronunciation.

CD 1, track 41   page 66, Prononciation

vivent	collectent
travaillent	habitent
vendent	cirent

2 Pose les questions à ton/ta partenaire. Utilise les dessins. A ↔ B.

In pairs, students take turns to ask and answer *Où habitent les enfants?* and *Que font-ils?* They use the picture prompts as the basis for their answers. They could also use the text in activity 1 for support. Refer students back to the **Pronunciation of verb endings** skills box and remind them to pay attention to their pronunciation in their dialogues.

3 Écoute. Quatre jeunes parlent de l'interview de Jasbir. Qui dit quoi?

Students listen to four young people talking about the interview with Jasbir (activity 1) and decide who says which of the English statements.

Answers: **Clément:** b, f; **Marine:** a, e; **Sadia:** d; **Aziz:** c

Students listen again and note down the French equivalents for the three English phrases.

Answers: j'ai trouvé ça effrayant / je pense que / cette interview m'a fait réfléchir

Students listen again to spot a comparative (*plus/moins que ...*) and an example of the imperfect tense.

Answers: **Comparative:** *Il y a beaucoup d'enfants dans le monde qui sont moins heureux que moi.* **Imperfect:** *Je ne savais pas qu'il y avait des enfants qui travaillent à mon âge!*

CD 1, track 42   page 67, activité 3

– Tu as entendu l'interview de Jasbir sur les enfants des rues, Clément?
– Oui, j'ai trouvé ça effrayant. Ils ont mon âge et ils vivent seuls dans la rue, c'est terrible. Et en plus, ils n'ont pas de famille, pas de maison. Ça me rend très triste.
– Et toi, Marine?
– Moi, je pense qu'on doit aider ces enfants. L'année dernière, j'ai donné de l'argent à une association qui construit des écoles. Je veux les aider à vivre mieux si je peux.
– Et toi, Sadia?
– Je ne savais pas qu'il y avait des enfants qui travaillent à mon âge! Ils travaillent toute la journée et n'ont pas le temps de jouer avec leurs copains comme moi. C'est incroyable!
– Aziz, et toi?
– Cette interview m'a fait réfléchir. J'ai beaucoup de chance. Il y a beaucoup d'enfants dans le monde qui sont moins heureux que moi. Ils travaillent et ils ne vont pas à l'école comme moi.

4 Lis le texte de Mélissa. Réponds aux questions en anglais.

Students read the text and answer the questions in English. Before they do so, revise the imperfect tense via the **Up, down** starter activity.

Answers: a *children who work;* b *between 6 and 15 years old;* c *up to 20 hours a day;* d *in carpet factories;* e *eye problems and respiratory diseases;* f *sad*

Students choose three verbs in the imperfect tense in Mélissa's text and translate them into English.

Students translate the underlined expressions in the text.

Answers: I read an article about / seven days a week / they were ill / respiratory diseases / I can eat what I want

4 Être ado, c'est quoi?

5 Écris un article. Compare ta vie et la vie des enfants des rues.
Students write an article comparing their life and the life of street children. They use ideas from activities 1 and 4.

◯ Students use the present tense and the imperfect, as in the text in activity 4: *J'ai lu un blog sur les enfants des rues. Ils travaillaient ... Ils habitaient ... Moi, je vais au collège ...*

⊕ Students add some comparisons with their own life: *Ma vie est plus facile. Moi, j'ai une maison et une famille, mais ils n'ont pas de maison ...*

6 Présente ton article à la classe.
Students make a presentation to the class, based on their article from activity 5. Encourage them to prepare cue cards or key words to refer to while they are speaking, instead of simply reading aloud their text. Allow them to practise in pairs before giving their presentation to the class. Remind students to pay attention to their pronunciation of verb endings.

Plenary
Students reflect on what they have learned about how children's lives can differ and how this makes them feel about their own life.

★ Students name three countries where children live on the streets.

◯ Students consider the street children they have learnt about and use the imperfect tense to explain what they had to do.

⊕ Students make up three sentences about their lives, using connectives and two tenses (present and imperfect).

4.6 Labo-langue
pages 68–69

Planner

Objectives
- Grammar: modal verbs; the imperfect tense; the imperative
- Skills: cultural awareness strategies
- Pronunciation: silent verb endings

Resources
- Student Book, pages 68–69
- CD 1, track 43
- Grammar and Skills Workbook, page 51
- Kerboodle, Unit 4
- Unit 4, Worksheets 7, 8

PLTS
- Creative thinkers, Reflective learners, Self-managers

Modal verbs 🖵

1 Put the words in the correct order.

Answers: **a** Je dois faire mon lit tous les jours. **b** Nous devons aider mes parents à la maison tous les week-ends. **c** Mon frère ne veut pas ranger sa chambre. **d** On peut aller au cinéma le week-end prochain. **e** Je dois tondre la pelouse pour mes parents. **f** Elle peut me faire confiance.

⊕ **t** Students translate the sentences into English.

Answers: **a** I must make my bed every day. **b** We must help our parents at home every weekend. **c** My brother does not want to tidy his room. **d** We can go to the cinema next weekend. **e** I have to mow the lawn for my parents. **f** She can trust me.

Imperfect tense 🖵

2 Complete the sentences using the correct form of the verb in brackets. Use the present tense or the imperfect tense.

Answers: **a 1** utilise, **2** utilisait; **b 1** écrit, **2** écrivait; **c 1** travaille, **2** travaillais; **d 1** va, **2** allait; **e 1** a, **2** avait

The imperative 🖵

t 3 Translate Tante Agathe's advice into French.

Answers: **a** Parle à tes parents. **b** Range ta chambre. **c** Travaille bien au collège. **d** Fais confiance à tes copains. **e** Aide ton petit frère. **f** Ne reste pas dans ta chambre.

Cultural awareness strategies

This section encourages students to think about strategies for developing their cultural awareness. Students work in pairs to consider aspects of life that have changed or remained the same over the past 30–40 years and compare their lists with the cultural changes mentioned on pages 64–65

Students are encouraged to use their findings to help them predict what they might read and hear in activities 3 and 4 on page 65.

Pronunciation: silent verb endings

6 Decide whether each verb is present or imperfect. Make two lists and read them aloud. Listen to check.

Answers: **Present:** 1 habitent; 2 utilisent; 4 rendent; 6 parlent; 7 doivent; 9 peuvent; 12 veulent;

Imperfect: 3 avaient; 5 allaient; 8 écoutaient; 10 travaillaient; 11 étaient

CD 1, track 43 — page 69, activité 4

1. habitent – present
2. utilisent – present
3. avaient – imperfect
4. rendent – present
5. allaient – imperfect
6. parlent – present
7. doivent – present
8. écoutaient – imperfect
9. peuvent – present
10. travaillaient – imperfect
11. étaient – imperfect
12. veulent – present

4.7 Extra Star — page 70

1 Find five sentences in the word snake and copy them out.

Answers: Mon père me traite comme un bébé. Je ne peux pas sortir. Les résultats scolaires sont importants. Je parle beaucoup avec mes parents. Je dois rentrer à l'heure.

2 Match the answers to the questions.

Answers: **1** f; **2** e; **3** b; **4** a; **5** d; **6** c

3 Write your own answers to the questions in activity 2.

Students write sentences about themselves in answer to the questions from activity 2.

4 Read Basile's email and answer the questions in English.

Answers: **a** a good relationship; **b** she trusts him; **c** 25 euros (per week); **d** magazines and cinema tickets; **e** his clothes; **f** when he washes the car; **g** it was his birthday; **h** his aunt

4.7 Extra Plus — page 71

1 Lis et trouve les verbes.

Students read the texts and choose the correct verbs from those listed to fill the gaps.

Answers: **a** avais; **b** regardait; **c** avait; **d** utilisait; **e** ai; **f** travaille; **g** écoute; **h** parle

t 2 Traduis les phrases de Monique et de Carla en anglais.

Students translate the sentences from activity 1 into English.

Answers: **Monique:** I was 14 years old in 1970. We watched just one TV channel. There were no computers. We used a different currency: the franc. **Carla:** I am 14 years old today. I work a lot on my computer. I listen to music on my MP4 player. I speak to my friends via text.

3 Lis le mail de Judith et trouve les expressions.

Students read the text and find the French equivalents for the English phrases.

Answers: **a** je me sentais seule; **b** j'étais souvent triste; **c** je ne parlais à personne; **d** j'ai envoyé une lettre; **e** je peux aider les autres; **f** m'a donné confiance en moi

4 Écris un paragraphe sur l'argent de poche.

Students write a paragraph about pocket money. Remind them to cover all the bullet points listed and to refer to the key language box for support.

4 Être ado, c'est quoi?

4.8 Lire
page 72

Resources
- Student Book, page 72
- Kerboodle, Unit 4

PLTS
- Independent enquirers

1 Clémence, a teenager, has written a review of the novel *Maïté Coiffure* by Marie-Aude Murail. According to Clémence, what are the four themes of the book?

Answers: **b** conflicts between parents and children; **c** relationships between teenagers; **e** career choice; **f** discovering a different environment

2 Choose words from the box to fill in the gaps in this summary of the book.

Answers: **a** stage; **b** coiffure; **c** change; **d** collègues; **e** métier; **f** collège; **g** opposés; **h** affronter

3 Does Clémence like the book? Find phrases in the text to justify your opinion.

Answers: Yes, she does: Ce livre est très bien pour les jeunes …; le thème … concerne tous les adolescents; cela peut arriver à n'importe quel jeune; J'ai aimé Louis, le personnage principal …

4.8 Vidéo
page 73

Resources
- Student Book, page 73
- Kerboodle, Unit 4 Video clip

PLTS
- Independent enquirers

Épisode 4: La jeunesse de Madame Tournemine
Thouraya and Jémilie are about to undertake the next challenge in the competition: this time, they need to research what it was like to be a teenager in the past. To find out, they are on their way to interview Madame Francette Tournemine, who is 72 and was a teenager during the 1950s. The girls have an interesting conversation with Madame Tournemine and learn a lot about life as a teenager in the past.

Video clip, Unit 4   page 73

(In the street)

Thouraya: J'aime beaucoup ce concours.

Jémilie: Moi aussi. C'est quoi, le nouveau défi?

Thouraya: « Comment c'était, d'être un ado dans le passé? »

Jémilie: Et qu'est qu'on fait ici?

Thouraya: Nous allons interviewer Madame Francette Tournemine. Elle a 72 ans. Elle va nous raconter comment c'était d'être un ado dans les années cinquante.

Jémilie: Super.

(In Madame Tournemine's house)

Thouraya: Madame Francette, bonjour. Est-ce que vous êtes née à Montpellier?

Francette: Non, je suis née dans un village près de la Rochelle. Mes parents avaient une ferme et je suis née à la ferme.

Jémilie: Est-ce que vous avez des frères et des sœurs?

Francette: Oui, j'ai un frère est une sœur qui avait 12 ans et 13 ans quand je suis née, et je vais pouvoir vous les montrer. Voilà. *(Shows them a photo)*

Thouraya: Est-ce que vous aviez de bonnes relations avec vos parents?

Francette: Oui, mais j'ai perdu ma maman à l'âge de 8 ans. Mon père s'est remarié – j'en avais 11 – et je ne m'entendais pas très bien avec ma belle-mère. Mais de toute façon, j'étais un enfant assez sage.

Jémilie: Est-ce que vous aviez le droit de sortir avec vos amis?

84

Francette:	Oui, j'avais le droit de sortir faire un tour en vélo, d'aller me baigner à la rivière …
Jémilie:	Vous sortiez le soir?
Francette:	Oui, j'allais aux bals, mais les parents étaient toujours là. C'étaient des bals de fêtes de village et tout le monde y allait.
Thouraya:	Qu'est-ce que vous faisiez quand vous sortiez seule avec vos amies?
Francette:	Il y avait très peu de choses qu'on pouvait faire sans chaperon. Donc on faisait des bêtises. Par exemple, je raccompagnais ma copine chez elle, elle me raccompagnait à ma maison, et je la raccompagnais à sa maison …
Jémilie:	Qu'est-ce que vous portiez comme vêtements quand vous sortiez?
Francette:	Je portais une robe, une jupe, un manteau, des gants et un chapeau. J'avais horreur des chapeaux.
Jémilie:	Donc pas de jeans?
Francette:	En France, les jeans n'existaient presque pas. Et pour les filles, les pantalons étaient interdits à l'école normale et j'ai lutté pour avoir le droit de porter des pantalons à l'école.
Thouraya:	Est-ce que vous aviez une télévision à la maison?
Francette:	Chez mes parents, nous n'avons jamais eu de télévision. Mon oncle a eu une télévision en 1953 – il était le seul dans son village et tout le monde venait voir les informations chez lui.
Thouraya:	Est-ce que vous alliez au cinéma?
Francette:	Oui, j'y allais de temps en temps et le premier film que j'ai vu c'était *La Belle et Le Clochard*. J'étais un peu déçue parce que c'était un film pour enfants et que je voulais voir un film d'adultes.
Jémilie:	Vous êtes née pendant la Seconde Guerre mondiale. Est-ce que vous aviez de quoi manger?
Francette:	J'habitais dans une ferme; nous avions de quoi manger, mais ce n'était pas comme ça pour tout le monde.
Thouraya:	Qu'est-ce que vous receviez comme cadeau de Noël?
Francette:	Si on avait de la chance, on recevait une orange comme cadeau.
Jémilie:	Vous rigolez!
Francette:	Non, pendant et après la guerre la vie était très difficile. Une orange et du chocolat, c'était vraiment le luxe.
Jémilie:	Est-ce que vous aidiez beaucoup à la maison?
Francette:	Non, pas tellement. Ma belle-mère ne voulait pas me laisser travailler. Mais j'aurais bien aimé apprendre toutes ces choses.
Thouraya:	Vous vouliez faire des tâches ménagères?
Francette:	Oui, j'aurais bien aimé.
Thouraya:	Est-ce que vous pensez que c'est mieux d'être ado aujourd'hui ou quand vous étiez jeune?
Francette:	Ce n'est pas si différent. Ce qui compte surtout, ce sont des amis.
Thouraya:	Oui, c'est vrai. Madame Francette, merci, c'était vraiment très intéressant.
Jémilie:	Oui, merci beaucoup pour l'interview.

1 Regarde l'épisode 4. Madame Tournemine (Francette) parle de quelle période dans sa vie?

Students watch the video and decide which period of the twentieth century is talked about.

Answer: b (les années 1950)

2 Madame Tournemine raconte sa jeunesse. De quels sujets (a–k) parle-t-elle? Choisis les six bonnes réponses.

Students decide which six of the topics listed are covered in Madame Tournemine's description of her youth.

Answers: a, b, c, e, g, j

3 Vrai ou faux? Corrige les phrases fausses en anglais.

Students decide whether the statements are true or false. Encourage them to give as much information as possible to explain the false statements.

*Answers: **a** vrai; **b** vrai; **c** faux (She was allowed to go out dancing at village fêtes, but her parents were present.); **d** vrai; **e** faux (Girls were banned from wearing trousers to school, but she fought to be allowed to wear them.); **f** faux (Her parents never had a TV set, but her uncle did, and everyone in the village came to his house to watch the news.); **g** vrai; **h** vrai*

4 À ton avis, la vie des ados est meilleure aujourd'hui qu'avant? Pourquoi?

In groups, students debate whether teenagers have a better life today than in the past. Remind students to use opinion phrases and to justify their opinions with reasons.

4 Être ado, c'est quoi?

4.9 Test

page 74

Resources
- Student Book, page 74
- CD 1, track 44

PLTS
- Creative thinkers, Reflective learners, Effective participators

AT levels
Approximate medal guidelines:
- (Foundation) L: 3; S: 4; R: 4; W: 4
- (Core) L: 3–4; S: 4; R: 4; W: 4
- (Higher) L: 4; S: 5; R: 5; W: 5

1 Listen to Isabelle, Yvan, Coralie and Nathan talking about pocket money. Copy out and fill in the grid in English. (See pages 60–61.)

Answers:

	How much?	Is it enough?	What chores do they do?	Extra details
Isabelle	25€ per month	yes	tidies her room, looks after her little brother	bought cinema tickets last weekend
Yvan	35€ per month	yes	mows lawn, gets good results at school	buys own clothes, e.g. bought T-shirt and jeans last weekend
Coralie	5€ per week	no	does shopping for grandmother, tidies room every weekend	must save up because would like to buy a smartphone
Nathan	15€ per month	yes	doesn't help much at home but sometimes does babysitting	did shopping for grandmother last Saturday

CD 1, track 44   page 74, activité 1

- Isabelle, parle-moi de ton argent de poche.
- Je gagne vingt-cinq euros par mois. Je dois ranger ma chambre et quelquefois, je dois garder mon petit frère. Vingt-cinq euros, je trouve que c'est assez parce que je peux acheter ce que je veux. Le week-end dernier, j'ai acheté des places de cinéma.
- Et toi, Yvan?
- Moi, mes parents me donnent vingt euros et ma grand-mère quinze euros. Donc, j'ai trente-cinq euros par mois. Je pense que c'est assez. Je dois tondre régulièrement la pelouse pour mes parents et avoir de bons résultats au collège! J'achète mes vêtements. Par exemple, le week-end dernier, j'ai acheté un T-shirt et un jean.
- Coralie, tu as combien d'argent de poche?
- J'ai cinq euros par semaine, ce n'est pas assez. J'aimerais avoir plus! Je dois faire les courses pour ma grand-mère et ranger ma chambre tous les week-ends. Je dois économiser parce que je voudrais acheter un smartphone.
- Et pour finir, Nathan?
- Je reçois quinze euros par mois et je pense que c'est bien, c'est assez pour moi. Je n'aide pas beaucoup à la maison mais quelquefois, je dois faire du baby-sitting. Samedi dernier, j'ai fait les courses pour ma grand-mère!

2 Prepare a short presentation. (See pages 58–59 and 62–65.)

Students prepare and present a short presentation about their relationship with their family and the pressures faced by teenagers today. Encourage them to draw on the language covered in the unit and to include a range of opinion phrases and reasons.

3 Read these two articles. Who says what? (See pages 58–59.)

Students read the texts and decide whether the English statements apply to Sophie or Léo.

Answers: **a** Sophie; **b** Léo; **c** Sophie; **d** Sophie; **e** Léo; **f** Léo; **g** Léo; **h** Sophie

4 Write an article for your school magazine comparing your lifestyle with that of your grandparents. (See pages 62–65.)

Remind students to cover all the bullet points and to draw on the language they have learned throughout the unit. Encourage them to develop their answers, using opinions, reasons, time expressions and different tenses.

5 En pleine forme!

Unit 5: En pleine forme! Overview grid

Page reference	Contexts and objectives	Grammar	Strategies and skills	Key language	AT levels*
76–77 **5.1 Tu manges bien?**	Talk about healthy eating	Impersonal structures	Dictionary skills. Use context to work out meaning	l'huile, le poulet, le yaourt, le beurre, les glaces, le fromage, le riz, l'eau, le poisson, les pommes de terre, le pain, les gâteaux, l'ananas, le coca, les carottes. Il faut manger cinq fruits ou légumes … Il ne faut pas/Il est important de ne pas manger trop de/d' … Il est nécessaire/essentiel de boire un litre/deux parts de/d' … par jour, une/deux fois par jour, à chaque repas, régulièrement … parce que c'est bon/ce n'est pas bon pour le cœur/le cerveau/la peau/les yeux/les dents/les cheveux/les os/les muscles. … parce qu'il y a des vitamines/des fibres/des protéines/trop de sucre/graisses.	L: 3–4 S: 3–4 R: 3–4 W: 3–4
78–79 **5.2 Comment vivre sainement?**	Discuss healthy lifestyles	The pronoun en	Build confidence in asking questions. Evaluate your performance	Je bois un litre/beaucoup d'eau par jour. Je mange cinq/beaucoup de fruits et légumes par jour. Je fais du sport/de la danse une/deux fois par semaine. Je joue au foot/tennis tous les jours/toutes les semaines. J'en mange/bois/fais … Je mange équilibré/sainement/à des heures régulières. Je dors huit heures par nuit.	L: 3–4 S: 3–4 R: 4–5 W: 4–5
80–81 **5.3 Attention: danger!**	Talk about how diet affects health	Perfect tense (revision). Expressions of quantity	Strategies for checking written work. Evaluate your performance	des céréales, du thé, un yaourt, un steak-frites, une tarte au citron, un hamburger, des pâtes, un gâteau, du jambon, une pomme, du fromage blanc, un jus d'orange. J'ai/Je n'ai pas/Tu n'as pas mangé/bu/pris … au (petit) déjeuner/goûter/dîner. trop de/d' … beaucoup de/d' … assez de/d' …, plus de/d' …, moins de/d' … Il faut/Il est important de manger/boire/prendre … graisses, produits gras, sucre, fruits et légumes, eau. C'est bien/Ce n'est pas bien parce que/qu' … … c'est trop gras/sucré. … c'est équilibré. … c'est bon/mauvais pour la santé/la peau/le cœur/les dents. … il y a des vitamines/protéines/fibres/risques d'obésité/de surpoids. Je pense que je mange/tu manges bien/mal. Je pense qu'il/elle mange assez bien.	L: 3–5 S: 4–5 R: 3–5 W: 4–5
82–83 **5.4 Ma vie changera!**	Talk about resolutions to be healthier	Future tense	Use connectives to extend sentences	Je mangerai plus de fruits et de légumes. Je ferai plus de sports. Je boirai moins de boissons sucrées. J'irai à l'école en vélo. Je mangerai moins de fast-food. Je jouerai au basket. Je regarderai moins la télé. Je dormirai huit heures par nuit. … parce que c'est important/essentiel/mauvais pour la santé/les résultats scolaires.	L: 3–5 S: 3–5 R: 3–6 W: 4–5
84–85 **5.5 Ce sera comment?**	Talk about what life will be like in the future	Develop knowledge of the future tense	Translate into French	un robot-cuisinier, un mini jardin potager, des insectes, des pauses-exercices, une pilule-repas. On mangera plus/moins de/d'… On mangera des insectes/pilules. On remplacera les repas par … Ce sera meilleur pour la planète. On aura/Il y aura des robots-cuisiniers.	L: 4–5 S: 4–5 R: 4–5 W: 4–5
86–87 **5.6 Labo-langue**	Grammar, language strategies and pronunciation	The pronoun en. Talking about the past. Talking about the future	Evaluating your performance. Pronunciation: the French r sound		
88–93 **5.7 Extra Star, Extra Plus 5.8 Lire, Vidéo 5.9 Test, Vocabulaire**	Reinforcement and extension; reading material; activities based on the video material; revision and assessment		**Lire:** Using a dictionary: R: 5–7 **Vidéo:** L: 4–6; S: 4–5		**Test:** L: 4–6 S: 4–6 R: 4–6 W: 4–6

*See teacher notes for alternative assessment options. Guidelines for the various assessment criteria are provided in the introduction of this Teacher Handbook.

87

5 En pleine forme!

Unit 5: Week-by-week overview

(Three-year KS3 route: assuming six weeks' work or approximately 10–12.5 hours)
(Two-year KS3 route: assuming four weeks' work or approximately 6.5–8.5 hours)

About Unit 5, *En pleine forme!*: In this unit, students work in the context of healthy living: they discuss healthy eating and lifestyles, how diet affects health, and talk about resolutions to be healthier and what life will be like in the future.

Students revisit impersonal structures, using them now in the context of healthy eating. They learn to use the pronoun *en* to say 'of it', 'of them', 'some' or 'any', and also learn to use expressions of quantity when talking about how diet affects health. The perfect tense with *avoir* is revised, giving students the opportunity to transfer new language into the past. Students are introduced to the future tense and this is developed further, allowing students to master both regular and irregular verbs in the singular and plural forms.

Evaluating performance is given a focus in this unit and students are invited to assess themselves and others in order to pinpoint areas for improvement in both spoken and written work. Students are provided with multiple opportunities to work on their writing skills: dictionary skills and strategies for checking written work are covered, and students also learn how to translate into French. Strategies for building confidence in asking questions and for using connectives to extend sentences also enhance students' spoken work. The pronunciation point focuses on the correct pronunciation of the French *r* sound.

Three-year KS3 route

Week	Resources
	*Material from the end-of-unit pages (**5.7 Extra Star/Plus**, **5.8 Lire** and **Vidéo**) may be used during week 6 or selectively during weeks 1–5 as time permits.*
1	5.1 Tu manges bien?
2	5.2 Comment vivre sainement? 5.6 Labo-langue, activity 1 5.6 Labo-langue, Evaluating your performance
3	5.3 Attention: danger! 5.6 Labo-langue, activities 2 and 3 5.6 Labo-langue, Evaluating your performance
4	5.4 Ma vie changera! 5.6 Labo-langue, activity 4 5.6 Labo-langue, Pronunciation: the French *r* sound
5	5.5 Ce sera comment?
6	5.7 Extra Star, Extra Plus 5.8 Lire 5.8 Vidéo 5.9 Test 5.9 Vocabulaire

Two-year KS3 route

Week	Resources
	*Material from the end-of-unit pages (**5.7 Extra Star/Plus**, **5.8 Lire** and **Vidéo**) may be used selectively during weeks 1–4 as time permits.*
1	5.1 Tu manges bien? (Omit activity 4)
2	5.2 Comment vivre sainement? 5.6 Labo-langue, activity 1 5.6 Labo-langue, Evaluating your performance
3	5.3 Attention: danger! (Omit activity 3) 5.6 Labo-langue, activities 2 and 3 5.6 Labo-langue, Evaluating your performance
4	5.4 Ma vie changera! (Omit activities 3 and 7) 5.6 Labo-langue, activity 4 5.6 Labo-langue, Pronunciation: the French *r* sound 5.9 Test 5.9 Vocabulaire

5.1 Tu manges bien?

pages 76–77

Planner

Objectives
- Vocabulary: talk about healthy eating
- Grammar: use impersonal structures
- Skills: develop dictionary skills; use context to work out meaning

Resources
- Student Book, pages 76–77
- CD 1, tracks 45–46
- Grammar and Skills Workbook, page 20
- Kerboodle, Unit 5

Key language

l'huile, le poulet, le yaourt, le beurre, les glaces, le fromage, le riz, l'eau, le poisson, les pommes de terre, le pain, les gâteaux, l'ananas, le coca, les carottes

Il faut manger cinq fruits ou légumes …

Il ne faut pas/Il est important de ne pas manger trop de/d'…

Il est nécessaire/essentiel de boire un litre/deux parts de/d'…

par jour, une/deux fois par jour, à chaque repas, régulièrement

… parce que c'est bon/ce n'est pas bon pour le cœur/le cerveau/la peau/les yeux/les dents/les cheveux/les os/les muscles.

… parce qu'il y a des vitamines/des fibres/des protéines/trop de sucre/graisses.

Grammar
- Impersonal structures

PLTS
- Activity 2: Independent enquirers
- Activity 4: Self-managers
- Activity 5: Team workers
- Plenary: Reflective learners

Homework and self-study
- Student Book, page 76, activity 2
- Student Book, page 77, activity 4
- Student Book, page 77, activity 6
- Grammar and Skills Workbook, page 20

Starters

See Kerboodle Starters bank for further details of **Up, down**.

- Hold a **Class discussion** in English about healthy eating and the various food groups. Compile a list on the board of the food groups that are essential for a healthy diet, and those which are less healthy.

- Play **Up, down**, using the recording of the text in activity 3. Students stand up whenever they hear an impersonal structure.

Plenaries

- **Reflecting on progress with dictionary skills.** Students produce a help sheet for Year 7 language learners at their school, providing some 'top tips' for using a dictionary. Encourage students to provide: personal examples of how they have found the dictionary to be useful; two examples of inference making/intelligent guessing in context in Units 1–4 of *Allez 2*; humorous examples of disastrous use of online translators.

1 Écoute et lis (1–15). Trouve les images dans la pyramide.

Do the **Class discussion** starter activity to introduce the topic of healthy eating and the food groups. Refer students to the list of food groups on the board and then ask them to compare this with the food pyramid on page 76. Can they see which groups are the equivalents of the English terms on the board?

Students then listen and find the picture for each of the French food words (which are in the same order as on the recording). They could do this in pairs, taking turns to point to the correct picture.

As a follow-up activity, ask students to consider how some of the foods are categorised in the pyramid. For example, potatoes are vegetables, but in the food pyramid they are classed as *Céréales*; cola is a drink, but in the food pyramid it is shown in the *Sucre et produits sucrés* section. Point out that it depends on the criteria being used to classify them. For example, it's true that cola is a drink, but it's also true that it contains a lot of sugar; botanically, potatoes are vegetables, but in terms of nutritional value, potatoes belong in the *Céréales* group. Ask students if they can identify other foods that might appear in different categories depending on the criteria used to

5 En pleine forme!

classify them. This could lead to an interesting cross-curricular discussion: for example, milk is a drink (*Boisson*) and also a dairy product (*Produit laitier*). What about cake(s) and ice cream?

Answers: **1** *l'huile – oil;* **2** *le poulet – chicken;* **3** *le yaourt – yoghurt;* **4** *le beurre – butter;* **5** *les glaces – ice cream;* **6** *le fromage – cheese;* **7** *le riz – rice;* **8** *l'eau – water;* **9** *le poisson – fish;* **10** *les pommes de terre – potatoes;* **11** *le pain – bread;* **12** *les gâteaux – cakes;* **13** *l'ananas – pineapple;* **14** *le coca – cola;* **15** *les carottes – carrots*

⭐ Students think of an extra item that could be added to each category.

🎵 **CD 1, track 45**   page 76, activité 1

1 L'huile, c'est une matière grasse.
2 Le poulet, c'est de la viande.
3 Le yaourt, c'est un produit laitier.
4 Le beurre, c'est une matière grasse.
5 Les glaces, c'est un produit sucré.
6 Le fromage, c'est un produit laitier.
7 Le riz, c'est des céréales.
8 L'eau, c'est une boisson.
9 Le poisson … c'est du poisson!
10 Les pommes de terre, ce sont des légumes … mais elles sont dans la catégorie « Céréales et dérivés ».
11 Le pain, c'est des céréales.
12 Les gâteaux, ce sont des produits sucrés.
13 L'ananas, c'est un fruit.
14 Le coca, c'est une boisson … mais c'est dans la catégorie « Produits sucrés ».
15 Les carottes, ce sont des légumes.

---

2   Regarde la pyramide et lis (a–f). C'est vrai ou faux?
Students look again at the food pyramid and decide whether the statements are true or false. Draw their attention to the glossed items of vocabulary. As a follow-up task, ask them to correct the false statements.

Answers: **a** *vrai;* **b** *vrai;* **c** *faux (5 par jour);* **d** *faux (à chaque repas);* **e** *faux (limiter la consommation);* **f** *vrai*

⭐ Students find the French for the listed items of vocabulary.

Answers: consommation, à chaque repas, à volonté

3   Écoute, lis et trouve les parties du corps.
Before starting work on activity 3, run through the grammar box on **Impersonal structures**, reminding students that they used these in Unit 3, when talking about the dangers of social networking sites. Do the **Up, down** starter activity, playing the recording an initial time for students to spot the impersonal structures.

Students then listen and read the text, and match the numbered French words highlighted in the text to the correct pictured body parts.

Answers: **1** *b;* **2** *g;* **3** *e;* **4** *f;* **5** *d;* **6** *c;* **7** *a*

As a follow-up task, use the recording for pronunciation practice of difficult sounds. Play the recording and ask students to listen out for the pronunciation of *les œufs* and *les os*. Elicit from the class the correct pronunciation of the singular and go on to emphasise the difference between the pronunciation of the singular and plural nouns:

un œuf [uneuf]   des œufs [dezeu]   les œufs [lezeu]
un os [unos]   des os [dezo]   les os [lezo]

🎵 **CD 1, track 46**   page 77, activité 3

C'est bon pour la santé? Pourquoi?
Il est essentiel d'avoir une alimentation équilibrée, riche en protéines (la viande, le poisson, les œufs) et en vitamines C et E (les fruits et les légumes). Il faut manger au moins cinq fruits et légumes par jour.
Il est important de manger des céréales (du pain, du riz, des pâtes) et des produits laitiers (des yaourts, du fromage) à chaque repas. Le pain et les céréales apportent des fibres et aident à avoir de beaux cheveux, une peau saine, un cœur en pleine forme et de beaux muscles!
Les produits laitiers apportent du calcium. Le calcium est très important pour les os et les dents. Quand on mange bien, notre cerveau fonctionne mieux.
En revanche, il est nécessaire de diminuer sa consommation des produits gras comme les frites et il est essentiel de boire de l'eau. Mais attention, il ne faut pas boire trop de boissons sucrées!

---

4   Relis et réponds aux questions en anglais.
Students read the text again and answer the questions in English. Before they do so, refer them to the skills box on **Using a dictionary** and encourage them to follow these tips when working out their answers.

Answers: **a** *meat, fish, eggs;* **b** *fruit and vegetables;* **c** *at least five;* **d** *bread, rice, pasta;* **e** *yoghurt, cheese;* **f** *it is essential to drink water, you mustn't drink too many sugary drinks*

t   As a Gold medal activity, ask students to translate the text into English.

Answer: It is essential to have a balanced diet, rich in protein (meat, fish, eggs) and in vitamins C and E (fruit and vegetables). You must eat at least five fruits and vegetables per day.

It is important to eat cereals (bread, rice, pasta) and dairy products (yoghurt, cheese) at each meal. Bread and cereals supply fibre and help (us) to have nice hair, healthy skin, a healthy heart and also good muscles. Dairy products supply calcium. Calcium is very important for bones and teeth. When we eat well, our brain works better.

On the other hand, it is necessary to/you must reduce your consumption of fatty products such as cakes and it is essential to drink water. But watch out – you mustn't drink too many sugary drinks!

5 À deux: « C'est bon pour la santé? Pourquoi? » A ↔ B.
In pairs, students discuss whether the foods covered in the spread are good for the health and why (not). Encourage them to bring impersonal structures into their dialogues and to draw on the reasoning in the text in activity 3. They also use the key language box for support.

◯ Students also say which part of the body each food is good for.

6 Écris un paragraphe: « Bien manger ».
Students write a paragraph about how to eat healthily, giving reasons for their statements. Encourage them to use impersonal structures in their writing and to use a range of phrases to justify what they say (*parce que*, *car*, etc.). Refer them to the key language box for support.

✚ Students also add what is not good and why.

Plenary

In pairs, students talk about healthy eating and reflect on whether their fluency has improved.

★ Students name five foods that are good for a healthy diet.

◯ Students use impersonal structures to give advice on what to eat and drink for a healthy diet.

✚ Students give reasons for their advice: for example, vitamins, protein.

5.2 Comment vivre sainement?

pages 78–79

Planner

Objectives
- Vocabulary: discuss healthy lifestyles
- Grammar: use the pronoun *en*
- Skills: build confidence in asking questions; evaluate your performance

Resources
- Student Book, pages 78–79
- CD 1, track 47
- Grammar and Skills Workbook, pages 22 and 53
- Kerboodle, Unit 5
- Unit 5 Worksheet 5 (ex. 1), 6

Key language
Je bois un litre/beaucoup d'eau par jour.
Je mange cinq/beaucoup de fruits et légumes par jour.
Je fais du sport/de la danse une/deux fois par semaine.
Je joue au foot/tennis tous les jours/toutes les semaines.
J'en mange/bois/fais …
Je mange équilibré/sainement/à des heures régulières.
Je dors huit heures par nuit.

Grammar
- The pronoun *en*

PLTS
- Activity 2: Independent enquirers
- Activity 4: Reflective learners
- Plenary: Creative thinkers

Homework and self-study
- Student Book, page 78, activity 1
- Student Book, page 79, activity 3
- Student Book, page 79, activity 5
- Grammar and Skills Workbook, pages 22 and 53

Starters

See Kerboodle Starters bank for further details of **Pictionary**.

- Hold a **Class discussion** about what comprises a healthy lifestyle. Ask students to think about aspects such as exercise, sleep and eating habits, and to think of good and bad examples of each.

- Play **Pictionary** to consolidate the key language introduced in activity 1.

5 En pleine forme!

> **Plenaries**
> - **Plenary people.** Inform the class at the beginning of the lesson that you will be requesting a team of 'plenary people' towards the end of the lesson. These students will act as 'experts' and will need to be prepared to answer questions from their peers on healthy eating and healthy lifestyles. Refer students back to the skills box on **Asking questions** on page 79 and give students five minutes to prepare some questions of their own. Ask then for volunteers to come to the front of the class to answer the questions raised by the class.
>
> If time permits and it is appropriate for the class, students could vote for who is the best expert in the field. Note: this plenary may be more beneficial after students have watched the Unit 5 video clip on page 91.

1 Lis les phrases a–j. C'est Monsieur Parfait ou Madame Terrible?

Before starting this activity, do the **Class discussion** starter activity to encourage students to think about what comprises a healthy or unhealthy lifestyle.

Students then look at the pictures of Monsieur Parfait and Madam Terrible, and read the statements. They decide which statements relate to which character. Ensure that students understand that Monsieur Parfait represents a healthy lifestyle, whilst Madame Terrible represents an unhealthy lifestyle.

Answers: **Monsieur Parfait**: a, e, f, h, i;
Madame Terrible: b, c, d, g, j

As a follow-up activity, students carry out a survey. They ask five classmates, *Que fais-tu pour vivre sainement?* Students base their answers on the phrases from activity 1.

2 Écoute l'interview: « Que fais-tu pour vivre sainement? » C'est Margaux (M), Robin (R), Léa (L) ou Sacha (S)?

Before playing the recording, do the **Pictionary** starter activity, to ensure that students are familiar with the lifestyle statements from activity 1. Students then copy the grid, listen, and note down the initial of each speaker to whom each statement applies. Point out that most of the statements apply to more than one person.

Once students have completed the activity, run through the grammar box on **The pronoun en**. Then play the recording again and challenge students to spot each use of the pronoun *en* (*J'en bois ..., J'en mange ..., J'en fais ..., J'en bois ...*).

*Answers: Je mange à des heures régulières: R, S;
Je bois beaucoup d'eau: M, S; Je fais du sport: M, L, S;
Je mange équilibré: R, L*

⭐ Students note down the three sports mentioned in the interview.

Answers: boxing, badminton, tennis

✚ t Students transcribe what Margaux says.

CD 1, track 47   page 78, activité 2

- Que font les jeunes pour vivre sainement et être en forme? Margaux, que fais-tu?
- Moi, je fais beaucoup de sport. Je fais de la boxe deux fois par semaine. En plus, je bois beaucoup d'eau. J'en bois au moins un litre et demi par jour.
- Et toi, Robin?
- Moi, je mange à des heures régulières parce que c'est important. Comme c'est très bon pour la santé, je mange équilibré et je mange beaucoup de fruits et de légumes. J'en mange au moins cinq par jour.
- Et toi, Léa?
- Moi, la semaine, je suis très active. Je joue au badminton ou au tennis, et je mange équilibré parce que c'est essentiel pour la santé.
- Et toi, Sacha?
- Moi, je fais beaucoup de sport car il faut bouger. J'en fais trois ou quatre fois par semaine. Avec ma famille, on mange à des heures régulières et je bois beaucoup d'eau. J'en bois deux litres par jour – c'est super important pour la santé!
- Super! Merci, les jeunes et ... continuez!

3 Lis. Recopie et remplis la grille.

Students read the interview with Maxime and copy and complete the grid. Ask them also to spot examples of *en* in the interview.

Answers: **Hours of sleep:** eight hours per night; **Sport:** a lot of sport, e.g. swimming (three times a week); **Fruit/Vegetables:** eats a lot of fruit/veg because is vegetarian; **Regular mealtimes:** yes, at midday and 7 p.m. every day; **Other details:** eats a balanced diet, drinks a lot of water (more than two litres per day); yesterday had rice and vegetables for dinner

⭐ t *Students translate the six questions from the interview.*

Answers: How many hours do you sleep per night? Do you do sport? Do you eat fruit and vegetables? Do you eat at regular hours? What else do you do to be fit? What did you eat yesterday?

○ **t** Students translate what Maxime says.

Answers: I sleep about eight hours a night. Yes, I do a lot (of it). For example, I swim. I do it three times a week. Yes, since I'm a vegetarian, I eat a lot of them. Yes, I eat at midday and 7 p.m. every day. I eat a balanced diet and I drink a lot of water. I drink more than two litres (of it) per day. Yesterday for dinner I ate rice and vegetables.

4 À deux. A pose les questions de l'activité 3. B répond. Utilise *en*. A ↔ B.

Before students begin this activity, refer them to the skills box on **Asking questions**. In pairs, students work to create a bank of questioning words that they will use in their dialogues. Remind students to pay attention to intonation at the end of their questions.

When carrying out the activity, less able students might wish to begin with (or stick to) the questions from the interview in activity 3. More able students will be able to adapt these questions and use the bank of questioning words which they have assembled.

○ Students add a time expression and a reason.

For a Gold medal, more able students could develop their answers further by using the past tense to say what they did last week.

Once students have completed the activity, refer them to the section on **Evaluating your performance** on page 87. Ask students to work through this section in pairs, evaluating their own performance, providing feedback to each other and discussing how they might improve on it.

5 Écris un blog: « Que fais-tu pour vivre sainement? »

Students write a blog about healthy living. Encourage them to draw on all the language covered in the spread.

○ Students use *en* and *il faut* in their writing.

✚ Students develop their answers further by using the past tense to say what they did last week.

Plenary

Students prepare a short report for a radio programme, talking about what they do to keep healthy. They should try to make it interesting for listeners by considering what would catch their attention and why.

★ Students use simple sentences.

○ Students build more complex sentences using connectives and giving reasons.

✚ Students add their opinion of whether or not their lifestyle is healthy.

5.3 Attention: danger!

pages 80–81

Planner

Objectives
- Vocabulary: talk about how diet affects health
- Grammar: revise the perfect tense; use expressions of quantity
- Skills: use strategies for checking written work; evaluate your performance

Resources
- Student Book, pages 80–81
- CD 2, track 2
- Grammar and Skills Workbook, pages 35, 36, 52 and 53
- Kerboodle, Unit 5
- Unit 5 Worksheets 4 (ex. 1), 5 (ex. 2–3)

Key language

des céréales, du thé, un yaourt, un steak-frites, une tarte au citron, un hamburger, des pâtes, un gâteau, du jambon, une pomme, du fromage blanc, un jus d'orange

J'ai/Je n'ai pas/Tu as/Tu n'as pas mangé/bu/pris … au (petit) déjeuner/goûter/dîner.

trop de/d' …, beaucoup de/d' …, assez de/d' …, plus de/d' …, moins de/d' …

Il faut/Il est important de manger/boire/prendre …

graisses, produits gras, sucre, fruits et légumes, eau

C'est bien/Ce n'est pas bien parce que/qu' …

… c'est trop gras/sucré. … c'est équilibré.

… c'est bon/mauvais pour la santé/la peau/le cœur/les dents.

… il y a des vitamines/protéines/fibres/risques d'obésité/de surpoids.

Je pense que je mange/tu manges bien/mal.

Je pense qu'il/elle mange assez bien.

Grammar
- The perfect tense (revision)
- Expressions of quantity

PLTS
- Activity 4: Team workers
- Activity 5: Independent enquirers
- Activity 7: Reflective learners

5 En pleine forme !

Homework and self-study
- Student Book, page 81, activity 5
- Student Book, page 81, activity 6
- Student Book, page 81, activity 7
- Grammar and Skills Workbook, pages 35, 36, 52 and 53

Starters

See Kerboodle Starters bank for further details of **Dominoes** and **Word tennis**.

- Play **Dominoes** using the food items presented in activity 1, to consolidate this vocabulary before students attempt activity 2.
- Revise the perfect tense with a game of **Word tennis**: decide whether to stick to the *je* form or whether to include other forms too. Students take it in turns to call out a perfect tense verb (e.g. *j'ai mangé, j'ai bu*).

Plenaries

- **Peer assessment.** Students work in the same groups of four as for the Plenary on page 81. They devise a simple code for marking: for example, SC = self correct, G = gender error, etc. Alternatively, they could use the school or department marking policy. Students take turns to give constructive written feedback on the analyses of diet written by their group members for activity 7 on page 81. Encourage students to include at least one hint for further improvement.

---

1 Trouve les paires.
Students match the French food items to the correct pictures.
Answers: **1** b; **2** h; **3** g; **4** i; **5** j; **6** f; **7** k; **8** l; **9** c; **10** a; **11** d; **12** e

2 Écoute l'interview de Léna. Qu'est-ce qu'elle a mangé et bu hier ?
Students listen and note down what Léna ate and drank for each meal. Before playing the recording, do the **Dominoes** starter activity to consolidate students' knowledge of the food items from activity 1.
Answers: **Breakfast:** cereal and orange juice; **Lunch:** chicken, vegetables, yoghurt; **4 o'clock snack:** apple; **Evening meal:** pasta, ham, fromage frais

t Students transcribe what Léna says.

CD 2, track 2   page 80, activité 2
- Alors, Léna qu'est-ce que tu as mangé et bu hier ?
- Au petit déjeuner, j'ai mangé des céréales et j'ai bu un jus d'orange. À midi, j'ai mangé du poulet avec des légumes et j'ai pris un yaourt. À quatre heures, au goûter, j'ai mangé une pomme. Et pour le dîner, on a mangé des pâtes avec du jambon et en dessert, du fromage blanc.
- Merci, Léna !

3 Lis le journal de Léna. En réalité, qu'est-ce qu'elle a mangé et bu hier ?
Students read Léna's diary to discover what she really ate and drank yesterday. They note down the correct food and drink items for each meal. Before they start on this activity, explain to students that in Léna's interview her diet sounded quite healthy, but that in her diary she has written down what she really ate and drank yesterday – which turns out to be quite different from what she said in the interview!
Answers: **Breakfast:** nothing; **Lunch:** hamburger, apple, cola; **4 o'clock snack:** chocolate cake, tea; **Evening meal:** steak and chips, lemon tart

4 À deux : « Qu'est-ce que tu as mangé et bu hier ? » A ↔ B.
In pairs, students take turns to ask and say what they ate yesterday. Before they do so, run through the grammar box on the **Perfect tense with *avoir***. Then do the **Word tennis** starter activity to give students some practice of the perfect tense.

The following two medal tasks take this activity further and recycle language from spread 5.1.

○ As a Silver medal task, students say whether their partner's diet yesterday was healthy or not: *C'est bon/Ce n'est pas bon pour la santé.*

✚ As a Gold medal task, they explain why: *... parce que c'est/ce n'est pas bon pour les dents.*

5 Lis l'analyse de l'alimentation de Léna. Trouve les expressions a–f dans le texte.
Students read the analysis of Léna's diet and match the English phrases (a–f) to their French equivalents (underlined within the text). Before they do this, refer students to the grammar box on **Expressions of quantity** as they will need these expressions when looking for the French equivalents of the phrases.
Answers: **a** il faut manger plus de céréales; **b** il est important de manger plus de fruits et de légumes; **c** il faut boire moins de boissons sucrées; **d** il est essentiel de manger le matin; **e** bien manger est essentiel; **f** il y a des risques de surpoids ou d'obésité si on en mange trop

⭐ Students note down the dangers of eating too much fat and sugar.

Answers: Fat is bad for the heart and there is the danger of becoming overweight or obese. Sugar is not good for the teeth.

t 6 Traduis l'analyse (activité 5) en anglais.

Students translate the text from activity 5 into English.

Answer: Léna didn't eat breakfast/didn't eat anything for breakfast. That isn't good because it's essential to eat in the morning. You/We must eat more cereals. They are good for the health.

Léna ate too many fatty foods, which are bad for the heart. There are risks of being overweight or obese if you eat too many of them. Also, she drank too much cola. You/We must drink fewer sugary drinks because they aren't good for the teeth.

Léna ate an apple at lunchtime. That's good, but she didn't eat enough fruit. It is important to eat more fruit and vegetables because they contain vitamins.

I think Léna eats quite badly/unhealthily. Healthy eating is essential for keeping fit.

7 Est-ce que tu as bien mangé hier?
Students write an analysis of what they ate yesterday, explaining why it is good or bad. They use activity 5 and the key language box for support.

Encourage them to use the perfect tense, to include other structures they have learnt in the unit such as *il faut/il est important de* + infinitive, and to extend their sentences by using connectives.

Once they have written their analysis, refer them to the skills box on **Checking your written work** and encourage them to work back through their writing, checking the points listed.

Then refer students to the section on **Evaluating your performance** on page 87: students reflect on what they have written and how they went about checking their work. They could work in pairs to discuss which writing strategies they have found most helpful and how they will try to apply these to future written tasks.

Plenary

In groups of four, students discuss what they ate and drank last weekend. Encourage them to use the language they have learnt in the unit in their discussion.

⭐ Students say what they ate and drank for the various meals last weekend.

◯ Students decide who has the best diet.

➕ Students give reasons for their choice.

5.4 Ma vie changera! pages 82–83

Planner

Objectives
- Vocabulary: talk about resolutions to be healthier
- Grammar: use the future tense
- Skills: use connectives to extend sentences

Resources
- Student Book, pages 82–83
- CD 2, tracks 3–4
- Grammar and Skills Workbook, page 34
- Kerboodle, Unit 5
- Unit 5 Worksheets 3, 4 (ex. 2)

Key language

Je mangerai plus de fruits et de légumes. Je ferai plus de sports. Je boirai moins de boissons sucrées. J'irai à l'école en vélo. Je mangerai moins de fast-food. Je jouerai au basket. Je regarderai moins la télé. Je dormirai huit heures par nuit.

... parce que c'est important/essentiel/mauvais pour la santé/les résultats scolaires.

Grammar
- The future tense

PLTS
- Activity 1: Creative thinkers
- Activity 2: Team workers
- Plenary: Reflective learners

Homework and self-study
- Student Book, page 83, activity 4
- Student Book, page 83, activity 5
- Student Book, page 83, activity 6
- Student Book, page 83, activity 7
- Grammar and Skills Workbook, page 34

5 En pleine forme!

Starters
- Practise the use of the first person future tense before students attempt activity 2. Call out a verb in the future tense (preferably one from the resolutions in activity 1) and ask students to call out the *je* form of the future tense of that verb: Teacher: *Je mange!* Student: *Je mangerai!* Teacher: *Je bois!* Student: *Je boirai!*, etc.
- Compile with the class a list of **Connectives** and write them on the board. Say a short phrase and ask a student to use a connective and then add another short phrase. Continue around the class as long as possible: *Je mangerai beaucoup de fruits ... et je boirai beaucoup de légumes ... mais je mangerai moins de fast-food ... car c'est mauvais pour la santé ...*, etc.

Plenaries
- **Using technology to set motivational goals.** Students create a personal timeline for change, using an online tool such as readwritethink. org/files/resources/interactives/timeline_2 or timeline.knightlab.com, which can be used in different languages and also has a video tutorial on how to upload clips, etc.

This plenary could be started in class on phones or tablets if available, and finished for homework. Students could use wordle.net or worditout.com for key vocabulary to start with, and could add images sourced from the Internet to illustrate each stage added at home. Everything should be labelled in the target language. Students should make it very clear when they want to achieve a goal by. As a homework extension activity, they could add how they will achieve their goals. This could also be linked to the Gold medal Plenary task on page 85 and might encourage more students to aspire to tackle it.

1 Écoute et lis (1–8). Trouve les paires.
Students listen and read the resolutions to be healthier. They match the resolutions with the correct pictures. Once students have done this, run through the grammar box on **The future tense**. Remind students that they are already familiar with the near future tense (*je vais* + infinitive), which enables them to say what they <u>are going to do</u>. Explain that the future tense enables them to say what they <u>will do</u> in the future. Ask students to look through the resolutions again and to spot the examples of the future tense. Draw their attention to the two irregular verbs used (*je ferai* and *j'irai*) and explain that these will need to be learnt (along with the future tense of *être*, *avoir* and other irregular verbs).

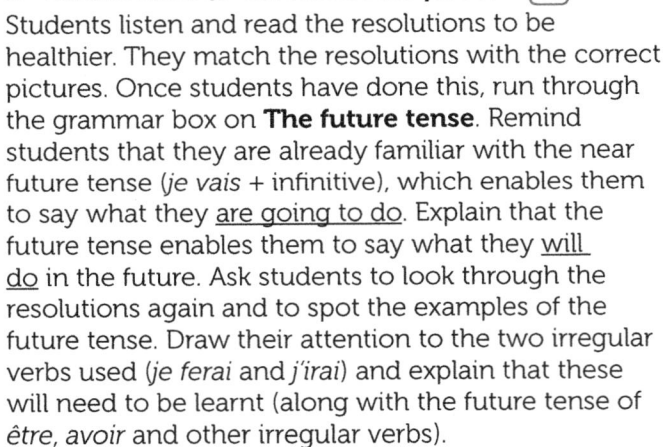

Answers: **1** b; **2** h; **3** d; **4** e; **5** g; **6** a; **7** c; **8** f

t Students translate the eight resolutions into English. Refer them to the grammar box on **The future tense** for support.

🎵 **CD 2, track 3**   page 82, activité 1

Mes nouvelles résolutions pour être en pleine forme!
1 Je mangerai plus de fruits et de légumes.
2 Je ferai plus de sport.
3 Je boirai moins de boissons sucrées.
4 J'irai à l'école à vélo.
5 Je mangerai moins de fast-food.
6 Je jouerai au basket.
7 Je regarderai moins la télé.
8 Je dormirai huit heures par nuit.

---

2 Choisis cinq résolutions de l'activité 1. Discute avec ton/ta partenaire.
Do the starter activity to practise the future tense before students embark on this pairwork task. Once students are happy with the formation of the *je* form, they take turns to say what they will do in the future, using the resolutions in activity 1 for support.

➕ Encourage students to add connectives (*mais, et, par contre*) and quantities (*plus/moins de*) to extend their sentences. Do the **Connectives** starter activity to provide support with this.

3 Écoute (1–4). Quatre jeunes parlent de leurs résolutions. Recopie et remplis la grille.
Students listen to four young people talking about their resolutions for the future. They copy the grid and decide which resolution applies to each speaker.

◎ Students note down extra details in the final column of the grid.

As a follow-up activity, play the recording again and ask students how many time expressions they can spot (five: *par jour, tous les jours, tous les week-ends, tous les jours, chaque semaine*).

t As a further follow-up task, ask students to transcribe one or more of the young people's responses.

Answers:

	Drink more water	Do more sport	Eat more fruit/veg	Extra details
1		✓	✓	will eat 5 fruits a day
2	✓			will walk to school every day
3		✓		will play football every weekend, go to school by bike every day
4		✓		will eat fewer hamburgers

CD 2, track 4   page 82, activité 3

1 – Alors, Charlotte, quelles sont tes résolutions pour la nouvelle année?
   – Moi, je mangerai cinq fruits par jour et je ferai plus de sport.
2 – Et toi, Djamela?
   – Moi, j'irai à l'école à pied tous les jours et je boirai plus d'eau.
3 – OK ... et Benjamin?
   – Moi, je jouerai au foot tous les week-ends et j'irai au collège à vélo tous les jours.
4 – Et pour finir, Hishem?
   – Moi, je ferai plus de sport chaque semaine et je mangerai moins de hamburgers!
   – Bravo, les jeunes, et merci!

4 Lis les résolutions et les questions (a–f). C'est qui?
Students read the two texts and answer the English questions.
Answers: **a** Isabelle; **b** Martin; **c** Martin; **d** Martin; **e** Isabelle; **f** Martin; **g** Martin

Students read the text again to spot the connectives.

Answers: connectives include *comme, et, car, donc*

t 5 Traduis les textes de Martin et d'Isabelle.
Students translate the two texts.

Answers: **Martin:** *As I am not fit, I will eat less chocolate and fewer chips. On the other hand, I will eat more fruit because it contains vitamins. Also, I will do more sport.* **Isabelle:** *I go out too often, nearly every evening, so I will go out less often, just at the weekend. I will go to the cinema once a week and I will be more hard-working. Yes, I will work more!*

6 Écris tes cinq résolutions pour la Nouvelle Année. Utilise les exemples de l'activité 4.
Students write their own resolutions for the New Year, basing them on the texts in activity 4.

Remind students to add reasons and to use a range of connectives.

7 Lis et réponds aux questions en anglais.
Students read the text about a programme against childhood obesity and answer the questions in English.

Answers: **a** She launched a programme against childhood obesity; **b** one in three; **c** more sport (at least one hour of sport a day at school); **d** she danced; **e** to encourage children to move/be active; **f** created a vegetable garden to encourage children to eat healthily

Students work out what *auront, seront* and *feront* mean. Refer them back to the grammar box on **The future tense**, and ask them to work out first which infinitives these verb forms are from. Ask them then to think about the usual verb endings in the present tense for these infinitives: can they work out which form of the verb these examples are in (*ils/elles* form)?

Plenary

Students say three things that they will do to change their lifestyle.

Students add time expressions.

Students also add reasons.

In pairs, students discuss their newly-acquired ability to talk about the future and discuss what they already knew about using the near future tense. Encourage students to practise using the two forms of the future and to explore the difference in sense and meaning between them.

5 En pleine forme!

5.5 Ce sera comment?

pages 84–85

Planner

Objectives
- Vocabulary: talk about what life will be like in the future
- Grammar: develop knowledge of the future tense
- Skills: translate into French

Resources
- Student Book, pages 84–85
- CD 2, track 5
- Grammar and Skills Workbook, page 34
- Kerboodle, Unit 5

Key language
un robot-cuisinier, un mini jardin potager, des insectes, des pauses-exercices, une pilule-repas
On mangera plus/moins de/d'... On mangera des insectes/pilules. On remplacera les repas par ... Ce sera meilleur pour la planète. On aura/Il y aura des robots-cuisiniers.

Grammar
- Develop knowledge of the future tense

PLTS and Numeracy
- Activity 4: Creative thinkers
- Activity 5: Creative thinkers
- Plenary: Reflective learners
- Numeracy: Activity 1: recognising large numbers

Homework and self-study
- Student Book, page 85, activity 3
- Student Book, page 85, activity 4
- Student Book, page 85, activity 5
- Grammar and Skills Workbook, page 34

Starters

See Kerboodle Starters bank for further details of **Word tennis**.

- Play **Word tennis** to consolidate the singular forms of the future tense. Divide the class into groups of three and put on the board a list of infinitives. Students take turns to say the *je*, *tu* and *il/elle/on* forms of each infinitive. More able students should be able to do this with the irregular verbs covered on page 82, as well as the regular verbs.

- Hold a **Class discussion** to generate ideas about what life might be like in 50 years' time. Write a list on the board and invite students to use some of these ideas if they need inspiration for their written work in activity 5.

Plenaries

- **Exit tickets.** At the start of the lesson hand out small pieces of card, the shape and size of a ticket. Ask students to write down from memory a sentence containing some new items of vocabulary that they have learnt in the past few lessons, focusing on the context of improving lifestyle and the future of the planet. At the end of the lesson, students read out the sentence on their 'ticket' with correct pronunciation in order to be able to 'exit' the lesson. Encourage more able students to challenge themselves, by being among the first to read out their sentence and then to act as co-teachers. You could also save some of the tickets to use in a starter activity for the next lesson; students could be asked to transcribe or translate them.

1 Lis. Corrige les erreurs dans les phrases a–f.
Students read the text and correct the errors in the English statements.

Answers: **a** 165 million children <u>don't eat enough</u>. **b** 42% live in Africa and <u>Asia</u>. **c** 43 million children under <u>five</u> are obese. **d** They <u>haven't done enough</u> sport. **e** In China, the number of obese children is <u>increasing</u>. **f** In America, the number of obese children is <u>going down</u>.

Students find four verbs in the future tense in the text.

Answers: pourra, sera, se passera, vivrons

t Students translate into English the questions at the end of the article.

Answers: Will everybody be able to have enough to eat in fifty years' time or will we all be obese? What will happen? How will we live?

t Students translate the whole article.

Answer:

Famine and obesity

Two world problems: are we dying of hunger or eating too much?

98

Today, 165 million children in the world do not develop well because they do not eat enough. 42% live in Africa and Asia. Famine remains a serious problem.

On the other hand, in the West, 43 million children under the age of five suffer from obesity because they eat too much and eat badly/haven't had a good diet, and because they don't do enough sport. In China, the number of obese children is increasing because their diet is richer than before, but in the USA the number is beginning to decrease because there are specialised programmes to inform young people.

Will everybody be able to have enough to eat in fifty years' time or will we all be obese? What will happen? How will we live?

2 Écoute (1–5). « Comment vivrons-nous dans cinquante ans? » Trouve une image pour chaque personne.

Students listen and choose the picture that illustrates what each speaker talks about.

t As a follow-up task, students could transcribe some or all of the young people's responses. Challenge them to spot the French for 'I don't agree' (*Non, je ne suis pas d'accord*). Which two people say it (Laëtitia and Hanane)?

Do the **Word tennis** starter activity to consolidate students' knowledge of the singular forms of the future tense. Then run through the grammar box on **The future tense**. Point out the plural endings to students (only the singular was covered in spread 5.4) and the stems of the irregular verbs that are featured. Then play the recording again and ask students to listen out for and note down any plural examples of the future tense (*habiteront, prépareront, remplaceront, mangerons*).

Answers: **1** c; **2** d; **3** b; **4** a; **5** e

CD 2, track 5   page 84, activité 2

1 – Alors, comment vivrons-nous dans cinquante ans? Mohamed?
  – Moi, je pense qu'il y aura des « robots-cuisiniers » qui habiteront chez nous et prépareront des repas équilibrés pour toute la famille.

2 – Olivia, qu'en penses-tu?
  – Moi, je pense qu'on ne mangera plus trois repas par jour. On aura des « pilules-repas » qui remplaceront certains repas. Ce sera plus rapide.
  – Oh, c'est intéressant!

3 – Tu es d'accord, Laëtitia?
  – Non, je ne suis pas d'accord. Moi, je pense qu'on aura un « mini jardin potager » dans notre cuisine et on aura toujours des légumes frais à la maison parce que c'est important pour la santé.
  – OK ...

4 – Et toi, Luc?
  – Moi, je pense qu'on mangera des insectes comme en Asie parce qu'ils sont riches en vitamines et en protéines. Nous mangerons moins de viande mais plus d'insectes.
  – Beurk! ...

5 – Tu es d'accord, Hanane?
  – Oh non, je ne suis pas d'accord! C'est dégoûtant! Moi, je pense qu'on mangera normalement mais qu'on fera du sport tous les jours. Il y aura dix minutes de « pauses-exercices » obligatoires toutes les deux heures au travail, à l'école ou dans la rue.

As a follow-up speaking activity, ask students to discuss how we might live in 50 years' time, using the pictures from activity 2 as prompts. More able students could also add reasons: **A** *On mangera des insectes! Tu es d'accord?* **B** *Oui, je suis d'accord! / Oui, je suis d'accord parce que c'est bon pour la santé.*

3 Lis. Qui dit les phrases a–f? C'est Justine, Romain ou les deux?

Students read the two texts and decide whether the English statements apply to Justine, Romain or both of them.

Answers: **a** Justine; **b** Romain; **c** Justine; **d** les deux; **e** Romain; **f** Justine

t Students translate the underlined expressions into English.

Answers: I think that in fifty years' time we will eat less meat; They will replace beef or pork; because insects don't need a lot of food or water; we will replace some meals with a pill; to help us to be healthy/fit; we will waste less time

4 Traduis en français.

Before students undertake this activity, refer them to the strategies box on **Translating into French** and encourage them to follow these tips as they carry out their translations. They should use the key language box to help them and will find it useful to look back at the texts in activity 3 for reference.

Answers: **a** *Je pense qu'on mangera/que nous mangerons moins de viande mais plus d'insectes. Ils sont très bons pour la santé parce qu'ils ont beaucoup de vitamines.* **b** *Les insectes sont riches en protéines donc ils remplaceront la viande.* **c** *On mangera/Nous mangerons une pilule par jour. La pilule-repas aura de bonnes valeurs nutritionnelles et remplacera un repas.*

5 En pleine forme!

5 Comment vivrons-nous dans cinquante ans? Écris un blog pour présenter tes idées.
Students write a blog to present their ideas about how we will live in 50 years' time. Encourage students to be as creative as possible with their ideas (they can draw on the ideas generated in the **Class discussion** starter activity if they need inspiration) and to use the language covered in the spread, as well as their own previously-learnt language. Remind them to use the future tense and to try to include examples of plural as well as singular forms.

Plenary

In pairs, students reflect on their progress in Unit 5, considering which tenses they have used. They try to use them in the medal activities.

- ★ Students discuss which foods are good for you and what you must eat to be healthier.
- ◎ Students discuss what life will be like in the future and what people will eat.
- ✚ Students make a list of resolutions for a healthier lifestyle.

5.6 Labo-langue
pages 86–87

Planner

Objectives
- Grammar: the pronoun *en*; talking about the past; talking about the future
- Skills: evaluating your performance
- Pronunciation: the French *r* sound

Resources
- Student Book, pages 86–87
- CD 2, track 6
- Grammar and Skills Workbook, page 53
- Kerboodle, Unit 5
- Unit 5 Worksheets 7, 8

PLTS
- Creative thinkers, Reflective learners, Self-managers

The pronoun *en*

1 Write answers to the questions. Replace the noun with the pronoun *en*.
Answers: **a** Oui, j'en mange beaucoup. **b** Non, il n'en fait pas toutes les semaines. **c** Oui, elle en fait. **d** Non, je n'en bois pas assez. **e** Non, je n'en mange pas. **f** Oui, j'en mange.

Talking about the past

2 Copy out the sentences. Put each verb into the perfect tense.
Answers: **a** a lancé; **b** as fini; **c** avons mangé; **d** ont choisi; **e** avez bu; **f** ai fait

3 Translate a–f into English.
Answers: **a** Michelle Obama launched/has launched a campaign against obesity. **b** Have you finished/Did you finish your work? **c** We ate/have eaten too many chips. **d** The children have chosen/chose chocolate cakes. **e** Have you drunk/Did you drink too many colas? **f** I did/have done a lot of sport this summer.

Talking about the future

4 Copy out the sentences. Put each verb into the future tense.
Answers: **a** aurons; **b** serai; **c** mangera; **d** boiront; **e** ferez; **f** irons; **g** viendras; **h** prendront

Evaluating your performance

This section encourages students to think about strategies for evaluating their performance in speaking and writing tasks. Once students have completed activity 4 on page 79, ask them to work in pairs and discuss the questions, evaluating themselves and providing feedback to each other.

Students are also encouraged to work through the second set of strategies after completing activity 7 on page 81.

Pronunciation: the French *r* sound

5 Listen and repeat.

CD 2, track 6   page 87, activité 5

je choisirai
il finira
nous irons
je verrai
je regarderai
tu seras
Je mangerai moins de frites.
Ce sera super.

100

5.7 Extra Star
page 88

1 Can you crack the code and find eight items of food and drink? Write out the words.
Explain to students that the vowels have been replaced with numbers and that once they have worked out which vowel each number represents, they will be able to substitute all instances of that number for the correct vowel.

Answers: **a** la viande; **b** le riz; **c** le poulet; **d** le coca; **e** le yaourt; **f** les fruits; **g** le poisson; **h** l'eau

2 Match the pictures to the words in activity 1.
Answers: **1** f; **2** d; **3** c; **4** h; **5** a; **6** g; **7** b; **8** e

3 Rewrite these sentences using correct word order.
Answers: **a** Je n'ai pas mangé au petit déjeuner. **b** Il faut manger au moins cinq fruits et légumes par jour. **c** Je fais beaucoup de sport parce qu'il faut bouger. **d** Je dors six heures par nuit mais ce n'est pas assez. **e** Je mangerai moins de produits gras. **f** Le calcium est essentiel pour les os.

t 4 Translate the sentences from activity 3.
Answers: **a** I didn't eat (anything) at/for breakfast. **b** We/You must eat at least five fruits and vegetables per day. **c** I do a lot of sport because we/you must be active. **d** I sleep six hours a night but it is not enough. **e** I will eat less fatty food/fewer fatty foods. **f** Calcium is essential for bones.

5 Affreux Jojo has written about a healthy lifestyle. Correct his seven <u>underlined</u> mistakes using words from the box.
Answers: **1** manger; **2** fruits et légumes; **3** boire; **4** vitamines; **5** du sport; **6** moins; **7** dormirai

5.7 Extra Plus
page 89

1 Trouve l'intrus.
Students find the odd one out in each set of four words and explain why it is the odd one out. Explain to students that there aren't necessarily any right or wrong answers – any answers will be accepted, as long as they can be justified.

Sample answers:
a l'eau – because it's a drink, or because it's the only one that begins with a vowel; or le sucre because it's the only sweet item
b le pain because it's the only one that isn't plural, or because it isn't a vegetable or fruit
c les œufs because they're not a part of the body
d j'ai mangé because it's the perfect tense; or je dors because it's the only verb that doesn't involve eating or drinking
e prendrai because it's the only future tense, or because it isn't an infinitive

2 Lis et réponds aux questions en anglais.
Students read the text and answer the questions in English.
Answers: **a** schools; **b** to live better and longer; **c** chefs; **d** to explain how to eat well, to prepare balanced dishes, to talk about good eating habits; **e** original dishes and different vegetables; **f** more than 500

t 3 Traduis le texte de Corinne en anglais.
Students translate Corinne's text into English.

Answers:
To be fit/healthy, I will do more sport and I will have balanced meals. Also, I will eat at least five fruits and vegetables per day.

I will eat dairy products because they contain calcium, which is good for the bones and teeth.

I think that it is important to eat at regular times. It is also essential to drink water to stay healthy. Yesterday, I drank two litres (of it).

4 Qu'est-ce que tu as mangé et bu le week-end dernier? Qu'est-ce qu'il faut faire pour être en forme? Quelles seront tes résolutions?
Students write about what they ate and drank last weekend, what they need to do to keep fit and what their resolutions are. This written task requires the use of three tenses (past, present and future) and will encourage students to write expansively, using all the language they have covered in this unit. Remind students to use impersonal structures, a range of connectives and to give plenty of opinions and reasons in their writing.

5 En pleine forme!

5.8 Lire
page 90

Resources
- Student Book, page 90
- Kerboodle, Unit 5

PLTS
- Independent enquirers

1 Read the text. Match these phrases (a–i) to the highlighted phrases in the text.

Students read the text about a Belgian NGO's football project in Togo. They match the English phrases with the highlighted French phrases in the text. Refer students to the skills box on **Using a dictionary** and encourage them to use the strategies on page 77 when looking up words.

As a follow-up task, discuss with the class the idea of physical activity being essential as part of a healthy lifestyle, building up personal confidence, opening doors, etc.

Answers: **a** a suivi des formations à l'arbitrage; **b** faire des études longues; **c** rendre les filles fortes sur le terrain et en dehors du terrain; **d** bâtir leur avenir; **e** réussir les épreuves; **f** essayer d'obtenir ce que nos mamans n'ont pas eu; **g** ils ont reconnu l'effet positif; **h** prêtes à faire des études supérieures; **i** Je découvre de nouveaux lieux

2 Choose a title (below) for each paragraph of the text (1–4). Careful: there are two titles that you will not need.

Answers: **1** Devenir footballeuse professionnelle à l'âge adulte; **2** Les opposants changent d'avis; **3** Une occasion pour voyager et apprendre; **4** Les projets à long terme des jeunes arbitres

3 Answer the questions in English.

Answers: **a** they considered football to be a violent sport that should only be played by boys; **b** she discovers/visits new places, she meets different people, she has confidence in herself; **c** continue to be a referee, study to be a journalist or interpreter

5.8 Vidéo
page 91

Resources
- Student Book, page 91
- Kerboodle, Unit 5 Video clip

PLTS
- Independent enquirers

Épisode 5: Manger équilibré
Zaied and Basile are undertaking the next challenge in the competition: this time they have to find out what foods are needed for a healthy diet. They go to the market to meet with Lyvia, a dietitian, who takes them through the various food groups needed in our everyday diet.

Video clip, Unit 5   page 91

(Outside the market)

Zaied: Qu'est-ce qu'on fait aujourd'hui, Basile?

Basile: C'est le concours … « Qu'est-ce qu'il faut manger pour être en forme? »

Zaied: Bon, c'est facile. Il faut manger de la nourriture!

Basile: Oui, mais quoi comme nourriture? Il ne faut pas manger des hamburgers et des frites tous les jours.

Zaied: Qu'est-ce qu'il faut manger alors?

Basile: On a rendez-vous avec Lyvia. Elle est diététicienne et elle va nous expliquer ce qu'il faut manger pour être en forme.

(They meet Lyvia)

Lyvia: Bon, Basile, qu'est-ce que tu as mangé aujourd'hui au petit déjeuner?

Basile: J'ai mangé des céréales avec du lait et j'ai bu du jus d'orange.

Lyvia: C'est pas mal, si les céréales ne sont pas trop sucrées. Et toi, Zaied?

Zaied: Moi, je prends un grand chocolat chaud et puis un pain au chocolat.
Lyvia: Hmm, c'est trop sucré tout ça. Le sucre, c'est mauvais pour la santé. Il est vital de manger équilibré, riche en vitamines et en fibres.
Zaied: Des fibres: il faut manger de fibres?
Lyvia: Oui, vous verrez. Si on mange bien, c'est délicieux et bon pour la santé.

(In the market)

Lyvia: Ici, il y a beaucoup de fruits et de légumes. Combien de fois par jour il faut manger des fruits et des légumes?
Basile: Il faut manger cinq fruits et légumes par jour.
Lyvia: Oui, c'est juste. Il est important donc de manger des fruits et des légumes – ils sont riches en vitamines, minéraux et aussi de nombreuses fibres.
Zaied: Des fibres, il y en a dans les fruits?
Lyvia: Oui, dans les fruits et légumes donc il y a de nombreuses fibres. Il est important d'en consommer à chaque prise de repas.
Basile: Il faut manger des légumes pour le petit déjeuner?
Lyvia: Oui, dans de nombreux pays on consomme des légumes. Mais si tu préfères, tu peux consommer des fruits.
Basile: Ah oui, comme des fraises ou une banane.
Lyvia: Oui, des fruits frais avec un yaourt. Le yaourt et les produits laitiers apportent donc du calcium qui est très important pour nos os et nos dents.
Zaied: Les produits laitiers contiennent du calcium?
Lyvia: Oui, ils contiennent du calcium et des protéines. La France est réputée pour ses nombreux fromages. Le fromage fait partie des produits laitiers.
Basile: J'adore le fromage et j'en mange à chaque repas.
Lyvia: Il est bon de manger du fromage, mais il ne faut pas en manger en trop grande quantité car il contient des graisses, et les graisses ne sont pas bonnes pour le cœur.
Zaied: Ouh, c'est trop compliqué tout ça! Il faut manger des produits laitiers mais pas trop.
Lyvia: Non, ce n'est pas compliqué. Le fromage blanc et les yaourts sont bons et contiennent moins de graisses. Quant aux autres fromages, il faut en manger, mais avec modération.
Zaied: Et les glaces, les glaces sont très bonnes.
Lyvia: Oui, mais les glaces, elles contiennent beaucoup de sucre, donc il faut limiter leur consommation.
Basile: À quoi servent les protéines?
Lyvia: Les protéines sont importantes pour nos cheveux, notre cœur et les muscles.
Zaied: Et où est-ce qu'on trouve les protéines?
Lyvia: Dans les viandes, le poulet, le poisson, les fruits de mer, le tofu, les œufs – tout ça en contient.
Zaied: Super. Je mangerai un hamburger à midi.
Lyvia: Il faut faire attention avec les hamburgers parce que le fast-food apporte trop de graisses et trop de sel. Mais un steak avec une grande salade et du riz serait équilibré pour la santé, n'est-ce pas?
Zaied: Et comme dessert?
Lyvia: Des fruits, ou des légumes ... ou un yaourt.
Basile: Ce n'est pas très compliqué. Je mangerai plus de fruits et légumes. Le matin, je prendrai un yaourt nature et des fruits. À midi, je mangerai du poulet ou de la viande avec du riz ou des pâtes et des légumes. Et le soir, je prendrai une grande salade ou une soupe de légumes.
Lyvia: Excellent, Basile. Des fruits et des légumes à volonté. Une fois par jour, de la viande. Du sucre avec modération. Et il ne faut pas oublier de boire de l'eau aussi. Il est essentiel pour la santé de consommer deux litres d'eau par jour.
Basile: D'accord, je boirai deux litres d'eau par jour.
Lyvia: Et toi, Zaied, qu'est-ce que tu mangeras?
Zaied: Moi, je mangerai plus équilibré parce que je fais de la boxe et c'est essentiel pour être en forme. Merci, Lyvia.
Lyvia: Merci à vous et bonne chance pour le concours.
Basile: Avec tout ça, je meurs de faim.
Zaied: Moi aussi. Ça me donne envie de manger des frites.
Basile: Zaied!

5 En pleine forme!

1 Regarde l'épisode 5. Qui est Lyvia?
Students watch the video and decide what Lyvia's profession is.
Answer: une diététicienne

2 Avant la rencontre avec Lyvia, qui mange quoi? C'est Zaied ou Basile?
Students note down whether Zaied or Basile normally consume the listed foods. Check students understand that they are listening for the boys' eating habits before their meeting with Lyvia, rather than their resolutions for the future.
Answers: **Basile**: a, b, e; **Zaied**: c, d, f

3 Lis les bonnes résolutions de Basile. Trouve les sept erreurs. Recopie et corrige le texte.
Students read the text detailing Basile's resolutions. They copy it out and correct the seven errors in it.
Answers: Je mangerai plus de fruits et de légumes. Le matin, je mangerai un yaourt (nature) et des fruits. À midi, je prendrai du poulet/de la viande avec du riz ou des pâtes et des légumes. Et le soir, je mangerai une grande salade ou une soupe de légumes. Je boirai aussi deux litres d'eau par jour.

4 Lis les phrases a–g. C'est vrai ou faux, selon la vidéo? Corrige les phrases fausses en anglais.
Students decide whether the statements are true or false. They correct the false sentences. Encourage them to give as much information as possible to explain the false items.
Answers: **a** faux (not good if breakfast cereal has sugar in); **b** vrai; **c** vrai; **d** vrai; **e** vrai; **f** faux (good for bones and teeth); **g** faux (not good for health because contain too much sugar)

5 Lyvia donne beaucoup de conseils. Pour toi, quel conseil est le plus facile?
In groups, students discuss which pieces of Lyvia's advice they personally find easiest to follow.

5.9 Test   page 92

Resources
- Student Book, page 92
- CD 2, track 7

PLTS
- Creative thinkers, Reflective learners, Effective participators

AT levels
Approximate medal guidelines:
- (Foundation) L: 4; S: 4; R: 4; W: 4
- (Core) L: 5; S: 5; R: 5; W: 4–5
- (Higher) L: 6; S: 6; R: 6; W: 5

1 Listen to three young people talking about their diet. Copy and fill in the grid in English. (See pages 80–83.)

Answers:

	Breakfast	Lunch	Dinner	Good or bad diet? Why?	Resolutions
Enzo	cereal + milk	hamburger + chips chocolate cake cola	pizza	bad – too much fat/sugar	will eat more vegetables, drink water, do more sport
Charlotte	nothing	veggie burger + chips ice cream	pasta with tomato sauce	bad – too much fast food and sweet food	will eat 5 fruit/veg per day, fewer cakes, will go to school by bike
Aziz	cereal + milk	spaghetti bolognese	chicken + carrots water	good – it is a balanced diet	will eat at least 5 fruit/veg per day will do 1 hour of sport per day

104

CD 2, track 7 — page 92, activitié 1

- Aujourd'hui, nous écoutons trois jeunes qui nous parlent de leur alimentation et de leurs nouvelles résolutions. Tout d'abord, Enzo, qu'est-ce que tu as mangé hier?
- Alors, j'ai mangé des céréales avec du lait le matin, puis à midi, un hamburger avec des frites et un gâteau au chocolat. J'ai aussi bu du coca et, le soir, j'ai mangé une pizza.
- OK, ce n'est pas super parce que tu manges trop de graisses et de sucre. Qu'est-ce que tu changeras?
- Je pense que je mangerai plus de légumes et que je boirai de l'eau. Je ferai aussi plus de sport parce que c'est important pour être en forme.
- Et toi, Charlotte?
- Moi, je n'ai rien mangé au petit déjeuner, mais à midi, j'ai mangé un végiburger avec des frites au McDo. Je suis végétarienne. J'ai aussi mangé une glace. Le soir, j'ai mangé des pâtes à la sauce tomate.
- Tu as mangé trop de fast-food et de produits sucrés, Charlotte! Ce n'est pas bon pour ta santé. Qu'est-ce que tu changeras pour manger mieux?
- Je pense que je mangerai cinq fruits et légumes par jour et je mangerai moins de gâteaux aussi. J'irai à l'école à vélo aussi.
- Et toi, Aziz?
- Alors, moi, je suis sportif donc ce matin, j'ai pris des céréales avec du lait. À midi, j'ai mangé des spaghettis bolognaises. Le soir, j'ai mangé du poisson avec des carottes et j'ai bu de l'eau mais pas de cocas parce que c'est mauvais pour les dents!
- Super! Tu as mangé très équilibré! C'est génial. Est-ce que tu changeras quelque chose?
- Oui, je pense que je mangerai plus de fruits, au moins cinq par jour, parce qu'ils ont beaucoup de vitamines. Et je ferai une heure de sport par jour aussi!
- Merci, les jeunes, et bon courage!

2 Answer these questions about healthy eating and your lifestyle. (See pages 76–83.)

Students prepare a presentation, answering the questions listed. They should use all three tenses (perfect, present and future) and should justify what they say with reasons, where appropriate.

3 Read the text and answer the questions in English. (See pages 76–83.)

Answers: **a** a healthy diet and doing sport; **b** because he was obese; **c** more fruit and vegetables, e.g. pineapple, carrots, potatoes; **d** 1½ litres of water; **e** he doesn't like them at all any more; **f** he'll go to school by bike, he'll play basketball (in a club)

4 Write an article for your school magazine, talking about a healthy lifestyle. (See pages 76–83.)

Students should include four paragraphs, covering the bullet points listed. Remind students that they should develop and extend their answers as much as possible and should include the structures, points and tenses shown in the boxes.

6 Rendez-vous

Unit 6: Rendez-vous — Overview grid

Page reference	Contexts and objectives	Grammar	Strategies and skills	Key language	AT levels*
94–95 **6.1 Alors, cette fête de fin d'année?**	Organise a party	Near future	Strategies to improve speaking Evaluate your performance	On va … envoyer les invitations, acheter la nourriture et les boissons pour le buffet, télécharger de la musique, décorer la salle, préparer le buffet, nettoyer! C'est une fête pour célébrer mon anniversaire. C'est samedi soir/à partir de 18 heures. Ça va être au collège/chez moi. Ça va être (vraiment) super/génial. Tu peux apporter du coca/des sandwichs. Je vais passer te chercher à 17 heures.	L: 4–5 S: 4–5 R: 3–5 W: 4–5
96–97 **6.2 On pourrait sortir?**	Suggest activities and make excuses	Conditional: *on pourrait* + infinitive	Conversation skills Evaluate your performance	On pourrait faire les magasins/faire un pique-nique/aller à un concert/aller à une fête/aller au bowling/aller au ciné/manger au McDo/regarder un DVD. Bof, je n'aime pas trop … Je ne sais pas … Ah non, c'est nul./Je déteste … Je ne peux pas parce que c'est trop cher/je n'ai pas beaucoup d'argent/j'ai horreur de danser/j'ai horreur du fast-food/je suis fatigué(e)/j'y suis allé(e) hier.	L: 3–6 S: 4–6 R: 3–5 W: 4–6
98–99 **6.3 Les festivals, j'adore!**	Talk about a festival or special event that you've been to	Perfect tense with *être* Imperfect tense	Cultural awareness strategies Evaluate your performance	Je suis allé(e) à la fête nationale/au festival de … On est allé(e)s à la Fête du Cinéma/de la Musique. J'y suis allé(e) avec mes copains/copines/parents … C'était génial/super/incroyable/gratuit. Il y avait un concert/un feu d'artifice/beaucoup de monde. Je suis resté(e)/On est resté(e)s trois jours/tout le week-end/juste le samedi. J'ai/On a dansé/chanté/mangé/vu/écouté … Je vais y retourner l'année prochaine/l'été prochain.	L: 5–6 S: 4–6 R: 4–6 W: 4–6
100–101 **6.4 Rencontre**	Communicate with people in formal situations	*Vous* form (present tense)	Formal and informal language Evaluate your performance	Je suis … depuis … ans/mois. C'est passionnant/excitant/intéressant mais c'est aussi fatigant/frustrant/prenant. Je commence à … heures. Je fais/lis/visite/travaille … L'année prochaine, nous allons organiser/faire …	L: 4–6 S: 4–6 R: 4–6 W: 4–6
102–103 **6.5 Calendrier des fêtes**	Talk about traditions and festivals	Use past and present tenses	Cultural awareness strategies	C'est nécessaire de se souvenir de la Guerre/de la Révolution. C'est important de penser à son amoureux(-euse)/s'amuser. Il y a des défilés/feux d'artifice/concerts. Il n'y a pas d'école. C'est un jour férié. On fait/mange/boit/danse/écoute/va/vient … C'était … Il y avait … Il faisait … On a fait/mangé/bu/dansé/écouté … On est allé(e)s/venu(e)s …	L: 4–5 S: 4–5 R: 4–5 W: 4–5
104–105 **6.6 Labo-langue**	Grammar, language strategies and pronunciation	Talking about the past: the perfect tense with *être* Conditional: *on pourrait* + infinitive Near future: *aller* + infinitive	Evaluating your own and others' performance Pronunciation: the perfect tense and the imperfect		
106–111 **6.7 Extra Star, Extra Plus** **6.8 Lire, Vidéo** **6.9 Test, Vocabulaire**	Reinforcement and extension; reading material; activities based on the video material; revision and assessment			**Lire:** R: 6–7 **Vidéo:** L: 4–5; S: 4–5	**Test:** L: 4–6 S: 4–6 R: 5–6 W: 4–6

*See teacher notes for alternative assessment criteria. Guidelines for the various assessment options are provided in the introduction of this Teacher Handbook.

Unit 6: Week-by-week overview

(**Three-year KS3 route**: assuming six weeks' work or approximately 10–12.5 hours)
(**Two-year KS3 route**: assuming four weeks' work or approximately 6.5–8.5 hours)

About Unit 6, Rendez-vous: In this unit, students work in the context of going out, meeting people and celebrating special events: they learn to organise a party, suggest activities and make excuses, and talk about cultural and other special events. They also learn how to communicate with people in formal situations and to discuss traditions and festivals in both France and Britain.

Students revisit the near future tense, using it now in the context of party preparations. They learn to use the conditional *on pourrait* + infinitive to make suggestions for going out. They revise and extend their knowledge of the perfect tense with *être*, and use the perfect tense alongside the imperfect. Work on tenses is developed further, with a focus on using the present and past tenses alongside each other. In addition, students learn to use the *vous* form of the present tense.

Evaluating performance is given a major focus again in this unit, and students are invited to assess themselves and others throughout, in order to pinpoint areas for improvement in both spoken and written work. They are also encouraged to develop their pairwork skills to help each other improve their own learning. Students are provided with multiple opportunities to develop their spoken and written work: they are offered strategies to help with planning and developing their spoken work, tips on developing conversation and are asked to consider the differences between formal and informal written language. Cultural awareness strategies also form a major part of the skills provision in this unit. The pronunciation point focuses on the perfect tense and the imperfect.

Three-year KS3 route

Week	Resources
	Material from the end-of-unit pages (**6.7 Extra Star/Plus**, **6.8 Lire** and **Vidéo**) may be used during week 6 or selectively during weeks 1–5 as time permits.
1	6.1 Alors, cette fête de fin d'année? 6.6 Labo-langue, activity 3 6.6 Labo-langue, Evaluating your own and others' performance
2	6.2 On pourrait sortir? 6.6 Labo-langue, activity 2 6.6 Labo-langue, Evaluating your own and others' performance
3	6.3 Les festivals, j'adore! 6.6 Labo-langue, activity 1 6.6 Labo-langue, Evaluating your own and others' performance 6.6 Labo-langue, Pronunciation: the perfect tense and the imperfect
4	6.4 Rencontre 6.6 Labo-langue, Evaluating your own and others' performance
5	6.5 Calendrier des fêtes
6	6.7 Extra Star, Extra Plus 6.8 Lire 6.8 Vidéo 6.9 Test 6.9 Vocabulaire

Two-year KS3 route

Week	Resources
	Material from the end-of-unit pages (**6.7 Extra Star/Plus**, **6.8 Lire** and **Vidéo**) may be used selectively during weeks 1–4 as time permits.
1	6.1 Alors, cette fête de fin d'année? (Omit activity 4) 6.6 Labo-langue, activity 3 6.6 Labo-langue, Evaluating your own and others' performance
2	6.2 On pourrait sortir? (Omit activity 2) 6.6 Labo-langue, activity 2 6.6 Labo-langue, Evaluating your own and others' performance
3	6.3 Les festivals, j'adore! (Omit activity 3) 6.6 Labo-langue, activity 1 6.6 Labo-langue, Evaluating your own and others' performance 6.6 Labo-langue, Pronunciation: the perfect tense and the imperfect
4	6.4 Rencontre 6.6 Labo-langue, Evaluating your own and others' performance 6.9 Test 6.9 Vocabulaire

6 Rendez-vous

6.1 Alors, cette fête de fin d'année?

pages 94–95

Planner

Objectives
- Vocabulary: organise a party
- Grammar: use the near future
- Skills: develop strategies to improve speaking; evaluate your performance

Resources
- Student Book, pages 94–95
- CD 2, tracks 8–9
- Grammar and Skills Workbook, pages 33 and 55
- Kerboodle, Unit 6

Key language

On va ...

envoyer les invitations, acheter la nourriture et les boissons pour le buffet, télécharger de la musique, décorer la salle, préparer le buffet, nettoyer!

C'est une fête pour célébrer mon anniversaire.
C'est samedi soir/à partir de 18 heures.
Ça va être au collège/chez moi.
Ça va être (vraiment) super/génial.
Tu peux apporter du coca/des sandwichs.
Je vais passer te chercher à 17 heures.

Grammar
- The near future

PLTS
- Activity 1: Independent enquirers
- Activity 5: Self-managers
- Plenary: Reflective learners

Homework and self-study
- Student Book, page 94, activity 2
- Student Book, page 95, activity 6
- Grammar and Skills Workbook, page 33

Starters

See Kerboodle Starters bank for further details of **Word tennis** and **Pictionary**.

- Play **Word tennis** to revise the near future (first introduced in *Allez 1*, Unit 7, in the context of holidays). Divide the class into two teams and ask students to call out near future phrases in the *je* form: *je vais aller – je vais prendre – je vais manger*, etc. Once students have mastered the *je* form, go on to the other forms.
- Play **Pictionary** to consolidate students' knowledge of the phrases for party organisation in activity 1.

Plenaries

- **Life across the world.** This plenary focuses on geographical knowledge and the development of empathy. Set the scene by asking students to imagine that they are in a different continent, organising a party for their year group at school. Before they start speaking, students spend a few minutes in groups noting down differences in climate and availability of clothing/food/drink and how this might affect what they might eat and wear to the party. They should also discuss transport to the event. More able students should be expected to add why there are such differences and might also want to include what they could do to raise funds for a community in another country.

1 Qu'est-ce qu'on va faire pour organiser la fête? Trouve les paires.

Before students start this activity, revise the near future tense with them by doing the **Word tennis** starter activity. Run through the grammar box on **The near future** and ensure students are secure with this. They then read the phrases about preparing for a party and match them to the pictures. Remind them to use their knowledge of cognates and the pictures for clues.

Note that, although *la nourriture* has been used here, it might be worth pointing out to students that *la bouffe* ('grub') is an informal/slang term for food and is widely used by young people in France.

Answers: **1** d; **2** b; **3** e; **4** f; **5** c; **6** a

2 Écoute. Qui va faire quoi? Choisis les bonnes images (a–f) de l'activité 1.

Do the **Pictionary** starter activity to consolidate the phrases for organising a party from activity 1. Students then listen to a group of teenagers discussing plans for organising a party. They identify which tasks each person will be doing, and note down the letters of the corresponding pictures from activity 1.

Answers: **Martin**: d, a; **Margaux**: b, c, a; **Amélie**: e, a; **Hugo**: f, a

As a Bronze medal task, ask students to note down how many people there are in each team.

Answers: 5 people in Martin's team; 4 people in Margaux's team; 3 in Amélie's team; 2 in Hugo's team

As a Silver medal task, ask students to note down where the party will take place

Answers: At school in the big hall – it's enormous, so there's lots of space for dancing.

CD 2, track 8   page 94, activité 2

- Alors, tout est prêt pour notre fête? On résume ... Qui va faire quoi? Martin, qu'est-ce que tu vas faire?
- Moi, je vais contacter toute la classe par mail et envoyer les invitations.
- Vous êtes combien dans ton équipe?
- On est cinq.
- Margaux, toi et ton équipe?
- Nous, on est quatre et on va faire les courses pour le buffet et acheter la nourriture – les pizzas, les chips, etc. – et les boissons.
- Et vous allez préparer le buffet?
- Ah oui, nous, on va faire les sandwichs ... tout ça.
- Amélie?
- On va organiser la sono et télécharger de la musique. On est trois dans mon équipe.
- OK ... Et qui va s'occuper de la décoration de la salle? Hugo?
- Oui, Léo et moi, on va décorer la salle. On va utiliser le grand foyer du collège – il est immense! On va avoir beaucoup de place pour danser!
- Et après la fête, qui va nettoyer?
- On va tous nettoyer!

3 Lis l'invitation et réponds aux questions en anglais.
Students read the invitation and answer the questions in English.

Answers: **a** *Saturday 21 June;* **b** *starts 6 p.m., finishes 11 p.m.;* **c** *in the school hall;* **d** *3 euros;* **e** *decorate room, do the shopping, organise the music;* **f** *cakes, crisps, fruit, pizzas (and drinks)*

4 Écoute, lis et note les mots (1–8).
Students listen and follow the dialogue. They choose words from the box to fill the gaps in the text. Make sure students understand that there are more words in the box than there are gaps to fill – two items in the box won't be needed.

Answers: **1** *fête;* **2** *vacances;* **3** *soir;* **4** *danser;* **5** *collège;* **6** *acheter;* **7** *boissons;* **8** *chercher*

As a follow-up Silver medal activity, ask students to spot some 'filler' words.

Answers: bof, ben, euh, bon

t As a follow-up Gold medal activity, ask students to translate the conversation into English.

Answer:
- Hello Lisa, are you going to come to the party that Hugo's organising?
- Hi Olivier. Oh, I'm not sure yet. What about you?
- Yes, of course I am! It's going to be great! It's to celebrate the summer holidays.
- Well ... I'm not sure. When is it exactly?
- Saturday evening, from 6 p.m. We're going to dance and have fun! Go on, come!
- Er ... I don't know, maybe ... where is it going to be?
- It's going to be in the main hall of the school.
- Do I need to bring something?
- Hugo's going to bring the food, but if you want, you can bring some drinks.
- OK, will you come and get me from my house?
- Yes. As the party starts at 6 p.m., I'll come and get you at 5.55 p.m. ... OK?
- Great, thanks, see you later!

CD 2, track 9   page 95, activité 4

- Allô, Lisa, tu vas venir à la fête qui est organisée par Hugo?
- Salut, Olivier. Bof, je ne sais pas encore. Et toi?
- Oui, bien sûr! Ça va être génial! C'est pour célébrer les grandes vacances.
- Ben ... je ne suis pas sûre. C'est quand exactement?
- Samedi soir, à partir de dix-huit heures. On va danser et s'amuser! Allez, viens!
- Euh ... je ne sais pas, peut-être ... ça va être où?
- Ça va être au grand foyer du collège.
- Il faut apporter quelque chose?
- Hugo va acheter la nourriture mais si tu veux, tu peux apporter des boissons.
- Bon, d'accord, tu vas passer me chercher chez moi?
- Oui. Comme la fête commence à dix-huit heures, je vais passer te chercher à dix-sept heures quarante-cinq ... OK?
- Super, merci, à plus!

5 À deux. Adaptez le dialogue. Utilisez les questions de l'activité 4 et changez les expressions soulignées.

In pairs, students carry out the role play from activity 4, using the questions and adapting the underlined expressions in the dialogue. Before they begin this activity, refer students to the box on **Speaking strategies** and encourage them to follow these tips in their dialogues. Refer them also to the section on **Evaluating your own and others' performance** on page 105 and ask them to provide feedback to each other once they have completed their dialogue.

109

6 Rendez-vous

For a Silver medal, ask students to say that they cannot go and explain why: e.g. *Je ne peux pas parce que je vais en vacances avec mes parents.*

6 Écris un mail pour inviter tes copains à ta fête d'anniversaire.
Student write an email, inviting their friends to their birthday party. They can refer to the phrases used in activities 1, 3 and 4 for support, as well as to the key language box.

Plenary

In pairs, students reflect on why confident use of the near future is important.

- Students say three things they are going to do to prepare for a party.
- Students ask and say when and where the party will be.
- Students add an opinion and tell their partner what time they will pick him/her up.

6.2 On pourrait sortir?

pages 96–97

Planner
Objectives
- Vocabulary: suggest activities and make excuses
- Grammar: use the conditional: *on pourrait* + infinitive
- Skills: develop conversation skills; evaluate your performance

Resources
- Student Book, pages 96–97
- CD 2, tracks 10–12
- Grammar and Skills Workbook, pages 42 and 55
- Kerboodle, Unit 6
- Unit 6 Worksheets 4 (ex. 3), 5 (ex. 1), 6 (ex. 1)

Key language
On pourrait faire les magasins/faire un pique-nique/aller à un concert/aller à une fête/aller au bowling/aller au ciné/manger au McDo/regarder un DVD.
Bof, je n'aime pas trop ... Je ne sais pas ... Ah non, c'est nul./Je déteste ...
Je ne peux pas parce que c'est trop cher/je n'ai pas beaucoup d'argent/j'ai horreur de danser/j'ai horreur du fast-food/je suis fatigué(e)/j'y suis allé(e) hier.

Grammar
- Conditional: *on pourrait* + infinitive

PLTS
- Activity 3: Creative thinkers
- Activity 4: Team workers
- Activity 5: Self-managers
- Plenary: Reflective learners

Homework and self-study
- Student Book, page 96, activity 1
- Student Book, page 96, activity 2

Starters
See Kerboodle Starters bank for further details of **Pictionary**.
- Play **Pictionary** to familiarise students with the phrases in activity 1.
- Hold a class **Brainstorming** session to compile a list of as many filler words as possible. Write them on the board for students to refer to in their pairwork dialogues in activity 4.

Plenaries
- **Improving pronunciation and accuracy.** Refer students back to the sections on **Silent verb endings** on page 69 and the **French r sound** on page 87 before starting this plenary. A mark scheme should be agreed by the students (with the help of the teacher, if needed). Working in groups of four, students use the dialogue *Chantal la Râleuse* on page 96 as a dictation task in the lesson after the text has been covered in class. The text should be photocopied and put on the classroom wall in several places (and possibly cut up into sections for less confident learners). Students take it in turns to go to the text, memorise a section and dictate it to their group. Another group should check the transcriptions and give constructive feedback.

1 Écoute et lis (1–8). C'est quelle image? Recopie les phrases.
Students listen and match the texts to the correct pictures. The activities should all be familiar to students or easy to guess: only *On pourrait ...* is really new. Before playing the recording, do the **Pictionary** starter activity to ensure students have a good grasp of the various phrases. They will then be able to focus

more on *On pourrait ...*, rather than worrying about the meaning of the phrases.

Once students have completed the task, ask if they can work out what *On pourrait ...* might mean. Encourage them to think about the context of what is being asked and how they might say these phrases in English ('We could ...'). Explain that this is called the conditional and is a polite way of suggesting an activity. Refer students to the grammar box on **On pourrait + infinitive**.

Answers: **1** d; **2** g; **3** f; **4** a; **5** c; **6** b; **7** e; **8** h

As a follow-up Bronze medal activity, ask students to work in pairs and read out each phrase, adding a time: e.g. *On pourrait faire les magasins à quinze heures.*

As a follow-up Silver medal activity, ask students to add who they might do the activities with: e.g. *On pourrait faire les magasins à quinze heures avec Pierre.*

CD 2, track 10   page 96, activité 1

1. On pourrait faire les magasins?
2. On pourrait faire un pique-nique?
3. On pourrait aller à un concert?
4. On pourrait aller à une fête?
5. On pourrait aller au bowling?
6. On pourrait aller au ciné?
7. On pourrait manger au McDo?
8. On pourrait regarder un DVD?

2 Écoute et lis le dialogue. Mets les excuses (a–d) dans l'ordre.

Students listen and read the dialogue. They put Chantal's excuses into the order in which she uses them in the text. Before playing the recording, challenge students to try to work out what *la Râleuse* means (in the dialogue title) when they listen to and read the dialogue (answer: 'grumbler').

Answers: c, d, a, b

CD 2, track 11   page 96, activité 2

– Salut, Chantal, ça va?
– Bof!
– Écoute, ce week-end, on pourrait faire un pique-nique avec Sacha et Matthias?
– Ah non, je déteste Sacha et Matthias. Ils m'énervent!
– OK, alors on pourrait aller au ciné?
– Désolée, c'est trop cher, le ciné. Je n'ai pas assez d'argent!
– Alors on pourrait aller en ville et faire les magasins?
– Tu rigoles, j'espère! Le samedi, il y a trop de monde dans les magasins!
– Bon, alors ... euh ... viens chez moi! On pourrait jouer aux jeux vidéo? J'ai un nouveau jeu qui s'appelle « Dansez! ». C'est génial!
– Non mais tu plaisantes! Danser, j'ai horreur de ça!
– OK, ciao ... Moi, je vais retrouver Sacha et Matthias!

Students note down Marion's four suggestions.

Answers: **1** have a picnic with Sacha and Matthias; **2** go to the cinema; **3** go shopping in town; **4** play her new video game called 'Dance!'

t Students translate the conversation into English.

Answers:
– Hi, Chantal, how are you?
– Oh!
– Listen, this weekend we could have a picnic with Sacha and Matthias?
– Oh no, I hate Sacha and Matthias. They get on my nerves!
– OK, so we could go to the cinema?
– Sorry, it's too expensive. I don't have enough money!
– OK, we could go into town and go shopping?
– You're joking, I hope! There are too many people in the shops on Saturdays!
– OK, so ... er ... come to my house! We could play video games? I have a new game called 'Dance'! It's great!
– No, you're joking! I can't stand dancing!
– OK, bye ... I'm going to see Sacha and Matthias!

3 Écoute. Axel veut sortir mais Morgane invente des excuses! Recopie et remplis la grille en anglais.

Students copy the grid, listen and note down Axel's sugggestions and Morgan's excuses for each. Before they do so, run through the **Developing conversation skills** box and ask students to listen out for 'filler words' and for the intonation used with *On pourrait ...?* in the recording.

Answers:

Suggestions	Excuses
Go into town with friends	Tired
Go bowling with Salomé	Went bowling yesterday with sister, hates Salomé
Have a picnic and then play volleyball on the beach	Hates volleyball
Come to your place and watch a DVD	Doesn't have any good films

Students spot 'filler' words in the recording.

Answers: Bof; Écoute; Bof; Allez!; Ah non; OK, alors; euh; euh; Ah non; Bon, alors; Bof ... j'sais pas; Écoute; alors

Students spot one verb in the perfect tense.

Answer: j'y suis allée hier avec ma sœur

t In pairs, students transcribe what Axel and Morgane say and then perform the dialogue. The class could vote for the best performance.

111

6 Rendez-vous

CD 2, track 12 — page 97, activité 3

- Salut, Morgane, tu vas bien?
- Salut, Axel ... Bof, comme ci comme ça!
- Écoute, on pourrait sortir en ville avec des copains?
- Bof, j'sais pas ... j'suis fatiguée aujourd'hui.
- Allez! On pourrait aller au bowling avec Salomé?
- Ah non, j'y suis allée hier avec ma sœur. Et en plus, je déteste Salomé!
- OK, alors on pourrait ... euh ... faire un pique-nique et après ... euh ... jouer au volley sur la plage?
- Ah non, j'ai horreur du volley!
- Bon, alors on pourrait regarder un DVD chez toi?
- Bof ... j'sais pas, je n'ai pas de bons films ...
- Écoute, nous, on veut s'amuser ... alors ciao, et à plus!

4 À deux. Écrivez un dialogue: A veut sortir mais B invente des excuses! Utilisez les activités 2 et 3.
In pairs, students write a dialogue, based on those in activities 2 and 3. Remind them to use filler words, and to use rising intonation when using *On pourrait ...?* Refer them to the key language box for support when making up their excuses. They can also use the list of filler words generated during the class **Brainstorming** starter activity.

Exemple: On pourrait ... avec ... On pourrait se retrouver à ... Je vais téléphoner à ...

○ Students include reasons for their excuses.

5 À deux. Faites le dialogue de l'activité 4.
In pairs, students read aloud the dialogue they wrote in activity 4. When they have done so, ask them to give feedback to each other, and refer them to **Evaluating your own and others' performance** on page 105.

⊕ Students memorise their dialogue and perform it.

Plenary

In pairs, students take turns to suggest activities and then give each other feedback on their intonation and pronunciation.

★ Students suggest three activities.

○ Students refuse two of their partner's suggestions and give reasons.

⊕ Students challenge themselves to keep the dialogue going as long as they can (until they run out of suggestions and excuses).

6.3 Les festivals, j'adore! pages 98–99

Planner

Objectives
- Vocabulary: talk about a festival or special event that you've been to
- Grammar: use the perfect tense with *être*; use the imperfect tense
- Skills: use cultural awareness strategies; evaluate your performance

Resources
- Student Book, pages 98–99
- CD 2, track 13
- Grammar and Skills Workbook, pages 14, 35–39, 54 and 55
- Kerboodle, Unit 6
- Unit 6 Worksheet 5 (ex. 2–3)

Key language
Je suis allé(e) à la fête nationale/au festival de ...
On est allé(e)s à la Fête du Cinéma/de la Musique.
J'y suis allé(e) avec mes copains/copines/parents ...
C'était en juillet/l'année dernière/le week-end dernier.
C'était génial/super/incroyable/gratuit.
Il y avait un concert/un feu d'artifice/beaucoup de monde.
Je suis resté(e)/On est resté(e)s trois jours/tout le week-end/juste le samedi.
J'ai/On a dansé/chanté/mangé/vu/écouté ...
Je vais y retourner l'année prochaine/l'été prochain.

Grammar
- Perfect tense with *être*
- Imperfect tense

PLTS
- Activity 1: Independent enquirers
- Activity 4: Team workers
- Activity 5: Creative thinkers, Reflective learners

Homework and self-study
- Student Book, page 99, activity 3
- Student Book, page 99, activity 5
- Grammar and Skills Workbook, pages 14, 35–39 and 54

Starters

See Kerboodle Starters bank for further details of **Up, down** and **Categorise**.

- Revise the perfect tense with *avoir* by playing **Up, down**. Read out the two blogs from activity 1 and ask students to stand up whenever they hear an example of the perfect tense with *avoir*. You could then go on to repeat this activity, this time asking students to stand up whenever they hear an example of the perfect tense wth *être*.

- Play **Categorise** to consolidate the difference between the perfect and imperfect tenses. Use the two tenses as the categories and ask students to write down as many *je*, *tu* or *il/elle/on* forms as they can think of.

Plenaries

- **Using persuasive language.** Students work in groups to compose a letter to the Prime Minister or their local MP, asking Parliament to consider the creation of an extra Bank Holiday for a national day to be celebrated in Britain. They should refer to the **Cultural awareness strategies** on page 99 and research information from other countries prior to starting the letter. Each group should appoint a spokesperson, who reads out the letter to the rest of the class; the class votes for the most convincing argument. If possible, ask a member of the wider community to visit the class to act as Prime Minister/local MP. If time permits, the class should reflect on tone of voice and intonation used by the readers and how effective this was in presenting their case. Note: this plenary could be combined with spread 6.4 or used after this point for less confident learners.

1 Lis les textes. Réponds aux questions en anglais pour Gwenaël et Mathilde.

Students read the texts about two people's experiences at music festivals and answer the questions for each person in English. Once they have done this, ask them to look back at the texts and identify what tenses are used in the texts (perfect and imperfect). Do the **Up, down** starter activity to revise the perfect tense with *avoir*. Then run through the grammar box on **The perfect tense with être** and remind students that they have already come across this with the verb *aller* in *Allez 1*, Units 7 and 8. Repeat the starter activity, this time practising the perfect tense with *avoir*.

Answers: **Gwenaël: a** to a music festival in Brittany; **b** with his big brother and four friends; **c** arrived on Friday and stayed for three days; **d** any two of: camping, danced in the mud, fireworks display; **e** they will go again next summer and you can come with us; **Mathilde: a** hip-hop dance festival in Paris; **b** with her two (girl) friends, Lola and Olivia; **c** arrived on Saturday morning and stayed for two days; **d** danced, saw incredible groups; **e** they will go again next year

Students make a list of the connectives and perfect tense verbs they spot in each text.

Answers:

Connectives: Gwenaël: *mais, et, et, parce que, parce qu', et;* **Mathilde:** *et, et, et, et*

Perfect tense verbs: Gwenaël: *Je suis allé, ma mère a payé, Je suis parti, On est arrivés, on a campé, On y est restés, on a dansé, il a plu, il y a eu, j'ai passé;* **Mathilde:** *Je suis rentrée, J'y suis allée, On est arrivées, on y est restées, On a dansé, on a vu, Ma sœur est venue, on est rentrées*

Students spot opinions and imperfect tense verbs in the blogs, and identify verbs that take *avoir* and *être* in the perfect tense.

Answers:

Opinions: Gwenaël: *c'était incroyable!, C'était très marrant, J'ai passé un week-end de rêve!;* **Mathilde:** *C'était vraiment top!, des groupes qui étaient absolument incroyables*

Imperfect tense verbs: Gwenaël: *C'était, Il y avait, c'était;* **Mathilde:** *C'était, étaient*

Perfect tense + avoir: Gwenaël: *ma mère a payé, on a campé, on a dansé, il a plu, il y a eu, j'ai passé;* **Mathilde:** *On a dansé, on a vu.*

Perfect tense + être: Gwenaël: *Je suis allé, Je suis parti, On est arrivés, On y est restés;* **Mathilde:** *Je suis rentrée, J'y suis allée, On est arrivées, Ma sœur est venue, on est rentrées*

t Students translate the texts into English.

Answers:

Gwenaël: *I went to a music festival in Brittany which is called 'The Old Ploughs'. It was a bit expensive, 106 euros, but my mum paid. I went with my big brother and four friends. We arrived on the Friday and we camped because camping is free when you have a ticket. We stayed for three days. There were more than 200,000 people there – it was amazing! It was really funny because we danced in the mud ... it rained the whole weekend! One evening there was a big firework display. I had an amazing weekend! We're going to go back there next year and you can come with us.*

Mathilde: *I got home yesterday evening from the hip-hop dance festival of Paris. It was really great! I went there with two friends, Lola and Olivia. We arrived on the Saturday morning and we stayed two days. We danced and we saw groups who were absolutely incredible. My sister came to meet us on the Sunday and we came home together in the evening. We're going to go back there next year, that's for sure!*

6 Rendez-vous

2 Écoute Julie, Tom et Hussein qui parlent de trois fêtes. Note les détails en anglais.

Students listen and note down for each person which festival they went to, when, for how long, which activities they did and any extra details. *La Fête de la Musique*, mentioned by Julie, is referring to the international event known as World Music Day, held in cities around the world on 21 June each year. What do students know about this?

Answers:

Julie: music festival/Music Day; 21 June; stayed for one day (just Saturday); went to free rock concert in town centre, danced till midnight; **other details:** it was fantastic, she went with her (girl) friends, will go again next year with her (girl) friends

Tom: Belgian national day; 21 July; stayed from 10 a.m. on Sunday morning till midnight on Sunday; ate chips (it's traditional), went to free concert in the park, watched big firework display in the evening; **other details:** it was great, fireworks were absolutely incredible, went with parents and cousins this year, will go again next year with friends because it will be more fun

Hussein: film festival (in Paris); last weekend in June; stayed all weekend, Saturday and Sunday; saw two films on Saturday and three films on Sunday; **other details:** tickets for the films weren't expensive, 3.50 euros per ticket, it was great, will go again next year because loves the cinema

⭕ Students note down the final question that the interviewer asks each person.

Answer: Will you go back (next year)?

➕ t Students transcribe what Julie, Tom or Hussein say. Students could work in pairs to do this: partner A transcribes the interviewer's lines, partner B transcribes the interviewee's lines, then they put the whole thing together and perform the interview. The class could vote for the best performance.

CD 2, track 13   page 99, activité 2

- Bonjour, les jeunes! Je voudrais vous poser quelques questions ... Julie, où es-tu allée cet été?
- Je suis allée à la Fête de la Musique avec toutes mes copines.
- C'était quand?
- C'était le 21 juin.
- Tu y es restée combien de temps?
- On y est restées juste le samedi.
- Qu'est-ce que vous avez fait?
- Comme il y avait un concert de rock gratuit au centre ville, on a décidé d'y aller. On a dansé jusqu'à minuit!
- C'était comment?
- C'était trop top!
- Tu vas y retourner l'année prochaine?
- Oui, bien sûr, on va y retourner avec mes copines!
- Merci!
- Et toi, Tom, tu es allé où?
- Chez moi, en Belgique, on a la Fête nationale belge. J'y suis allé avec mes parents et mes cousins.
- C'était quand?
- C'était le 21 juillet. C'était super.
- Tu y es resté toute la journée?
- On est arrivés le dimanche matin à dix heures et on est rentrés le soir, à minuit.
- Qu'est-ce que tu as fait?
- Bien sûr, on a mangé les traditionnelles frites! Il y avait aussi un concert gratuit dans le parc. Et le soir, on a vu un grand feu d'artifice. C'était absolument incroyable!
- Tu vas y retourner?
- Oui, je vais y retourner l'année prochaine, mais avec mes copains. Je pense que ce sera plus marrant!
- Et toi, Hussein, où es-tu allé?
- Je suis allé à Paris avec mes copains pour la Fête du Cinéma.
- C'était quand?
- Le dernier week-end de juin.
- Tu es resté à Paris tout le week-end?
- Bien sûr, on y est restés les deux jours, le samedi et le dimanche.
- Qu'est-ce que tu as fait?
- J'ai vu deux films le samedi, et trois films le dimanche parce que les places n'étaient pas chères. On a payé trois euros cinquante la place! C'était super!
- Tu vas y retourner l'année prochaine?
- Oui, je vais y retourner parce que j'adore le cinéma!
- Merci à tous!

Cultural awareness strategies

This section encourages students to consider some of the cultural events mentioned in the unit and to compare them with their own culture. Students could work in pairs or small groups to discuss the questions raised in the box.

Students will be familiar with most of the types of events mentioned so far in the unit: for example, music/dance/film festivals. Talk now about those that students might not be familiar with: for example, the Belgian national day (mentioned by Tom in the recording). What do students think of having a national day for the UK? Can they think of any problems? For example, the UK comprises Scotland, Northern Ireland, Wales, and England, so it might be difficult and even controversial for the separate countries to agree on a date and how to celebrate it. Also, each country already has a special day (St George's Day, St Andrew's Day, St Patrick's Day, and St David's Day), but these are not bank holidays and there are not usually any major events held on these days.

If there are different religious/cultural groups in the class, encourage them to talk about special celebrations/festivals that are important to them.

Students might not be aware of the popularity and high profile of cinema in France. Talk about France as the 'birthplace of cinema' and see if anyone in the class can remember anything about the Lumière brothers (see Unit 1).

Note that the box encourages students to look at the festivals on spread 6.5 too, as those who are following a two-year KS3 might otherwise miss that spread. Spread 6.5 focuses entirely on festivals/celebrations. Even if you are following a two-year KS3 with your class and would normally omit spread 5, you might still like to use some of the material selectively so that students don't miss out on the cultural aspects.

3 Lis les questions et trouve les réponses.
Students match the questions to the correct answers. Before they embark on this task, run through the grammar box on **Perfect or imperfect?** Check students' understanding of the use of each tense and remind them to look closely at the verb forms when matching up the questions and answers. Draw students' attention to the glossed items of vocabulary (phrases including *y*).

Answers: **1** c; **2** f; **3** e; **4** g; **5** a; **6** b; **7** d

t As a follow-up activity, ask students to translate the questions (Silver medal) or the questions and answers (Gold medal) into English.

Answers:
1 *Where did you go?* **c** *I went to the Music Festival in town.*
2 *Who with?* **f** *I went with my sister.*
3 *When was it?* **e** *It was last weekend.*
4 *How long did you stay there?* **g** *We stayed there the whole weekend because on the Sunday evening there was a big firework display!*
5 *What did you do?* **a** *We danced, sang and ate sandwiches.*
6 *How was it?* **b** *It was absolutely fantastic.*
7 *Will you go back there?* **d** *Yes, I'll go back there next year with my friends.*

4 Imagine que tu es allé(e) à un festival. Réponds aux questions de l'activité 3.
Students work in pairs and take turns to ask and answer the questions from activity 3. They use the phrases highlighted in the answers from activity 3 and adapt the rest of the sentence each time.
To develop their language further (Bronze medal), students could add extra details and opinions: *Hier, je suis allé(e) à … avec … C'était …!*

○ Students add what they liked best.

For a Gold medal, ask students to use the perfect tense, the imperfect and the near future in their answers: *Hier, je suis allé(e) à … avec … C'était …! L'été prochain, je vais …*

5 Imagine que tu es allé(e) à un festival. Écris un blog.
Students write a blog about their experiences at a festival. They use the language covered in the spread and refer to the blogs in activity 1 as a model. They then swap with a partner and evaluate each other's work. Refer students to the section on **Evaluating your own and others' performance** on page 105 and ask them to provide feedback to each other.

> **Plenary**
> Students consider what it means to be 'culturally aware'. They write down two things.
> ☆ Students name three festivals.
> ○ Students choose one festival and say they went to it, when it was and who they went with.
> ✚ Students describe what they did there and add their opinion.

6.4 Rencontre
pages 100–101

> **Planner**
>
> **Objectives**
> - Vocabulary: communicate with people in formal situations
> - Grammar: use the *vous* form of the verb
> - Skills: use formal and informal language; evaluate your performance
>
> **Resources**
> - Student Book, pages 100–101
> - CD 2, track 14
> - Grammar and Skills Workbook, pages 4 and 55
> - Kerboodle, Unit 6
> - Unit 6 Worksheet 4 (ex. 2)

115

6 Rendez-vous

Key language

Je suis ... depuis ... ans/mois.

C'est passionnant/excitant/intéressant mais c'est aussi fatigant/frustrant/prenant.

Je commence à ... heures.

Je fais/lis/visite/travaille ...

L'année prochaine, nous allons organiser/faire ...

Grammar

- *Vous* form (present tense)

PLTS

- Activity 2: Independent enquirers
- Activity 5: Team workers
- Activity 6: Self-managers, Reflective learners

Homework and self-study

- Student Book, page 100, activity 1
- Student Book, page 101, activity 4
- Grammar and Skills Workbook, page 4

Starters

- Practise the *tu* form in preparation for the grammar box on **Tu and vous**. Call out a verb in the *je* form and elicit the *tu* form from students. Continue around the class until students are happy with the *tu* form.
- Consolidate students' knowledge of formal and informal language: put on the board a list of phrases using *tu* and *vous*, as follows:

  Pourriez-vous me parler de ...?

  Bonjour, Monsieur/Chère Marie

  Merci

  À plus! Bisous!

  Recevez mes sincères salutations

  Quand travaillez-vous?

  Que faîtes-vous?

  Tu travailles quand?

  Je vous remercie

  Tu peux me parler de ...?

  Salut, Marie

  Tu fais quoi?

Ask students to work in pairs to put the phrases into formal and informal language categories, and also to match up the pairs. More able students could also be asked to translate the sentences into English.

Plenaries

- **Formal and informal language**. Relate students' current learning to the learning to come by using the *Lire* page on page 108 about volunteers working on the Schiltigheim Youth Council. Refer students particularly to activity 3 on page 108, which focuses on people being voted onto a youth council.

  This plenary is difficult to conduct in French but, as most British schools incorporate a student voice into their development plans, students may be able to express simple opinions on how useful they find the student council at their own school.

- Students review their understanding of the *tu* and *vous* forms of verbs and write a list in French of people they know whom they would address using the *vous* form. Ask them to reflect on their understanding of use of register and the type of language that they consider appropriate or inappropriate in certain situations.

1 Lis la lettre et trouve les expressions a–h.

Students read the formal letter and find in the text the French equivalents for the English phrases. Remind students to use their reading strategies (particularly looking at the language either side of words that they recognise) when trying to identify the French phrases.

Answers: **a** Merci pour votre lettre; **b** Je serais ravi; **c** pour répondre à vos questions; **d** dans la salle de réception de la Mairie; **e** deux représentants; **f** notre réunion; **g** Pourriez-vous m'envoyer; **h** Recevez mes sincères salutations

Students note down what the Mayor asks for.

Answers: a list of questions by email

2 Lis le mail de Julie et réponds aux questions.

Students read Julie's email and answer the questions in English.

Answers: **a** the mayor; **b** 27 March at 2 p.m.; **c** a list of questions (by email); **d** two people from the Children's Council; **e** tomorrow

Students analyse the email to decide what marks it out as being informal. This would be good done in pairs, enabling students to share their ideas.

Answers: Salut; exclamation marks; use of the tu form; C'est génial, n'est-ce pas?; Tu peux ...?; Bisous et à plus!

t Students translate the email into English.

Answer:
Hi Mohammed!
Are you OK? I've received a reply from the mayor! We've got a meeting on 27 March at 2 p.m. I'm going to send (him) our questions by email. Two people from the Children's Council are going to be at the meeting too.
It's great, isn't it? Can you call me tomorrow?
Love, and see you later!
Julie

Formal and informal language

Students look back at both the formal letter in activity 1 and the informal email in activity 2, noting the difference in language style of both. Ask them to look at the examples in the skills box and to find similar examples in the letter and the email. In addition, encourage them to look closely at the salutation (*Chère Julie/Salut*), the use of *notre* in the mayor's letter (i.e. the *nous* form) contrasted with *on* and the informal expressions in Julie's email: for example, the smiley emoticon, *c'est génial, non?*

3 Traduis la lettre de l'activité 1 en anglais.

Before students begin this activity, do the starter activity to consolidate their knowledge of formal and informal language (see **Starters**). Students then translate the letter from activity 1 into English. Remind them to refer to the skills box on **Formal and informal language**, and to use the English phrases in activity 1 for support.

Answer:
Montpellier, 2 March
Dear Julie,
Thank you for your letter dated 20 February. I would be delighted to receive/meet you on Tuesday 27 March at 2 p.m. in the reception room at the Town Hall to answer your questions. Two representatives of the Children's Council will be present at our meeting. Could you send me a list of your questions by email?
Yours faithfully ...

4 Écoute et lis l'interview de Monsieur le Maire. Trouve les paires.

Students listen to and read the interview with the Mayor. Alternatively, students read and match up the texts, and then listen to check their answers.

Answers: **1** e; **2** c; **3** f; **4** d; **5** b; **6** a

As a follow-up Silver medal activity, ask students whether the interview is formal or informal. How can they tell?
Answers: formal – e.g. use of vous, polite pourriez-vous ..., je vous remercie instead of merci

As a follow-up Gold medal activity, students translate the interview into English.

Answer:
- *Good afternoon, Mr Mayor. Since when have you been mayor?*
- *I've been mayor for two years.*
- *Do you like your work/job?*
- *Yes, it's exciting, but it's also very time-consuming.*
- *Could you describe a typical day?*
- *Usually, I start at 8 a.m. I have meetings and visits, I work on projects ... but what I like best in my job are the weddings that I sometimes have to celebrate.*
- *Why have you created a Children's Council?*
- *Because I think it's very important to listen to young people.*
- *Which project are you going to work on this year?*
- *Next year we are going to organise a big drama festival. That is going to be our big project of the year!*
- *Thank you, Mr Mayor.*
- *Thank you.*

CD 2, track 14   page 101, activité 4
- Bonjour, Monsieur le Maire. Depuis quand êtes-vous maire?
- Je suis maire depuis deux ans.
- Vous aimez votre travail?
- Oui, c'est passionnant mais c'est aussi très prenant.
- Pourriez-vous décrire une journée typique?
- D'habitude, je commence à huit heures. J'ai des réunions et des visites, je travaille sur des projets ... mais ce que je préfère dans mon travail, ce sont les mariages que je dois célébrer parfois!
- Pourquoi avez-vous créé un Conseil des Enfants?
- Parce que je pense que c'est très important d'écouter les jeunes.
- Sur quel projet allez-vous travailler cette année?
- L'année prochaine, nous allons organiser un grand festival de théâtre. Ça va être notre grand projet de l'année!
- Je vous remercie, Monsieur le Maire.
- Merci à vous.

5 À deux. Inventez et écrivez l'interview d'une personne célèbre. Utilisez l'interview de l'activité 4. Adaptez les expressions soulignées.

Before students embark on this activity, do the starter activity revising the *tu* form and then run through the *tu* form and *vous* form verbs in the grammar box on **Tu and vous**. Ask students to look back at the sentences in activity 4 and to spot all the examples of *vous*-form verbs.

In pairs, students then make up and write down and interview with a famous person. They adapt the underlined phrases from the interview in activity 4. Remind students to use the *vous* form and other aspects of formal language in their interviews.

117

6 Rendez-vous

- ⭐ Students use connectives in their interview.
- ◯ Students add what they did last week.

6 À deux. Faites l'interview de l'activité 5.
In pairs, students read out their dialogues from activity 5. When they have done so, refer students to **Evaluating your own and others' performance** on page 105 and encourage them to provide feedback to each other.

➕ Students learn their interview by heart and perform it. This could be a class activity, with students voting for the best performance (containing the most formal language, most instances of the *vous* form, etc.).

Plenary

In pairs, students discuss when to use formal and informal language and reflect on why they need to know both forms of language.

- ⭐ Students say a sentence or a question and their partner decides if it is formal or informal.
- ◯ Students consider how they would start and end a formal letter.
- ➕ Students choose five French expressions that could be used in a formal situation and their partner translates them.

6.5 Calendrier des fêtes

pages 102–103

Planner

Objectives
- Vocabulary: talk about traditions and festivals
- Grammar: use past and present tenses
- Skills: develop cultural awareness strategies

Resources
- Student Book, pages 102–103
- CD 2, tracks 15–16
- Grammar and Skills Workbook, pages 43 and 54
- Kerboodle, Unit 6
- Unit 6 Worksheets 3, 4 (ex. 1), 6 (ex. 2–3)

Key language

C'est nécessaire de se souvenir de la Guerre/de la Révolution.

C'est important de penser à son amoureux(-euse)/ s'amuser.

Il y a des défilés/feux d'artifice/concerts.

Il n'y a pas d'école. C'est un jour férié.
On fait/mange/boit/danse/écoute/va/vient …
C'était … Il y avait … Il faisait …
On a fait/mangé/bu/dansé/écouté …
On est allé(e)s/venu(e)s …

Grammar
- Past and present tenses

PLTS and Numeracy
- Activity 2: Independent enquirers
- Activity 4: Creative thinkers
- Activity 5: Effective participators
- Numeracy: Activity 1: recognising dates, presenting survey results in a chart

Homework and self-study
- Student Book, page 102, activity 2
- Student Book, page 103, activity 4
- Grammar and Skills Workbook, pages 43 and 54

Starters

See Kerboodle Starters bank for further details of **Loto**.

- Hold a **Class discussion** to share knowledge of the festival days presented in activity 1. Can students identify the English equivalents? Explain to students that there are many public holidays (*jours fériés*) in France to mark important events in the nation's history. Can they think of any similar days in Britain that are significant, but that are not public holidays (e.g. St George's Day, St Andrew's Day, St David's Day, St Patrick's Day, etc.)?
- Play **Loto** to practise the numbers for dates.

Plenaries

- **Analysing progress with the language**. Give students some questions for reflection: Are they better at adapting and recycling language in different tenses than they were a few months ago? How is their understanding of types of verb growing? Are they better at spotting patterns? Are they continuing to gather useful phrases from listening and reading activities to use in improving their speaking and writing? Are they using technology to help them? If so, how, and what ideas can they share with their peers?

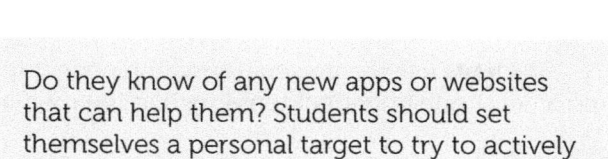

Do they know of any new apps or websites that can help them? Students should set themselves a personal target to try to actively use previously-learnt language in a new context and review this a month later.

1 Écoute, lis et trouve les paires.

Before students attempt this activity, ask them to work in pairs and to try to work out what each of the festival days might be in English. Remind them to use their knowledge of cognates and to use other language that they might already know, as well as the pictures, to help them. Students won't know *muguet* in caption d, but encourage them to work it out from the picture (although they may not know the name of the plant lily-of-the-valley in English either).

Do the **Class discussion** starter activity to share knowledge of the various festival days. It would also be a good idea to do the **Loto** starter activity at this point, to revise numbers for the dates. Draw students' attention particularly to the exception to the rule: *le premier mai*.

Students then listen to the recording and match the festivals to the correct dates. Refer them then to the **Cultural awareness strategies** and ask them to discuss in pairs whether the festivals in activity 1 are celebrated in the UK and what they know about them. They could research any that they do not know about.

Note that *la Fête du travail* and *la Fête du muguet* are both on 1 May, but the festivals have different origins. *La Fête du travail* has its origins in the nineteenth century, when workers campaigned for more reasonable working hours: it is also known as Labour Day in some parts of the world. *La Fête du muguet* is a much older festival, celebrating the arrival of spring.

Answers: **1** d; **2** c; **3** a; **4** e; **5** b

As a Bronze medal activity, students could listen out for the name of Isabelle's boyfriend.

Answer: Martin

CD 2, track 15   page 102, activité 1

– Salut, Maude, tu es encore en vacances?
– Salut, Isabelle. Oui, c'est le premier mai, la Fête du travail. C'est un jour férié et il n'y a pas école, c'est super! On offre du muguet, c'est un porte-bonheur!
Tu sais, il y a beaucoup de fêtes en France …
Par exemple, le huit mai, on fête la victoire de la Seconde Guerre mondiale, en 1945.
Il y a aussi le 11 novembre, c'est l'Armistice de la guerre de 1914 à 1918. C'est très important de se souvenir.
Et il y a la Fête nationale aussi …
– C'est quand?
– C'est le 14 juillet. On célèbre la prise de la Bastille de 1789. Il y a des défilés et des feux d'artifice.
– Le 14 février aussi, c'est important!
– Pourquoi?
– Parce que c'est la Saint-Valentin, la fête des amoureux. C'est important de penser à son amoureux!
– Ah, oui, toi et Martin, ton petit copain!

As a follow-up speaking activity, students could work in groups and carry out a survey into the class's favourite festival (of those presented in activity 1). They ask *Quelle est ta fête préférée?* They could present the results in a pie chart.

2 Lis. C'est Thomas ou Salomé?

Students read the two texts about favourite festivals and answer the questions in English. As a follow-up task, can students identify what the English equivalent of Thomas's favourite festival is (April Fools' Day)?

Answers: **a** Thomas; **b** Thomas; **c** Salomé; **d** Salomé; **e** Thomas; **f** Salomé

Students find in the texts connectives and time expressions.

Answers: **Connectives:** *parce qu'* (two instances), *et* (several instances), *donc*; **Time expressions:** *l'année dernière* (two instances), *toute la journée, le soir, jusqu'à une heure du matin*

Students find in the text verbs in the imperfect tense.

Answers: c'était fantastique; il faisait super beau

Students find in the text verbs in the present and perfect tenses.

Answers: **Present:** *c'est, on fait, on colle, c'est, c'est, c'est, il y a;* **Perfect:** *j'ai mis, elle n'a rien vu, elle a gardé, mon pére et moi avons beaucoup ri, Antoine a joué, je suis allée, on a vu, on a dansé, j'ai adoré, j'ai vu, on a dansé*

3 Écoute et lis l'interview de Sophiane. Note les mots 1–8.

Students listen and read the interview with Sophiane. They note down the missing words from the interview, choosing from those in the box. Alternatively, students could do this first as a reading task, and then listen to check their answers.

Once students have completed this activity, run through the grammar box on **Present and past tenses**. Check students' understanding and ask them to look back through the interview and identify all the examples of verbs in the present, imperfect and perfect tenses.

6 Rendez-vous

Answers: **1** mois; **2** boire; **3** onze ans; **4** semaine; **5** difficile; **6** mère; **7** trois; **8** cadeaux

t Students translate the underlined phrases into English.

Answers: You're a Muslim; we must not eat or drink; I observed Ramadan; it was too difficult (to fast) every day; we can eat and drink as we want; we celebrate for three days

> **CD 2, track 16   page 103, activité 3**
>
> – Bonjour, Sophiane. Tu es musulman. Tu fais le Ramadan?
> – Oui. Pendant un mois, on « jeûne », c'est-à-dire on ne doit pas manger ou boire de l'aube au coucher du soleil. Moi, j'ai fait le Ramadan pour la première fois l'année dernière, quand j'avais onze ans, mais juste un jour par semaine parce que c'était trop difficile tous les jours. Après le coucher du soleil, on peut manger et boire comme on veut. Ma mère a préparé beaucoup de plats cette année. Quand c'est la fin du Ramadan, l'Aïd el-Fitr, on fait la fête pendant trois jours et on a des cadeaux.
> – Merci, Sophiane!
> – De rien! À bientôt!

4 Écris un article sur ta fête préférée.
Students write an article about their favourite festival. Encourage them to come up with their own ideas, but to use language from the texts in activities 2 and 3 for support. They should include opinions with reasons where possible.

Students use the present tense, the perfect tense and at least one imperfect tense verb in their writing.

5 Fais une présentation de ta fête préférée. Utilise ton article de l'activité 4.
In groups, students prepare a presentation about their favourite festival. They use their articles from activity 4 as the basis of the presentation. Alternatively, give each group a different festival to present and encourage students within each group to share their ideas and pool language and phrases. Students make their presentations to the class, and the class votes for its favourite festival, based on the information and arguments presented.

Plenary

In pairs, students discuss the main tenses: how are they formed and what are the key points about each one?

- Students say what their favourite festival or special day is and when it takes place.
- They add what they did last year on this occasion, who they were with and give their opinion.
- Students write a tourist leaflet advertising a local festival. Encourage them to be creative and give examples of what usually happens and what happened last year.

6.6 Labo-langue

pages 104–105

Planner

Objectives

- Grammar: talking about the past: the perfect tense with *être*; the conditional: *on pourrait* + infinitive; the near future: *aller* + infinitive
- Skills: evaluating your own and others' performance
- Pronunciation: the perfect tense and the imperfect

Resources

- Student Book, pages 104–105
- CD 2, tracks 17–18
- Grammar and Skills Workbook, page 55
- Kerboodle, Unit 6
- Unit 6 Worksheets 7, 8

PLTS

- Creative thinkers, Reflective learners, Self-managers

Talking about the past: the perfect tense with être

Refer students to the 'Mrs Van Der Tramp' mnemonic in the grammar box. Students could make up/perform a rap using 'Mrs Van Der Tramp' and the list of verbs.

1 Copy out Samuel's text. Put each infinitive into the perfect tense.

Answers:

La semaine dernière, je <u>suis allé</u> à un festival de hip-hop. Mon copain Luc <u>est venu</u> au festival avec moi. On <u>est partis</u> le vendredi matin et on <u>est arrivés</u> au camping le vendredi soir.
Nos copines de classe Alice et Clara <u>sont arrivées</u> le samedi. Mais Alice <u>est tombée</u> et elle <u>est allée</u> à l'hôpital! Clara <u>est partie</u> avec elle.
Luc et moi, nous <u>sommes restés</u> tout le week-end au festival. Luc <u>est rentré</u> le dimanche soir. Moi, je <u>suis rentré</u> le lundi matin.

The conditional: *on pourrait* + infinitive

2 Replace the pictures with words and write sentences in French.

Students can use a question mark or a full stop at the end of their sentences.

Answers: **a** On pourrait aller au cinéma. **b** Mon frère pourrait faire les magasins. **c** Je pourrais aller au bowling. **d** On pourrait/Nous pourrions faire un pique-nique. **e** Tu pourrais/Vous pourriez aller à une fête. **f** Ils/Elles pourraient manger au McDo.

The near future: *aller* + infinitive

3 Unscramble the sentences and rewrite them using correct word order.

Answers: **a** On va aller à la Fête de la Musique ce week-end. **b** Sacha va acheter des pizzas pour la fête. **c** Qui va préparer les sandwichs? **d** Je vais passer te chercher. **e** On va télécharger de la musique. **f** Tu ne vas pas décorer la salle?

t As a follow-up task, ask students to translate the sentences into English.

Answers: **a** We are going to go to the Music Festival/Music Day this weekend. **b** Sacha is going to buy pizzas for the party. **c** Who is going to prepare the sandwiches? **d** I will come and pick you up. **e** We are going to download some music. **f** Aren't you going to decorate the room?

Evaluating your own and others' performance

This section encourages students to evaluate their own performance and that of others. Ask students to work in pairs and to try out some of the pairwork suggestions to aid their learning.

Students are encouraged to try out the evaluation strategies with the writing activity on page 99, and with the speaking activities on pages 95, 97 and 101.

Pronunciation: the perfect tense and the imperfect

4 Try to pronounce these verbs, then listen and repeat.

CD 2, track 17 — page 105, activité 4

1. je dansais
2. j'ai dansé
3. j'étais
4. j'ai été
5. il arrivait
6. il est arrivé

5 Listen (1–8). Is it the perfect tense or the imperfect?

Answers: **1** imperfect; **2** perfect; **3** imperfect; **4** imperfect; **5** perfect; **6** perfect; **7** perfect; **8** imperfect

CD 2, track 18 — page 105, activité 5

1. je regardais
2. j'ai écouté
3. je mangeais
4. il allait
5. j'ai mangé
6. il est allé
7. j'ai regardé
8. elles dansaient

6 Rendez-vous

6.7 Extra Star
page 106

1 Suggest an activity for each picture. Begin each suggestion with *On pourrait* + infinitive.

Students can use a question mark or a full stop at the end of their sentences.

Answers: **a** On pourrait aller au bowling? **b** On pourrait aller au cinéma? **c** On pourrait aller au concert? **d** On pourrait regarder la télé. **e** On pourrait faire les magasins/aller en ville? **f** On pourrait faire un pique-nique?

2 The lines of this conversation are mixed up! Write them out in the correct order.

Answers: 3, 8, 6, 9, 2, 5, 1, 7, 4 (NB: 5 and 1 could precede 9 and 2)

3 Read Charly's text and answer the questions in English.

Answers: **a** Quebec/Canada; **b** 24 June; **c** last year; **d** his brother; **e** saw rock groups, there was a big parade in the streets; **f** there was a huge firework display; **g** next year

6.7 Extra Plus
page 107

1 Lis le poster et trouve les paires (1–6 et a–f). Recopie les six phrases.

Students read the poster advertising a music festival and match the sentence halves.

Answers: **1** d; **2** e; **3** c; **4** a; **5** b; **6** f

t 2 Traduis les phrases de l'activité 1 en anglais.

Students translate the sentences from activity 1 into English.

Answers: **1** The first festival was in 1989. **2** More than 60 artists will sing over three days. **3** It is 45€ for one day. **4** With your ticket, camping is free. **5** You can book on the Internet. **6** The weekend pass is 81€.

3 Lis le texte de Justine et réponds aux questions en anglais.

Students read the text and answer the questions in English.

Answers: **a** the Armistice/end of the First World War; **b** to remember wars and the history of your country in general; **c** it is a bank/public holiday; **d** a procession and a minute's silence at the war memorial; **e** she took part in the procession and read a poem in front of the mayor; **f** stressed but excited; **g** she will go to Belgium to visit the main monuments of the Great War and learn more about the war.

4 Imagine que tu vas organiser une fête.

Students write a description of the party they are going to organise. Remind them to cover all the bullet points, and to use a range of tenses: the bullet points allow for the present, perfect, imperfect and near future. More able students could also try to bring in the conditional where appropriate.

6.8 Lire
page 108

Resources	PLTS
• Student Book, page 108 • Kerboodle, Unit 6	• Independent enquirers

@ 1 Read the web page about Schiltigheim youth council. Find these words in French in the text.

Provide students with some cultural background to the text: *La Course des Brasseurs* (the Brewers' Race) is mentioned. This is an annual running race, so called because Schiltigheim was once known as *la Cité des Brasseurs* (City of the Brewers) because of the breweries that were established there.

As a follow-up task, discuss with the class what youth councils do. The one in Schiltigheim, in the Alsace region, is particularly active. Can they find out about any in their local area?

Answers: **a** élus; **b** un tournoi; **c** (la) croissance; **d** (le) soutien; **e** guerres (la guerre); **f** pistes cyclables (la piste cyclable)

2 Which eight of the following activities are young councillors involved with? Find phrases in the text to justify your answers.

Answers: **a** *bénévolat à la Course des Brasseurs;* **c** *animations à destination des aînés;* **d** *organisation d'une scène ouverte pour la fête de la musique; partenariat avec l'Opéra National du Rhin;* **f** *tournoi inter-Conseils de Jeunes;* **g** *projet de repas avec les chercheurs du CNRS;* **h** *plantation de 52 arbres et suivi de leur croissance;* **i** *avec l'aide des enfants de l'école primaire; soutien au collège Leclerc;* **j** *prévention routière, pistes cyclables.* 'Trips abroad' (b) and 'encouraging healthy eating' (e) are not mentioned.

3 Imagine that you have been voted onto a youth council in your own town. List the activities you would like to be involved with. Give reasons for your choices.

Encourage students to be imaginative and to draw on the language used in the text for support.

6.8 Vidéo   page 109

Resources
- Student Book, page 109
- Kerboodle, Unit 6 Video clip

PLTS
- Independent enquirers

Épisode 6: Les fêtes
The friends are gathered together for the next challenge in the competition: to guess which festivals and traditions are being described. Basile mentions that he loves festivals and that he went to Paris to celebrate 14 July (Bastille Day) last year. He describes the procession and fireworks that he saw and tells his friends what the festival is in memory of (the storming of the Bastille in 1789). The group then goes on to answer the questions for the competition, identifying various different festivals (April Fool's Day, Music Day, Remembrance Day).

Video clip, Unit 6 page 109

Jémilie:	C'est quoi, le nouveau défi, Clarisse?
Clarisse:	« En France, il y a beaucoup de fêtes. Est-ce que vous pouvez deviner de quelle fête on parle? »
Basile:	Ah oui! J'adore les fêtes et les festivals. L'année dernière, je suis allé à Paris pour fêter le 14 juillet.
Maxime:	Qu'est-ce que tu as fait?
Basile:	J'y suis allé avec mes parents. On a passé deux jours dans un hôtel. Le matin, j'ai vu un défilé et tout le monde était déguisé.
Jémilie:	Qu'est-ce que tu as fait le soir?
Basile:	J'ai vu un grand feu d'artifice.
Zaied:	Mais pourquoi est-ce qu'on fête le 14 juillet?
Basile:	C'est la fête nationale française pour célébrer la prise de la Bastille en 1789.
Jules:	Ça suffit. Il faut faire le défi.
Maxime:	Clarisse, qu'est-ce qu'il faut faire?
Clarisse:	Ici, nous avons quelques informations sur des fêtes. Il faut deviner de quelle fête on parle.
Thouraya:	D'accord. On est prêts?
Clarisse:	« Pour cette fête, on colle un poisson en papier dans les dos des copains. »
Maxime:	Ah oui. L'année dernière, j'ai mis un poisson en papier dans le dos de ma mère et elle n'a rien vu. J'ai beaucoup ri!
Clarisse:	Oui, mais c'est quelle fête?
Maxime:	C'est le premier avril.
Jules:	Oui, le premier avril!
Clarisse:	Deuxième question: « Cette fête a lieu au mois de juin dans toute la France. Il y a des concerts gratuits et beaucoup de gens jouent de la musique dans la rue. »
Jémilie:	Ah oui, je sais, je sais. C'est le 21 juin – la Fête de la Musique.
Zaied:	Oui. Je pense qu'elle a raison. Cet été, il y avait un concert et j'y suis allé avec mon frère. J'ai adoré le concert.
Jémilie:	Ah, moi aussi. J'y suis allée avec ma sœur. Et il y avait beaucoup de musiciens qui jouaient dans les rues aussi.
Thouraya:	Et la troisième question?
Clarisse:	« Cette fête est une fête très sérieuse. Ce jour-là, on pense à tous les morts de la Première et la Seconde Guerre mondiale. »
Basile:	Cette question est plus difficile.

6 Rendez-vous

Maxime:	La Seconde Guerre mondiale a eu lieu de 1939 à 1945 et la Première Guerre mondiale de 1914 à 1918.	Clarisse:	La dernière question est: « Quelle est ta fête préférée? »
Zaied:	À l'école on a étudié la Première Guerre mondiale. Je pense que la Première Guerre mondiale s'est terminée le 11 novembre.	Thouraya:	Pour moi, c'est le 14 février, le Saint Valentin.
		Maxime:	Ah non, pour moi, c'est la Fête de la Musique, le 21 juin.
Basile:	Ah oui, on a signé l'armistice à onze heures le onzième jour du onzième mois.	Zaied:	Je pense que la fête à la fin du Ramadan, Aïd el-Fitr, est très importante. C'est une fête musulmane et la date change chaque année.
Jémilie:	C'est le 11 novembre donc.		
Maxime:	Oui, c'est ça. Et c'est très important de se souvenir de la guerre et tous les gens qui sont morts.	Clarisse:	Qu'est-ce que j'écris donc?
		Basile:	Qu'on aime toutes les fêtes?

1 Regarde l'épisode 6. On parle de quelles fêtes? Trouve les six fêtes dans la liste.
Students watch the video and note down the letters of the six festivals that are mentioned. As a follow-up task, ask them to provide English equivalents for all the listed festivals.
Answers: b, c, e, f, g, i

2 Qui a fait quoi? Relie les quatre jeunes aux dates et aux activités. Écris des phrases en anglais.
Students match the four young people to the correct dates and activities. They write full sentences in English.
Answers: On 21 June, on Music Day, Zaied went to a concert with his brother/Jémilie went to a concert with her sister. On 14 July, Bastille Day, Basile went to Paris and stayed in a hotel. He saw a parade and fireworks. On 1 April, Maxime stuck a paper fish on his mother's back.

3 Les jeunes parlent de l'Armistice. Trouve et note les mots et les dates (a–k).
Students read the transcript of a section of conversation from the video clip and decide which words from the box are needed to fill the gaps. They could attempt this activity from memory, and then watch the video to check their answers.
Answers: a Première; b Seconde; c 1939; d 1945; e 1914; f 1918; g le onze novembre; h l'Armistice; i onze; j onzième; k onzième

4 Quelle est la fête préférée, ou la plus importante, pour Maxime, Thouraya et Zaied? Écris des phrases en français.
Students write sentences about each person's favourite festival. Again, they could attempt this activity from memory, and then watch the video to check their answers.
Answers: Pour Maxime, c'est la Fête de la Musique, le 21 juin, et le 11 novembre est très important aussi. Pour Thouraya, c'est la Saint-Valentin, le 14 février. Pour Zaied, c'est l'Aïd el-Fitr, la fête à la fin du Ramadan.

5 Parle de ta fête préférée.
In groups, students discuss their own favourite festivals. Encourage them to give reasons for their preference, to describe what they did for their chosen festival last year, and how they found it.

6.9 Test   page 110

Resources
- Student Book, page 109
- CD 2, track 19

PLTS
- Creative thinkers, Reflective learners, Effective participators

AT levels
Approximate medal guidelines:
- (Foundation) L: 4; S: 4; R: 4; W: 4
- (Core) L: 5; S: 5; R: 5; W: 4–5
- (Higher) L: 6; S: 6; R: 6; W: 5

1 Listen to five young people talking about weekend activities. Copy and fill in the grid in English. (See pages 94–97.)

Answers:

	Suggestion	Yes or no? (✓ or ✘)	If no, what is their excuse? If yes, what will they do?
1	go to the cinema	✘	is going to music festival in Brittany
2	go bowling (with Ophélie and Léa)	✘	went bowling yesterday (with brother), doesn't like Ophélie – she gets on his nerves
3	organise a party for the end of the school year	✓	it's a great idea, will buy food/drinks and download music
4	go to town, go shopping	✘	has no money at the moment
5	go to town, have lunch at McDonald's	✘	had a burger yesterday evening, has no money at the moment

CD 2, track 19   page 110, activité 1

1. – Salut, Robin, qu'est-ce qu'on fait ce week-end? On pourrait aller au cinéma?
   – Oh, non, je suis désolé. Ce week-end, je vais aller à un festival de musique en Bretagne!
2. – Brice, qu'est-ce que tu fais ce week-end? On pourrait aller au bowling avec Ophélie et Léa?
   – Ben, non, j'y suis allé hier avec mon frère. Et en plus, je n'aime pas Ophélie, elle m'énerve. Alors, non merci!
3. – Amélie, qu'est-ce que tu fais ce week-end? Je pourrais organiser une fête de fin d'année avec toute la classe.
   – C'est une super idée! Moi, je vais acheter la nourriture et les boissons et télécharger de la musique!
4. – Faïsa, ce week-end, on pourrait aller en ville et faire les magasins?
   – Non, tu rigoles! Je n'ai pas d'argent en ce moment, alors faire les magasins, non merci!
5. – Martin, on pourrait aller en ville et manger au McDo à midi?
   – Ben, écoute, j'ai mangé un hamburger hier soir! Et en plus, je n'ai pas beaucoup d'argent en ce moment, désolé!

2 Give a short presentation about your favourite festival or celebration. (See pages 98–99.)

Encourage students to cover all the bullet points and to use the full range of tenses, as indicated in the prompts: present, perfect (with *avoir* and *être*), imperfect, near future and conditional).

3 Read Thouraya's interview and answer the questions in English. (See pages 100–101.)

Answers: **a** the mayor of her town; **b** 3 years ago; **c** working with children/young people because it is important to listen to them; **d** very long days and a lot of meetings which are sometimes very boring; **e** a new swimming pool for the town; **f** organising an international dance festival

4 Write about an outing or a special event that you attended. (See pages 98–99.)

Students use the suggestions from activity 2. Remind them to develop their answers, using opinions, time expressions and different tenses, and to mention whether they will go back again and who with.

125

7 Autour du monde

Unit 7: Autour du monde — Overview grid

Page reference	Contexts and objectives	Grammar	Strategies and skills	Key language	AT levels*
112–113 **7.1 On voyage comment?**	Talk about how you travel and compare means of transport	Negatives: *ne ... jamais/ni ... ni ...*	Use comparisons to develop writing and speaking	*le train, le car, le bateau, l'avion, le métro, le vélo, le bus, la voiture ... Je prends/J'utilise/Je préfère ... Mon moyen de transport préféré, c'est ... parce que ... C'est (plus/moins) polluant, cher, rapide, facile, pratique, relaxant, écolo(gique), bon/meilleur pour la santé.*	L: 3–5 S: 4–5 R: 4–5 W: 4–5
114–115 **7.2 Pour les vacances, on réserve?**	Buy tickets and talk about travel plans	Present tense of *choisir* and *partir*	24-hour clock	*un aller-retour, un aller simple, départ, arrivée, compostez votre billet, tarif étudiant, plein tarif, billet valable 30 jours Je voudrais un billet pour Marseille, s'il vous plaît. Un aller simple ou un aller-retour? Vous avez des réductions pour les étudiants? Vous avez votre carte-étudiant? C'est combien? C'est 25 euros avec la réduction-étudiant. À quelle heure part le train? Il part à ... du quai numéro 2 et il arrive à Marseille à ...*	L: 4–5 S: 3–5 R: 4–5 W: 4–5
116–117 **7.3 On part en vacances?**	Plan a holiday	Correct tenses with *si* and *quand*	The French *r* sound Super Strategies	*Quand j'aurai dix-huit ans, j'irai/je partirai en vacances en/au ... avec ... On prendra l'avion/le bateau/le train ... Si on ... Si on peut/Si on a le temps, on visitera/ira/fera ... J'espère que je verrai ... J'espère qu'il fera beau/chaud. Ce sera intéressant/excitant/génial ...*	L: 4–5 S: 4–5 R: 4–5 W: 4–5
118–119 **7.4 Et tes vacances, c'était comment?**	Describe a past holiday	Perfect and imperfect tenses	Grammar memorisation strategies Translation skills	*les vacances sportives/de luxe/« aventure »/au vert/en colonie/linguistiques Je suis allé(e)/parti(e) ... J'ai passé une/deux semaine(s) ... J'ai fait/visité/nagé/joué ... J'ai pris des photos. C'était ... enrichissant, incroyable, excitant, relaxant, fatigant, barbant.*	L: 4–5 S: 4–5 R: 4–5 W: 4–5
120–121 **7.5 Voyage dans le temps!**	Talk about transport in books and films	Use different tenses	Understand more complex reading texts	*J'ai lu un livre qui s'appelle ... J'ai vu un film qui raconte l'histoire de ... C'était (vraiment) amusant/intéressant/génial ... Les personnages sont marrants/intéressants ... J'ai adoré le personnage principal/l'histoire/les animations. Si tu aimes ..., tu aimeras/adoreras ...*	L: 4–6 S: 4–6 R: 5–6 W: 4–6
122–123 **7.6 Labo-langue**	Grammar, language strategies and pronunciation	Negatives Present tense of *-ir* verbs Perfect and imperfect tenses *Si* (if) and *quand* (when)	Super Strategies Pronunciation: *u* and *ou*		
124–129 **7.7 Extra Star, Extra Plus 7.8 Lire, Vidéo 7.9 Test, Vocabulaire**	Reinforcement and extension; reading material; activities based on the video material; revision and assessment		**Lire:** R: 6–7 **Vidéo:** L: 4–6; S: 4–5		**Test:** L: 4 S: 4–6 R: 5–6 W: 5–6

*See teacher notes for alternative assessment options. Guidelines for the various assessment criteria are provided in the introduction of this Teacher Handbook.

126

Unit 7: Week-by-week overview

(Three-year KS3 route: assuming six weeks' work or approximately 10–12.5 hours)
(Two-year KS3 route: assuming four weeks' work or approximately 6.5–8.5 hours)

About Unit 7, *Autour du monde*: In this unit, students work in the context of travel, transport and holidays: they talk about how they travel and compare means of transport. They learn to buy tickets and talk about travel plans, and also learn to plan a holiday, describe a past holiday and talk about transport in books and films.

Students extend their knowledge of negatives, learning how to use *ne … jamais* and *ne … ni … ni*. They revisit *-ir* verbs in the form of *choisir* and *partir*, and learn to use the correct tenses with *si* and *quand*. They continue to develop their use of tenses, and are now given the opportunity to use all four (present, perfect, imperfect and future) in one productive task.

Students are introduced in this unit to Super Strategies, which they can apply to different types of activities across the four skills. In this unit, they are encouraged to identify and apply language patterns in various ways, and to zoom in on key words when listening, areas in written work where they know they usually make mistakes, pronunciation sounds they find tricky, and on task instructions in general. In addition, students are given the opportunity to use comparisons to develop their writing and speaking, to develop confidence when using the 24-hour clock, to work on grammar memorisation strategies and translation skills, and to work on skills to help them improve their understanding of more complex reading texts. The pronunciation point focuses on the correct pronunciation of the French *r* sound, this time in the context of the future tense.

Three-year KS3 route

Week	Resources
	Material from the end-of-unit pages (*7.7 Extra Star/Plus*, *7.8 Lire* and *Vidéo*) may be used during week 6 or selectively during weeks 1–5 as time permits.
1	7.1 On voyage comment? 7.6 Labo-langue, activity 1
2	7.2 Pour les vacances, on réserve? 7.6 Labo-langue, activity 2
3	7.3 On part en vacances? 7.6 Labo-langue, activity 4 7.6 Labo-langue, Super Strategies 7.6 Labo-langue, Pronunciation: the French *r* sound
4	7.4 Et tes vacances, c'était comment? 7.6 Labo-langue, activity 3
5	7.5 Voyage dans le temps!
6	7.7 Extra Star, Extra Plus 7.8 Lire 7.8 Vidéo 7.9 Test 7.9 Vocabulaire

Two-year KS3 route

Week	Resources
	Material from the end-of-unit pages (*7.7 Extra Star/Plus*, *7.8 Lire* and *Vidéo*) may be used selectively during weeks 1–4 as time permits.
1	7.1 On voyage comment? (Omit activity 4) 7.6 Labo-langue, activity 1
2	7.2 Pour les vacances, on réserve? (Omit activity 5) 7.6 Labo-langue, activity 2
3	7.3 On part en vacances? (Omit activity 4) 7.6 Labo-langue, activity 4 7.6 Labo-langue, Super Strategies 7.6 Labo-langue, Pronunciation: the French *r* sound
4	7.4 Et tes vacances, c'était comment? 7.6 Labo-langue, activity 3 7.9 Test 7.9 Vocabulaire

7 Autour du monde

7.1 On voyage comment?
pages 112–113

Planner

Objectives
- Vocabulary: talk about how you travel and compare means of transport
- Grammar: use negatives: *ne ... pas/jamais/ ni ... ni ...*
- Skills: use comparisons to develop writing and speaking

Resources
- Student Book, pages 112–113
- CD 2, tracks 20–21
- Grammar and Skills Workbook, page 5
- Kerboodle, Unit 7
- Unit 7 Worksheet 6 (ex. 1)

Key language
le train, le car, le bateau, l'avion, le métro, le vélo, le bus, la voiture

Je prends/J'utilise/Je préfère ... Mon moyen de transport préféré, c'est ... parce que ...

c'est (plus/moins) polluant, cher, rapide, facile, pratique, relaxant, écolo(gique)/bon/meilleur pour la santé.

Grammar
- Negatives: *ne ... pas/jamais/ni ... ni ...*

PLTS and Numeracy
- Activity 4: Independent enquirers
- Activity 5: Team workers
- Activity 6: Creative thinkers
- Numeracy: Activity 5: presenting survey results as a chart

Homework and self-study
- Student Book, page 112, activity 3
- Student Book, page 113, activity 6
- Student Book, page 113, activity 7
- Grammar and Skills Workbook, page 5

Starters
See Kerboodle Starters bank for further details of **Dominoes** and **Up, down**.
- Play **Dominoes** with the modes of transport.
- Reinforce comparisons by playing **Up, down**. Read out the text from activity 3, or play the recording from activity 4, and ask students to stand up whenever they hear a comparison phrase.

Plenaries
- **Independent learning strategies**. This plenary encourages students to reflect on prior learning.

In groups, students reread the interview with the mayor on page 100 (spread 6.4) and revisit the vocabulary section 'Meeting people in formal situations' on page 111. Using the results from the *sondage* in activity 5 on page 113 (this may need collating as a whole class first), students then discuss transport in their local environment and suggest an improvement to the infrastructure that they could take to either the mayor or a local politician. They then discuss in pairs how successful they have been in their preparation for this task, focusing particularly on their speaking and presentation skills.

1 Trouve les paires.
Students read the French modes of transport and match them to the correct pictures. Once they have done this, check answers as a class and discuss how they worked them out. Some are cognates, some they will have come across before, but some will be new. Draw students' attention to the false friend *le car*. Did they work out this one correctly? How did they do it? By guessing? By a process of elimination?
Answers: **1** h; **2** d; **3** f; **4** c; **5** a; **6** g; **7** b; **8** e

2 Écoute. Recopie et remplis la grille avec les moyens de transport (1–8) de l'activité 1.
In preparation for this activity, do the **Dominoes** starter activity to reinforce the new vocabulary presented in activity 1. Then ask students to look at the two phrases in the answer grid: *Je prends* and *J'aime prendre*. Make sure they understand what they are listening for: i.e. how the speakers travel and how they <u>like</u> to travel. Remind students to listen out for these phrases, as they will help them focus on categorising correctly the modes of transport cited by each speaker. Students then listen and identify which modes of transport each speaker mentions, and note down the corresponding letters of the pictures from activity 1.

Answers:

	Lola	Hugo	Karim	Sandrine	Robin
Je prends	6, 1	6, 8	8, 1	7, 1	6, 3
J'aime prendre	2, 4	2	3	2, 4	5, 2

Students note down any extra details from the recording.

CD 2, track 20   page 112, activité 2

– Lola, quels moyens de transport prends-tu d'habitude?
– Je prends le bus et la voiture tous les jours.
– Quels moyens de transport aimes-tu prendre?
– J'adore prendre l'avion ou le bateau.
– Et toi, Hugo?
– Moi, je prends le bus ou le métro pour aller au collège mais j'aime bien prendre l'avion quand je vais en vacances!
– Karim?
– Moi, je prends le métro ou la voiture pour aller au collège mais j'aime aussi prendre le vélo! C'est plus amusant!
– Sandrine, et toi?
– Je prends le car et la voiture tous les jours mais j'aime bien prendre l'avion ou le bateau quand je vais en vacances!
– Robin, qu'est-ce que tu préfères comme moyen de transport?
– Moi, je prends le bus et le vélo tous les jours mais pour aller en vacances, j'aime prendre le train ou l'avion. C'est super rapide!
– Merci à tous!

3 Lis. Trouve les expressions a–f dans le texte.

Students read the text and find the French equivalents for the English phrases. Once they have done this, run through the skills box on **Comparisons** and ask students to read through the text again and spot all the examples of comparisons.

Answers: **a** on utilise les transports en commun; **b** c'est plus pratique; **c** moins cher que la voiture; **d** c'est très écologique; **e** la voiture électrique; **f** le moyen de transport le plus rapide

Students find at least three connectives in the text. Ask them to provide translations for each.

Answers: comme (such as, like), ou (or), parce que (because), et (and), ou (or), et (and), car (as, since), en revanche (on the other hand), et (and)

4 Écoute et remplis la grille en anglais pour Aïsha, Benjamin et Nolan.

Students listen and complete the grid. They note down which mode of transport each speaker takes to school and why, what their favourite mode of transport is with reasons, and any extra details.

Answers:

	Transport to school + reasons	Favourite transport + reasons
Aïsha	bus – cheap and practical, mum takes her to bus stop by car	boat – relaxing
Benjamin	bike – environmentally friendly, not polluting, good for the health	plane – very fast
Nolan	by bike – lives 5 minutes away from school, it's easy and good for the health	electric car – it's environmentally friendly

	Extra details
Aïsha	travelled by boat to Britain last year – it was great
Benjamin	went to Guadeloupe by plane last year – loved it
Nolan	plane is too polluting; mum has an electric car – it's great in town

Students transcribe what Aïsha says.

CD 2, track 21   page 113, activité 4

– Alors, Aïsha, quels moyens de transport prends-tu pour aller au collège?
– Moi, je prends le bus tous les jours parce que ce n'est pas cher et parce que c'est pratique. Ma mère m'emmène à l'arrêt de bus en voiture.
– Quel moyen de transport tu préfères?
– J'aime prendre le bateau parce que c'est relaxant. L'année dernière, j'ai pris le bateau pour aller en Grande-Bretagne. C'était génial! Je pense que le bateau, c'est mon moyen de transport préféré!
– Et toi, Benjamin?
– J'aime prendre le vélo pour aller au collège parce que c'est très écolo. Ça ne pollue pas et en plus, c'est bon pour la santé. L'année dernière, on est allés en vacances en Guadeloupe donc on a pris l'avion. J'ai adoré ça! C'était très rapide! L'avion, c'est mon moyen de transport préféré pour aller en vacances.
– Et toi, Nolan, tu préfères l'avion ou la voiture?
– Je trouve que l'avion, c'est trop polluant. Moi, je préfère la voiture électrique parce que c'est plus écologique. Ma mère a une petite voiture électrique et c'est génial, surtout en ville! Tous les jours, je prends mon vélo parce que j'habite à cinq minutes du collège donc c'est facile et c'est bon pour la santé!

7 Autour du monde

5 Sondage. Pose les questions (1–3) à cinq personnes.

Before students embark on this groupwork activity, do the **Up, down** starter activity to consolidate students' knowledge of comparisons. Once they are sure of how to use comparisons, students ask five classmates the three questions listed and note down the results. They could present their findings in the form of a bar or pie chart. Refer students to the key language box for support.

Students say how they went on holiday last year.

6 Lis la conversation et réponds aux questions en anglais.

Students read the conversation and answer the questions in English. Encourage students to use their reading strategies when working out the answer to question e. They know that *car* means 'coach' and they know the word *camping*, so what do they think *camping-car* might mean?

Once students have completed the activity, run through the grammar box on **Negatives**. Ask students to look back through the text in activity 6 and spot the examples of *ne … ni … ni …* and *ne … jamais*. As a follow-up task, ask students to make up some short sentences of their own, using the negative structures and other modes of transport from activity 1.

Answers: **a** in Quebec; **b** by plane; **c** train or car; **d** it's too expensive and too polluting; **e** camper van; **f** very long and boring

Students translate Tom's lines into English.

Answers:
– Hi Chiara! You're lucky! We take neither the plane nor the boat. We always take the train or the car! I've never taken the plane.
– Because my parents think that the plane is too expensive and too polluting. They're very environmentally friendly! Last year, when we went to Spain, we took the camper van. It was very long and boring!
– OK. See you later!

7 Écris un blog sur les moyens de transport. Réponds aux questions de l'activité 5.

Students write a blog about the various modes of transport. They use the questions in activity 5 as the structure for their writing. Encourage students to use the texts in activities 3 and 6 for support, as well as the key language box, and remind them to use comparisons in their writing.

To encourage students to develop and extend their writing, ask them to use at least two connectives (Bronze medal), use at least one negative expression (Silver medal) and to add where they travelled to last year and how they went (Gold medal).

Plenary

In pairs, students review what they have learnt about transport.

- Students name at least five means of transport and say which they prefer.
- Students add a reason for their choice.
- Students compare different means of transport.

7.2 Pour les vacances, on réserve?

pages 114–115

Planner

Objectives
- Vocabulary: buy tickets and talk about travel plans
- Grammar: use *choisir* and *partir* in the present tense
- Skills: develop confidence with the 24-hour clock

Resources
- Student Book, pages 114–115
- CD 2, tracks 22–23
- Grammar and Skills Workbook, pages 26, 28 and 30
- Kerboodle, Unit 7
- Unit 7 Worksheet 3 (ex. 1)

Key language

un aller-retour, un aller simple, départ, arrivée, compostez votre billet, tarif étudiant, plein tarif, billet valable 30 jours

Je voudrais un billet pour Marseille, s'il vous plaît. Un aller simple ou un aller-retour?

Vous avez des réductions pour les étudiants? Vous avez votre carte-étudiant?

C'est combien? C'est 25 euros avec la réduction-étudiant.

À quelle heure part le train? Il part à ... du quai numéro 2 et il arrive à ... à ...

Grammar

- Present tense of *choisir* and *partir*

PLTS and Numeracy

- Activity 3: Team workers
- Activity 6: Creative thinkers

- Plenary: Reflective learners
- Numeracy: Activities 2 and 3: recognising and using 24-hour clock times

Homework and self-study

- Student Book, page 115, activity 4
- Student Book, page 115, activity 6
- Grammar and Skills Workbook, pages 26, 28 and 30

Starters

See Kerboodle Starters bank for further details of **Loto** and **Dominoes**.

- Play **Loto** with numbers up to 60: play several rounds, using numbers between 1 and 20, 30 and 40, and 50 and 60 for each separate round.
- To practise converting 12-hour clock times to the 24-hour clock, write on the board a series of 12-hour clock times and ask students to call out in turn what the 24-hour clock equivalent is.
- Play **Dominoes** to revise country names.

Plenaries

- **Cross-curricular links with Maths, Geography and Science**. To reinforce links across the curriculum, ask students to reflect on the environmental impact of tourism. More able learners could also research statistics for tourist destinations and see if they can find any changing patterns: e.g. Where do French people choose to go on holiday and how do they travel there? Have there been any recent changes and if so, why? They should use as much French as possible to report their findings, but the main focus should be on how they link their learning of other subjects to their study of French and French-speaking countries across the world.

1 Regarde les billets et trouve les expressions a–h.
Students look at the two tickets and find the French equivalents for the English words and phrases. Remind them to focus on cognates, and other words that they recognise, when decoding new vocabulary.

Answers: **a** un aller-retour; **b** un aller simple; **c** départ; **d** arrivée; **e** compostez votre billet; **f** tarif étudiant; **g** plein tarif; **h** billet valable 30 jours

2 Écoute et lis. Mets les phrases du dialogue dans le bon ordre.
Students listen and read the dialogue. Explain that the sentences of the dialogue are in the wrong order on page 114 and draw their attention to the glossed vocabulary (*du quai numéro 2*). Students note down the correct order for the sentences. For a more challenging version of this activity, students reorder the sentences before listening to check their answers.

Once students have completed this activity, refer them to the skills box on **The 24-hour clock**. Check their understanding of this concept and do the starter activity to practise converting 12-hour clock times to the 24-hour clock, in preparation for activity 3. Ask them to look back at the dialogue in activity 2 and to spot the examples of 24-hour clock times. Can they say what the equivalent times would be in the 12-hour clock? (10:42 a.m.; 4:34 p.m.)

Answers: c, f, b, a, d, i, e, g, h

t Students translate the dialogue into English.

Answers:
- Hello. I'd like a ticket to Marseille, please.
- Yes, a single or return?
- A return. Do you have discounts for students?
- Yes, of course. Do you have your student card?
- Yes, here it is. How much is that?
- It's 25 euros with the student discount.
- What time does the train leave?
- It leaves at 10:42 from platform 2, and it arrives at Marseille at 16:34.
- Perfect! Thank you. Goodbye.

CD 2, track 22   page 114, activité 2

- Bonjour, monsieur. Je voudrais un billet pour Marseille, s'il vous plaît.
- Oui, un aller simple ou un aller-retour?
- Un aller-retour. Vous avez des réductions pour les étudiants?
- Oui, bien sûr, vous avez votre carte-étudiant?
- Oui, voilà. C'est combien?
- C'est vingt-cinq euros avec la réduction-étudiant.
- À quelle heure part le train?
- Il part à 10 h 42 du quai numéro 2 et il arrive à Marseille à 16 h 34.
- Parfait! Merci, monsieur. Au revoir.

7 Autour du monde

3 À deux. Adaptez le dialogue de l'activité 2 pour acheter les billets a–c.
Before students embark on this activity, do the **Loto** starter activity to practise numbers up to 60, which will help students with saying the 24-hour clock times. In pairs, students then adapt the dialogue from activity 2, using the information in the ticket prompts provided.

4 Lis les dialogues 1 et 2. Vrai, faux ou pas mentionné?
Before starting this activity, do the **Dominoes** starter activity to revise country names. Students then read the two dialogues and decide whether the English statements relating to each text are true, false or not mentioned in the text. As a follow-up task, students correct the false statements.
Answers: **1 a** *vrai;* **b** *pas mentionné;* **c** *vrai;* **d** *faux (the car);* **2 a** *faux (the second person prefers the boat; but eventually suggests the car and the Shuttle);* **b** *vrai;* **c** *faux (it's fast but a bit expensive);* **d** *vrai*

5 Écoute Maman, Papa, Marion et Vincent. Qui choisit quoi?
Students listen and decide who chooses which type of holiday (a–c). Explain to students that one holiday type is chosen by two people.
Answers: **a** *Marion;* **b** *Papa et Maman;* **c** *Vincent*

⭐ Students note down where the family decides to go in the end.
Answer: camping in Antibes

◯ Students note down the reasons each person gives for their choice.
Answers: **a** *Marion: wants to travel by plane and stay in a hotel;* **b** *Papa: loves camping; Maman: can also see the animals at Marineland;* **c** *Vincent: loves animals and the countryside, and can go horse riding every day*

〰 CD 2, track 23   page 115, activité 5

- Alors, les enfants, on choisit quoi cette année pour nos vacances en famille? Vincent?
- Moi, j'adore les animaux et la campagne donc je choisis les vacances à la ferme. En plus, on peut faire de l'équitation tous les jours! Ce sera super!
- Ah non, c'est ennuyeux, la campagne! Je déteste … et j'ai peur des chevaux! Alors non, non, et non … Moi, je choisis la Guadeloupe parce que je veux voyager en avion et en plus, loger dans un hôtel. Ce sera génial!
- Mais l'hôtel, c'est très cher, Marion, donc ce n'est pas possible. Mais si on choisit le camping à Antibes, on pourra aussi voir des animaux à Marineland.
- Tu as raison, ma chérie. Et en plus, j'adore camper … et vous, les enfants?
- Bof!
- Oh, quel enthousiasme! Alors, on choisit quoi?
- On choisit le camping à Antibes pour deux semaines. Ce sera très relaxant pour tout le monde! OK?
- OK!

---

6 Choisis une destination pour les vacances. On voyage comment? Écris un dialogue comme dans les activités 4 et 5.
Students write a dialogue similar to those in activities 4 and 5. They could work in pairs to do this, each writing the lines for one person. Before they start on this, run through the grammar box on *Choisir* and *partir*. Remind students that they have come across *–ir* verbs before (e.g. *choisir* and *finir* in *Allez 1*, Unit 7) and check that they are secure with the verb endings before they write their dialogues.

7 À deux. Faites les dialogues de l'activité 6.
In pairs, students read aloud their dialogues. This could be done in front of the class, with students voting for the holiday plans they most like the sound of, or those with the most persuasive arguments.

Plenary

Students pick out the most important vocabulary from pages 114–115 and make some notes to help an absent friend catch up. Remind them to include *–ir* verbs.

⭐ Students explain the 24-hour clock to a partner.

◯ In pairs, students talk about booking a holiday: they decide where to go and how to travel.

➕ Students develop their conversation further by discussing the advantages and disadvantages of different ways to travel.

132

7.3 On part en vacances?

pages 116–117

Planner

Objectives
- Vocabulary: plan a holiday
- Grammar: use the correct tenses with *si* and *quand*
- Skills: pronounce the French *r* sound; use Super Strategies

Resources
- Student Book, pages 116–117
- CD 2, tracks 24–26
- Grammar and Skills Workbook, pages 34 and 41
- Kerboodle, Unit 7
- Unit 7 Worksheets 4 (ex. 1), 5 (ex. 3), 6 (ex. 2)

Key language
Quand j'aurai dix-huit ans, j'irai/je partirai en vacances en/au ... avec ...
On prendra l'avion/le bateau/le train ...
Si on peut/Si on a le temps, on visitera/ira/fera ...
J'espère que je verrai ...
J'espère qu'il fera beau/chaud.
Ce sera intéressant/excitant/génial ...

Grammar
- Correct tenses with *si* and *quand*

PLTS
- Activity 2: Team workers
- Activities 3, 4 and 5: Reflective learners, Self-managers
- Plenary: Reflective learners, Self-managers, Effective participators

Homework and self-study
- Student Book, page 117, activity 3
- Student Book, page 117, activity 5
- Grammar and Skills Workbook, pages 34 and 41

Starters

See Kerboodle Starters bank for further details of **Word tennis** and **Tongue twisters**.

- Play **Word tennis** to revise the future tense: write on the board various infinitives (relating to the topic) and ask students to call out the *on* form of the future tense for each. See how long the class can keep going without getting one wrong.
- Provide students with some French **Tongue twisters** using the *r* sound, and have them practise them in small groups.

Plenaries

- **Reflection on progress with speaking.** Following on from the plenary on page 117, ask students to record their presentations on their phones at home and bring them to class. Allow time at the end of the lesson for them to listen to each other's recordings in pairs, and to provide feedback on their improving speaking skills. They should note any errors of pronunciation and practise saying these words or phrases to each other until they are perfect.

Encourage students to use target language questions and statements in their feedback. They should be familiar with the following from *Allez 1: Qu'est ce que tu as appris aujourd'hui et comment?* Encourage them also to use other phrases such as: *Tu peux parler clairement. Ta prononciation est incorrecte/plutôt correcte/correcte. Tu peux faire des phrases correctes! Tu sais comment utiliser les verbes ... Ta grammaire est correcte!*

1 Écoute et lis le dialogue. Qui dit quoi? Papa, Maman, Maëva ou Noa?

Students listen and read the dialogue. They decide which speaker would be likely to say each of the English statements.

Answers: **a** Maman; **b** Papa; **c** Maman; **d** Papa; **e** Maëva; **f** Noa

(t) Once students have done this, run through the grammar box on **Si (if) and quand (when)**. Ask them to look back through the dialogue to spot the *si* and *quand* phrases, and to translate them into English. Draw students' attention to the difference in tense usage between French and English when using *quand: Quand* **on sera** *dans le Devon* = 'When **we are** in Devon', rather than 'When **we will be** in Devon'.

Answers:
Si on veut arriver vite, on prendra l'avion. (If we want to arrive quickly, we will take the plane.)

Mais quand on sera dans le Devon, qu'est-ce qu'on fera? (But what will we do when we are in Devon?)

S'il fait beau, on ira à la plage et on visitera les villes de la région. (If the weather is fine, we will go to the beach and we will visit the towns of the region.)

Et quand on sera à Londres, on visitera Big Ben et la Maison du Parlement. (And when we are in London, we will visit Big Ben and the Houses of Parliament.)

133

7 Autour du monde

Exploit the dialogue further with additional comprehension questions, or ask students to make up questions for each other. For example: Why will they go in July? (because it's after the exams); What two reasons are given for taking the plane? (it's fast, they can get low-cost tickets to London); How will they travel around in England? (they will hire a car); How long will they stay in each place? (a week in Devon, five days in London); What will they do in Devon? (go to the beach if weather is good, visit towns, eat afternoon teas); What will they do in London? (visit Big Ben and Houses of Parliament, go shopping, speak English).

As an additional folllow-up task, use the recording for further practice: students practise the dialogue in groups of four, then read along with the recording. They then perform to the class, which votes for the best performance.

CD 2, track 24   page 116, activité 1

- Maman, on ira où en vacances cet été?
- Je pense qu'on ira en Angleterre. Ce sera bien pour votre anglais, les enfants, non?
- Et on partira quand?
- On partira juste après les examens, en juillet!
- Super! Mais on voyagera comment?
- Si on veut arriver vite, on prendra l'avion. Il y a des vols « low cost » pour Londres qui ne sont pas trop chers et on louera une voiture pour visiter la région.
- Oui, super! Et on restera combien de temps?
- Je pense qu'on restera une semaine dans le Devon et cinq jours à Londres.
- Oui, c'est génial! Mais quand on sera dans le Devon, qu'est-ce qu'on fera?
- Ça dépendra du temps. S'il fait beau, on ira à la plage et on visitera les villes de la région. On prendra aussi des « afternoon teas ». J'adore les scones avec de la crème!
- Super! On logera où? Dans un camping ou à l'hôtel?
- Je pense qu'on logera dans un gîte dans le Devon et dans un hôtel à Londres!
- Et quand on sera à Londres, on visitera Big Ben et les Maisons du Parlement. Ce sera génial! Et on fera du shopping!
- *England*, on arrive! Je parlerai anglais tout le temps. J'adore l'anglais! Ce sera super pour mes examens!

The French r sound

Ask students to practise making the French *r* sound in pairs and to provide feedback on each other's pronunciation. Do the **Tongue twisters** starter activity and then play the recording and encourage students to repeat each word in turn, again evaluating each other's pronunciation. Check that students know the meaning of all the future tense verbs listed and ask them to spot them in the dialogue in activity 1. They should remember them from Unit 5, but refer them to section on **The future tense** on page 123 if they need a reminder.

CD 2, track 25   page 116, Prononciation

on ira
on partira
on sera
on restera
on fera
on prendra

2 À deux. A pose les questions de l'activité 1. B répond. A ↔ B.

Before students start this activity, do the **Word tennis** starter activity to revise the future tense. In pairs, students then take turns to ask and answer the questions that are highlighted in the dialogue in activity 1. Remind students to focus on their pronunciation of the French *r* sound.

○ Students add opinions.

⊕ Students use a *si* clause and a *quand* clause in their dialogues.

3 Lis le texte et réponds aux questions en anglais.

Students read the text and answer the questions in English. Draw their attention to the glossed vocabulary for support. Before students start on this, refer them to the section on **Super Strategies** on page 123. Ask them to read the tips on **Zooming in** and to apply them when working on the text. Once they have answered the questions, ask them to read the text again, this time identifying the tenses and verb endings as specified on page 123.

Answers: **a** *to Australia, with his friends;* **b** *Airbus A380;* **c** *less expensive;* **d** *loves diving;* **e** *watch the sunset;* **f** *the East Coast*

⭐ **t** Students translate the underlined expressions into English.

Answers: When I'm 18; If I can; we'll travel; we'll visit; we'll go; If we have time; I hope that I will see …

4 Écoute et écris la transcription: « Mes vacances en Corse ».

Students listen and transcribe the recording. Before they do so, refer them to the section on **Super**

134

Strategies on page 123 and encourage them to apply their knowledge of language patterns to help them transcribe what they hear. Remind them also to zoom in on where they usually make mistakes.

CD 2, track 26   page 117, activité 4

Quand j'aurai dix-huit ans, j'irai en vacances en Corse avec mes copains et on fera du camping parce que c'est moins cher. S'il fait beau, on ira à la plage tous les jours. Quand on sera à Ajaccio, on visitera le musée Napoléon! Si on a le temps et l'argent, on fera de la plongée. J'espère qu'il fera beau!

---

5 Écris un paragraphe comme dans les activités 3 et 4. Utilise les expressions soulignées de l'activité 3.

Students write a paragraph about their holiday plans, along the same lines as those in activities 3 and 4. They use the underlined expressions from activity 3 as the basis for their writing and the key language box for support. Refer students again to the section on **Super Strategies** on page 123 and challenge them to use the verbs they find most difficult. Remind them also to zoom in on where they usually make mistakes.

○ Students add opinions.

Plenary

Students prepare a short talk on a holiday they would like to go on and present it to their partner.

★ Students say where they will go and what they will do.

○ Students add a reason for their choice.

✚ Students use *si, quand* and at least two connectives to make their talk more interesting.

Once they have given their presentation, they give each other constructive feedback on fluency, pronunciation and use of the future tense.

7.4 Et tes vacances, c'était comment?
pages 118–119

Planner

Objectives
- Vocabulary: describe a past holiday
- Grammar: use the perfect and imperfect tenses
- Skills: use grammar memorisation strategies; develop translation skills

Resources
- Student Book, pages 118–119
- CD 2, tracks 27–28
- Grammar and Skills Workbook, pages 14, 35–39 and 56
- Kerboodle, Unit 7
- Unit 7 Worksheets 4 (ex. 2), 5 (ex. 2), 6 (ex. 3)

Key language

les vacances sportives/de luxe/« aventure »/au vert/ en colonie/linguistiques

Je suis allé(e)/parti(e) ...

J'ai passé une/deux semaine(s) ...

J'ai fait/visité/nagé/joué ... J'ai pris des photos.

C'était ... enrichissant, incroyable, excitant, relaxant, fatigant, barbant.

Grammar
- Perfect and imperfect tenses

PLTS
- Activity 5: Self-managers
- Activity 6: Creative thinkers
- Plenary: Reflective learners

Homework and self-study
- Student Book, page 119, activity 3
- Student Book, page 119, activity 5
- Student Book, page 119, activity 6
- Grammar and Skills Workbook, pages 14, 35–39 and 56, activity 3

Starters

See Kerboodle Starters bank for further details of **Up, down**.

- Play **Up, down** to reinforce students' knowledge of when to use the perfect tense or the imperfect. Play the recording from activity 1 and ask students first to stand up every time they hear a perfect tense verb. Then play it again to test awareness of imperfect tense verbs. Check students' understanding by eliciting what each tense is used for.

- Hold a **Class discussion** to recall the memorisation strategies covered in *Allez 1* and *Allez 2*. Write them on the board and encourage students to refer to them when working in pairs on the **Grammar memorsiation strategies**.

7 Autour du monde

Plenaries

- **Hot seat.** Ask for volunteers who are prepared to be 'tested' by their peers on their understanding of the imperfect and perfect tenses. The rest of the class notes down English questions to put to the volunteers, such as: What type of holiday do you prefer? Why? Where did you go on holiday last year? What was it like? How long did you stay there? The first volunteer sits at the front of the class and answers the English questions in French. If he/she answers correctly (answers may need checking for accuracy), he/she stays in the hot seat; if the answer is grammatically incorrect, another volunteer takes his/her place.

1 Écoute (1–6). « Tu préfères quel type de vacances »?

Students listen, and copy and complete the grid. They note down the type of holiday each person went on, how long it was and what they thought of it. Most of the holiday types should either be familiar to students, or they should be able to decode them fairly easily, using the photos as clues.

Once students have completed the activity, run through the grammar box on **Perfect tense or imperfect?** and do the **Up, down** starter activity to reinforce this.

Answers:

	Type of holiday	How long was last year's holiday?	Opinion
1	f	2 weeks	rewarding
2	a	3 weeks	great
3	c	2 weeks	tiring, exciting
4	b	1 week	(absolutely) incredible
5	e	1 month	(really) super/great
6	d	10 days	really relaxing, a bit boring

Students also note down where each person went.

Answers: **1** England; **2** Paris; **3** Morocco; **4** Seychelles; **5** Alps; **6** Brittany

---

CD 2, track 27   page 118, activité 1

1 – Alors, Joséphine, tu préfères quels types de vacances?
– Moi, j'adore apprendre les langues. J'étudie l'anglais, l'allemand et l'espagnol au collège et l'année dernière j'ai fait un stage linguistique de deux semaines en Angleterre. C'était très enrichissant!

2 – Et toi, Tanguy?
– Moi, j'adore le sport donc je préfère les vacances sportives. L'année dernière, j'ai fait un stage de volley à Paris pendant trois semaines. C'était génial.

3 – Et toi, Zinedine?
– Moi, j'aime l'aventure ... Partir en safari ou en excursion, par exemple. L'année dernière, j'ai fait une grande randonnée de deux semaines au Maroc. C'était fatigant mais super excitant.

4 – Et toi, Ophélie?
– Moi, j'adore rester dans des hôtels de luxe. En juillet dernier, on est restés une semaine dans un hôtel quatre étoiles aux Seychelles. C'était absolument incroyable!

5 – Marion?
– Moi, j'adore partir avec des copains. Je suis fan des colonies de vacances. Les dernières vacances, je suis allée en colo dans les Alpes pendant un mois. C'était vraiment super!

6 – Et pour finir, Oliver?
– Mes parents sont très écolo donc on part toujours à vélo, à la campagne, pour passer des vacances au vert. L'année dernière, on est restés dix jours dans une ferme en Bretagne. C'était vraiment relaxant mais un peu barbant aussi!

Grammar memorisation strategies

In pairs, students make a list of the rules for using the perfect tense and the imperfect. Students may need prompting to remember all the rules connected with the perfect and imperfect tenses. For example:

- which verbs take *avoir* and *être* in the perfect tense
- conjugation of *avoir* and *être*
- how to form regular past participles (*-er*, *-ir*, *-re* verbs)
- irregular past participles
- agreement of the past participle with *être* verbs
- how to use negatives in the perfect tense (negative goes around the auxiliary verb)
- when to use the perfect tense and when to use the imperfect
- how to form the imperfect tense – any exceptions? (only exception is *être*)

Do the **Class discussion** starter activity to help with this.

Students go on to discuss how they have gone about memorising these rules and what strategies

136

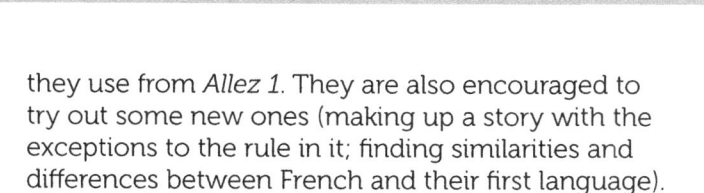

they use from *Allez 1*. They are also encouraged to try out some new ones (making up a story with the exceptions to the rule in it; finding similarities and differences between French and their first language).

2 À deux. A pose les questions 1–3. B répond. A ↔ B.
In pairs, students take turns to ask and answer the questions listed. They use the key language box for support and refer to the grammar box to check their tense usage.

○ Students add extra details such as how long they stayed, who they went with and what they thought of it.

3 Lis les textes. Vrai, faux ou pas mentionné?
Students read the two texts and answer the questions in English. As a follow-up task, ask them to correct the false sentences.

Answers: **a** *faux (two weeks);* **b** *pas mentionné;* **c** *faux (over 50);* **d** *faux (eight hours);* **e** *vrai;* **f** *pas mentionné*

Exploit the text further by asking some additional comprehension questions, or ask students to make some up for each other. For example:

Sacha: Where did Sacha stay on the first night? (in a camp below Kilimanjaro); What did they do the next day? (went to the Tsavo national park); What four animals did Sacha photograph? (rhinos, lions, elephants, zebras).

Natasha: At the hotel, how long did they have to wait for their room? (two hours); How far away from the hotel was the beach? (20 minutes); What was the problem with the sea? (full of jellyfish).

4 Écoute et trouve les sept erreurs dans la traduction.
Students listen and find the seven errors in the English translation.

Answers (corrections underlined): I spent <u>a week</u> in Spain, but what a nightmare! On <u>Saturday</u>, when we arrived at the airport, our flight was <u>two</u> hours late.

CD 2, track 28   page 119, activité 4

J'ai passé une semaine en Espagne mais quel cauchemar!
Le samedi, quand on est arrivés à l'aéroport, notre vol avait deux heures de retard!
Ensuite, à l'hôtel, la chambre de mes parents n'était pas prête. On a attendu une heure!
Finalement, l'eau de la piscine était très froide et la plage était à une demie-heure à pied. C'était vraiment nul!

Then, at the hotel, <u>my parents' bedroom</u> was not ready. We waited <u>an hour</u>. Finally, the <u>pool water</u> was very cold and the beach was half an hour away <u>on foot</u>! It was really rubbish!

5 Traduis le texte de l'activité 4 en français.

Students translate the text from activity 4, remembering to correct the seven mistakes. Before they start, refer them to the skills box on **Translating into French** and encourage them to follow these strategies when translating the text. Talk particularly about the pitfalls of using online translation tools and warn pupils against this. When students have completed their translation, play the recording from activity 4 again so that they can listen and check their text against the original.

Answer: J'ai passé une semaine en Espagne mais quel cauchemar! Le samedi, quand on est arrivés à l'aéroport, notre vol avait deux heures de retard! Ensuite, à l'hôtel, la chambre de mes parents n'était pas prête. On a attendu une heure! Finalement, l'eau de la piscine était très froide et la plage était à une demie heure à pied. C'était vraiment nul!

6 Écris un article sur tes vacances de rêve ☺ ou tes vacances catastrophiques ☹.
Students write their own article about a dream or disastrous holiday. They use the expressions from activities 2, 3 and 4, and refer to the key language box for support. Remind them to think carefully about tense usage and to check back to the grammar box if they need help.

Plenary

In pairs, students explain when to use the perfect tense and the imperfect, and how each tense is formed. They give examples.

★ Students choose a verb and use it in the perfect tense.

○ Students add a description in the imperfect tense.

✚ **t** Students give each other an English sentence in the perfect tense and one in the imperfect tense, and they translate them into French using the correct tenses. Students then check each other's translations and provide feedback.

7 Autour du monde

7.5 Voyage dans le temps!
pages 120–121

Planner

Objectives
- Vocabulary: talk about transport in books and films
- Grammar: use different tenses
- Skills: understand more complex reading texts

Resources
- Student Book, pages 120–121
- CD 2, track 29
- Grammar and Skills Workbook, pages 14 and 43
- Kerboodle, Unit 7
- Unit 7 Worksheets 3 (ex. 2), 4 (ex. 3), 5 (ex. 1)

Key language

J'ai lu un livre qui s'appelle …

J'ai vu un film qui raconte l'histoire de …

C'était (vraiment) amusant/intéressant/génial …

Les personnages sont marrants/intéressants …

J'ai adoré le personnage principal/l'histoire/les animations.

Si tu aimes …, tu aimeras/adoreras …

Grammar
- Use different tenses

PLTS
- Activity 2: Creative thinkers
- Activity 4: Effective participators
- Plenary: Reflective learners

Homework and self-study
- Student Book, page 120, activity 1
- Student Book, page 121, activity 2
- Student Book, page 121, Plenary
- Grammar and Skills Workbook, pages 14 and 43

Starters

See Kerboodle Starters bank for further details of **Odd one out** and **Categorise**.

- Play **Odd one out** to check students' knowledge of the four different tenses: use sets of conjugated verbs, with the odd one out being in a different tense each time. Challenge students to identify both the odd tense and the majority tense in each set.
- Play **Categorise** to brainstorm positive and negative adjectives that students could use to describe their chosen book or film in activity 4 and in the Plenary. (Remove the adjectives from the board before students embark on the Plenary, to encourage them to use memorised language.)

Plenaries

- **Film/book reviews: self-assessment of written work.** Following on from the Plenary on page 121, hold a target language discussion to explore areas in which students feel they could improve their written work. Start the process by asking: *Tu amélioras ton orthographe?* Possible student responses include: *Je sais comment améliorer ma technique à l'écrit. Je peux écrire des phrases correctes/des phrases fantastiques … Je connais l'accord des noms et des adjectifs. Mon orthographe est correcte/plutôt correcte …* Take this further by encouraging students to make a list of areas for personal improvement and focusing on these in future written tasks. Personal targets for improving their writing skills could include: *Je dois écrire des mots/des phrases sans erreurs. Je dois vérifier mon orthographe*, etc.

1 Lis et trouve les expressions a–h dans le texte.
Students read the texts and find the French equivalents for the English phrases. Once students have done this, ask them to read the text again, this time paying more attention to the detail. Refer students to the glossed vocabulary and encourage them to draw on their reading strategies when decoding unknown vocabulary.

Answers: **a** *un roman d'aventures;* **b** *il raconte le voyage de Phileas Fogg;* **c** *ils ont pris le bateau;* **d** *les avions n'existaient pas;* **e** *[ils] ont voyagé pendant quatre-vingts jours;* **f** *en quelques jours;* **g** *quand Jules Verne a écrit;* **h** *si tu aimes les aventures*

⭐ Students note down the nationalities of the two main characters.

Answers: English and French

◎ 🔍 Students find examples of the four tenses used in the text. Before they do this, run through the grammar box on **Using different tenses** and check students' understanding.

Answers: **Present:** *s'appelle, il raconte, c'est, on fait, tu aimes, c'est;* **Perfect:** *j'ai lu, a fait, j'ai adoré, il est arrivé, ils ont pris, ils ont voyagé, ont voyagé, ont voyagé, a écrit;* **Imperfect:** *n'existaient pas, était;* **Future:** *tu adoreras*

⊕ t Students translate the text into English. Refer them to the grammar box and remind them to take care when translating the different tenses.

Answer: I have read an adventure novel by Jules Verne, which is called 'Around the world in 80 days'. It tells the story of the journey of Phileas Fogg, an English gentleman who went round the world with his French servant, Passepartout. I loved this book because Fogg and Passepartout had lots of adventures during their journey. They took the boat and the train because planes did not yet exist in 1870. They even travelled on elephants' backs! In the film based on the novel, the characters also travelled by hot-air balloon ... but that's just in the film, not in the novel! Fogg and Passpartout travelled for 80 days. It's quicker today because we go round the world in just a few days! When Jules Verne wrote this book, Fogg and Passepartout's journey was science fiction. If you like adventures, you will love this story! It's exciting!

2 Lis et trouve les sept erreurs dans la traduction.

Students read the French text and compare it with the English translation. They identify the seven mistakes in the translation.

Note that in the English-language version of the film *Cars*, the main character is called Lightning McQueen, but in the French version he is called Flash McQueen. Flash McQueen has been used in both the French text and the English translation to avoid confusion.

Answers (corrections underlined):

I like <u>cars</u> so I loved the series of Cars films. The hero, Flash McQueen, and the <u>main</u> characters are <u>cars</u>. A lot of adventures happen to Flash McQueen!

The <u>first</u> film was good but I preferred Cars 2 because we discover many <u>countries</u>. The <u>cars</u> travel to France, Japan, Italy and Great Britain. The story is really <u>funny</u> and the animations are fantastic. If you like cars, you will love this film! I hope there will be a sequel, Cars 3!

★ Students spot connectives in the text and provide translations for them.

Answers: donc (therefore/so), et (and), mais (but), parce qu' (because), et (and), et (and)

3 Écoute (1–5). Ils aiment a ou b? Pourquoi? Recopie et remplis la grille en anglais.

Students listen, and copy and complete the grid. They note down whether each speaker likes *Cars* (a) or *Le Tour du monde en 80 jours* (b), and their reasons.

Answers:

	Likes ...	Because ...
1	b	exciting story
2	a (Cars 2)	loves 3D films, animations were excellent
3	a (Cars 1)	loves cartoons (Cars 2 not as funny as Cars 1)
4	b	loves history, will go round the world like Fogg when has money
5	b	loves adventure novels

⊕ t Students choose three of the speakers and transcribe what they say.

CD 2, track 29   page 121, activité 3

1 Moi, j'ai préféré le livre de Jules Verne parce que l'histoire est passionnante.
2 J'ai adoré le film *Cars 2* parce que j'adore regarder des films en 3D. Les animations de *Cars 2* étaient excellentes!
3 Moi, mon film préféré c'est *Cars 1*. J'adore les films d'animation. J'ai vu *Cars 2* aussi mais c'était moins amusant.
4 J'adore l'histoire donc j'ai beaucoup aimé le livre de Jules Verne. Je ferai le tour du monde comme Fogg quand j'aurai de l'argent!
5 J'adore les romans d'aventure donc j'ai lu *Le Tour du monde en 80 jours* trois fois.

4 Présente un livre ou un film à ton/ta partenaire. Utilise les activités 1 et 2.

In pairs, students present a book or film of their own choice to each other. Do the **Categorise** starter activity to get students thinking about adjectives. Refer them also to the key language box for support and remind them to draw on the language in the texts from activities 1 and 2. Challenge more able students to include reasons for their opinions.

Plenary

Students choose either the book or the film from pages 120–121 and prepare to write about it. They write from memory a list of positive and negative adjectives to use, plus qualifiers. When they have written their texts, they swap with a partner and provide feedback to each other.

★ Students describe what the story is about.

◎ Students add whether they have read the book or seen the film.

⊕ Students add their opinion and explain why they did or didn't like it.

139

7 Autour du monde

7.6 Labo-langue

pages 122–123

Planner

Objectives
- Grammar: negatives; present tense of -ir verbs; the perfect tense and the imperfect tense; si (if) and quand (when)
- Skills: Super Strategies
- Pronunciation: u and ou

Resources
- Student Book, pages 122–123
- CD 2, tracks 30–31
- Grammar and Skills Workbook, pages 56–57
- Kerboodle, Unit 7
- Unit 7 Worksheets 7, 8

PLTS
- Creative thinkers, Reflective learners, Self-managers

Negatives

1 Translate into French.
Answers: **a** Je ne prends ni le train ni le bus. **b** Mon frère n'a jamais pris l'avion. **c** Je n'aime ni les vacances sportives ni les colonies. **d** Je ne prends plus le bateau parce que ce n'est pas pratique. **e** Si on prend l'avion, on n'aura pas de voiture. **f** Mon copain Mat n'a jamais visité Londres.

Present tense of -ir verbs

2 Choose the correct verb to complete each sentence.
Students choose the correct verb from one of the three highlighted options. As a follow-up task, ask students to translate each sentence into English.
Answers: **a** part (The train leaves at 5 p.m.) **b** choisit (My brother chooses sporty holidays.) **c** choisit (We choose the train to go to Spain.) **d** partent (My friends are leaving for England in July.) **e** choisissent (The children choose the boat.) **f** finit (The film finishes at 8 p.m.)

The perfect tense and the imperfect tense

3 Choose the correct tense to complete each sentence.
Answers: **1** je suis allé; **2** j'ai fait; **3** C'était; **4** on jouait; **5** on mangeait; **6** on visitait; **7** J'ai passé

Si (if) and quand (when)

4 Put each highlighted verb into the present tense or the future. Write out the sentences.
Ask students to compare English tenses after 'if' and 'when' with French tenses after si and quand: English uses the present tense after both 'if' and 'when', whereas French uses the future tense after 'when'.
Answers: **a** as, auras; **b** arrivera, ira; **c** veux, prendra; **d** a, fera; **e** aurai, partirai; **f** sera, visitera

Super Strategies

This section encourages students to think about strategies for identifying and applying language patterns across the four skills (listening, speaking, reading and writing). They are also encouraged to zoom in on particular points and areas where they know they often make mistakes or find things tricky. Remind students to put these strategies into action in all their receptive and productive work.

Students are encouraged to try out the new strategies in activities 3, 4 and 5 on page 117.

Pronunciation: u and ou

5 Listen (1–10) and repeat. Is it u or ou?
Answers: **1** u; **2** ou; **3** ou; **4** u; **5** u; **6** ou; **7** ou; **8** ou; **9** u; **10** u

CD 2, track 30		page 123, activité 5
1 tu	5 bus	9 polluant
2 vous	6 écoute	10 aventure
3 nous	7 je voudrais	
4 plus	8 aller-retour	

6 Listen and repeat.
To encourage students to round their lips tightly when pronouncing u, suggest imagining that they are going to whistle or blow out a candle. Also encourage them to practise in front of a mirror to make sure their lips are in the right shape, i.e. tightly rounded and pointing forwards.

CD 2, track 31	page 123, activité 6
tu as lu	vous avez attendu
je voudrais un aller-retour	nous avons vu le bus
on utilise la voiture	c'est plus polluant

7.7 Extra Star

page 124

1 Find the odd one out in each set of words. Explain in English why it is the odd one out.

For odd one out activities, emphasise to students that there are not any 'right' or 'wrong' answers: all answers will be accepted, as long as they can justify them. The most obvious answers are given here.

Answers: **a** les vacances (the others are all means of transport); **b** un voyage (the others are all types of accommodation); **c** on va (it's the only verb in the present tense); **d** polluant (others are all types of holidays); **e** ennuyeux (others are all positive)

2 This train traveller has been given the wrong ticket! Read the conversation and find the six mistakes on the ticket.

Answers: traveller's destination is Montpellier, not Lyon; should be a return ticket, not a single; the price is 75€, not 115€; it should say student price on the ticket, not full price; departure time should be shown as 11 h 45; arrival time should be shown as 15 h 55.

3 Read these holiday plans. Find the missing words 1–7 in the box.

Answers: **1** irai; **2** prendrai; **3** fait; **4** irons; **5** ferons; **6** fera; **7** verrai

t 4 Translate the text from activity 3 into English.

Answer: Next year, I will go to Guadeloupe to see my aunt who lives in Basse-Terre. I will take the plane at Paris with all my family. If the weather is nice, we will go to the beach every day and we will go diving. I hope that it will be nice weather and that I will see some dolphins!

5 Write about your holiday plans for next year.

Encourage students to cover all the bullet points, using the future tense and including *si* and *quand* structures with the correct tense.

7.7 Extra Plus

page 125

1 Trouve les paires.
Students match the French times to the digital clocks.
Answers: **1** b; **2** e; **3** f; **4** c; **5** a; **6** d

t 2 Trouve les paires et traduis les phrases en anglais.
Students match the sentence beginnings to the endings and then translate the sentences into English.
Answers: **1** c; **2** d; **3** a; **4** e; **5** b; **6** f
1 When I am 16, I will go on holiday with my friends.
2 If I go to England, I will spend two days in London.
3 If it is nice weather, we will go to the beach every day.
4 When we go to London, we will take a low-cost flight.
5 If you like animation films, you will love the film *Cars*.
6 If my brother has time, he will also visit Scotland.

3 Lis et trouve les mots (1–10).
Students read the text and fill the gaps with the correct words from the box.
Answers: **1** populaires; **2** ai; **3** s'appelle; **4** adoré; **5** avion; **6** voulait; **7** rapides; **8** plus; **9** aimes; **10** adoreras

t As a follow-up task, ask students to translate the text into English. Make sure they have filled in the gaps correctly before they do the translation.

Answer:
Modes of transport are very popular at the cinema. I have seen the 3D animation film called *Planes*. It's the first film of the *Planes* trilogy.

I loved the main character who is called Dusty Crophopper. He's a little plane who is always a bit sad. In the first film, he wanted to fly with the fastest planes and be champion. His best friend was called Skipper. He was an old plane who no longer worked because he had retired.

The second film tells the story of Dusty, who decides to become a firefighter so that he can save his little airport! If you like animation films, you will love this film!

4 Écris un blog sur les vacances.
Students write a blog describing last year's holiday, next year's holiday and their dream holiday. Encourage them to use all four tenses if possible and to include at least two sentences using *si* and two using *quand*.

7 Autour du monde

7.8 Lire
page 126

Resources
- Student Book, page 126
- Kerboodle, Unit 7

PLTS
- Independent enquirers

1 *Planète Jeune* is a travel and discovery magazine for young people. For each idea in the editor's mind map, find the corresponding paragraph in the text advertising this issue.

Answers: **1** transport/technologie – Est-ce que les automobiles de demain se conduiront seules?; **2** bracelets et colliers: que signifient-ils pour les jeunes? – Les ados du monde; **3** jeunes Français au Japon – carnet de voyage; **4** Paul et Jeanne L + enfants – direction le soleil et le sable chaud …; **5** jeunes musiciens en Afrique – Une belle leçon d'espoir

2 Advertising texts often talk to the reader directly, using words such as 'you', 'us' and 'our'. Find examples of *te/t'* and *nous* in the text. Copy out the phrases and translate them into English.

Answers: Planète Jeune te propose de tenter l'expérience – Planète Jeune gives you the chance to experience it; tu trouveras dans l'article un lien pour le site web – you will find a link to the website in the article; De drôles de vacances qu'ils nous font partager – An unusual holiday that they're going to share with us; Dominique t'invite à assister aux répétitions – Dominique invites you to attend his rehearsals; Les ados du monde nous montrent les accessoires qu'ils portent au poignet ou autour du cou – The teenagers of the world show us the accessories they wear on their wrist or around their neck; Ils nous ont envoyé un carnet de voyage – They sent us a travel journal

3 True or false? For the false statements, find words from the text to justify your answer.
Answers: **a** false – sur simulateur, bien entendu; **b** false – Pas de chameaux; **c** true; **d** true; **e** false – Il habite à Kinshasa; **f** true

7.8 Vidéo
page 127

Resources
- Student Book, page 127
- Kerboodle, Unit 7 Video clip

PLTS
- Independent enquirers

Épisode 7: Se déplacer à Montpellier
To undertake the next challenge of the competition, the friends have to try to use as many modes of transport as possible within half an hour. For each environmentally-friendly mode of transport they will receive double points. They split into two groups (girls and boys) and set off. The girls take the tram and the bus, and finally run too. The boys use hire bikes, and then Segways. Jules, however, trumps them all – he phones them at the end of the half-hour from a plane!

Video clip, Unit 7   page 127

(*In gardens close to* Place de la Comédie)
Zaied: Jules, c'est quoi, le prochain défi? Je suis très impatient!
Thouraya: Oui, ce concours est vraiment extra.
Max: Écoutez donc. Jules va nous lire le défi.
Jules: « À Montpellier il y a plusieurs moyens de transport et beaucoup sont écologiques. Combien de moyens de transport pouvez-vous utiliser en une demi-heure? Vous recevrez un point pour chaque moyen de transport utilisé et deux points s'il est écologique! »
Jémilie: Excellent, et on peut travailler en équipe.
Jules: 3, 2, 1. C'est parti! *(Blows whistle)*

(*In* Place de la Comédie)

Clarisse: Les transports en commun comme le tramway sont pratiques et moins polluant que la voiture.
Jémilie: Et moins chers aussi.
Thouraya: Venez, on va prendre le tramway.

(At the ticket machine)

Clarisse: Un aller simple coûte combien?
Jémilie: Un aller simple coûte 1,50 euros.
Thouraya: Est-ce qu'il y a un tarif spécial pour les jeunes?
Jémilie: C'est gratuit jusqu'à l'âge de trois ans. Et il y a un ticket avec dix voyages pour 10 euros.
Clarisse: On va prendre ça, alors, parce que après, on va prendre le bus.
Jémilie: D'accord.
Basile: Moi, je préfère prendre mon skate pour aller à l'école. C'est beaucoup plus pratique et plus écologique que d'aller en voiture avec mon père.
Maxime: Ça me fait penser … Les Vélomaggs. Et si on louait des Vélomaggs?
Jules: J'ai une autre idée. Je vous rejoindrai plus tard.
Maxime: D'accord. À tout à l'heure.
Thouraya: Les tramways à Montpellier sont aussi très beaux car chaque ligne a un dessin et une couleur différente.
Zaied: Ça coûte combien pour louer un Vélomagg?
Maxime: Ça coûte 1,50 euros pour une heure, mais il faut payer par carte bleue.
(*Maxime and Basile get on bikes*)
Maxime: Allez, Zaied, on y va.
Zaied: Mais je ne sais pas monter à vélo!

(At the bus stop)

Clarisse.: Les bus à Montpellier sont très écologiques.
Thouraya: Ah oui, ils roulent au gaz naturel.
Jémilie: Et on peut utiliser le même ticket que pour le tramway.

(Boys on Segways)

Zaied: Alors, tu parles! Le Segway, c'est super.
Basile: Ah oui, on peut faire le tour de Montpellier en Segway.
Maxime: C'est rapide et moins polluant qu'une voiture ou un taxi.
Zaied: C'est le meilleur moyen de transport.
Jémilie: On a cinq minutes pour rejoindre les autres. Courez.
Thouraya: Courir, c'est très rapide et super écolo.
Jémilie: Mais très fatigant.

(Boys arrive back where they left Jules)

Jémilie: On a gagné?
Basile: Mais il est où, Jules?
Clarisse: Il n'est pas avec vous?
(*Maxime's phone rings*)
Jules: Salut l'équipe.
Thouraya: Où es-tu, Jules?
Jules: Je suis dans un avion.
Thouraya: Mais ce n'est pas très écologique, Jules.
Jules: Non, mais c'est très rapide, super moderne et il y a un aéroport à Montpellier. C'est le meilleur moyen de transport. À demain!
Clarisse: Mais qui a gagné le défi?
Maxime: Je pense que c'est Jules qui a gagné.
Thouraya: Mais ce n'est pas écolo du tout!

1 Regarde l'épisode 7. Quel moyen de transport gagne <u>deux</u> points?

Students watch the video and decide which type of transport will gain two points. Make sure students realise they are looking for a general type of transport rather than a specific mode.

Answer: un moyen de transport écologique

2 C'est quel moyen de transport? Trouve les paires.

Students match the photos with the French modes of transport.

Answers: **a** le tramway; **b** le skateboard; **c** le Vélomagg'; **d** le bus; **e** le Segway; **f** la voiture; **g** le taxi; **h** courir; **i** l'avion

3 Réponds aux questions en anglais.

Students answer the questions in English. They could attempt this activity from memory and then watch the video again to check their answers.

Answers: **a** because they want to take the bus afterwards, and the tickets can be used for both; **b** by skateboard; **c** each line is a different colour and has different artwork on the side; **d** 1,50 euro an hour; **e** he says he can't ride a bike; **f** Segway; **g** running; **h** by plane

7 Autour du monde

4 Quel est le moyen de transport le plus écologique en ville, à ton avis? Pourquoi?
In groups, students discuss which modes of transport about town they consider to be the most environmentally friendly. Encourage them to give reasons for their opinions and to use comparatives where appropriate.

7.9 Test
page 128

Resources
- Student Book, page 128
- CD 2, track 32

PLTS
- Creative thinkers, Reflective learners, Effective participators

AT levels
Approximate medal guidelines:
- (Foundation) L: 3; S: 4; R: 4; W: 4
- (Core) L: 3–4; S: 4–5; R: 5; W: 5
- (Higher) L: 4; S: 5; R: 6; W: 6

1 Listen (1–4). How do they travel to school? How do they like to travel on holiday? Copy and fill in the grid. (See pages 112–113.)
Answers:

	Transport to school	Holiday transport	Reasons
1	bus, car	plane	loves plane because very fast
2	bike	train, boat	train is more relaxing (but it's a bit expensive)
3	bus	plane	fast, practical (but expensive)
4	tube/underground	car	less polluting than plane

CD 2, track 32   page 128, activitié 1

1 – Bonjour, Clément, tu utilises quel moyen de transport d'habitude?
   – Moi, je prends le bus et la voiture pour aller au collège mais j'adore prendre l'avion quand on part en vacances parce que c'est très rapide pour voyager.
2 – Et toi, Lucile?
   – Moi, je prends le vélo pour aller au collège mais je préfère prendre le train ou le bateau quand on va en vacances en famille!
   – Ah oui … et pourquoi?
   – Le train, c'est plus relaxant … mais c'est un peu cher!
3 – Et toi, Marie, tu aimes prendre le train pour partir en vacances?
   – Non, moi, je préfère prendre l'avion parce que c'est pratique et rapide. Par contre, c'est cher. Tous les jours, je prends le bus pour aller au collège.
4 – Et toi, Jamel?
   – Moi, je préfère prendre la voiture quand je pars en vacances parce que c'est moins polluant que l'avion. Mais quand je vais au collège, je prends le métro tous les jours.

2 Prepare a short talk about holidays. (See pages 115–117.)
Students prepare a presentation, drawing on the key language covered in the unit. They use the present, past and future tenses and should try to include structures with *si* and *quand*.

3 Read Zaied's email and answer the questions in English. (See pages 118–119.)
Answers: **a** two weeks; **b** train and boat, because plane was too expensive; **c** no, it was too long and he was ill on the boat because the sea was rough; **d** the rooms weren't ready, had to wait for two hours; **e** visited Brighton, went on excursions, took some fantastic photos; **f** go back to England and visit London

4 Write about a past holiday that you enjoyed and a holiday you will have when you are eighteen. (See pages 116–119.)
Encourage students to cover as many of the bullet points as they can and to use the full range of tenses. Remind them to develop their writing as much as possible, extending their answers by using connectives and giving reasons for their opinions.

8 Chez moi, ça veut dire quoi?

Unit 8: Chez moi, ça veut dire quoi? Overview grid

Page reference	Contexts and objectives	Grammar	Strategies and skills	Key language	AT levels*
130–131 **8.1 Un toit à moi**	Describe what type of home you live in	y Present tense with depuis	Translation strategies Super Strategies	J'habite dans une caravane/une cabane/une yourte/un igloo/une hutte en terre/un appartement/une maison jumelée/une cité/la banlieue de Paris/un bidonville. J'habite sur une péniche/la rivière. J'y habite depuis …	L: 3–4 S: 3–4 R: 4 W: 3–4
132–133 **8.2 Dessine-moi une maison!**	Describe rooms in a house	Regular -re verbs in the present tense	Recognise and compare writing styles	la salle de bains (attenante), les WC, la cuisine, la chambre de mon frère/de ma sœur/d'amis/de mes parents, l'entrée, la buanderie, le garage, le bureau, la véranda, le jardin, la salle à manger, le séjour Au rez-de-chaussée/A l'étage/A gauche/A droite/En face/A côté/Entre et … il y a/on a/nous avons/se trouve … D'abord, … Puis, … Ensuite, … Après, … Pour finir, …	L: 4–6 S: 3–4 R: 4–5 W: 3–4
134–135 **8.3 Ne pas déranger!**	Describe a bedroom, items in it and their location	Prepositions	Extending your range of vocabulary Debate a point	une table de nuit, une lampe de chevet, un lit, un bureau, une chaise pivotante, un ordi, une lampe de bureau, une étagère, une console de jeux vidéo, un fauteuil poire le coin nuit, le coin divertissement, le coin travail sur, sous, devant, derrière, à côté, en face, entre Je (ne) partage (pas) ma chambre. J'ai une chambre à moi. Je suis pour/contre parce que … Ça rapproche. On rigole. On apprend à cohabiter. On n'est jamais seul. On se dispute. C'est facile/difficile pour les devoirs. On a un espace privé. On est obligé de supporter les mauvaises habitudes de l'autre.	L: 3–5 S: 3–4 R: 3–6 W: 3–5
136–137 **8.4 La maison de mes rêves**	Describe the type of home you would like to have	Si clauses + imperfect tense and conditional	Develop knowledge of connectives to extend sentences	Si j'avais de l'argent, j'aurais … Si j'avais … Si j'étais riche, j'achèterais … Si j'étais riche, je voudrais acheter … Si je gagnais à la loterie, j'aimerais faire construire … un loft en ville, une péniche sur la Seine, une maison sur la plage, un chalet à la montagne, une villa dans la banlieue de Paris, une grande ferme à la campagne S'il/Si elle était/avait/gagnait …, il/elle habiterait dans …/… il/elle achèterait/aurait/aimerait … Ce serait grand/beau/moderne … Il y aurait … parce que/car …	L: 5–6 S: 5–6 R: 5–6 W: 5–6
138–139 **8.5 Chez moi, ça m'inspire!**	Describe places in detail and express how you feel about them	Work with different structures from the unit	Memorisation strategies Extend your range of vocabulary		L: 3–4 S: 3–4 R: 5–6 W: 4–6
140–141 **8.6 Labo-langue**	Grammar, language strategies and pronunciation	Regular -re verbs in the present tense Prepositions Si clauses + imperfect and conditional	Super Strategies Pronunciation: i and y		
142–147 **8.7 Extra Star, Extra Plus 8.8 Lire, Vidéo 8.9 Test, Vocabulaire**	Reinforcement and extension; reading material; activities based on the video material; revision and assessment		**Lire:** R: 6–7 **Vidéo:** L: 4–6; S: 4–5		**Test:** L: 5–6 S: 4–6 R: 5–6 W: 4–6

*See teacher notes for alternative assessment criteria. Guidelines for the various assessment options are provided in the introduction of this Teacher Handbook.

8 Chez moi, ça veut dire quoi?

Unit 8: Week-by-week overview

(**Three-year KS3 route: assuming six weeks' work or approximately 10–12.5 hours**)
(**Two-year KS3 route: assuming four weeks' work or approximately 6.5–8.5 hours**)

About Unit 8, Chez moi, ça veut dire quoi?: In this unit, students work in the context of houses and homes: they describe what type of home they live in, the rooms in a house, a bedroom (including furniture and other items and their location) and the type of home they would like to have. They also describe places in detail and express how they feel about them.

Students revisit *y*, this time using it to say where they live and since when (using *depuis* + the present tense). They extend their knowledge of regular *-re* verbs in the present tense and consolidate their use of the perfect and imperfect tenses. *Si* clauses are revisited, this time giving students the opportunity to use them with the imperfect tense and the conditional. Students also work on prepositions, using them to describe the location of items in a room.

There is a focus again on Super Strategies in this unit, which students can apply this time when working out meaning when reading and when memorising difficult language. Translation skills are also reinforced, and students are given the opportunity to develop their writing skills via strategies to extend vocabulary and to extend sentences by using connectives. A literacy strand is present throughout the unit, allowing students a chance to recognise and compare writing styles, whilst students' spoken productive work is enhanced by skills to debate a point. The pronunciation point focuses on *i* and *y*.

Three-year KS3 route

Week	Resources
	*Material from the end-of-unit pages (**8.7 Extra Star/Plus**, **8.8 Lire** and **Vidéo**) may be used during week 6 or selectively during weeks 1–5 as time permits.*
1	8.1 Un toit à moi 8.6 Labo-langue, Super Strategies
2	8.2 Dessine-moi une maison! 8.6 Labo-langue, activity 1
3	8.3 Ne pas déranger! 8.6 Labo-langue, activity 2
4	8.4 La maison de mes rêves 8.6 Labo-langue, activity 3 8.6 Labo-langue, Pronunciation: *i* and *y*
5	8.5 Chez moi, ça m'inspire!
6	8.7 Extra Star, Extra Plus 8.8 Lire 8.8 Vidéo 8.9 Test 8.9 Vocabulaire

Two-year KS3 route

Week	Resources
	*Material from the end-of-unit pages (**8.7 Extra Star/Plus**, **8.8 Lire** and **Vidéo**) may be used selectively during weeks 1–4 as time permits.*
1	8.1 Un toit à moi 8.6 Labo-langue, Super Strategies
2	8.2 Dessine-moi une maison! 8.6 Labo-langue, activity 1
3	8.3 Ne pas déranger! 8.6 Labo-langue, activity 2
4	8.4 La maison de mes rêves (Omit activity 4) 8.6 Labo-langue, activity 3 8.6 Labo-langue, Pronunciation: *i* and *y* 8.9 Test 8.9 Vocabulaire

8.1 Un toit à moi

pages 130–131

Planner

Objectives
- Vocabulary: describe what type of home you live in
- Grammar: use *y*; use the present tense with *depuis*
- Skills: develop translation strategies; use Super Strategies

Resources
- Student Book, pages 130–131
- CD 2, track 33
- Grammar and Skills Workbook, pages 22, 25, 40 and 59
- Kerboodle, Unit 8

Key language

J'habite dans une caravane/une cabane/ une yourte/un igloo/une hutte en terre/ un appartement/une maison jumelée/une cité/ la banlieue de Paris/un bidonville. J'habite sur une péniche/la rivière. J'y habite depuis ...

Grammar
- *y*
- *Present tense with depuis*

PLTS and Numeracy
- Activity 3: Effective participators, Team workers
- Activity 5: Self-managers
- Activity 6: Creative thinkers
- Numeracy: Activity 3: presenting survey results in a chart or graph

Homework and self-study
- Student Book, page 131, activity 4
- Student Book, page 131, activity 5
- Student Book, page 131, activity 6
- Grammar and Skills Workbook, pages 22, 25 and 40

Starters

See Kerboodle Starters bank for further details of **Dominoes** and **Up, down**.

- Play **Dominoes** to revise the vocabulary for accommodation types and areas to live from *Allez 1*, Unit 3: *une maison individuelle, une maison jumelée, un appartement, un pavillon, à la campagne, à la montagne, en ville, dans un village, en banlieue.*
- Play **Up, down** to reinforce students' knowledge of *y* and *depuis*. Play the recording from activity 2 and ask students to stand up every time they hear a phrase containing *y* or *depuis*.

Plenaries

- **La Plenum-Pyramide**. Remind students of their work on comparisons on spread 7.1 (page 112) and encourage them to reflect on the value of comparing: *Tu as fait une comparaison (Plenary, page 131). C'est important de faire des comparaisons? On doit souvent comparer des choses dans la vie? On doit comparer les maisons des enfants qui vivent dans d'autres pays du monde avec les maisons d'ici? Pourquoi? Dessine une pyramide et cite trois choses que tu as apprises, deux choses que tu dois faire pour améliorer ton travail et une question.*

  If it is too difficult for some students to conduct this plenary in French, ask them to consider in English how their minds have been changed during their work on this unit.

1 Trouve les paires.

Do the **Dominoes** starter activity to revise the conventional accommodation types covered in *Allez 1*, Unit 3, before students read the French terms and match them to the correct photos. Remind them to use their reading strategies when working out the meaning of the French terms: cognates and near-cognates, familiar language, picture clues, etc. Once they have done this, ask them, in pairs, to try to work out the English equivalent for each accommodation type. Then hold a class discussion about the various accommodation types presented here and how they differ from each other. Can students identify what types might exist in Britain and France, and which might be more likely to be found in other parts of the world, such as in developing countries? Remind them to use their cultural awareness strategies and to draw on what they know of the world in general.

Answers: **a** 6; **b** 5; **c** 4; **d** 7; **e** 3; **f** 2; **g** 1; **h** 8

8 Chez moi, ça veut dire quoi?

2 Écoute (1–8). Où habitent-ils? Recopie et remplis la grille.

Students listen, and copy and complete the grid in English.

Students add any extra details they hear in the recording (i.e. more exact details about where they live). For this part of the activity, refer students to the phrases in the prompts box. These terms are all mentioned in the recording; ask students to work in pairs to decode them, using a dictionary if necessary, and then check answers with the class before playing the recording again. NB: point out to students that *une cité* is a false friend (not a city, but a housing estate).

t Students choose three people and transcribe what they say.

Answers:

	Where?	When?/For how long?	Extra details
1	a flat	since two years old	housing estate in Paris suburbs
2	sometimes in a modern house, sometimes in an igloo	lives in igloo when travelling	lives in north of Canada
3	mud hut	has always lived there	lives in Senegal, West Africa
4	yurt	lives there in winter	lives in Mongolia; a yurt is a traditional tent; lives in town in the summer
5	caravan	for three years	lives there with family
6	houseboat	for ten years	on the Mekong river in Vietnam
7	semi-detached house	for six months	lives in Leeds, England
8	shack	for four years	lives in shantytown in Port-au-Prince, Haiti

CD 2, track 33   page 130, activité 2

1 Salut! Je m'appelle Nico. J'habite dans un appartement dans une cité, dans la banlieue de Paris. J'y habite depuis l'âge de deux ans.
2 Parfois, tu habites dans une maison moderne. Parfois, tu habites dans un igloo, dans le nord du Canada. Tu y habites quand tu voyages.
3 Il habite dans une hutte en terre au Sénégal, en Afrique de l'Ouest. Il y habite depuis toujours.
4 Elle habite dans une yourte, une tente traditionnelle, en Mongolie. Elle y habite en hiver. En été, elle habite en ville.
5 Nous habitons dans une caravane, ma famille et moi. Nous y habitons depuis trois ans.
6 Vous habitez sur une péniche sur la rivière Mékong, au Vietnam. Vous y habitez depuis dix ans.
7 Ils habitent dans une maison jumelée à Leeds, en Angleterre. Ils y habitent depuis six mois.
8 Elles habitent dans une cabane dans un bidonville à Port-au-Prince, en Haïti. Elles y habitent depuis quatre ans.

3 Sondage: « Où habites-tu? »

In groups, students choose a home from those in activity 1 and take turns to survey their group about where everyone lives. Encourage students to choose a different home each time they are surveyed, as this will extend their practice of the vocabulary. Students note down the answers they are given and write a short report detailing the results. They could also present their results in the form of a bar or pie chart. To aid students in their spoken work, refer them to the conjugation of *habiter* in the grammar box on **J'y habite depuis** ... To reinforce students' knowledge of this, play the recording from activity 2 again and ask students to note down all the different conjugated examples of *habiter* that they hear.

Students add more details, including how long they have lived there. For this, they will need to use *y* and *depuis*. Run through the grammar box on **J'y habite depuis** ... Remind students that they have already come across the pronoun *y* (meaning 'there') in the context of going somewhere. This time, it is being used in the context of living somewhere. Check students' understanding of *depuis* (covered in *Allez 1*, in the context of how long you have known someone (Unit 2), and in the context of how long you have been doing certain sports (Unit 8)), and remind them to use the present tense with *depuis*. Then do the **Up, down** starter activity to consolidate students' recognition of this structure.

4 Trouve les expressions a–g dans les paragraphes 1–5.

Students read the five paragraphs and find the French equivalents for the English phrases. Before they do so, refer them to the section on **Super Strategies** on page 141. Here, they are given advice on combining Super Strategies when reading: looking for cognates, and combining this with what they already know, their knowledge of the world and the context. Encourage them to use these strategies when decoding vocabulary in activity 4.

Answers: **a** *rapide et peu chère à construire;* **b** *construites en brique et en bois;* **c** *construite avec des blocs de neige compacte;* **d** *une tente traditionnelle en peau d'animal ou en feutre;* **e** *construite avec des matériaux récupérés;* **f** *le manque d'hygiène;* **g** *peuvent être utilisées comme moyen de transport*

Students add two more English phrases (h and i) for their partner to find in the texts and make a note of the answers.

As a Gold medal follow-up activity, ask students to analyse their answers to activity 4, reflecting on whether there was a 'clue' or 'trigger' word that helped them find the French for each expression.

5 Relis les paragraphes 1–5.

Before students start this activity, refer them to the skills box on **Translation strategies**. Ask them to follow these tips when translating the texts and also to refer to the section on **Super Strategies** on page 141.

- **t** Students translate two of the paragraphs into English.
- **t** Students translate three or more paragraphs.

Answers:

1 *I live in a mud hut in the countryside in Senegal, in West Africa. I have always lived here. A mud hut is quick and cheap to build. In town it is different. The houses are modern and built of brick and wood.*

2 *Usually I live in a modern house but sometimes, when we go on hunting trips, I live in an igloo, in the north of Canada. I have lived there since the age of eleven. An igloo is a small circular house built with blocks of compacted snow.*

3 *I live in a yurt (a traditional tent made of animal skin or felt) in Mongolia. Yurts are the traditional dwellings/homes of Mongolian and Turkish nomads from Central Asia. I have always lived here ... but only in winter. In summer, my family and I live in a house in town.*

4 *I live in a shack in a shantytown in Port-au-Prince, in Haiti. My shack is built with recycled materials.*

I have lived here since I was six months old. Here, there is rubbish in the streets and the lack of hygiene is a big problem.

5 *I live on a houseboat on the Mekong river in Vietnam. A houseboat is a boat with a flat bottom. Houseboats can be used as a means of transport but they are often used as permanent places to live. I have lived here for ten years.*

6 Écris un paragraphe: « Les Maisons du monde ».
Students write a paragraph about different types of home around the world. They include a description of their own home. For a Bronze medal, students use phrases from pages 130–131; for a Silver medal they use and <u>adapt</u> phrases; and for a Gold medal, they write sentences using *On habite* ... and add their own ideas.

Plenary

When undertaking the medal activities, students think about young people living in other parts of the world and how their lives might be affected by different weather conditions.

- ★ Students list as many different types of homes as they can.
- ◯ Students give a description of one of them.
- ✚ Students add what type of home they live in and how long they have been living there. They compare it with one of the other homes they have learnt about on pages 130–131.

8.2 Dessine-moi une maison!

pages 132–133

Planner

Objectives
- Vocabulary: describe rooms in a house
- Grammar: use regular -re verbs in the present tense
- Skills: recognise and compare writing styles

Resources
- Student Book, pages 132–133
- CD 2, track 34
- Grammar and Skills Workbook, pages 27–28
- Kerboodle, Unit 8
- Unit 8 Worksheets 4 (ex. 3), 5 (ex. 1)

Key language
la salle de bains (attenante), les WC, la cuisine, la chambre de mon frère/ma sœur, la chambre d'amis, la chambre de mes parents, l'entrée, la buanderie, le garage, le bureau, la véranda, le jardin, la salle à manger, le séjour

Au rez-de-chaussée/À l'étage/À gauche/À droite/ En face/À côté/Entre ... et ...,

... il y a/on a/nous avons/se trouve ...

D'abord, ... Puis, ... Ensuite, ... Après, ... Pour finir, ...

Grammar
- Regular -re verbs in the present tense

PLTS
- Activity 3: Team workers
- Activity 4: Independent enquirers
- Plenary: Reflective learners, Self-managers

Homework and self-study
- Student Book, page 133, activity 4
- Student Book, page 133, activity 5
- Grammar and Skills Workbook, pages 27–28

8 Chez moi, ça veut dire quoi?

> **Starters**
> See Kerboodle Starters bank for further details of **Dominoes** and **Word tennis**.
> - Play **Dominoes** to help students learn the various rooms and areas of a house, as presented in activity 1.
> - Play **Word tennis** to help reinforce the endings of -re verbs. Students work in pairs and take turns to say each form of the verb *prendre*. Do the same with *vendre*, once covered.
>
> **Plenaries**
> - **Analysing different styles of writing**. Students reflect on their reading skills in English and discuss the following questions in pairs:
> - Does the knowledge they have gained from reading a wide range of texts (in other subjects as well) improve their understanding of structure, vocabulary, grammar and punctuation?
> - How quickly do they recognise the style of writing and <u>how</u> do they do this? (Encourage students to think about their skills of looking at the layout, headings and subheadings, picture clues, etc.)
>
> The first part of this plenary may have to be conducted in English but encourage simple target language phrases to be used where possible: *J'ai bien regardé le contexte/le style/ le plan. Pour mieux comprendre les mots nouveaux, j'ai fait des suppositions ...*

1 Voilà le plan de la nouvelle maison de Nina. Lis et relie. 🔑
Students look at the house plan and match the French terms to the correct numbered rooms or areas on the plan. Remind them to use their strategies for decoding unknown vocabulary, such as identifying cognates and near-cognates, looking for familiar language and using context and general knowledge to help them.
Answers: **1** f *(l'entrée);* **2** c *(la cuisine);* **3** m *(la salle à manger);* **4** g *(la buanderie);* **5** h *(le garage);* **6** b *(les WC);* **7** n *(le séjour);* **8** k *(la véranda);* **9** l *(le jardin);* **10** e *(la chambre de mes parents);* **11** j *(la chambre d'amis/le bureau);* **12** i *(la chambre de ma sœur);* **13** a *(la salle de bains);* **14** d *(la chambre de mon frère)*

2 Nina décrit sa nouvelle maison. Écoute et vérifie tes réponses (activité 1).
Students listen to Nina talking her friend Conrad through a guided video tour of her new home. Students listen for the names of the rooms and their numbers, which correspond to the plan on page 132 (and which Nina has also emailed to Conrad). They check their answers to activity 1.

⊙ Students listen to the recording again and note down what Nina says at the beginning that she has done.
Answer: She's made a plan of her house and a video to show what her new home is like.

⊕ Students note down what Nina would like her bedroom to have.
Answer: An en-suite bathroom like her parents'.

🎵 **CD 2, track 34   page 132, activity 2**

Salut, Conrad. C'est Nina. Tu me manques drôlement. Me voilà devant ma nouvelle maison. J'ai fait un plan de la maison et une petite vidéo pour te faire voir mon nouveau « chez moi ».

Alors ... on va commencer au rez-de-chaussée. D'abord, il y a le numéro un, l'entrée ... et puis à droite, on a le numéro deux, la cuisine. C'est une cuisine ouverte sur le numéro trois, la salle à manger. À côté de la cuisine, il y a le numéro quatre, la buanderie ... et le cinq, c'est le garage.
Ensuite, je passe devant les WC (c'est le numéro six) et après, nous avons ... le numéro sept, le séjour. C'est sympa, hein? ... Et là, si j'ouvre la fenêtre, on peut voir la véranda (le numéro huit) et le jardin (le neuf). Maintenant, je vais monter à l'étage. À gauche, nous avons la chambre de mes parents, c'est le numéro dix. À côté de la chambre de mes parents se trouve la chambre d'amis ou le bureau. C'est le numéro onze. Et en face de la chambre de mes parents, il y a le numéro douze, la chambre de ma sœur. La salle de bains (numéro treize) est entre la chambre de ma sœur et la chambre de mon frère (le quatorze). Et, pour finir, il y a ma chambre. J'aimerais bien avoir une salle de bains attenante ... comme mes parents. Voilà, c'est tout. J'espère que tu as aimé la visite virtuelle de chez moi et que tu vas venir bientôt. Salut!

3 À deux. A décrit sa maison et B dessine! A ↔ B.
Before students embark on this activity, do the **Dominoes** starter activity, to help students learn the various rooms and areas of the house presented in activity 1. In pairs, students then describe the layout of their own home to their partner, who draws a plan of it. Refer them to the key language box which will help them to describe the location and order of the rooms.

4 Lis le texte de Louka. Trouve les expressions a–f qui sont <u>soulignées</u> dans le texte. 🔑
Students read the text about Louka's move to a new city. They match the underlined phrases in the text to their English equivalents. Once they have done this, refer students to the grammar box on **Regular -re verbs in the present tense** and check their

understanding. Ask them if they can think of another -re verb that they already know (*prendre*), and explain that *vendre* takes the same endings. Ask them to read through the text again, this time spotting the examples of -re verbs (*nous vendons, on vend, je prends*). Then do the **Word tennis** starter activity to reinforce students' knowledge of the verb endings.

Draw students' attention to the use of *depuis* and the imperfect tense in *l'appart que j'habitais depuis dix ans*. Elicit from students what they already know about *depuis* (refer them back to page 130 if they need a reminder) and then explain that it can also be used with the imperfect tense to describe a continuous action further back in the past

As a follow-up activity, elicit from students the difference in use between the two past tenses (perfect and imperfect): the perfect tense is used for describing completed actions in the past, whilst the imperfect is used for describing feeling and emotions in the past. Ask them then to read the text again, this time finding examples of both tenses and explaining why each example is in the perfect tense or the imperfect (refer them back to Unit 7, pages 118–123, if they need a reminder). They could do this in pairs or in small groups.

Answers: **a** *l'appart que j'habitais depuis dix ans;* **b** *J'étais beaucoup plus à l'aise;* **c** *J'avais peur de quitter;* **d** *ce changement a été difficile mais pas impossible;* **e** *mon père m'a aidé à m'inscrire au club de foot de la région;* **f** *nous avons fait quelques voyages pour explorer Marseille*

To exploit the text further, give students the following statements and ask them to identify whether they are true (*vrai*), false (*faux*) or not mentioned in the text (*pas mentionné*):

a Louka was scared to leave Paris, his apartment and his friends.

b Before the move, he visited his new school and the new apartment.

c Louka's father helped him to join a basketball club.

d Shopping for things for his room made him more enthusiastic about the move.

e Louka told all his friends he was moving.

⭐ Students correct the false sentences.

◎ Students make up some new questions of their own for their partner.

➕ **t** Students choose a paragraph and translate it into English.

Answers: **a** *vrai;* **b** *faux (before the move, he visited his new school and the new <u>house</u>);* **c** *faux (his father helped him to join a <u>football</u> club);* **d** *pas mentionné;* **e** *pas mentionné*

Translation: One Saturday last year, my parents came to talk to me in my room in our apartment in Paris.

"Louka, I've found a new job. We're selling the apartment and moving," said my father.

"What? We're selling the apartment? To go where?" I asked.

"To Marseille," he replied.

At first, I was shocked. I was scared of leaving Paris, of leaving the apartment I had lived in for 10 years. I was scared of leaving my classmates and my football friends.

Before the move, we had a few trips to explore Marseille. I was a lot more comfortable because I visited my new school and my new house. My father helped me to join the local football club. Next, I went shopping for my new room with my mother.

It's true that moving house can be stressful. For my parents and me, this change was difficult but not impossible. Marseille is tremendous and I keep in contact with my friends from Paris. I have the best of both worlds!

5 Décris ces propriétés (a et b).

Students read the notices and write a description of each of the properties advertised for sale. Encourage students to be as expansive as possible in their writing and to refer to the key language box for support when describing the location of the rooms.

⭐ Students list the rooms.

◎ Students imagine and describe the layout of the building.

➕ Students use sequencers to develop their description.

Different styles of writing

Students look at the texts in activities 4 and 5. Elicit from students what types of texts they think they are before they start reading them and how they differ from each other: i.e. the abbreviated style of the property adverts is very different from the narrative style of Louka's text about moving house. Refer students also to the house plan on page 132 and discuss with them how it conveys information in a graphic form rather than in writing.

It would be worth returning to this section later on in the unit, after students have worked on the haiku poems (page 138) and descriptions of paintings (page 139). It would also be worthwhile comparing the type of language used in a debate (page 135) with the language of a property advertisement or a poem/ piece of descriptive writing.

t If appropriate for the class, compare the style of punctuation in French direct speech (see the short excerpt in *SOS déménagement*) with English punctuation. Students may have covered this in English lessons. If so, they could translate this excerpt of direct speech into English, changing the French style of punctuation to English style.

8 Chez moi, ça veut dire quoi?

French style:

« Louka, j'ai trouvé un nouvel emploi. Nous vendons l'appartement et nous déménageons, a dit mon père.
— Quoi? On vend l'appart? Pour aller où?, j'ai demandé.
— À Marseille », a-t-il répondu.

English style:

"Louka, I've found a new job. We're selling the flat and moving," said my father.
"What? We're selling the flat? To go where?" I asked.
"To Marseille," he replied.

> **Plenary**
>
> Students reflect on what they can now say and write in French that they couldn't before. They analyse their progress and set themselves a target to help them improve.
>
> ⭐ Students list as many different rooms as they can.
>
> ⊙ Students use simple sentences to say what rooms they have in their home.
>
> ➕ Students describe the layout of their home, adding extra details, such as which floor the rooms are on. They use sequencers and imagine they are giving a guided tour.

8.3 Ne pas déranger! pages 134–135

Planner

Objectives

- Vocabulary: describe a bedroom
- Grammar: use prepositions
- Skills: extend your range of vocabulary; debate a point

Resources

- Student Book, pages 134–135
- CD 2, tracks 35–36
- Grammar and Skills Workbook, page 21
- Kerboodle, Unit 8
- Unit 8 Worksheets 3 (ex. 2–3), 4 (ex. 2), 5 (ex. 2), 6 (ex. 1)

Key language

une table de nuit, une lampe de chevet, un lit, un bureau, une chaise pivotante, un ordi, une lampe de bureau, une étagère, une console de jeux vidéo, un fauteuil poire

le coin nuit, le coin divertissement, le coin travail

sur, sous, devant, derrière, à côté, en face, entre

Je (ne) partage (pas) ma chambre. J'ai une chambre à moi. Je suis pour/contre parce que …

Ça rapproche. On rigole. On apprend à cohabiter. On n'est jamais seul. On se dispute. C'est facile/difficile pour les devoirs. On a un espace privé. On est obligé de supporter les mauvaises habitudes de l'autre.

Grammar

- Prepositions

PLTS

- Activity 4: Independent enquirers
- Activity 7: Effective participators
- Plenary: Reflective learners, Self-managers

Homework and self-study

- Student Book, page 134, activity 3
- Student Book, page 135, activity 4
- Student Book, page 135, activity 6
- Grammar and Skills Workbook, page 21

Starters

See Kerboodle Starters bank for further details of **Dominoes** and **Word tennis**.

- Play **Dominoes** to revise and check understanding of the prepositions presented in the grammar box.
- Play **Word tennis** to consolidate students' knowledge of the items in a bedroom.

Plenaries

- **Sticky notes**. After students have completed the Plenary on page 135, ask them to use target language phrases for their written feedback to their partners: *Ton orthographe est … Tu peux écrire des phrases correctes. Tu connais l'accord des noms et des adjectifs. Tu sais comment améliorer ta technique à l'écrit. Tu dois écrire des mots sans erreurs. Tu dois vérifier ton orthographe.* Ask students to write their feedback on sticky notes and to refer to them when completing future written tasks.

1 Trouve les paires.

Students look at the picture of the room and match the numbered items to the correct French terms. Remind them to use their reading strategies (cognates, familiar language, context, etc.) when decoding the items of vocabulary.

Answers: **1** c (un lit); **2** a (une table de nuit); **3** b (une lampe de chevet); **4** i (une console de jeux vidéo); **5** j (un fauteuil poire); **6** d (un bureau); **7** f (un ordi); **8** g (une lampe de bureau); **9** e (une chaise pivotante); **10** h (une étagère)

2 Écoute (1–10) et vérifie.

Students listen and check their answers.

Run through the grammar box on **Prepositions** and remind students that these are used for saying where something is. Most of these prepositions will be familiar to students, but do the **Dominoes** starter activity to reinforce this knowledge. Then ask students to use the picture of the room for pairwork practice of prepositions: they take turns to ask and say where the various bedroom items are: *La lampe de chevet est sur la table de nuit*. Alternatively, students could write gap-fill sentences for each other: *La lampe de chevet est ... la table de nuit*.

CD 2, track 35   page 134, activité 2

1 Alors d'abord, dans ma chambre, il y a un lit, bien sûr.
2 Il y a une table de nuit à côté ...
3 ... et sur la table de nuit, il y a une lampe de chevet, pour lire.
4 Puis, j'ai une console de jeux vidéo ...
5 et un fauteuil poire, pour être confortable quand je joue.
6 Pour finir, il y a ... un bureau ...
7 ... où j'ai mon ordi ...
8 ... et ma lampe de bureau.
9 Devant le bureau, il y a une chaise pivotante ...
10 ... et à côté, il y a une grande étagère. Voilà, c'est tout!

3 Lis et réponds aux questions. C'est Lila, Zachary ou les deux?

Students read the texts about Lila and Zachary's rooms, and answer the questions in English. As a follow-up Bronze medal activity, students explain in English how they worked out the answers. They could work in pairs to do this.

Answers: **a** Zachary; **b** Lila; **c** Lila's; **d** both; **e** Lila; **f** Zachary; **g** both

t Students translate the phrases in bold.

Answers: I shared my room when I was little. I am lucky. I have my own room. My room is strictly out of bounds to ... I have personalised my room. I would like to have ... I'm unlucky. I have to share ... I have decorated our room with ... The problem is that ...

t Students translate either Lila's or Zachary's text.

Answers:

Lila: I shared my room when I was little, but now I'm lucky because I have my own room. My new room is quite small but it's my private space and my refuge. My room is strictly out of bounds to my little sister. I have personalised my room with holiday photos, postcards and posters on the walls. I would like to have a TV, but my parents don't agree. I have my computer and my CD player, that's all.

Zachary: I'm unlucky. I have to share my room with my big brother. Like my cousin Lila, we have personalised our room. I love skateboarding, so I've decorated our room with graffiti and there are skateboards attached to the walls. We have bunk-beds, a sofa, a large wardrobe, a desk and two netbooks/mini-laptops. We also have a flat-screen TV. The problem is, my brother likes watching TV late in the evening, so I can't sleep!

4 Partager une chambre ou avoir une chambre à toi? Recopie et remplis la grille avec « Les arguments » de la boîte.

Students read the arguments for and against sharing a room or having your own room. They copy and complete the grid with the appropriate arguments for each option. Most of the vocabulary should be either familiar to students, or decodable, using their reading strategies.

Answers:

Partager une chambre		Avoir une chambre à toi	
Pour	Contre	Pour	Contre
Ça rapproche. On apprend à cohabiter/partager. On rigole.	On n'est jamais seul. (could be either for or against) C'est difficile pour les devoirs. On se dispute. On n'a pas d'espace privé. On est obligé de supporter les mauvaises habitudes de l'autre. Ce n'est pas pratique pour recevoir des amis.	C'est facile pour les devoirs. On ne se dispute pas. On a un espace privé. On n'est pas obligé de supporter les mauvaises habitudes de l'autre. C'est pratique pour recevoir des amis.	Ça ne rapproche pas. On est toujours seul. (could be either for or against) On ne rigole pas.

153

8 Chez moi, ça veut dire quoi?

5 Partager une chambre: ils sont pour ou contre? Écoute le débat (1–4).

Students listen to the debate and note down whether each person is for or against sharing a room (or neither).

Answers: **1** against; **2** (rather/quite) for; **3** (completely) against; **4** neither (for nor against)

○ Students note down the arguments for or against given by each person.

Answers:

1 **Against:** shared a room with sister when she was little; didn't like it; it's difficult to do homework and it's not practical for having friends over; you have no private space

2 **For:** shared with his brother for two years and liked it; you have a laugh/fun and it brings you closer together. **Against:** can't be alone when you want

3 **Against:** has to share with two sisters; hates it; they argue, can never be alone and have no private space; would like to have her own room

4 **For:** (Has a room of his own and quite likes it); it's easy to do homework and you can be alone when you want. **Against:** you don't learn to share

As a Gold medal follow-up task, students could note down any verbs in the past tense (perfect, imperfect) and in the conditional.

Answers: **Perfect:** je n'ai pas aimé, j'ai partagé, j'ai bien aimé; **Imperfect:** je partageais, j'étais; **Conditional:** je voudrais

---

CD 2, track 36   page 135, activité 5

1 Moi, je suis contre car je partageais ma chambre avec ma sœur quand j'étais petite. Je n'ai pas aimé ça. Le problème, quand on partage une chambre, c'est que d'abord, c'est difficile pour les devoirs ... puis, ce n'est pas pratique pour recevoir des amis ... et pour finir, on n'a pas d'espace privé.

2 Je suis plutôt pour. J'ai partagé ma chambre avec mon grand frère pendant deux ans et j'ai bien aimé. L'inconvénient, c'est qu'on ne peut pas être seul quand on veut. Par contre l'avantage, c'est qu'on rigole et puis, ça rapproche.

3 Je suis tout à fait contre parce que je dois partager ma chambre avec mes deux sœurs. Je déteste ça. On se dispute et puis, on n'est jamais seules et on n'a pas d'espace privé. Je voudrais avoir une chambre à moi.

4 Je ne suis ni pour, ni contre. J'ai une chambre à moi et j'aime bien. D'un côté, c'est facile pour les devoirs et on peut être seul quand on veut. Mais d'un autre côté, on n'apprend pas à partager.

---

6 Écris une lettre au magazine *Monde des Ados* sur le thème: « Ma chambre, mon refuge ».

Students write a letter to the magazine *Monde des Ados* on the theme of 'My bedroom, my refuge'. Before students start, do the **Word tennis** starter activity to consolidate their knowledge of the items in a bedroom. Then refer them to **Extend your vocabulary** and encourage them to look up new vocabulary for use in their letters, either on French shopping websites, or in the dictionary. To emphasise the point, challenge students to find as many different words as they can in French for things that you can sit on: for example, *une chaise pivotante*, *une chaise berçante/à bascule* (rocking chair), *un fauteuil* (armchair), *un fauteuil poire* (beanbag), *un tabouret* (stool), *une chaise longue*, *une chaise pliante* (folding chair), *un banc* (bench), *un canapé/un sofa*, *un transat* (deckchair).

★ Students describe their room and how they have personalised it.

○ Students say whether or not they share a bedroom, giving the advantages and disadvantages. Refer students to the key language box if they need ideas.

✚ Students add whether they are for or against sharing a bedroom, giving reasons. Encourage students to use sequencers and to use a range of tenses in their justifications, where appropriate.

7 Prépare un débat: « Partager une chambre: pour ou contre? »

Students prepare arguments for a debate on the pros and cons of sharing a room.

★ Students decide whether they are for or against and give some supporting arguments.

○ Students use sequencers to present three arguments. Refer them to the key language box on page 132 for a reminder.

✚ Students explain the pros and cons of sharing a room. They use the key language box for ideas, or think up their own arguments.

✎ As a follow-up task and to continue with the literacy theme of looking at different styles of language, compare the language of a debate (persuasive, sequencing points, agreeing and disagreeing) with the language of the texts on pages 134–135 (abbreviated property advertisements and the narrative style in Louka's text).

154

> **Plenary**
>
> ⭐ Students describe the contents of their bedroom (real or imagined).
>
> ◎ Students sequence three arguments for or against sharing a bedroom.
>
> ➕ Students say whether they are for or against sharing a bedroom and explain why.
>
> Students read their partner's text and decide whether they have achieved the medal they were aiming for. They provide their partner with some written feedback to help them improve.

8.4 La maison de mes rêves
pages 136–137

Planner

Objectives
- Vocabulary: describe the type of home you would like to have
- Grammar: use *si* clauses (imperfect tense and conditional)
- Skills: develop knowledge of connectives to extend sentences

Resources
- Student Book, pages 136–137
- CD 2, track 37
- Grammar and Skills Workbook, pages 39 and 42
- Kerboodle, Unit 8
- Unit 8 Worksheets 3 (ex. 1), 4 (ex. 1), 6 (ex. 2–3)

Key language
Si j'avais de l'argent, j'aurais …
Si j'avais un emploi bien payé, j'achèterais …
Si j'étais riche, je voudrais acheter …
Si je gagnais à la loterie, j'aimerais faire construire …
un loft en ville, une péniche sur la Seine, une maison sur la plage, un chalet à la montagne, une villa dans la banlieue de Paris, une grande ferme à la campagne
S'il/Si elle était/avait/gagnait …,
… il/elle habiterait dans …
… il/elle achèterait/aurait/aimerait …
Ce serait grand/beau/moderne …
Il y aurait … parce que/car …

Grammar
- *Si* clauses + imperfect tense and conditional

PLTS
- Activity 2: Effective participators
- Activity 5: Creative thinkers
- Activity 6: Team workers

Homework and self-study
- Student Book, page 136, activity 1
- Student Book, page 137, activity 5
- Grammar and Skills Workbook, pages 39 and 42

Starters
See Kerboodle Starters bank for further details of **Word tennis**.

- Hold a class **Brainstorming** session to compile a list of connectives for use in students' written and spoken productive work. Write these on the board for students to refer to when completing activities 5 and 6.
- As a class, play **Word tennis** to think of possible nouns and verbs that could be used to describe the house of their dreams in activities 5 and 6. Write on the board the sentence *Il y aurait [1] parce qu'il/elle aime/adore [2]*. Ask students first to think of nouns (rooms or areas of the house) for gap [1], and then move on to verbs for gap [2]. Compile a list of each on the board, for students to refer to in activities 5 and 6. Possible items: Gap [1]: *une salle de jeux, une bibliothèque, une piscine, une gymnase, une salon de coiffure/beauté, un cinéma, un laboratoire, un atelier, des étables, des champs.* Gap [2]: *jouer au snooker, lire, nager, faire de la musculation, être bien soigné(e), regarder les films, faire des expériences, dessiner/peindre, faire de l'équitation, faire des randonnées.*

8 Chez moi, ça veut dire quoi?

Plenaries
- **Extending sentences**. Students discuss in pairs how using connectives can extend sentences. They produce the longest sentence they can. This could be in the form of a 'Grow-me' sentence (for an example, see *Allez 1* Grammar and Skills Workbook, page 51). Students consider how what they have learnt today connects to what they already know, and then review their strengths: *Mes points forts: Je peux utiliser des conjonctions. Je peux écrire des phrases longues et variées ...*

1 Lis et trouve les paires.

Students read the texts and match them to the correct photos. They should be able to do this without too much support, as much of the language for the acommodation types and locations will be familiar to them.

Answers: **1** e; **2** a; **3** b; **4** c; **5** d; **6** f

To add a cultural/literacy focus, explain to students that a *pied-à-terre* is someone's second residence, which is not their main home. Point out that it is one of a huge number of expressions in French that have been borrowed by and used in the English language – usually because the equivalent expression does not exist in English. Ask students to work in pairs to try to think of some more: for example, *carte blanche, bête noire, pièce de résistance*.

Once students have matched the texts to the photos, revise *si* + present tense and future tense, as covered in Unit 7 and check students are secure with this structure. Then run through the grammar box on **Si clauses** and check students' understanding of the tense usage here. Remind students that they have already come across the conditional in the form of *je voudrais* and *on pourrait* and explain how to form it – by adding the imperfect tense endings on to the future stem of the verb. Remind students that the future stem is usually the infinitive (minus the final *-e* for *-re* verbs), but that a few verbs have irregular future stems (e.g. *pouvoir – on pourrait*).

Ask students now to look back at the texts in activity 1 and to spot the examples of *si* + imperfect tense and conditional.

2 En groupe : « La maison de mes rêves. »

In groups, students consolidate what they have learnt about *si* + imperfect and conditional by practising the structure productively, using the accommodation types and locations from activity 1. They discuss the house of their dreams, saying what they would do if they were wealthy. Refer students to the grammar box and the key language box for support.

As a Silver medal follow-up task, students could explain why this would be their dream home (using *parce que* ...), and as a Gold medal task, they could adapt some of the structures on page 136 by adding something new.

3 Écoute (1–6). Recopie et remplis la grille en anglais.

Students listen, and copy and complete the grid. They note down each speaker's dream home and his/her reason.

○ Students note down any extra details.

✚ **t** Students choose three people and transcribe what they say.

	Dream home	Reason	Extra details
1	(Big) farm in the countryside	Loves animals	Would have a (little) farm shop selling products from the farm, e.g. eggs and cheese
2	A loft apartment in town	Loves cultural activities	Would buy it if he won the lottery; would go to the cinema, theatre and art galleries; it would be his urban pied-à-terre
3	A houseboat on the Seine	Loves Paris	The Seine is very beautiful, especially at night when the water reflects the lights of Paris
4	A beach house	Would like to a have a beautiful sea view	Would have a beach house built if she had a very well-paid job; would swim every day
5	A mountain chalet	Likes to breathe fresh/pure air	Would go hiking in summer and skiing in winter
6	A villa (big detached house) in the suburbs of Paris	Would go to Paris for entertainment and stay at home to relax	It would be the best of both worlds

156

CD 2, track 37   page 137, activité 3

1 Comme j'adore les animaux, je voudrais habiter dans une grande ferme à la campagne. J'aurais un petit magasin où je vendrais les produits de la ferme, comme les œufs et le fromage. Ce serait la maison de mes rêves.

2 Si je gagnais à la loterie, j'achèterais un loft en ville parce que j'adore les activités culturelles. J'irais au cinéma, au théâtre et dans les galeries d'art. Ce serait mon pied-à-terre urbain.

3 Si j'étais riche, j'achèterais une péniche sur la Seine parce que j'adore Paris. La Seine est très belle, surtout la nuit quand l'eau reflète les lumières de Paris.

4 Si j'avais un emploi très bien payé, je voudrais faire construire une maison sur la plage car j'aimerais avoir une maison avec une belle vue sur la mer. Je nagerais tous les jours.

5 Si j'avais de l'argent, je voudrais acheter un chalet à la montagne car j'aime respirer l'air pur. Je ferais des randonnées en été et du ski en hiver.

6 Quand je pense à la maison de mes rêves, j'imagine une villa dans la banlieue de Paris. J'irais à Paris pour me divertir et je resterais chez moi pour me relaxer. Je prendrais le meilleur des deux mondes!

4 Lis cette description d'une maison de rêve. Vrai, faux ou pas mentionné?

Students read the text and decide whether the English statements are true, false or not mentioned in the text. Encourage students to correct the false sentences.

Answers: **a** *faux (dreams of having a beautiful, solid house made of brick);* **b** *vrai;* **c** *pas mentionné;* **d** *faux (only has one room);* **e** *pas mentionné;* **f** *vrai*

○ Students make up some extra questions about the text, with answers, and challenge their partner to answer them.

t As a Gold medal follow-up task, challenge students to translate the final paragraph into English. There are two *si* clauses in this paragraph: the first one with imperfect and conditional (as covered in the grammar box), and the second one with present tense and future (as covered in Unit 7).

Answer: If I were rich, I would buy a house like that. If I work hard at school, I will perhaps have a well-paid job and I will be able to buy the house of my dreams.

5 Choisis ou invente un personnage. Décris la maison de tes rêves.

Before students embark on this activity, do the **Word tennis** starter activity to generate a list of vocabulary items that students can use to describe the house of their dreams. Students then choose a real or made-up character and describe the house of his or her dreams. For this task, students will need to use the third person of the conditional. Remind them of the correct endings and refer them to the key language box for support. Refer students also to the skills box on **More connectives**, do the **Brainstorming** starter activity to generate more ideas, and encourage them to use as wide a range of connectives as they can in their writing.

6 À deux: « La maison de mes rêves ». Continuez le dialogue de l'activité 2.

In pairs, students discuss their dream home. They develop their responses from activity 2 further, by adding reasons and extra details. Encourage students to refer to the texts in activity 4 for ideas and language, and to include a range of connectives to make their spoken work more interesting.

Plenary

★ Students list as many dream homes as they can.

○ Students use a sentence containing a *si* clause to say what kind of dream home they would have.

✚ Students explain their choice of dream home.

8.5 Chez moi, ça m'inspire!   pages 138–139

Planner

Objectives
- Vocabulary: describe places in detail and express how you feel about them
- Grammar: work with different structures from the unit
- Skills: use memorisation strategies; extend your range of vocabulary

Resources
- Student Book, pages 138–139
- CD 2, track 38
- Grammar and Skills Workbook, pages 27–28
- Kerboodle, Unit 8
- Unit 8 Worksheet 5 (ex. 1, 3)

8 Chez moi, ça veut dire quoi?

Grammar
- Work with different structures from the unit

PLTS
- Activity 2: Creative thinkers
- Ativity 3: Team workers
- Activity 4: Independent enquirers
- Activity 5, Gold medal: Self-managers
- Plenary: Creative thinkers, Reflective learners, Team workers, Self-managers

Homework and self-study
- Student Book, page 138, activity 2
- Student Book, page 139, activity 4
- Student Book, page 139, activity 5
- Grammar and Skills Workbook, pages 27–28

Starters
- Students work in pairs to identify language from the haiku poems in activity 1 that they find hard to remember. They then use these in their own haiku poems in activity 2
- As a class, brainstorm adjectives (particularly colours) for use in activity 5.

Plenaries
- **Extending vocabulary: prefixes and suffixes**. Students work in pairs to create a poster in French to help younger students gain confidence in understanding the value of vocabulary learning. This could be started in class and finished at home. Students should provide specific examples of prefixes and suffixes from the units already covered in *Allez 2* and should consider how they might teach the grammar they have learnt. Is there anything they might alter from the way they have been taught? They should also refer to the **Super Strategies** to encourage younger students to link their learning of other subjects to their study of French.
- Students present their poster to another pair for feedback. At the end of the lesson or start of the next one, whole-class feedback would be useful as review. Ask students to say which posters they think are particularly useful and to give reasons for their choice.

1 Écoute et lis les poèmes. Relie chaque poème à une image.
Students listen and read the poems. They match each poem (1–5) to the correct picture (a–d).
Answers: **1** b; **2** a; **3** c; **4** b; **5** d

Students list any cognates, near-cognates or words that they can guess.

Students work out what *je vois* and *j'entends* mean ('I see' and 'I hear'). Refer them to the grammar box on **Regular -re verbs in the present tense** and elicit from students examples of other *-re* verbs that they know of (*prendre* (point out to students that this is irregular), *descendre*, *vendre*). Refer them back to page 132 if they need a reminder.

Students translate two or three of the poems.

Translations:
1. I see the stars / They are neon lights that shine / When I go into town
2. I see the cars / I hear the traffic / When I go into town
3. That makes me smile / A country landscape / Beneath the beautiful sun
4. When I go into town / The silhouette/outline of the buildings / That's my horizon/That's what I see
5. That makes me dream / A rural night/A night in the country / (The) stars, (the) trees

CD 2, track 38   page 138, activité 1

1. Je vois les étoiles
   Ce sont les néons qui brillent
   Quand je vais en ville.

2. Je vois les voitures
   J'entends la circulation
   Quand je vais en ville.

3. Ça me fait sourire
   Un paysage campagnard
   Sous le beau soleil.

4. Quand je vais en ville
   La silhouette des immeubles
   C'est mon horizon.

5. Ça me fait rêver.
   Une nuit campagnarde
   Les étoiles, les arbres.

Explain to students that texts 1–5 are all examples of Haiku poems. A haiku is of Japanese origin and comprises just 17 syllables in three lines: five syllables on line 1, seven syllables on line 2, and five syllables on line 3. For more information on haiku poems, give students the following text and comprehension questions:

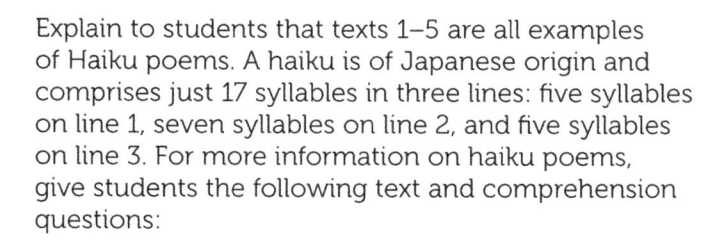

Poésie: le haïku
Un haïku est un court poème d'origine japonaise, de dix-sept syllabes. On peut écrire un haïku en trois lignes: une première ligne de cinq syllabes, une deuxième de sept syllabes et, pour finir, une troisième encore composée de cinq syllabes.

L'inspiration des auteurs de haïku vient des saisons ou de la nature. Un haïku doit donc contenir un mot qui fait référence à la nature ou à une des quatre saisons (l'automne, l'hiver, le printemps, l'été). Cette forme de poésie exprime des émotions et un moment dans le temps.

a What is a haiku?
b Where do haiku poems come from?
c What form does a haiku poem take?
d Where does the inspiration for haiku poems come from?
e What must a haiku poem include?
f What do haiku poems express?

Answers: **a** *a short poem (of Japanese origin) with 17 syllables;* **b** *Japan;* **c** *three lines: first line of five syllables, second line of seven syllables and third line of five syllables;* **d** *from seasons or nature;* **e** *a word that refers to nature or the four seasons;* **f** *emotions or a moment in time*

2 Écris un haïku comme dans l'activité 1.

Students write their own haiku poem, using those in activity 1 as a model. Refer students to **Super Strategy: memorising difficult language** and do the starter activity to give students the opportunity to identify items of vocabuary that they would like to incorporate into their poems. Students might also need to be provided with a framework or other support on which to base their writing. For example:

(Quand) je vais en ville/à la campagne	
je vois	
j'entends	les voitures
il y a	les arbres
c'est/ce sont	
ça me rend	triste, content(e)
ça me fait	sourire, rêver, pleurer
et, aussi, mais, ...	

⭐ Students write one haiku (about the countryside or a town).

◯ Students write two haiku (one about the countryside and one about a town).

➕ Students research their own vocabulary and use it in their poem.

3 Lis ton haïku à haute voix.

In groups, students choose a group leader who decides who will read first, second, and so on.

⭐ Students read out their haiku poem to the group.

◯ Students read out both of their poems. The group members discuss them and choose a favourite.

➕ **t** In groups, students translate their group's poems into English.

4 Lis les deux descriptions. Recopie et remplis la grille en anglais.

Students read the descriptions of the two Van Gogh paintings, and copy and complete the grid in English. They note down what each painting shows, which colours it uses and other details from the texts. On a first reading, ask students to find the cognates, near-cognates and any other words that they can guess.

Answers:

	What does the painting show?	Colours and other details
1	The town/an urban scene/ Paris	The colours are the colours of the town: grey and blue, with some spots of yellow and green. We see the roofs of Paris and Notre Dame cathedral on the horizon. Van Gogh was inspired by the view of Paris that he had from the window of his apartment in the Rue Lepic.
2	A country landscape at Auvers-sur-Oise	The painting shows a vast and open landscape. We see fields and on the horizon there is a line of trees between the earth and the sky. The colours are the colours of the countryside: blue and green with some spots of yellow and orange.

8 Chez moi, ça veut dire quoi?

t Students translate the underlined phrases into English.

Answers: Van Gogh painted the town; he painted the countryside; The first painting is an urban landscape; The colours are the colours of the town; some spots of yellow and green; We can see; on the horizon; The second painting is a rural lansdcape which is called; This landscape is; The colours are the colours of the countryside; with spots of

t Students translate the three *si* sentences (in italics in the texts).

Answers: If you had lots of money, which painting would you buy and why? If Van Gogh painted this painting today, there would be many more buildings and skyscrapers. If Van Gogh painted this painting today, the landscape would be practically identical.

5 Écris une description du tableau de Cézanne ou de Gauguin.
Students write their own description of a painting by Cézanne or Gauguin. They look at the paintings and use and adapt the underlined expressions in activity 4. Do the starter activity to brainstorm adjectives that students could use in their descriptions and provide additional vocabulary support if necessary. For example:

des maisons, des toits, des arbres, des champs, des collines, un cheval, le ciel
le bleu, le vert, le violet
bleu(e)(s), bleuâtre(s), bleu ciel, rouge(s), rougeâtre(s)
à côté, à gauche/droite, sur, sous, devant, derrière

Students use prepositions and colour adjectives in their description. Refer students back to page 134 for a reminder of prepositions.

As a Gold medal activity, students could research other language to use in their description. Refer them to the skills box on **Extend your vocabulary** and encourage them to try out these strategies when being more creative in their descriptions.

Plenary

In groups, students describe another painting of their choice. Before they begin, they decide which language and grammar would win a Bronze, Silver and Gold medal and make a note of their targets. Once they have written their description, they appoint a group leader to read it aloud to the class. The class votes for the best descriptions.

Ask students to prepare for this plenary ahead of the lesson: in an earlier lesson, set students a homework task to find a picture/print-out of a painting of their choice. Each group member could bring a different one. Better still, they could find a painting online using their phones.

8.6 Labo-langue
pages 140–141

Planner

Objectives
- Grammar: regular *-re* verbs in the present tense; prepositions; *si* clauses: the imperfect tense; *si* clauses: the conditional
- Skills: Super Strategies
- Pronunciation: *i* and *y*

Resources
- Student Book, pages 140–141
- CD 2, track 39
- Grammar and Skills Workbook, pages 58–59
- Kerboodle, Unit 8
- Unit 8 Worksheets 7, 8

PLTS
- Creative thinkers, Reflective learners, Self-managers

Regular *-re* verbs in the present tense

1 Copy and complete each sentence using the correct form of the verb provided.

t As a follow-up task, ask students to translate the sentences into English.

Answers: **a** descends; **b** vends; **c** entend; **d** entendons; **e** descendez; **f** vendent

Translations: **a** I go down to the ground floor. **b** Are you selling your caravan? **c** He hears the birds in the fields. **d** We hear the traffic in town. **e** You go down to go to the toilet. **f** They sell houses and flats.

160

Prepositions

2 Copy and complete the sentences. Translate the English prepositions into French.

As a follow-up task, ask students to translate the sentences into English.

Answers: **a** devant; **b** en face; **c** sur; **d** sous; **e** à gauche, à droite; **f** entre

Translations: **a** I have a dressing table in front of a big lit-up mirror. **b** There is a flat-screen TV and opposite there is a bed. **c** On the bedside table, I have a bedside lamp. **d** Under the bedside table, there is a pile of books. **e** In my closet, there are my shoes on the left, and there are my clothes on the right. **f** Between my desk and my wardrobe, there is a beanbag.

Si clauses: the imperfect tense

Check students' understanding of the use of the imperfect tense and the conditional after *si*.

Si clauses: the conditional

3 Copy and complete these sentences. Replace each infinitive with the imperfect tense (see page 140) or the conditional.

Answers: **a** je gagnais, je ferais; **b** tu avais, tu aimerais; **c** il était, il habiterait; **d** nous avions, nous achèterions; **e** vous habitiez, vous habiteriez; **f** elles voudraient, elles gagnaient

4 Translate a–f from activity 3 into English.

Answers: **a** If I won the lottery, I would have an eco-house built. **b** If you had the money, you would like to buy a houseboat on the Thames. **c** If he were rich, he would live in a villa/large detached house. **d** If we had a well-paid job, we would buy a flat in town. **e** If you lived in the African countryside, you would live in a mud hut. **f** They would like to buy a chalet in the mountains if they won a lot of money.

Super Strategies

This section encourages students to think about strategies for working out the meaning of unfamiliar language when reading. They are advised to look for cognates and to use them in combination with what they already know, their knowledge of the world and the context.

Students are encouraged to try out the strategies in activities 4 and 5 on page 131.

Pronunciation: *i* and *y*

5 Read aloud these sentences. How many long 'ee' sounds are there? Listen to check.

Students listen and identify the long 'ee' sounds.

Answers (in bold): **a** J'hab**i**te sur une pén**i**che sur la r**i**v**i**ère, à Par**i**s. **b** Il **y** a une cu**i**s**i**ne et derr**i**ère, **i**l **y** a une buander**i**e. C'est très prat**i**que. **c** Le b**i**donv**i**lle? J'**y** hab**i**te depu**i**s s**i**x ans et dem**i**. **d** S**i** j'éta**i**s r**i**che, j'hab**i**tera**i**s dans un loft en v**i**lle. C'est très ch**i**c, à mon av**i**s.

◼ CD 2, track 39 page 141, activité 5

a J'habite sur une péniche sur la rivière, à Paris.
b Il y a une cuisine et derrière, il y a une buanderie. C'est très pratique.
c Le bidonville? J'y habite depuis six ans et demi.
d Si j'étais riche, j'habiterais dans un loft en ville. C'est très chic, à mon avis.

8.7 Extra Star
page 142

1 Unscramble these words and match them to the pictures. Write the words out correctly.

Answers: **1** c – une lampe de bureau; **2** a – une étagère; **3** f – un lit; **4** d – une chaise pivotante; **5** b – un ordi; **6** e – un fauteuil poire

2 What do you have in your room? What would you like to have? Copy and complete these sentences.
Students complete the sentences with their own ideas.

3 Read Adam's description of his home and look at the plan.
Students work out what each room is (1–15) and make a list in English.

Answers: **1** les WC/toilet; **2** le séjour/living room; **3** la véranda/conservatory; **4** la buanderie/utility room; **5** la cuisine/kitchen; **6** la salle à manger/dining room; **7** le garage/garage; **8** le jardin/garden; **9** le bureau ou la chambre d'amis/office or guest room; **10** la salle de bains attenante/en-suite bathroom (in parents' bedroom); **11** la chambre de mes parents/my parents' room; **12** les deux balcons/two balconies; **13** la salle de bains/bathroom; **14** la chambre de ma sœur/my sister's room; **15** ma chambre/my room

4 Describe where you live. You can make it up if you like!
Students write a description of their home, detailing the type of accommodation, what rooms there are and their locations. Refer students to the text in activity 3 for support.

8 *Chez moi, ça veut dire quoi?*

8.7 Extra Plus
page 143

1 C'est quelle pièce? Écris en français.
Students look at the pictures and write the names of the rooms in French.
Answers: **a** la chambre de ma sœur; **b** la cuisine; **c** la salle à manger; **d** la salle de bains; **e** le séjour; **f** la chambre d'amis/le bureau

2 Lis l'article de Basile et réponds aux questions en anglais.
Students read the text and answer the questions in English.
Answers: **a** in a big old brick house, has lived there since childhood; **b** in an environmentally-friendly house made of wood (his house would use renewable energy); **c** in a forest, because he likes to go walking/hiking and breathe fresh air; **d** in other parts of the world, e.g. Mongolia, Africa (African countryside), northern Canada; **e** yurts/traditional tents made out of natural materials, mud huts, igloos; **f** igloos, made with blocks of compacted snow, have no impact on environment, built/lived in by Inuits when they go on hunting trips in northern Canada

3 Dessine la maison de tes rêves (ou trouve une photo) et écris la description.
Students draw (or find a photo of) the house of their dreams and write a description of it. Encourage them to include as many of the points mentioned as possible.

8.8 Lire
page 144

Resources
- Student Book, page 144
- Kerboodle, Unit 8

PLTS
- Independent enquirers

1 Read the story. Choose a heading (a–e) for each paragraph (1–5).
Explain to students that the text is adapted from a traditional story from Burkina Faso and refer them to the information box.
Answers: **1** c; **2** e; **3** b; **4** d; **5** a

2 Find these phrases in French in the story.
Answers: **a** commence à tomber; **b** arrive en courant; **c** il n'a pas aidé; **d** caché derrière; **e** ont peur; **f** il ne fait pas de bruit; **g** de loin

3 Answer the questions in English.
Answers: **a** He says he is ill. **b** because he didn't help with the building; **c** to get food; **d** The monkey and the cat dare to go near the hut, then they run away when they hear the flute; the hyena is too scared even to go near the hut and runs away on hearing the flute from a distance.

As a follow-up task, hold a class discussion about the story. Ask students how they feel about the hare's behaviour. Do they admire him? Is he the hero of the story or the villain? Do students think the story has a moral or a deeper meaning? Does it simply illustrate human relationships, where often it is the crafty trickster who gets away with things at the expense of those who work hard and play by the rules? Or perhaps it shows that hard work isn't always enough and that if you want to succeed, you sometimes have to be bold and take risks?

8.8 Vidéo
page 145

Resources
- Student Book, page 145
- Kerboodle, Unit 8 Video clip

PLTS
- Independent enquirers

Épisode 8: L'art de la rue
Clarisse and Thouraya are discussing the next challenge of the competition. This time it focuses on the urban environment. Clarisse mentions that she loves the historic centre of Montpellier, with its narrow streets and old buildings. Thouraya says she loves street art and the girls go into a café to interview Julie, a street artist. With her, they create an image of a face to be pasted onto on the wall of a house nearby.

Video clip, Unit 8 page 145

Clarisse: C'est quoi, ce nouveau défi?

Thouraya: C'est sur l'environnement urbain. « Qu'est-ce que vous aimez le plus comme environnement urbain à Montpellier? »

Clarisse: Moi, j'adore le centre historique. Toutes les petites rues et les anciens immeubles.

Thouraya: Moi, ce que j'aime, c'est l'art de la rue. J'adore les peintures murales et les trompes l'œil.

Clarisse: Tu as raison, c'est beau et très intéressant.

Thouraya: Si j'avais une maison à moi, je la peindrais avec un grand trompe l'œil. Sur les murs je peindrais des arbres et des collines, et sur le toit, le ciel.

Clarisse: T'es trop romantique, toi! Mais qu'est-ce qu'on fait ici?

Thouraya: On va faire de l'art de la rue avec Julie.

(In Julie's house)

Thouraya: Salut, Julie. Je te présente ma copine, Clarisse.

Julie: Bonjour, Clarisse.

Thouraya: Julie, quand as-tu commencé à peindre?

Julie: Je fais de la peinture depuis l'âge de neuf ans. J'ai commencé à faire des yeux, des regards et des émotions.

Clarisse: Est-ce que tu as étudié la peinture?

Julie: J'ai pris des cours d'art plastique pendant un an.

Thouraya: Et qu'est-ce que tu prépares ici?

Julie: Je prépare un visage que l'on va peindre noir et blanc, avec des couleurs vives uniquement pour les yeux, comme de l'orange et du vert pomme. Quand il sera terminé, on le découpera aux ciseaux et on ira le coller sur la maison à côté. Vous voudriez m'aider?

Thouraya: Oui, bien sûr.

Clarisse: Bien sûr.

Clarisse: Est-ce que tu fais d'autres choses artistiques?

Julie: Oui, je fais des bijoux, de la sculpture et plein de petites choses artisanales. Vous pouvez voir là-bas. Je fais aussi des T-shirts ...

Clarisse: Est-ce que tu les vends?

Julie: Oui, sur les marchés.

Julie: Est-ce que vous voudriez m'aider à le coller sur le mur?

T & C: Bien sûr.

Julie: D'abord, il faut le découper ... Alors, ici à droite, j'ai préparé la colle. J'ai mis de la poudre et j'ai rajouté au-dessus de l'eau tiède.

Clarisse: Pourquoi est-ce que tu aimes peindre les visages?

Julie: Depuis que je suis petite, j'ai toujours été fascinée par le regard des gens.

Thouraya: Les plantes servent à quoi?

Julie: À faire la chevelure, bien sûr.

Clarisse: Oui, je vois. C'est super – une fille avec les cheveux fleuris.

Thouraya: Je vais l'appeler Mademoiselle Fleurie.

Julie: Quand je me promène en ville, j'aime beaucoup repérer les endroits où je pourrais coller des visages. J'aime beaucoup la ville de Montpellier parce qu'il y a beaucoup de « street artists ».

Clarisse: Est-ce que la maison de tes rêves serait remplie de visages?

Julie: Oui, si j'avais beaucoup d'argent, la maison de mes rêves aurait beaucoup de jardinières où je pourrais peindre des visages en-dessous. Et j'inviterais des artistes à peindre sur les murs.

Thouraya: Merci beaucoup, Julie. Chaque fois que je passerai devant, je dirai bonjour à Mademoiselle Fleurie.

1 Regarde l'épisode 8. Qui aime ça (a–f) à Montpellier? C'est Clarisse ou Thouraya?

Students watch the video and decide whether each of the items listed appeals to Clarisse or to Thouraya.

Answers: **Clarisse:** b, c, e; **Thouraya:** a, d, f

2 Julie parle de quoi? Trouve les paires.

Students match the photos to the correct French phrases in the box.

Answers: **a** des petites choses artisanales, par exemple des bijoux; **b** des T-shirts; **c** des peintures; **d** un visage; **e** une grande feuille de papier; **f** des plantes pour la chevelure

8 Chez moi, ça veut dire quoi?

3 Recopie le texte et choisis les bons mots.
Students copy out the text and choose the correct word or phrase from each pair of options.

Answers: Julie est artiste. Elle fait de la peinture depuis <u>longtemps</u>. Elle a étudié <u>l'art plastique</u> pendant un an. Son projet aujourd'hui, c'est de coller un visage sur <u>une maison</u>. Ce visage est noir et blanc, <u>avec des</u> couleurs pour les yeux. Pour faire <u>les cheveux</u>, elle utilise des plantes. Julie crée d'autres choses, par exemple <u>des bijoux</u>, de la sculpture, des T-shirts.

Elle vend ses créations <u>sur les marchés</u>. Julie aime Montpellier car il y a beaucoup <u>d'art de la rue</u>.

4 Imagine que ton groupe va créer une peinture murale dans ta ville ou ton village.
Students imagine that they are going to create a mural in their own town or village. In groups, they discuss what they will paint and which colours they will use. Encourage them to use *On pourrait ...* and to give reasons for their suggestions.

8.9 Test   page 146

Resources
- Student Book, page 145
- CD 2, track 40

PLTS
- Creative thinkers, Reflective learners, Effective participators

AT levels
Approximate medal guidelines:
- ★ (Foundation) L: 5; S: 4; R: 4–5; W: 4
- ◉ (Core) L: 5–6; S: 5; R: 5; W: 5
- ✚ (Higher) L: 6; S: 6; R: 6; W: 6

1 Listen to Quentin and anwer these questions in English. (See pages 130–137.)
Answers: a semi-detached house; b five years; c in a house in London; d prefers his house in France because he has his own bedroom and it's really comfortable; e any four of: kitchen, living room, dining room, three bedrooms, bathroom; f a garden; g a big modern house in the Paris suburbs; if he were rich, he would have ten bedrooms for his family and all his friends, and a big garden where he would be able to play tennis every day

〜 CD X, track XX   page 146, activité 1

Salut! Je m'appelle Quentin et j'habite dans une maison jumelée, dans le sud de la France. J'y habite depuis cinq ans mais quand j'étais petit, j'habitais dans une maison à Londres. En Angleterre, je partageais une chambre avec mon petit frère. Je préfère ma maison en France parce que j'ai une chambre à moi. Je l'ai personnalisée avec des photos, des posters et mes objets préférés. Maintenant, c'est vraiment confortable.

Chez moi, au rez-de-chaussée, il y a la cuisine, le séjour et la salle à manger. Au premier étage, il y a trois chambres et la salle de bains. J'aimerais bien avoir un jardin!

La maison de mes rêves serait une grande maison moderne dans la banlieue de Paris. Et si j'étais riche, je voudrais avoir dix chambres pour ma famille et tous mes amis et un grand jardin où je pourrais jouer au tennis tous les jours.

2 Take a standpoint for or against sharing a bedroom. Argue your case in a debate. (See pages 134–135.)
Students give three arguments to support their standpoint and should try to include at least one past tense and a verb in the conditional.

3 Read Sofia's text and answer the questions in English. (See pages 130–137.)
*Answers: a a young girl and her little sister, who live in a shack in a shantytown in Port-au-Prince – they have been living there for four years; b because she lives in a little two-storey house and is safe/secure; c there's a kitchen, living room and dining room; d there are two bedrooms and a bathroom; e has to share a room with her sister so has no private space, but it's comfortable and big enough for both of them; f **When she was little:** a big, beautiful house where she would have a room of her own; **Now:** a house that she would have built for the two girls in Haiti*

4 Write about where you live and compare it to your dream home. (See pages 130–137.)
Encourage students to cover as many of the points listed as they can and to develop and extend their writing as far as possible.

9 Un métier, un rêve!

Unit 9: Un métier, un rêve! Overview grid

Page reference	Contexts and objectives	Grammar	Strategies and skills	Key language	AT levels*
148–149 **9.1 Quel métier fais-tu?**	Talk about jobs and the qualities needed for certain jobs	Masculine and feminine forms of jobs	Ask and answer questions. Super Strategies	archéologue, journaliste, réalisateur/réalisatrice, photographe, médecin, chef cuisinier, chirurgien/chirurgienne, vétérinaire Il/Elle travaille dans un cabinet médical/un bureau/un restaurant/une piscine. C'est un métier qui est passionnant/stressant/varié/fatigant. C'est un métier qui demande du courage/de l'énergie. Pour être … il faut avoir de la patience/être créatif/aimer voyager/aimer le contact avec les gens.	L: 3–5 S: 3–5 R: 4–5 W: 4–5
150–151 **9.2 Le métier de mes rêves!**	Talk about ideal jobs	Imperfect tense and the conditional (revision). Use different tenses together	Improve speaking and writing	footballeur professionnel, astronaute, pompier, pilote, professeur, danseur/danseuse, dentiste, pâtissier/pâtissière, écrivain Quand j'avais dix ans, je voulais devenir … Quand j'étais petit(e), je rêvais d'être/de travailler … Maintenant, j'ai changé d'avis/je pense que … parce que … Plus tard, j'aimerais/je voudrais/je préférerais … aller/être/travailler/voyager … parce que/car …	L: 4–6 S: 5–6 R: 5–6 W: 5–6
152–153 **9.3 Grandes ambitions!**	Talk about ambitions	Si clauses + imperfect tense and conditional (revision)	Translation strategies	Si je gagnais des millions/j'étais riche, je ferais le tour du monde/je donnerais de l'argent à des associations caritatives/j'achèterais un jet privé/je construirais des écoles en Afrique/je créerais des centres pour les animaux en danger/j'aurais une Ferrari avec chauffeur/j'aurais un studio d'enregistrement/j'organiserais des méga-fêtes.	L: 5–6 S: 4–6 R: 5–6 W: 5–6
154–155 **9.4 Les petits boulots!**	Talk about part-time jobs	Quand with different tenses	Combine tenses to improve speaking and writing	vendeur/vendeuse, serveur/serveuse, plagiste, maître-nageur, jardinier/jardinière, baby-sitter Quand j'avais onze ans, j'étais … Quand j'étais plus jeune, je faisais du baby-sitting/je travaillais pour … L'été dernier/L'année dernière, j'étais/j'ai fait/j'ai travaillé … En ce moment, je suis/je fais/je travaille … Quand j'aurai seize ans/L'année prochaine, je serai/je ferai/je travaillerai …	L: 4–6 S: 4–6 R: 5–6 W: 4–6
156–157 **9.5 Échec et réussite**	Talk about success and failure	Use different tenses	Motivation strategies	J'ai choisi … parce que … Je l'adore pour son talent/son intelligence/son courage/sa détermination. Il/Elle a eu des difficultés/problèmes dans sa vie. Il/Elle était …	L: 5–6 S: 4–6 R: 4–6 W: 4–6
158–159 **9.6 Labo-langue**	Grammar, language strategies and pronunciation	Job titles. The imperfect tense and the conditional. Using *quand* with different tenses	Super Strategies. Pronunciation: tongue-twisters		
160–165 **9.7 Extra Star, Extra Plus 9.8 Lire, Vidéo 9.9 Test, Vocabulaire**	Reinforcement and extension; reading material; activities based on the video material: revision and assessment		**Lire:** R: 6–7 **Vidéo:** L: 4–6; S: 4–5		Test: L: 5–6 S: 5–6 R: 5–6 W: 5–6

* See teacher notes for alternative assessment options. Guidelines for the various assessment criteria are provided in the introduction of this Teacher Handbook.

165

9 Un métier, un rêve!

Unit 9: Week-by-week overview

(Three-year KS3 route: assuming six weeks' work or approximately 10–12.5 hours)
(Two-year KS3 route: assuming four weeks' work or approximately 6.5–8.5 hours)

About Unit 9, *Un métier, un rêve!*: In this unit, students work in the context of jobs and ambitions: they talk about jobs, the qualities needed for certain jobs, ideal jobs, ambitions and part-time jobs. They also discuss success and failure and what these signify for them in life.

This unit places a major focus on the uses of tenses. Students revisit the imperfect tense and the conditional, this time in the context of what their ideal jobs used to be and would be in the future. They develop this further, by revising *si* + imperfect and conditional, and using *quand* with the imperfect tense as well as with the future tense. Students are given the opportunity throughout to use a range of tenses (present, perfect, imperfect and future, as well as the conditional) together in one spoken or written piece. Masculine and feminine forms of job titles are also introduced and practised throughout.

Strategies in this unit focus mainly on improving speaking and writing: students are given the opportunity to work on asking and answering questions, and to consider the key elements for improving their productive work (using a variety of tenses, adding connectives and expressing and justifying opinions). Translation strategies offer students the chance to focus in detail on their written work, whilst Super Strategies help students to reflect on how they approach certain tasks. The pronunciation point focuses on general pronunciation, in the form of tongue-twisters.

Three-year KS3 route

Week	Resources
	Material from the end-of-unit pages (9.7 Extra Star/Plus, 9.8 Lire and Vidéo) may be used during week 6 or selectively during weeks 1–5 as time permits.
1	9.1 Quel métier fais-tu? 9.6 Labo-langue, activity 1 9.6 Labo-langue, Super Strategies
2	9.2 Le métier de mes rêves! 9.6 Labo-langue, activity 2
3	9.3 Grandes ambitions!
4	9.4 Les petits boulots! 9.6 Labo-langue, activity 3 9.6 Labo-langue, Pronunciation: tongue-twisters
5	9.5 Échec et réussite
6	9.7 Extra Star, Extra Plus 9.8 Lire 9.8 Vidéo 9.9 Test 9.9 Vocabulaire

Two-year KS3 route

Week	Resources
	Material from the end-of-unit pages (9.7 Extra Star/Plus, 9.8 Lire and Vidéo) may be used selectively during weeks 1–4 as time permits.
1	9.1 Quel métier fais-tu? (Omit activity 5) 9.6 Labo-langue, activity 1 9.6 Labo-langue, Super Strategies
2	9.2 Le métier de mes rêves! (Omit activity 3) 9.6 Labo-langue, activity 2
3	9.3 Grandes ambitions! (Omit activity 4)
4	9.4 Les petits boulots! (Omit activity 5) 9.6 Labo-langue, activity 3 9.6 Labo-langue, Pronunciation: tongue-twisters 9.9 Test 9.9 Vocabulaire

9.1 Quel métier fais-tu?

pages 148–149

Planner

Objectives
- Vocabulary: talk about jobs and the qualities needed for certain jobs
- Grammar: use masculine and feminine forms of jobs
- Skills: ask and answer questions; use Super Strategies

Resources
- Student Book, pages 148–149
- CD 2, tracks 41–42
- Kerboodle, Unit 9
- Unit 9 Worksheets 3 (ex. 1), 5 (ex. 1), 6 (ex. 2)

Key language

archéologue, journaliste, réalisateur/réalisatrice, photographe, médecin, chef cuisinier, chirurgien/chirurgienne, vétérinaire

Il/Elle travaille dans un cabinet médical/un bureau/un restaurant/une piscine.

C'est un métier qui est passionnant/stressant/varié/fatigant.

C'est un métier qui demande du courage/de l'énergie.

Pour être ..., il faut avoir de la patience/être créatif/aimer voyager/aimer le contact avec les gens.

Grammar
- Masculine and feminine forms of jobs

PLTS and Numeracy
- Activity 1: Independent enquirers
- Activity 6: Self-managers
- Activity 7: Team workers
- Numeracy: Activity 2: recognising ordinal and cardinal numbers

Homework and self-study
- Student Book, page 149, activity 4
- Student Book, page 149, activity 6

Starters

See Kerboodle Starters bank for further details of **Pictionary** and **Categorise**.

- Play **Pictionary** to help students learn the job titles. In addition to drawing a picture, ask students to write *m* or *f* next to the picture so that their group can state the correct form of the job title.
- Play **Categorise** to practise asking questions using the various different formats: inversion, *Est-ce que* and question words. Use these three formats as the different categories, and ask students to note down five examples of each in turn. They can refer to these lists when formulating their own questions in activity 7.

Plenaries

- **Ways of expressing opinions**. In groups, students consider how to present a visual depiction of their thoughts on current news items, or issues that concern or excite them in the local community. Ask them to think about how to get their opinions across in photo format, or as a poster campaign or a mural: *Les photos ... On pourrait prendre ... parce que ... Les peintures murales ... On pourrait peindre ... parce que ...* Students could use the text from activity 4 on page 149 and the Unit 8 video clip (page 145) to help them with ideas.

1 Trouve les paires.

Students look at the photos and match them to the correct French professions. Encourage them to look for cognates and near-cognates, and to use the pictures as clues.

Answers: **1** d; **2** f; **3** b; **4** h; **5** a; **6** c; **7** e; **8** g

2 Écoute et vérifie.

Students listen and check their answers to activity 1. Before playing the recording, recap on ordinal numbers and explain that students will need to listen out for a combination of ordinal and cardinal numbers when checking which job comes in which place in popularity.

Run through the grammar box on **Job titles**. Point out that the definite article is not used with job titles in French, but that many titles have a masculine and feminine form. Explain also that some jobs do not change according to gender: for example, *archéologue, journaliste, médecin, vétérinaire, photographe*.

9 Un métier, un rêve!

CD 2, track 41   page 148, activité 2

Alors, voici le résultat du sondage sur les huit métiers les plus populaires en France en ce moment.
En huitième position, c'est chirurgien ou chirurgienne.
Puis le numéro sept, c'est médecin …
… devancé par réalisateur ou réalisatrice en six …
… et archéologue en cinquième position.
Le numéro quatre, c'est vétérinaire.
Les trois grands gagnants sont:
journaliste, qui arrive en troisième position, …
… chef cuisinier en deux …
… et le métier le plus populaire en ce moment, photographe.
Voilà! Et toi, quel métier tu voudrais faire plus tard?

3   À deux: « Quel métier fait ton père? Quel métier fait ta mère? » Inventez! Utilisez les photos de l'activité 1.
Do the **Pictionary** starter activity to help students learn the jobs. Once students are secure with these, they discuss in pairs which (imaginary) jobs their parents do, using the photos and texts in activity 1 as prompts. Remind them to use the correct masculine or feminine form if applicable.

4   Lis le texte de Sami. Trouve les expressions a–h en français.
Students read the text about *Reporters Sans Frontières* and find the French equivalents for the English phrases. Once students have done this, talk to the class about *Reporters Sans Frontières*. It is an *ONG* (*Organisation humanitaire non gouvernementale*), or NGO in English. Have they heard of it? What do they think the organisation does? Compare it with *Médecins Sans Frontières*, which they might have heard of. Ask students to suggest the possible advantages of these sorts of organisations.
Answers: **a** j'ai toujours aimé; **b** je ne voulais pas travailler tout le temps dans un bureau; **c** c'est un métier qui est assez fatigant; **d** qui demande beaucoup d'énergie; **e** pour être journaliste; **f** il faut être créatif; **g** la qualité essentielle est; **h** il faut avoir du courage

t   As a follow-up Gold medal activity, students translate the text into English.

Answer: I am a journalist. I work for 'Reporters Without Borders'. I have always liked travelling and I didn't want to work in an office all the time, so I love my job. I take photos, I write articles and I travel abroad a lot. It's an exciting and very varied job. On the other hand, it is a job which is quite tiring and which requires a lot of energy. To be a journalist, you have to be creative but I think that the essential quality is to like contact with people. You also have to have courage because there are risks!

5   Écoute Lucie, Enzo et Camille. Recopie et remplis la grille en anglais.
Students listen, and copy and complete the grid. They note down the jobs that each speaker's parents do, their opinion of it and the qualities needed. As a follow-up task, ask students to spot how to say 'when he/she was younger' and 'when they were young' and elicit which tense this is in (imperfect).

○   Students also note down the jobs the parents did when they were younger.

t   As a Gold medal follow-up activity, ask students to transcribe what Lucie says.

Answers:

	Parents' jobs	Opinion/ qualities needed	Job when younger
Lucie	Dad: video clips director Mum: works at home	Dad likes his job because you need to be creative	Dad worked at McDonald's
Enzo	Mum: doctor	Work is tiring but exciting because she likes to help people who are ill	Worked at swimming pool
Camille	Parents own restaurant: dad is chef, mum works in the restaurant	Very tiring (because have to work evenings/ weekends) but they love the contact with people	Both mum and dad worked in the school canteen

CD 2, track 42   page 149, activité 5

– Que font tes parents dans la vie? … Lucie?
– Mon père est réalisateur de clips vidéo. Il aime beaucoup son travail parce qu'il faut être très créatif. Ma mère travaille à la maison.
– Et ton père, quand il était plus jeune, il travaillait?
– Ah, oui, quand il était étudiant, il travaillait au McDo.

– Merci! Et toi, Enzo, tes parents, que font-ils?
– J'habite avec ma mère parce que mes parents sont divorcés. Elle est médecin et elle travaille dans un cabinet médical au centre-ville. Elle trouve que son travail est assez fatigant mais il est aussi passionnant parce qu'elle aide des personnes qui sont malades.
– Et quand elle était plus jeune, elle travaillait?
– Oui, elle travaillait dans une piscine.
– Et toi, Camille?
– Mes parents ont un restaurant. Mon père est chef-cuisinier et ma mère travaille dans le restaurant. C'est un métier qui est très fatigant parce qu'il faut travailler le soir et les week-ends mais ils adorent le contact avec les gens.
– Et quand ils étaient jeunes, ils travaillaient?
– Oui, ma mère travaillait à la cantine du collège! Et mon père aussi!

6 Écris un paragraphe sur le métier d'une personne célèbre.

Students write about the job of a famous person. Encourage them to do some research and to describe the job that their chosen person does now and which qualities are needed for their job. Refer students to the text in activity 4 and to the key language box for support. Before students start planning or writing, refer them to the section on **Super Strategies** on page 159 and encourage them to try out some of these when describing the job of their chosen famous person.

Students also include what job their chosen person did when he/she was younger. Remind them to use the imperfect tense for this.

7 À deux: le jeu des dix questions! Qui suis-je?

Students imagine they are the person they wrote about in activity 6. In pairs, they take turns to ask and answer questions to work out who their partner is pretending to be. Before they start, refer students to the skills box on **Asking questions** and remind them to use the various different formats for asking questions when they do the activity. Do the **Categorise** starter activity to provide them with more support. Refer students also to the section on **Super Strategies** on page 159 and encourage them to try out some of these when asking questions to guess their partner's chosen famous person.

Plenary

In pairs, students recap on what they have learnt in the unit.

- Students name a job and their partner adds the qualities needed:
- Students think of an adult they know, say what job they do and add the qualities needed for their job.
- Students add where this person used to work when they were younger.

9.2 Le métier de mes rêves!

pages 150–151

Planner

Objectives
- Vocabulary: talk about ideal jobs
- Grammar: revise the imperfect tense and the conditional; use different tenses together
- Skills: improve speaking and writing

Resources
- Student Book, pages 150–151
- CD X, track XX
- Grammar and Skills Workbook, pages 39, 41, and 42
- Kerboodle, Unit 9
- Unit 9 Worksheets 3 (ex. 2–3), 4 (ex. 1), 5 (ex. 2), 6 (ex. 1, 3)

Key language
footballeur professionnel, astronaute, pompier, pilote, professeur, danseur/danseuse, dentiste, pâtissier/pâtissière, écrivain

Quand j'avais dix ans, je voulais devenir …
Quand j'étais petit(e), je rêvais d'être/de travailler …
Maintenant, j'ai changé d'avis/je pense que … parce que …
Plus tard, j'aimerais/je voudrais/je préférerais …
… aller/être/travailler/voyager … parce que/car …

Grammar
- Imperfect tense and conditional (revision)
- Use different tenses together

PLTS and Numeracy
- Activity 3: Independent enquirers
- Activity 4: Reflective learners, Team workers
- Plenary: Reflective learners
- Numeracy: Activity 4: presenting survey findings as a chart or graph

169

9 Un métier, un rêve!

Homework and self-study
- Student Book, page 151, activity 3
- Student Book, page 151, activity 5
- Grammar and Skills Workbook, pages 39, 41 and 42

Starters

See Kerboodle Starters bank for further details of **Categorise** and **Dominoes**.

- Play **Categorise** to consolidate students' knowledge of the imperfect tense and the conditional. Ask students to note down five different verbs in the *je* form for each category (imperfect or conditional). With more able students, move on to the *tu* form and then the *il/elle/on* form. Challenge them to include irregular verbs in their lists.

- Play **Dominoes** to check students' knowledge of the various job titles in activities 1 and 2: *footballeur professionnel, astronaute, pompier, pilote, professeur, danseur/danseuse, dentiste, pâtissier/pâtissière, écrivain*.

Plenaries

- **Nous allons faire une révision.** As a review to demonstrate growing understanding, students practise forming different tenses. Provide pairs of students with two dice and ask them to note down six verbs from previous units. They number the verbs and take turns to roll a die to determine which verb to conjugate. Their partner states which tense to use; they should cover at least the present, perfect and future tenses and, depending on the confidence of the class, possibly the imperfect and conditional too. Tell students to start with the *je* form, but encourage them to move on to the *il/elle/nous/ils/elles* forms, using a second die for the pronouns.

- Students then reflect on and review their understanding of moving from singular to plural forms in the various tenses: *J'ai utilisé le présent, le passé et le futur. Nous avons utilisé facilement le présent, le passé et le futur.* Reassure students that they will continue to work on combining tenses and refer them to activity 7 and the skills box on **Using different tenses** on page 155.

---

1 Lis. C'est qui?
Students read the texts and answer the English questions with the correct name. Remind students to look for cognates and any other language that they recognise, as well as using context and the pictures for clues.
Answers: **a** Salomé; **b** Sacha; **c** Sacha; **d** Robin; **e** Salomé; **f** Robin

Run through the grammar box revising **The imperfect tense and the conditional** and check students' understanding of when each tense is used: imperfect – to say what you used to do or what used to happen and to describe what someone or something was like; conditional – to say what you would like or would do. Do the **Categorise** starter activity to give students the opportunity to practise producing the imperfect and the conditional.

Students find examples in the texts of each of the present, perfect and imperfect tenses, and of the conditional.
Answers: **Present:** *c'est; je pense;* **Perfect:** *j'ai pensé;* **Imperfect:** *j'avais; je voulais; j'étais; je voulais; ce n'était pas; j'avais; je voulais;* **Conditional:** *j'aimerais; mon rêve serait; je voudrais; j'aimerais; je voudrais; ce serait; je préférerais; j'aimerais*

t Students translate what Sacha says.
Answer: When I was ten, I wanted to be a firefighter like my dad but I thought it would be very difficult. Now I think that I would prefer to be a vet because I would like to work in Africa with wild animals.

2 Écoute les interviews (1–4). Recopie et remplis la grille en anglais.
Students listen, and copy and complete the grid in English. They note down what job each speaker wanted to do when he/she was younger, and what he/she would like to be now, using the English job titles in the box. Before playing the recording, ask students to check that they know the French equivalents of all these job titles. Some are cognates and some they will know already. The **Dominoes** starter activity will help with this.

Students note down any extra information from the recording.

t Students transcribe what Anaïs says.

Answers:

	Wanted to be	Would like to be	Extra information (silver medal)
1	dancer	English teacher	languages are important; loves children
2	pilot	doctor	wanted to travel around world; now wants to help sick people (and work for an NGO such as MSF)
3	pastry chef/cake maker	still wants to be pastry chef/cake maker	always wanted to eat cakes; would like to have a big shop where he can sell his cakes
4	author	dentist	loved Harry Potter; now wants to work in a surgery

CD 2, track 43   page 150, activité 2

– Bonjour à tous! Je suis au collège Saint-Exupéry et je voudrais savoir quels étaient les métiers de rêve de nos collégiens quand ils étaient petits et bien sûr quels sont leurs métiers de rêve aujourd'hui.
1 – Alors, Sylvie, que voulais-tu faire quand tu étais toute petite?
   – Je voulais devenir danseuse.
   – Et maintenant?
   – Je crois que j'aimerais être professeur d'anglais parce que les langues sont super importantes. En plus, j'adore les enfants!
2 – Et toi, Hugo?
   – Moi, quand j'avais dix ans, je rêvais d'être pilote de ligne pour voyager dans le monde entier.
   – Et maintenant, tu veux toujours être pilote?
   – Ben, non, pas vraiment … maintenant, je préférerais être médecin parce que je voudrais aider les personnes malades et travailler pour une ONG comme Médecins Sans Frontières.
3 – Et toi, Zinedine?
   – Moi, avant, je voulais être pâtissier parce que je voulais toujours manger des gâteaux!
   – Et maintenant, tu veux toujours devenir pâtissier?
   – Oui, je veux toujours être pâtissier et je voudrais avoir une grande pâtisserie où je vendrai mes gâteaux!
4 – Et toi, Anaïs?
   – Quand j'étais petite, je voulais devenir écrivain comme J. K. Rowling parce que j'adorais Harry Potter. Mais maintenant, mon rêve serait d'être dentiste et de travailler dans un cabinet médical!
   – Ah, oui, c'est différent! … Merci à tous et j'espère que vous réaliserez tous vos rêves!

3   Lis le texte de Jémilie. Trouve et note les mots 1–8. Utilise les mots de la boîte.

Students read the text and fill the gaps with the appropriate words from the box. Remind students to look carefully at the surrounding language and grammatical structures when making their choice; they should ensure they choose the correct type of word (noun or verb), and the correct form and tense of verbs, as well as considering context and meaning.

Answers: **1** étais; **2** actrice; **3** travailler; **4** voulait; **5** écrivain; **6** professeur; **7** aimerais; **8** réalisatrice

t Students translate the highlighted phrases into English.

Answers: I used to love the theatre/acting; I wanted to act; because I wanted to be the star of a series; she has changed her mind; because she loves literature; he would prefer to work; because he would like to earn money

4   Sondage. Pose les questions 1 et 2 à cinq personnes. Note les réponses.

In groups, students ask five classmates what job they used to want to do when they were younger, and what they would like to do in the future. They use the imperfect tense and the conditional. Remind students to give reasons for what they say and refer them to the key language box for support. Refer students to the skills box on **Improving your speaking and writing** and encourage them to use these strategies when giving their responses to the survey. Once students have carried out the survey, they could present their findings in a pie chart or graph.

5   Qu'est-ce que tu voulais faire quand tu étais petit(e)? Et maintenant? Écris un article.

Students now put into writing what job they used to want to do and what they would like to do now. They could use their responses from activity 4, or could come up with new ideas to practise using a range of vocabulary. They refer to the texts in activities 1 and 3 as models, and use the key language box for support. Refer students again to the skills box on **Improving your speaking and writing** and encourage them to use these strategies when writing their article.

9 Un métier, un rêve!

○ Students also say what their friend used to want to do and what he/she would like to do now. Check that students remember the third person endings of the conditional before they do this. The text in activity 3 is a good reference pont.

⊕ Students add the qualities needed for each job they mention in their text.

Plenary

In pairs, students work on perfecting their pronunciation and support each other with helpful feedback.

★ Students name at least five jobs they have come across in the unit.

○ They add what they would like to do and explain why.

⊕ Students add what they wanted to do when they were younger.

9.3 Grandes ambitions!

pages 152–153

Planner

Objectives
- Vocabulary: talk about ambitions
- Grammar: use *si* clauses (imperfect tense and conditional)
- Skills: use translation strategies

Resources
- Student Book, pages 152–153
- CD 2, tracks 44–45
- Grammar and Skills Workbook, pages 39 and 42
- Kerboodle, Unit 9

Key language
Si je gagnais des millions/j'étais riche, je ferais le tour du monde/je donnerais de l'argent à des associations caritatives/j'achèterais un jet privé/je construirais des écoles en Afrique/je créerais des centres pour les animaux en danger/j'aurais une Ferrari avec chauffeur/j'aurais un studio d'enregistrement/j'organiserais des méga-fêtes.

Grammar
- *Si* clauses + imperfect tense and conditional (revision)

PLTS
- Activity 1: Independent enquirers
- Activity 2: Team workers
- Activity 5: Creative thinkers

Homework and self-study
- Student Book, page 153, activity 3
- Student Book, page 153, activity 5
- Grammar and Skills Workbook, pages 39 and 42

Starters

See Kerboodle Starters bank for further details of **Odd one out** and **Pictionary**.

- Play **Odd one out** to revise the imperfect tense and the conditional. Use sets of conjugated verbs, with the odd one out being in a different tense each time.

- Play **Pictionary** to help students learn the conditional phrases from activity 1. Challenge students to guess while their partner is still drawing – how quickly can they guess the correct phrase?

Plenaries

- **Translating**. Students search online for a poem, recipe or short text (e.g. a review of a computer game or film) to translate into English. They should look for something that motivates them to translate. This could be set as a homework from the previous lesson, to save time in class.

- Once students have completed their translations, they assess their partner's translation against the **Translation strategies** on page 153. Does the translation make good sense in English? Students should also refer to the **Grammar and Skills Workbook** (pages 59 and 63), and reflect on the strategies listed and their progress with this skill.

1 Écoute l'interview de Maëlle. Mets les phrases a–h dans le bon ordre.

Students listen and note down the order in which the French phrases are mentioned in the interview. Once they have done this, discuss the recording and the texts in more detail. Students should remember *associations caritatives* from *Allez 1*, so draw their attention to *Les Restos du Cœur* mentioned in the audio. Point out that this is a charity providing free meals to people in need, literally 'Restaurants of the Heart', and draw a comparison with soup kitchens. Can students work out what *un studio d'enregistrement* might be ('recording studio')? Remind them to look at other language for clues: here, does *je suis musicienne* in the recording help them? As a follow-up task, ask them to work out which text each of the photos relates to (not all of the texts have a photo).

Answers: f, d, g, h, b, c, e, a

CD 2, track 44   page 152, activité 1

- Bonjour. Maëlle, si tu gagnais des millions, qu'est-ce que tu ferais?
- Ben, moi, je pense que si je gagnais beaucoup d'argent, je ferais d'abord le tour du monde avec toute ma famille.
  Puis, j'aurais une Ferrari avec chauffeur et j'achèterais aussi un jet privé pour voyager … Et j'achèterais des téléphones portables à toute ma famille!
  Tous les mois, j'organiserais des méga-fêtes pour mes copains. Chez moi, j'aurais un grand studio d'enregistrement parce que je suis musicienne.
  Mais, bien sûr, il faut aussi aider les autres. C'est important. Donc je donnerais de l'argent à des associations caritatives comme les Restos du Cœur et je construirais des écoles en Afrique. Et pour finir, je créerais des centres pour les animaux en danger. Voilà!
- Bravo, quel programme! Merci, Maëlle!
- De rien! Merci à vous!

Students listen out for connectives and the French for 'Don't mention it' (*De rien!*).

Students note down why Maëlle wants a recording studio.

Answer: because she's a musician

Students translate texts a–h into English.

Answers: **a** I would create centres for animals in danger. **b** I would have a recording studio at my house. **c** I would give money to charities. **d** I would have a Ferrari with a chauffeur and I would buy a private jet. **e** I would build schools in Africa. **f** I would go round the world with my family. **g** I would buy mobile phones for all my family. **h** I would organise mega-parties for my friends.

2 Pose la question à ton/ta partenaire. A ↔ B.

Before students embark on this activity, run through the grammar box on *Si* **clauses** and remind them to use the imperfect and conditional with this structure. Do the **Odd one out** starter activity to revise the imperfect tense and the conditional and the **Pictionary** starter activity to reinforce the conditional phrases from activity 1. In pairs, students then take turns to ask and answer *Si tu gagnais des millions, qu'est-ce que tu ferais?* They use the texts in activity 1 as prompts, or could make up their own sentences.

Students add reasons to their responses.

3 Lis l'interview de Harim. Vrai, faux ou pas mentionné?

Students read the interview with Harim and decide whether the English statements are true, false or not mentioned in the text. As a follow-up task, students make up their own statements about the text and their partner decides whether they are true, false or not mentioned.

Students correct the false statements.

Answers: **a** *vrai;* **b** *faux (to change the world);* **c** *vrai;* **d** *faux (create jobs and listen to young people);* **e** *pas mentionné;* **f** *vrai;* **g** *faux (he would build hospitals)*

4 Écoute et lis le poème. Traduis en anglais.

Students listen and read the poem. They then translate the poem into English. Ask students to focus on the *si* clauses and to take care when translating the imperfect tense and the conditional. Refer them to the skills box on **Translation strategies** and encourage them to try to use these when writing their translation.

If students are following the 2-year KS3 and are likely to have to omit spread 9.5, it might be worth referring them at this point to the **Motivation strategies** on page 156. These Super Strategies can be applied to almost any task.

Students add another verse to the poem, in the same style.

Answer:

If I had money, I would have a lot of friends … but can we buy friendship?
If I had money, I would be intelligent … but can we buy intelligence?
If I had money, I would never be ill … but can we buy health?

9 Un métier, un rêve!

If I had money, I would buy the oceans and the mountains ... but can we buy our planet?
No, you will never be able to buy the most beautiful things with money!

> **CD 2, track 45** **page 153, activité 4**
>
> Si ...
> Si j'avais de l'argent, j'aurais beaucoup d'amis ... mais est-ce qu'on peut acheter l'amitié?
> Si j'avais de l'argent, je serais intelligent ... mais est-ce qu'on peut acheter l'intelligence?
> Si j'avais de l'argent, je ne serais jamais malade ... mais est-ce qu'on peut acheter la santé?
> Si j'avais de l'argent, j'achèterais les océans et les montagnes ... mais est-ce qu'on peut acheter notre planète?
> Non, tu ne pourras jamais acheter les plus belles choses avec de l'argent!

5 Complète les phrases 1 et 2. Écris <u>trois</u> ambitions pour chaque phrase.
Students use the sentence starters *Si j'étais riche, ...* and *Si j'étais président(e), ...* as the basis of the structure for a written piece on their dreams and ambitions. They draw on the language covered in the spread. Encourage them to use sequencers and connectives and to pay attention to the tenses they use after *si*.

◎ Students add reasons for their ambitions.

As a spoken follow-up task, students prepare a short presentation entitled « Si je gagnais à la loterie, ... » They use language from the spread and take ideas from activities 1, 3 and 4. More able students could add reasons, and also describe what they wanted to do when they were younger.

Plenary

Students imagine that a journalist is going to record them talking about money. In groups, they nominate the best speaker and the class then votes for the four speakers with the most convincing accents to talk to the journalist.

★ Students make four statements about what they would do if they had the money.

◎ Students add reasons for their choices.

✚ Students add what they have done in the past for charity.

9.4 Les petits boulots! pages 154–155

Planner

Objectives
- Vocabulary: talk about part-time jobs
- Grammar: use *quand* with different tenses
- Skills: combine tenses to improve speaking and writing

Resources
- Student Book, pages 154–155
- CD 2, tracks 46–48
- Grammar and Skills Workbook, pages 34, 39 and 41
- Kerboodle, Unit 9
- Unit 9 Worksheets 4 (ex. 2), 5 (ex. 3)

Key language
vendeur/vendeuse, serveur/serveuse, plagiste, maître-nageur, jardinier/jardinière, baby-sitter
Quand j'avais onze ans, j'étais ...
Quand j'étais plus jeune, je faisais du baby-sitting/ je travaillais pour ...
L'été dernier/L'année dernière, j'étais/j'ai fait/ j'ai travaillé ...
En ce moment, je suis/je fais/je travaille ...
Quand j'aurai seize ans, ...
L'année prochaine, je serai/je ferai/je travaillerai ...

Grammar
- *Quand* with different tenses

PLTS
- Activity 1: Independent enquirers
- Activity 6: Effective participators
- Activity 7: Creative thinkers
- Plenary: Self-managers

Homework and self-study
- Student Book, page 154, activity 3
- Student Book, page 155, activity 7
- Grammar and Skills Workbook, pages 34, 39 and 41

Starters

See Kerboodle Starters bank for further details of **Word tennis** and **Categorise**.

- Play an adapted version of **Word tennis** to revise the use of *quand* + future tense (first covered in Unit 7). In pairs, students take turns to say each element of a quand clause: *Quand – j'irai – en Angleterre, – je visiterai – Londres*. Students can make up their own sentences, or put some options on the board if they need inspiration.
- Play **Categorise** to practise the different tenses required for activities 6 and 7. Students note down five conjugated verbs in each of the present, perfect, imperfect and future tenses, plus the conditional.

Plenaries

- **Switching tenses**. Students reflect individually on how being able to switch tenses confidently improves their written and spoken French. They should look through their exercise books carefully: *Ce que j'ai appris, c'est…* Working in small groups, students then give each other supportive feedback and suggestions for further improvement, backed up by examples from their work: *On s'évalue en groupes. Pour développer … Écris une chose qu'il/elle a bien faite. Écris une chose qu'il/elle pourrait faire pour s'améliorer.*

1 Lis et trouve les paires.
Students read the French job titles and match them to the correct photos. Encourage students to use their reading strategies to decode words that they do not know: can they spot any cognates (*baby-sitter, serveur/serveuse*)? Can they see the stems of words they do know (e.g. *vend-* from *vendre* in *vendeur/vendeuse*; *plag-* from *plage* in *plagiste*; *nag-* from *nager* in *maître-nageur*, etc.)

Answers: **1** b; **2** d; **3** a; **4** f; **5** e; **6** c

2 Écoute et vérifie.
Students listen and check their answers to activity 1.

CD 2, track 46   page 154, activité 2

Le numéro 1, vendeur ou vendeuse, c'est B.
Le 2, serveur ou serveuse, c'est D.
Et le numéro 3, plagiste, c'est A.
Le 4, maître-nageur, c'est F.
Le 5, jardinier ou jardinière, c'est E.
Et le dernier, baby-sitter, ben, c'est facile! C'est la lettre C, bien sûr!

---

3 Lis le texte d'Inès. Trouve et note les verbes 1–10.
Students read the text and fill the gaps with the correct verbs from the box. Advise students to read the text carefully and to pay close attention to the tense required in each gap. Refer them to the skills box on **Using different tenses** if they need a reminder.

Answers: **1** avais; **2** travaillais; **3** étais; **4** avait; **5** a travaillé; **6** était; **7** ont travaillé; **8** aurai; **9** aimerais; **10** travaillerai

⭐ Students find connectives and time expressions in Inès' text and give their English translations.

Answers: **Connectives:** et (and), en plus (what's more), parce que (because), ou (or), mais (but); **Time expressions:** quand (when), de temps en temps (from time to time), l'été dernier (last summer), tout le mois de juillet (the whole of July), l'année prochaine (next year), pendant (during)

◯ Students find in the text verbs in four tenses (imperfect, perfect, future, present) and the conditional.

Answers: **Imperfect:** j'avais, je travaillais, j'étais, je gardais, mon cousin avait, je gagnais, il était, Eliot était, c'était; **Perfect:** mon frère a travaillé, ils ont travaillé; **Future:** j'aurai, je pourrai, j'aurai, je travaillerai, on verra; **Present:** je peux, j'adore, je ne veux pas, c'est; **Conditional:** j'aimerais

4 Écoute et vérifie.
Students listen and check their answers to activity 2.

CD 2, track 47   page 154, activité 4

Moi, quand j'avais treize ans, je travaillais de temps en temps. J'étais baby-sitter pour ma tante. Je gardais mon cousin qui avait huit ans et je gagnais un peu d'argent de poche.
L'été dernier, mon frère, qui est plus âgé que moi, a travaillé tout le mois de juillet. Il était vendeur de glaces sur une plage et son copain Eliot était plagiste – en plus, ils ont travaillé sur la même plage, c'était sympa!
Moi, l'année prochaine, quand j'aurai seize ans, je pourrai travailler pendant les vacances parce que j'aurai l'âge légal. Si je peux choisir, j'aimerais être vendeuse dans un magasin de vêtements parce

9 Un métier, un rêve!

que j'adore la mode, ou je travaillerai dans un camping. Je ne veux pas travailler sur une plage comme mon frère parce que c'est trop fatigant. On verra!

○ ✂ **t** Students translate Inès' text into English. Refer them again to the skills box on **Using different tenses** and encourage them to think carefully about how the different tenses should be translated.

Answer: When I was thirteen, I used to work from time to time. I was a babysitter for my aunt. I used to look after my cousin who was eight and I used to earn a bit of pocket money. Last summer, my brother, who is older than me, worked all July. He was an ice cream seller on a beach and his friend Eliot was a beach attendant – and what's more, they worked on the same beach, it was nice! Next year when I am sixteen I will be able to work during the holidays because I will be of the legal age. If I can choose, I would like to be a sales assistant in a clothes shop, because I love fashion, or I will work on a campsite. I don't want to work on a beach like my brother because it's too tiring. We'll see!

5 Écoute l'interview de Paul. Vrai ou faux?
Students listen to the interview with Paul and decide whether the French statements are true or false.

○ Students correct the false statements.

*Answers: **a** faux (14); **b** vrai; **c** faux (he looks after his little brother); **d** vrai; **e** faux (beach attendant); **f** faux (he'll continue babysitting)*

○ **t** Students transcribe what Paul says.

⎍ **CD 2, track 48**   page 155, activité 5

- Bonjour, Paul, tu as quatorze ans! Est-ce que tu fais des petits boulots pour gagner un peu d'argent?
- Bonjour! Oui, de temps en temps, je suis jardinier pour ma grand-mère et les week-ends, je fais du baby-sitting pour aider mes parents. Je garde mon petit frère qui a cinq ans. Mais je ne gagne pas beaucoup d'argent!
- Est-ce que tu travailleras quand tu auras seize ans?
- Bien sûr! Moi, quand j'aurai seize ans, je travaillerai pendant les deux mois de vacances. J'aimerais être plagiste parce que j'adore être au bord de la mer. En plus, je pourrai travailler au soleil! Et si je peux, pendant la semaine, je continuerai à faire du baby-sitting pour mes parents parce que je gagne un peu d'argent!

6 Note tes réponses aux questions 1–3 et prépare une présentation. Tu peux inventer!
Before students embark on this activity, focus on the grammar box on **Using *quand* with different tenses**. Elicit from the class where they have come across this structure before (in the context of planning a holiday in Unit 7) and ask students to give some examples (e.g. *Quand on ira en Angleterre, on prendra le Shuttle*). Do the **Word tennis** starter activity to practise *quand* + future tense. Then introduce *quand* + imperfect tense. Ask students to look back at the text in activity 3 and spot the examples of *quand* + imperfect tense (*Moi, quand j'avais treize ans, je travaillais de temps en temps*) and *quand* + future tense (*Moi, l'année prochaine, quand j'aurai seize ans, je pourrai travailler pendant les vacances*).

When students are secure with the two formats, they prepare a presentation about part-time jobs, answering the three questions. They will need to use a range of tenses (perfect and imperfect for question 1; present for question 2; future for question 3); the **Categorise** starter activity will provide students with practice of the various tenses, if they need it. Encourage them to include both forms of the *quand* structure if they can. Students could make their presentations to the class or to small groups.

○ Students answer questions 1–3 about a friend, using the third person and appropriate tenses.

7 Écris un article sur tes petits boulots. 🖊
Students now put into writing their ideas from activity 6. They use the key language box and the text from activity 3 for support. Remind them to try to use four tenses and the conditional, and to include both forms of *quand* clause where appropriate.

> **Plenary**
>
> In pairs, students discuss the use of *quand* with different tenses and write down what they both think is the best way to remember this structure. They share their ideas with another pair.
>
> ★ Students make a sentence using *quand* in the imperfect tense.
>
> ○ Students add a sentence using *quand* in the future tense.
>
> ○ Students add a sentence using the perfect tense to say what job someone did last summer.

9.5 Échec et réussite

pages 156–157

Planner

Objectives
- Vocabulary: talk about success and failure
- Grammar: use different tenses
- Skills: use motivation strategies

Resources
- Student Book, pages 156–157
- CD 2, track 49
- Grammar and Skills Workbook, page 60
- Kerboodle, Unit 9

Key language

J'ai choisi ... parce que ...

Je l'adore pour son talent/son intelligence/son courage/sa détermination.

Il/Elle a eu des difficultés/problèmes dans sa vie.

Il/Elle était ...

Grammar
- Use different tenses

PLTS
- Activity 1: Independent enquirers
- Activity 4: Effective participators
- Activity 6: Creative thinkers
- Plenary: Self-managers

Homework and self-study
- Student Book, page 156, activity 2
- Student Book, page 157, activity 5
- Student Book, page 157, activity 6
- Grammar and Skills Workbook, page 60, activity 2

Starters
- Students work in pairs to research famous people, their qualities and the difficulties they have faced during their life. They could do this simply as a discussion about people they already know about, or could do some research using the Internet or magazine/newspaper articles.
- Hold a **Class discussion** about the **Motivation stategies**. Can students think of any others? How do they see themselves implementing these strategies into their language learning?

Plenaries
- **A final review.** Students write a text in French to a member of their family, telling them what they have achieved in their French studies. Display some examples to help less confident students: *Aujourd'hui au collège, j'ai parlé clairement avec un bon accent et j'ai fait des phrases complètes! J'ai appris et adapté le présent, le passé composé et le futur. Maintenant, je peux parler avec confiance et sans faire beaucoup d'erreurs. Je dois utiliser plus de phrases longues et détaillées/plus de conjonctions ...*

Students should present all the things they have learnt in recent months in a format of their choice, rank-ordering their importance. They then consider what they want to go on to achieve, setting themselves a final target: *Je vais continuer à/de ...* The text should be shown to their family at home.

1 Lis le texte. Vrai, faux ou pas mentionné?

Students read the text about Bill Gates and J. K. Rowling, and decide whether the English statements are true, false or not mentioned in the text. As a follow-up task, ask students to correct the false statements. As a Silver medal follow-up task, ask students to find in the text the French for 'one of the richest businessmen in the world' (*un des hommes d'affaires les plus riches du monde*) and 'one of the most famous authors in the world' (*un des écrivains les plus célèbres du monde*).

Answers: **a** *faux (they had a lot of problems <u>before</u> they were rich and famous);* **b** *faux (it wasn't very successful);* **c** *vrai;* **d** *vrai;* **e** *pas mentionné;* **f** *faux (she sold over 450 million books);* **g** *pas mentionné*

2 Traduis le texte de l'activité 1 en anglais.

Student translate the text from activity 1 into English. Refer them to the **Translation strategies** on page 153 and encourage them to follow these tips when working on their translation.

Translation:

Bill Gates and J. K. Rowling are rich and famous today, but before their success they had (some) problems.

When Bill Gates created his first business, he did not have much success. Then he founded Microsoft and he became one of the richest businessmen in the world.

9 Un métier, un rêve!

J. K. Rowling was a single mother who did not have a lot of money. She wrote the Harry Potter stories and sold more than 450 million books. She became one of the most famous authors in the world.

Bill Gates and J. K. Rowling succeeded because they were determined, motivated, courageous and passionate about what they did. They never abandoned their dreams. Determination, talent, intelligence and courage are essential in order to succeed.

3 Écoute (1–3). Eliot, Alice et Pierre parlent des personnalités qu'ils admirent. Recopie et remplis la grille en anglais.

Students listen, and copy and complete the grid. They note down which famous person each speaker talks about, what difficulties they faced during their life and what qualities they admire in them. As a follow-up task, ask students to spot how to say 'when he was alive' (*quand il était vivant*) and 'all his life' (*toute sa vie*) in Pierre's speech about Van Gogh.

Once students have completed the activity, refer them to the **Motivation strategies** and encourage them to take these on board throughout their language learning. Do the **Class discussion** starter activity and see if students can come up with any further ideas.

Problems in life? Answers:

	Who?	Qualities	Problems in life
1 Eliot	Einstein	intelligence, etermination	When he was little, he didn't speak and his teachers said he was lazy and not very intelligent
2 Alice	Jennifer Lopez	determination, talent	Left home at 19; lived in a dance studio because had no money for an apartment
3 Pierre	Van Gogh	determination, courage, talent	Very poor all his life; never had any money because no one wanted to buy his paintings; only sold one painting when he was alive

CD 2, track 49   page 156, activité 3

1 – Bonjour, Eliot, de quelle personnalité aimerais-tu parler?
– Je voudrais parler d'Albert Einstein.
– Pourquoi as-tu choisi Einstein?
– J'ai choisi Einstein parce que c'était un homme très intelligent. Il est devenu un grand scientifique et je l'admire pour son intelligence et sa détermination!
– Il a eu des difficultés dans sa vie?
– Ah oui, quand il était petit, il ne parlait pas et ses professeurs disaient qu'il était paresseux et qu'il n'était pas très intelligent!

2 – Et toi, Alice, de quelle personnalité voudrais-tu parler?
– J'aimerais parler de Jennifer Lopez.
– Pourquoi tu as choisi Jennifer Lopez?
– Parce que c'est une danseuse et une chanteuse que j'adore. J'aime sa détermination et son talent.
– Elle a eu des difficultés dans sa vie?
– Oui, quand elle avait dix-neuf ans, elle a quitté sa famille parce qu'elle voulait devenir danseuse. Pendant des mois, elle a habité dans un studio de danse parce qu'elle n'avait pas assez d'argent pour acheter un appartement. Aujourd'hui, elle est très célèbre et j'adore ses chansons!

3 – Et toi, Pierre?
– Moi, c'est Vincent Van Gogh que j'admire.
– Pourquoi est-ce que tu admires Van Gogh?
– Je l'admire parce que c'est un artiste que j'adore. J'adore le dessin et il m'a beaucoup influencé.
– Mais il a eu aussi des difficultés dans sa vie?
– Ah oui, toute sa vie, il a été très pauvre et il n'a jamais eu d'argent parce que personne ne voulait acheter ses peintures. Il a vendu une seule peinture quand il était vivant mais il a continué à peindre toute sa vie – il n'a jamais abandonné. J'admire sa détermination, son courage et son talent.

4 Choisis une personnalité, fais des recherches et réponds aux questions. Utilise les expressions soulignées.

Before students embark on this activity, do the research starter activity to give students the opportunity to find out about some famous people. Students then prepare a presentation about the famous person of their choice, detailing what he/she does/did, what qualities he/she has/had and giving reasons for their choice of person. Students use the speech bubbles given as a model and also refer to the text in activity 1 for support. Encourage students to draw on the language covered in the unit, using a range of tenses, *quand* + imperfect tense and job titles where appropriate.

➕ In pairs, students present their research and say what they want to achieve. Encourage them to evaluate each other's performace and provide feedback.

5 Lis les opinions des trois jeunes. Ils parlent de quels titres (a–d)?
Students read the young people's opinions and identify which kinds of success (a–d) are important to each person.
Answers: **Mehdi:** c, d; **Sacha:** b; **Noémie:** a, c, d

◯ Students find examples of four tenses (present, perfect, imperfect and future) in the texts.
Answers: **Present:** c'est, on aime, on aime, je crois, il faut, c'est, ce n'est pas, c'est, qui t'aiment, tu as, tu aimes, je pense, on fait, c'est; **Perfect:** j'ai eu; **Imperfect:** j'étais; **Future:** on travaillera, on sera, qui seront, tu seras, on aura, on gagnera, on pourra

➕ t Students translate the three highlighted *si* clauses into English. Remind them to think carefully about the tenses that are used and how these translate into English.
Answers: *if you like your job, you will work more and you will be happy!; If you have good friends and a family whom you love, you will be happy!; if you study, you will have a good job and earn money*

6 Complète les phrases 1–4 et écris un paragraphe: « Réussir, c'est quoi pour toi? »
Students use the sentence starters as the basis for the structure of their writing and the texts from activity 5 as a model.

◯ Students use a *si* clause and a future tense in their writing.

Plenary

In groups, students discuss what 'success' is for them. After completing the medal tasks, they write on a sticky note a target that they would like to achieve in their life, add the date and hand it in. Ensure there is a ready supply of sticky notes and keep the completed ones for review with the class at a later date. It might also be interesting to pass them on to whoever will be teaching the class next year, as students' targets are likely to change even more as time goes on.

⭐ Students say what the most important thing is for them to succeed in life.

◯ Students add a reason for their choice and use a *si* clause in their response. Remind them to check their tense usage.

➕ Students add an example of a famous person who overcame problems and explain why they were successful. Encourage them to use examples of both the perfect and imperfect tenses and to try to use *si* and *quand* phrases.

9.6 Labo-langue
pages 158–159

Planner

Objectives
- Grammar: job titles; the imperfect tense and the conditional; using *quand* with different tenses
- Skills: Super Strategies
- Pronunciation: tongue-twisters

Resources
- Student Book, pages 158–159
- CD 2, track 50
- Grammar and Skills Workbook, pages 60–61
- Kerboodle, Unit 9
- Unit 9 Worksheets 7, 8

PLTS
- Creative thinkers, Reflective learners, Self-managers

Job titles

t **1 Translate these sentences into French.**
Answers: **a** *Mon père est médecin.* **b** *Elle est actrice.* **c** *Ma sœur est coiffeuse.* **d** *Ma mère est avocate.* **e** *Mon frère est infirmier.* **f** *Tu es vétérinaire?/Es-tu vétérinaire?*

The imperfect tense and the conditional

2 Put each infinitive into the imperfect tense or the conditional. Write out the sentences.

t As a follow-up task, ask students to translate the sentences into English.

9 Un métier, un rêve!

Answers: **a** Si j'<u>étais</u> célèbre, je <u>gagnerais</u> beaucoup d'argent. (If I were famous, I would earn a lot of money.) **b** Si j'<u>avais</u> seize ans, je <u>travaillerais</u> pendant les vacances. (If I were sixteen, I would work during the holidays.) **c** Si mon père <u>était</u> premier ministre, il <u>créerait</u> des écoles. (If my father were prime minister, he would create schools.) **d** Si je <u>gagnais</u> des millions, j'<u>aurais</u> un jet privé et je <u>ferais</u> le tour du monde. (If I earned millions, I would have a private jet and I would do a world tour/go round the world.)

Using *quand* with different tenses

3 Put each infinitive into the imperfect tense or the future tense. Write out the sentences.

t As a follow-up task, ask students to translate the sentences into English.

Answers: **a** Quand j'<u>étais</u> plus jeune, je <u>voulais</u> être footballeur. (When I was younger, I wanted to be a footballer.) **b** Quand mon père <u>était</u> jeune, il <u>travaillait</u> sur une plage. (When my father was young, he used to work on a beach.) **c** L'année prochaine, quand j'<u>aurai</u> dix-huit ans, je <u>ferai</u> le tour du monde. (Next year, when I'm 18, I'll go round the world.) **d** Demain, quand on <u>arrivera</u> à Londres, on <u>ira</u> voir Big Ben. (Tomorrow, when we arrive in London, we will go to see Big Ben.)

Super Strategies

This section encourages students to think about combining strategies and applying them whatever the task, when reading, writing or speaking. They are particularly encouraged to try out the strategies in activities 6 and 7 on page 149.

Students are advised to use their background knowledge, to zoom in on useful structures and vocabulary, to apply patterns and grammar rules, to add extra details to personalise their text, and to use what they already know to overcome problems.

Pronunciation: tongue-twisters

4 Listen and repeat these tongue-twisters!

Discuss with the class the importance of developing a really good French accent by putting together everything they have learnt about French pronunciation in *Allez 1* and *2*.

Students use the *virelangues* (tongue-twisters) to help them practise. Encourage them to say the tongue-twisters slowly at first, concentrating on pronouncing everything clearly and correctly. Challenge them to learn them by heart and to try to say them as quickly as they can.

t As a follow-up task, challenge students to translate the tongue-twisters into English.

Answers: **a** Are the socks of the archduchess dry? Extra-dry! **b** Poor little fisherman, be patient in order to catch several little fish. **c** In the police station, when one police officer laughs, all the police officers in the police station laugh. **d** A pastry chef who was making pastries/cakes at the home of a wallpaperer* said one day to the wallpaperer who was wallpapering: is it better to make pastries at the home of a wallpaperer who is wallpapering or to wallpaper at the home of a pastry chef who is making pastries? (*tapissier can be a painter and decorator or someone who puts wallpaper up (a wallpaperer?), or it can be an upholsterer or a tapestry maker ...)

CD 2, track 50   page 159, activité 4

a Les chaussettes de l'archiduchesse sont-elles sèches? Archi-sèches!
b Pauvre petit pêcheur, prends patience pour pouvoir prendre plusieurs petits poissons.
c Dans la gendarmerie, quand un gendarme rit, tous les gendarmes rient dans la gendarmerie.
d Un pâtissier qui pâtissait chez un tapissier qui tapissait dit un jour au tapissier qui tapissait: vaut-il mieux pâtisser chez un tapissier qui tapisse ou tapisser chez un pâtissier qui pâtisse?

9.7 Extra Star   page 160

1 Find the ten jobs in the word snake.
Answers: archéologue; premier ministre; professeur; vendeuse; journaliste; photographe; chanteur; vétérinaire; médecin; plagiste

t 2 Write out these sentences with the words in the correct order. Translate the sentences into English.

Answers: **a** Ma mère est professeur et elle travaille dans un collège. (My mother is a teacher and she works in a secondary school.) **b** Quand mon père était jeune, il travaillait dans une piscine. (When my father was young, he used to work at a swimming pool.) **c** Pour être vétérinaire, il faut aimer les animaux. (To be a vet, you have to like animals.) **d** Quand j'avais cinq ans, je voulais devenir footballeur. (When I was five, I wanted to be a footballer.)

3 Read Benjamin's email and answer the questions in English.

Answers: **a** because he's got a job/has had a job for a week; **b** in a clothes shop; **c** in a cake shop; **d** last weekend; **e** cakes; **f** in August; **g** go to England with some friends

4 Write five suggestions to complete this sentence.

Students write their own endings to the sentence starter, *Si je gagnais au loto, …* Remind them to use the conditional in the second half of the sentence.

9.7 Extra Plus

page 161

1 Ils font quel métier? Quelles qualités sont nécessaires?

Students write sentences, identifying the job title in each photo and describing the qualities necessary for the job (accept any appropriate qualities for each job). Encourage students to try different structures: for example, *Pour être* + job, *il faut être* + adjective/*il faut avoir* + noun/*il faut aimer … C'est un métier qui demande* + noun.

Answers: **a** *Je suis chirurgien.* **b** *Je suis réalisatrice.* **c** *Je suis chef cuisinier.* **d** *Je suis archéologue.*

t 2 Trouve les paires et écris les phrases. Traduis les phrases en anglais.

Students match the sentence halves and then translate the sentences into English.

Answers: **1** c; **2** d; **3** e; **4** b; **5** a

1 *Quand j'avais six ans, je voulais devenir danseuse.* (When I was six, I wanted to be a dancer.) **2** *Si j'étais riche, je donnerais de l'argent à des associations caritatives.* (If I were rich, I would give money to charities.) **3** *Ma mère est médecin et elle travaille dans un cabinet médical.* (My mother is a doctor and she works in a surgery.) **4** *Pour être médecin, il faut aimer les gens.* (To be a doctor, you have to/it is necessary to like people.) **5** *C'est un métier qui demande beaucoup d'énergie.* (It is a job which demands/requires a lot of energy.)

3 Lis et réponds aux questions en anglais.

Students read the text and answer the questions in English.

Answers: **a** to become rich and famous (like Michael Jackson); **b** he travelled everywhere, sang, danced and earned a lot of money and Océane loved him. **c** Was Michael Jackson happy? **d** she thinks that money isn't the most important thing; **f** a job that is exciting and enriching; **f** she would help charities and create hospitals for children in Africa; **g** she will work during the holidays/do voluntary work

t 4 Traduis les phrases en français. Trouve les expressions dans l'Unité 9.

Students translate the sentences into French, using language from the unit.

Answers: **a** *Mon père est médecin. Il travaille dans un hôpital. Quand il avait dix-huit ans, il était maître-nageur.* **b** *Quand j'aurai seize ans, je travaillerai pendant les vacances. J'aimerais aussi voyager et faire le tour du monde.* **c** *Quand j'avais dix ans, je voulais devenir photographe. Je rêvais de travailler avec des animaux mais maintenant j'ai changé d'avis. Je voudrais être professeur parce que j'adore les enfants mais je pense que c'est un métier qui demande beaucoup d'énergie.*

9.8 Lire

page 162

Resources	PLTS
• Student Book, page 162 • Kerboodle, Unit 9	• Independent enquirers

@ 1 In excerpt 1, it is January 1914 and Hadrien is back at school after the Christmas holiday. Before you read it, try to predict what might be mentioned (such as classmates, subjects …).

Refer students to the cultural information box and explain that the reading text comprises two excerpts from a novel, *14–14*, by Silène Edgar (see interview on page 36 (Unit 2 *Lire*)) and Paul Beorn. The book is about two boys of the same age who live in the same French village in Picardie: Adrien lives there in 2014, Hadrien in 1914. They correspond with each other via a magic letterbox. For Hadrien, the First World War is about to begin.

Students should undertake this activity before they read the text. Encourage them to think carefully about what life would have been like in 1914 and what types

9 Un métier, un rêve!

of things are likely to be mentioned. Ideas might include: Hadrien's classmates, their clothes, what the classroom looks like, school equipment, school subjects.

2 Read excerpt 1. Did you predict correctly? Find the phrases that tell you about a–e. They are highlighted in yellow.

Answers: **a** *maître Pierre, maître Julien;* **b** *le petit Marcelin;* **c** *la petite salle;* **d** *le poêle ronronne;* **e** *encre fraîche, les encriers*

3 In excerpt 2, Hadrien talks about his future plans. Match phrases a–f to the phrases highlighted in blue.

Answers: **a** *avec soin;* **b** *intégrer;* **c** *le rêve;* **d** *toute une affaire;* **e** *lauréats;* **f** *grâce à*

4 Read excerpt 2 again. Answer these questions in English.

Answers: **a** several months; **b** end of June; **c** they get books, dictionaries and a savings account; **d** postman, policeman, railway worker; **e** small local secondary school (petit lycée), larger secondary school (lycée), engineering college (École des arts et métiers); **f** he wants to become an engineer/civil engineer

9.8 Vidéo   page 163

Resources
- Student Book, page 163
- Kerboodle, Unit 9 Video clip

PLTS
- Independent enquirers

Épisode 9: Quiz: Le métier!
The group of friends are in the conference room of the town hall, ready to undertake the final challenge of the competition: they have to choose the ideal job for themselves and their friends. They take turns to question each other and guess what each person's ideal job would be. In so doing, they discuss the characteristics needed for each job, their likes and dislikes and their hopes for the future.

Video clip, Unit 9   page 163

(At the conference room of the town hall)

Thouraya: Qu'est-ce qu'on fait ici, Jules?
Basile: On va assister à une conférence?
Maxime: Non. C'est le nouveau défi. « Quel est le métier de tes rêves? Choisissez le bon métier pour vos copains. »
Zaied: Quoi? Comment on va faire ça?
Jules: On va faire « le speed dating des métiers ».
Maxime: Pour commencer, à toi, Zaied.
Zaied: Moi?
Jémilie: Quand tu étais petit qu'est-ce que tu voulais faire comme métier?
Zaied: Je voulais devenir footballeur professionnel.
Clarisse: Est-ce que tu fais toujours beaucoup de sport?
Zaied: Oui, je fais de la boxe trois fois par semaine et je joue au football.
Thouraya: Est-ce que tu aimes manger?
Zaied: Oui, j'aime manger et j'aime cuisiner aussi.
Jules: Ça y est. Trois questions. Maintenant il faut le deviner.
Thouraya: Chef cuisinier.
Jémilie: Boxeur?
Clarisse: Footballeur professionnel.
Zaied: Mais je ne veux pas être ni chef cuisinier ni footballeur ni boxeur.
Clarisse: Tu veux faire quoi donc?
Zaied: Je veux devenir professeur d'éducation physique car j'aimerais travailler avec les enfants et j'aime beaucoup le sport.
Jémilie: Excellent. Pour ce métier il faut avoir beaucoup d'énergie et toi, tu as toujours beaucoup d'énergie.
Thouraya: Quand j'étais petite je voulais être médecin mais cela ne m'intéresse plus.
Maxime: Quelles sont les qualités qu'il faut pour le métier de tes rêves?

Thouraya:	Il faut être créative, patiente et je rêve d'être célèbre.
Basile:	Créative, patiente, célèbre … Tu aimes la musique?
Thouraya:	Ah oui, j'aime beaucoup la musique.
Zaied:	Je sais!
Maxime:	Artiste.
Basile:	Rock star.
Jules:	Chef d'entreprise?
Zaied:	Coiffeuse.
Thouraya:	Quoi? Rock star? Je ne sais même pas chanter, moi, et coiffeuse ne m'as jamais intéressée. Maxime a raison: mon métier de rêve serait d'être artiste.
Maxime:	Quand j'étais plus jeune, je voulais être archéologue car j'aimais beaucoup les programmes d'archéologie.
Clarisse:	Est-ce que tu aimes toujours l'histoire?
Maxime:	Oui, bien sûr. Mais pour faire ce métier, il faut être créatif aussi.
Jémilie:	Est-ce qu'il faut avoir un diplôme pour faire ce métier?
Maxime:	Je ne pense pas. Mais j'irai à l'université pour étudier.
Clarisse:	Musicien.
Thouraya:	Professeur d'histoire.
Jémilie:	Réalisateur.
Maxime:	Oui, Jémilie a raison. J'aimerais être réalisateur de programmes d'histoire à la télé. C'est un métier très intéressant et on peut voyager partout dans le monde.
Jules:	C'est le dernier tour. Il nous reste deux minutes seulement.
Clarisse:	Quand j'avais dix ans, je voulais être vétérinaire parce que j'aime beaucoup les animaux.
Zaied:	Est-ce que tu voudrais toujours travailler avec les animaux?
Clarisse:	Non, pas du tout. Mais pour faire ce métier, il faut être scientifique.
Jules:	Scientifique. Est-ce qu'il faut être en forme pour faire ce travail?
Clarisse:	Oui, pour faire ce travail il faut être scientifique et il faut aimer voyager aussi.
Girls:	Clarisse veut être astronaute.
Clarisse:	Oui, je veux être astronaute et voyager dans la station spatiale ou vers les étoiles.
Zaied:	Être astronaute! Tu es vraiment courageuse, Clarisse.
Clarisse:	Ah oui, mais ça va être difficile. Mais c'est mon rêve!

1 Regarde le début de l'épisode 9. Les jeunes arrivent dans la salle de conférences de l'hôtel de ville. Qu'est-ce qu'on fait ici?

Students watch the final episode of the video drama and identify what the friends are doing at the conference room of the town hall.

Answers: C'est pour le dernier défi: ils doivent choisir le métier idéal pour leurs copains/copines. (It's for the final challenge: they have to choose the ideal job for themselves and their friends.)

2 Relie les caractéristiques (a–m) aux quatre jeunes: Zaied, Thouraya, Maxime, Clarisse. Attention: <u>deux</u> caractéristiques correspondent à <u>deux</u> jeunes.

Students match the characteristics listed to the correct person. Make sure they are aware that two of the characteristics apply to two people. One characteristic (a) is not needed at all.

Answers: **Zaied:** *e, g, j, m;* **Thouraya:** *a, b, h, k;* **Maxime:** *d, f, h;* **Clarisse:** *c, f, i, l*

3 Qu'est-ce que les quatres jeunes voulaient faire quand ils étaient petits? Et maintenant?

Students identify which jobs each person wanted to do when they were younger and which they would like to do now. They choose one job from a–h and one from i–o.

Answers: **Zaied:** *e, m;* **Thouraya:** *f, i;* **Maxime:** *a, o;* **Clarisse:** *h, j*

4 Choisis un métier de l'activité 3. À ton avis, quelles qualités sont nécessaires pour faire ce métier? Aimerais-tu faire ce métier plus tard? Pourquoi?

Students choose a job they would like to do from those listed in activity 3. In groups, they discuss the necessary qualities for their chosen job and say whether they would like to do this job in the future. Encourage them to justify their opinions with reasons.

9 Un métier, un rêve!

9.9 Test
page 164

Resources
- Student Book, page 164
- CD 2, track 51

PLTS
- Creative thinkers, Reflective learners, Effective participators

AT levels
Approximate medal guidelines:
- (Foundation) L: 4–5; S: 4–5; R: 4–5; W: 4–5
- (Core) L: 5; S: 5; R: 5; W: 5
- (Higher) L: 6; S: 6; R: 6; W: 6

1 Listen (1–4). Four young people are being interviewed about their jobs. Copy and fill in the grid in English. (See pages 148–151 and 154–155.)

Answers:

	Job	Likes/Dislikes it? Reasons?	Used to …	Dream job
1	journalist	loves it – it's a fascinating job, very varied, requires a lot of energy, he travels a lot	worked in McDonald's, was babysitter for parents' friends at weekends	journalist
2	doctor	likes and dislikes it – likes helping sick people but it's tiring and stressful and you need lots of energy and patience	worked in clothes shop and was a lifeguard at a swimming pool during summer holidays	teacher or dancer
3	sales assistant in sports shop	doesn't like it – boring and tiring	was babysitter – looked after his little brother at weekends when parents were working	vet
4	PE teacher in a school	loves it – exciting, likes working with children, it's a bit tiring because you need energy and patience	waitress in restaurant at weekends	teacher

CD 2, track 51   page 164, activity 1

1
- Bonjour, Adrien, quel métier fais-tu?
- Moi, je suis journaliste.
- Est-ce que tu aimes ton métier?
- Bien sûr, j'adore mon métier. C'est un métier passionnant, très varié et qui demande aussi beaucoup d'énergie. Mais ce que j'aime le plus, c'est que je voyage beaucoup.
- Avant d'être journaliste, quel petits boulots as-tu fait quand tu étais plus jeune?
- Quand j'avais seize ans, tous les étés je travaillais au McDo et les week-ends, je faisais du baby-sitting pour des amis de mes parents.
- Si tu pouvais choisir le métier de tes rêves, ce serait quoi?
- Je serais journaliste! Je ne voudrais pas changer!

2
- Et toi, Isabelle, quel métier fais-tu?
- Moi, je suis médecin. Je travaille dans un cabinet médical.
- Tu aimes ton métier?
- Oui et non. J'aime mon métier parce qu'on aide les gens qui sont malades, mais je trouve que c'est trop fatigant et très stressant. Il faut beaucoup d'énergie et de patience!
- Avant d'être médecin, tu as fait des petits boulots?
- Oui, je voulais gagner un peu d'argent, donc pendant les vacances d'été, je travaillais dans un magasin de vêtements. J'étais aussi maître-nageur dans une piscine. C'était génial.
- Si tu pouvais choisir le métier de tes rêves, ce serait quoi?
- Je ne pense pas que je serais médecin mais peut-être professeur ou danseuse. Pourquoi pas? J'adore la danse!

3
- Et toi, Maxime?
- Moi, je suis vendeur dans un magasin de sport.
- Tu aimes ton métier?
- Non, pas du tout. C'est très ennuyeux et c'est fatigant aussi.
- Tu as fait d'autres petits boulots avant d'être vendeur?
- Non, pas vraiment ... Mais quand j'avais seize ans, j'étais baby-sitter. Je gardais mon petit frère quand mes parents travaillaient les week-ends!
- Si tu pouvais choisir le métier de tes rêves, ce serait quoi?
- J'aimerais être vétérinaire parce que j'adore les animaux!

4
- Et toi, Caroline, quel métier fais-tu?
- Moi, je suis prof d'EPS dans un collège.
- Tu aimes ton travail?
- Oui, j'adore mon métier. C'est passionnant parce que ce que je préfère, c'est travailler avec les enfants. C'est un peu fatigant parce qu'il faut de l'énergie et de la patience!
- Et avant, tu avais un petit boulot?
- Oui, quand j'avais dix-huit ans, j'étais serveuse dans un restaurant. Je travaillais tous les week-ends.
- Si tu pouvais choisir le métier de tes rêves, ce serait quoi?
- Je pense que je serais prof, comme aujourd'hui!
- Merci à tous! Et travaillez bien!

2 Prepare a presentation about jobs you used to do and your ambitions. (See pages 150–155.)
Remind students to cover all the bullet points, use the full range of tenses required and to develop and extend their speaking as much as possible.

3 Read Karim's text and answer the questions in English. (See pages 148–153.)
Answers: a he wanted to be a singer because his dream was to be famous and earn a lot of money; b he's a music teacher in a secondary school; c he wanted to be prime minister and change the world/earn millions; d he has chosen to work in the medical field because it's an exciting and enriching job and because you help sick people; e to be a doctor in Africa and work for Médecins Sans Frontières/help sick children; f build/create schools and hospitals

4 Imagine you are a famous person who has achieved success in the world of business, entertainment, sport or humanitarian work. Write a short magazine article about your career. (See pages 148–155.)
Remind students to cover all the bullet points, use the full range of tenses required, use connectives, give opinions and reasons and to develop and extend their writing as much as possible.

Grammar and Skills Workbook Answers

Each page of grammar activities in the Workbook suggests a cross-reference to an appropriate point in the Student Book where the activities may be used. Cross-references to the Workbook grammar and skills activities are also suggested in the Planner sections throughout this Handbook. However, these are just our suggestions and you may choose to use the Workbook activities at other points, depending on the needs of your students.

Parts of a verb Workbook page 4

1 a Il; b Ils; c Elle; d je; e Elles; f nous

2 a tu fais; b allez-vous; c vous aimez; d tu as; e vous habitez

t *Suggested translations:* a Hi, Maxime, what are you doing? b Fabien and Zoë, when are you going to London? c Sir, do you like visiting Britain? d Mum, have you got my passport? e Mr and Mrs Lebrun, do you live in a flat?

3 a 6; b 3; c 7; d 1; e 2; f 5; g 4

Negatives Workbook page 5

1 **Positive:** a, d, f, g, i; **Negative:** b, c, e, h, j
b On <u>ne</u> roule <u>pas</u> à gauche en France. c Mon ami <u>n'a jamais</u> pris l'avion. e On <u>n'a rien</u> fait hier soir. h Elle <u>ne</u> va <u>plus</u> à la maison des jeunes. j Il <u>ne</u> prend <u>ni</u> le train <u>ni</u> le bus.

2 a Non, je <u>ne</u> prends <u>pas</u> le bus. b Non, je <u>n'</u>utilise <u>jamais</u> mon vélo. c Non, je <u>n'ai pas</u> regardé de film. d Elle <u>ne va</u> ni à Paris <u>ni à Nice</u>. e Non, on <u>ne va plus en ville</u>. f Je <u>ne fais rien</u>.

3 **t** a On ne va pas/Nous n'allons pas à Paris. b Mon ami(e) ne va plus en vacances. c On ne fait rien/Nous ne faisons rien ce soir. d Elle ne prend jamais l'avion. e Il n'a pas regardé de film(s). f Je n'aime ni le train ni le bus.

Present tense of *avoir* Workbook page 6

Answers:

1 1 as; 2 ai; 3 Avez; 4 ai; 5 a; 6 avons; 7 ont; 8 a
1 c; 2 h; 3 e; 4 f; 5 a; 6 g; 7 b; 8 d

2 a ai; b avons; c as; d a; e ont

3 **t** a J'ai une grande collection de BD. b Elle a quatorze ans. c Nous avons/On a beaucoup de gadgets. d Tu as soif./Vous avez soif. e (Est-ce que) Tu as/Vous avez vu le documentaire? f Qu'est-ce qu'il a fait?

Present tense of *être* Workbook page 7

1 a suis pas fan! b es née, Lucile? c est situé dans les Alpes. d sont des Français célèbres. e sommes très différents. f êtes allés en Irlande?

2 **Horizontalement:** 8 est; 6 suis; 1 sont; 4 moi; **Verticalement:** 2 tu; 7 il; 5 ils; 1 sommes; 3 êtes

Connectives (1)

Workbook page 8

1   a mais; b Cependant; c et; d Par contre;
    e En revanche; f Comme; g pourtant; h donc

2   a cependant; b et; c Par contre; d mais; e donc;
    f car; g Comme; h parce qu'; i En revanche

A	C	E	C	G	P	I	L	N	P
E	N	R	E	V	A	N	C	H	E
R	S	U	P	X	R	Z	B	D	F
H	J	L	E	M	C	O	M	M	E
C	A	R	N	O	O	Q	T	W	Y
A	C	E	D	O	N	C	G	I	K
E	L	N	A	P	T	R	T	V	X
T	Z	B	N	D	R	M	A	I	S
F	H	J	T	L	E	N	P	R	T
V	X	P	A	R	C	E	Q	U	'

Connectives (2)

Workbook page 9

1   a C'est mon père qui aime les comédies. b La France est un pays qui utilise l'euro. c Marion Cotillard est une actrice française qui est née en 1975. d Lucky Luke est un cowboy imaginaire qui est le personnage principal d'une BD. e Le capitaine Haddock est un personnage de BD qui est le meilleur ami de Tintin.

2   a Astérix est un personnage de BD que j'aime beaucoup. b J'ai un smartphone que j'adore.

c Les Misérables est un livre que Victor Hugo a écrit. d C'est un film que je trouve ennuyeux. e Chez nous, il y a un uniforme qu'on porte à l'école.

3   **t** a What is important is Marie Curie's work on radioactivity. b What interests me is the history of France. c The thing I admire is Jean-Paul Gaultier's style. d The thing that I hate is electronic music.

4   Students' own answers.

Questions

Workbook page 10

1   **t** a Est-ce que tu fais du sport? Do you do (any) sport? b Est-ce que tu parles espagnol? Do you speak Spanish? c Est-ce que Léa aime manger les fruits? Does Léa like eating fruit? d Est-ce que vous avez travaillé en France? Have you worked in France?

2   **t** a Aimes-tu ton travail? Do you like your work? b Avez-vous de l'argent? Have you any money?

c Dois-tu passer un examen? Do you have to take an exam? d As-tu étudié les sciences? Did you study science?

3   a 3 Est-ce que tu aimes les légumes? b 6 Qu'est-ce qu'elle a inventé? c 1 Dois-tu parler d'autres langues? d 5 Quelles études vas-tu faire? e 4 Quand as-tu commencé ce travail? f 2 Pourquoi as-tu choisi ce métier?

187

Grammar and Skills Workbook Answers

Direct object pronouns
Workbook page 11

1 Moi, j'aime les dessins animés parce que je <u>les</u> trouve amusants. En revanche, les émissions de télé-réalité, je <u>les</u> trouve bêtes. Je préfère la musique, surtout le hip-hop. Ah oui, ce genre de musique, je **l'**adore. Les magazines? Je ne **les** lis pas souvent, mais j'aime lire des romans. La série *Oksa Pollock* est fantastique – je **l'**aime bien. Le dernier livre de cette série, je **le** lis en ce moment.

2 **a** les; **b** la; **c** les; **d** le; **e** l'; **f** l'

3 Students' own answers.

4 **t** **a** I find you/think you are very calm. **b** Comedies amuse us. **c** My parents treat me like a baby. **d** Léa et Max, I'm waiting (I'll wait) for you at the café.

Indirect object pronouns
Workbook page 12

1 **a** 5 me; **b** 3 te; **c** 8 lui; **d** 1 leur; **e** 7 lui; **f** 2 vous; **g** 6 nous; **h** 4 me

2 **a** Elle lui parle. **b** Nous lui donnons 10 euros. **c** Je lui ai envoyé des SMS. **d** Je ne leur ai pas téléphoné. **e** Ils lui font confiance.

3 Students' own answers.

Opinions (present tense)
Workbook page 13

1 **Positive:** a, b, f, g; **Negative:** c, d, e, h

2 **a** J'adore regarder les jeux télévisés. **b** Je n'aime pas écouter la musique punk. **c** Je déteste lire les romans historiques. **d** Tu aimes lire/regarder les BD?

3 Students' own answers.

Opinions (mixed tense)
Workbook page 14

1 **a** 6; **b** 4; **c** 2; **d** 8; **e** 1; **f** 7; **g** 3; **h** 5

2

Perfect	Imperfect	Present	Future
d, e, g	e, f, h	a, b, c, f, h	c

3 **a** J'ai lu ce livre deux fois parce que je l'<u>ai trouvé</u> captivant. I (have) read the book twice because I found it captivating. **b** Il ne prend pas le train parce qu'il <u>préfère</u> voyager en bus. He doesn't take the bus because he prefers to travel by train. **c** Elle a <u>détesté</u> le concert. C'<u>était</u> nul. She hated the concert – it was rubbish. **d** On va en Suisse – ce <u>sera</u> vraiment incroyable. We're going to Switzerland – it will be really incredible. **e** Salomé n'<u>a</u> pas <u>aimé</u> le documentaire. Moi non plus. Salomé didn't like the documentary. Nor did I.

faire + infinitive
Workbook page 15

1 **a** 3; **b** 5; **c** 1; **d** 6; **e** 2; **f** 4

2 **1** a; **2** f; **3** d; **4** b; **5** e; **6** c

3 Students' own answers.

Adjectives (agreement)

Workbook page 16

1

masculine singular	feminine singular	masculine plural	feminine plural	English meaning
démodé	démodée	démodés	démodées	*old-fashioned*
divertissant	divertissante	divertissants	divertissantes	*entertaining*
éducatif	éducative	éducatifs	éducatives	*educational*
enfantin	enfantine	enfantins	enfantines	*childish*
ennuyeux	ennuyeuse	ennuyeux	ennuyeuses	*boring*
essentiel	essentielle	essentiels	essentielles	*essential*
gris	grise	gris	grises	*grey*
rapide	rapide	rapides	rapides	*fast, quick*

2 a amusants; **b** divertissante; **c** informatifs; **d** bleu, démodé; **e** pratiques, ennuyeux

3 a essentielles; **b** éducative; **c** passionnantes; **d** nulles; **e** travailleuse, travailleurs

Adjectives (position and agreement)

Workbook page 17

1 a vieux; **b** gentil; **c** vieux; **d** vieille, verte; **e** nouvelles, bleues; **f** belle, petite; **g** bel; **h** grand, moderne

2 a J'aime la nouvelle tablette rouge. **b** Je n'aime pas les vieux ordinateurs gris. **c** Elle a un gros chien noir. **d** Tu aimes mes nouveaux jeux vidéo? **e** Ma vieille tablette a un petit écran.

3 a le vieux; **b** la nouvelle; **c** les petits; **d** les vertes

4 a 3; **b** 1; **c** 2

Comparative and superlative

Workbook page 18

1 True: a, b, c; **False:** d, e, f.

As a follow-up task, students correct the false statements.

2 a pratique; **b** polluants; **c** chers; **d** meilleur; **e** dangereuses

3 Students' own answers.

Demonstrative adjectives

Workbook page 19

1 a ces; **b** cet; **c** cette; **d** ce; **e** ces; **f** cette

2 a cette; **b** cet; **c** ces; **d** ce

Grammar and Skills Workbook Answers

Impersonal structures
Workbook page 20

1 a 4; b 6; c 8; d 2; e 7; f 1; g 5; h 3

2 **(t)** a Il est nécessaire de boire de l'eau. b Il est difficile d'écouter régulièrement. c Il est essentiel de ne pas oublier son/ton/votre mot de passe. d Il est impossible de manger trop de produits sucrés! e Il faut parler français en classe. f Il ne faut rien oublier.

3 Students' own answers.

Prepositions
Workbook page 21

1 J'habite <u>dans</u> un appartement (a) <u>**au** centre de</u> notre village, <u>en face</u> (b) <u>**des**</u> magasins. Je vais (c) <u>**aux**</u> magasins assez souvent. Notre appartement est (d) <u>**au**</u> rez-de-chaussée. Ma chambre est <u>à gauche</u> (e) <u>**des**</u> WC et <u>en face</u> (f) <u>**de la**</u> salle de bains. C'est très pratique le matin! <u>Dans</u> ma chambre, le lit est <u>à côté</u> (g) <u>**de la**</u> fenêtre. <u>Sur</u> la table, <u>à droite</u> (h) <u>**de l'**</u>étagère, il y a mon ordinateur. Je n'ai pas de télé.

(t) I live in a flat in the centre of our village, opposite some shops. I go to the shops quite often. Our flat is on the ground floor. My bedroom is to the left of the toilet and opposite the bathroom. It's very handy in the morning! In my bedroom, the bed is next to the window. On the table, to the right of the shelves, there is my computer. I don't have a TV.

2 a de limiter; b à aller; c de jouer; d à écouter; e de rester; f à choisir

Pronouns (en, y)
Workbook page 22

1 a Oui, j'en mange cinq par jour. b Oui, j'en ai assez. c Non, je n'en fais pas. d Oui, j'en ai bu un litre. e Oui, il y en a trois sur la table. f Non, je n'y vais pas.

2 a Oui, il y en a. b Il y en a trois. c Non, il y en a quatre. d Oui, j'en ai trouvé. e Non, je n'en ai pas acheté.

3 Students' own answers.

Expressions of frequency
Workbook page 23

1 a 3; b 7; c 1; d 5; e 2; f 4; g 6; 1 = TOUS LES JOURS

2 a 3; b 6; c 1; d 5; e 2; f 4

(t) a I go to the sports centre very often. b It is important to drink water regularly. c Sometimes we go swimming. d In winter, I go skiing once a week. e You must eat at least five fruits and vegetables a day. f At breakfast, I always eat cereal.

3 Students' own answers.

Reflexive verbs
Workbook page 24

1 a 6; b 3; c 1; d 9; e 4; f 7; g 2; h 5; i 8

2 a m'; b s'; c te; d s'; e vous; f nous; g se; h me; i me; j se

3 a Nous nous amusons./On s'amuse. b Je m'inspire de (+ name). c Elle se prépare pour la fête. d Je veux me protéger en ligne. e Je ne veux pas me séparer de mon smartphone/portable.

190

Present tense of -er verbs
Workbook page 25

1 **a** rentre; **b** préfères; **c** achètent; **d** rêve; **e** utilisez; **f** espère

2 **a** on; **b** je; **c** Tu; **d** Vous; **e** Fabien; **f** Mes parents

3 **a** 2 commences; **b** 5 arrivent; **c** 1 espérez; **d** 6 logeons; **e** 4 reflète; **f** 3 essaie

Present tense of -ir verbs
Workbook page 26

1 **a** 4 finissons; **b** 6 choisissent; **c** 2 grossit; **d** 5 rougissent; **e** 1 réfléchissez; **f** 3 remplis

2 **Horizontalement: 2** réfléchit; **4** elles; **7** finissons; **8** choisissez; **11** ils; **12** remplit;
   Verticalement: 1 réussissent; **3** tu; **5** grossir; **6** Nous; **9** Elle; **10** Il

Present tense of -re verbs
Workbook page 27

1 **a** 3; **b** 5; **c** 7; **d** 6; **e** 4; **f** 1; **g** 8; **h** 2

2 **a** attendons; **b** répond; **c** perds; **d** descendez; **e** entends; **f** vendent; **g** prenons; **h** mets

3 **t** **a** Je réponds toujours à ses textos/SMS. **b** Elle ne perd jamais son portable/smartphone. **c** Nous descendons la rue maintenant. **d** Qu'est-ce qu'on met pour le concert? **e** Mes copains/copines attendent le bus en ville. **f** Vous/Est-ce que vous prenez l'ascenseur? Je/Moi, je descends l'escalier.

Present tense of regular verbs
Workbook page 28

1
je réussis	réussir	I succeed/am succeeding
tu préfères	préférer	you prefer
il attend	attendre	he waits/is waiting
elle choisit	choisir	she chooses/is choosing
on travaille	travailler	we/you/they work/are working
nous vendons	vendre	we sell/are selling
vous finissez	finir	you finish/are finishing
ils voyagent	voyager	they travel/are travelling
elles répondent	répondre	they reply/are replying

V	O	Y	A	G	E	N	T	I	L
E	A	T	R	B	C	D	R	E	P
N	A	R	É	G	H	I	A	J	R
D	T	L	U	N	O	P	V	R	É
O	T	S	S	U	I	V	A	Y	F
N	E	Z	S	H	S	J	I	L	È
S	N	N	I	P	I	R	L	S	R
S	D	O	S	R	T	V	L	R	E
E	F	I	N	I	S	S	E	Z	S
Z	R	É	P	O	N	D	E	N	T

2 **a** 6 comprends; **b** 5 renvoie; **c** 2 désespérons; **d** 1 promettent; **e** 3 redescend

Grammar and Skills Workbook Answers

Present tense of irregular verbs (1) — Workbook page 29

1 a Le week-end, je <u>vais</u> au centre sportif. (aller)
b À la piscine, on <u>fait</u> de la natation. (faire) c On <u>va</u> au café. Tu <u>bois</u> de la limonade? (aller) (boire)
d Mon copain et moi, nous <u>buvons</u> du thé. (boire) e Qu'est-ce que vous <u>faites</u>? (faire) f Nous <u>traduisons</u> une histoire en anglais. (traduire)
g Mes profs <u>disent</u> que j'<u>écris</u> très bien parce que je <u>lis</u> beaucoup de livres. (dire) (écrire) (lire) h Nos voisins <u>construisent</u> une maison. Ils <u>font</u> beaucoup de bruit! (construire) (faire)

2 a lis; b écris, écrivent; c vais; d fait, faisons; e dites; f boit

3 a What are you reading/do you read? b I'm writing my diary and my sisters are writing emails. c In summer I go to the seaside. d When it is very hot, we do nothing. e What are you saying/do you say? f Usually we drink cola.

Present tense of irregular verbs (2) — Workbook page 30

1 a 3; b 5; c 9; d 7; e 10; f 1; g 8; h 2; i 6; j 4

2 a sors; b devient, voit; c part; d savons; e reçoivent

3 Students' own answers.

Modal verbs — Workbook page 31

1 a veux; b doit; c peux; d dois; e peut; f veulent; g voulons; h devez.

t As a follow-up task, ask students to translate the sentences.

2 a Je dois tondre la pelouse. b Je ne dois pas jouer sur mon ordi le soir. c Je peux économiser. d Je ne peux pas sortir avec mes copains. e Je ne veux pas garder mon petit frère.

3 Students' own answers.

Imperative — Workbook page 32

1 a 6; b 3; c 8; d 1; e 9; f 2; g 10; h 7; i 5; j 4

2 c, g, i

3 a Discute de tes problèmes. b Demande à tes parents. c Ne parle pas de ton prof! d Finis tes devoirs dans ta chambre. e Aide tes copains/copines/ami(e)s.

Near future tense — Workbook page 33

1 a On va manger de la pizza. b Ils vont écouter de la musique. c Je ne vais pas faire la vaisselle. d Vous allez nettoyer la salle.

2 a allons; b vas; c vais; d vont; e va; f va; g allez; h vont

3 Students' own answers.

Future tense — Workbook page 34

1 a 1 mangerai; b 2 changera; c 3 réussiras; d 4 dormiront; e 5 attendra; f 6 prendrez

2 **t** a mangerons (We will eat less fast food.) b boira (He won't drink any sugary drinks.) c achèteront (They will buy a large house.) d partirez (When will you go/are you going on holiday?) e travaillerai (I will not work in an office.) f répondras (I hope you will reply to my emails.)

3 **t** a ferons (Next year we will do more sport.) b ira (My teacher will go to school by bike.) c viendront (My grandparents will come to the restaurant.) d verras (You will see your cousins for the first time.) e serez (In 10 years you will be very rich!) f enverrai (I'll send an email every day.)

Perfect tense with *avoir* (1)

Workbook page 35

1 **a** ai; **b** a; **c** as; **d** ont; **e** avons; **f** avez

2 **a** attendu; **b** choisi; **c** écouté; **d** inventé; **e** perdu; **f** préparé; **g** rempli; **h** répondu

3 **t** **a** (Est-ce que) Tu as/Vous avez attendu le prof? **b** Ils ont/On a perdu une bouteille de coca. **c** Nous avons/On a choisi de la musique pour la fête. **d** Lucie a adoré le repas – elle a trouvé le dessert délicieux. **e** J'ai dormi longtemps – Je n'ai rien entendu. **f** Il n'a pas réfléchi et il a envoyé une photo en ligne.

Perfect tense with *avoir* (2)

Workbook page 36

1 **a** 2 eu; **b** 4 écrit; **c** 6 dû; **d** 5 pu; **e** 1 lu; **f** 3 bu

2 **t** **a** Il <u>a bu</u> du coca. (He drank/has drunk some cola.) **b** Qu'est-ce que tu <u>as dit</u>? (What did you say?) **c** Je n'<u>ai</u> rien <u>fait</u>. (I didn't do/haven't done anything.) **d** Nous <u>avons lu</u> des BD. (We (have) read comic books.) **e** Ils <u>ont ouvert</u> les portes. (They (have) opened the doors.) **f** Elle n'a pas <u>pris</u> le train. (She didn't take/hasn't taken the train.)

3 **a** a acheté; **b** n'ai pas compris; **c** a construit; **d** as écrit; **e** avez gagné; **f** n'ont pas mangé; **g** avons mis; **h** ont vu

Perfect tense with *être*

Workbook page 37

1 **a** suis; **b** sommes; **c** sont; **d** es; **e** est; **f** êtes

2 **a** allée; **b** partie; **c** venus; **d** né; **e** devenue; **f** montés

3 Students' own answers.

Perfect tense with *avoir* and *être*

Workbook page 38

1

infinitive	meaning to ...	past participle	avoir/être
attendre	wait (for)	attendu	avoir
boire	drink	bu	avoir
choisir	choose	choisi	avoir
descendre	go down	descendu	être
faire	do, make	fait	avoir
finir	finish	fini	avoir
manger	eat	mangé	avoir
monter	go up	monté	être
naître	be born	né	être
partir	leave	parti	être
payer	pay	payé	avoir
perdre	lose	perdu	avoir
regarder	watch	regardé	avoir
sortir	go out	sorti	être
tomber	fall	tombé	être
venir	come	venu	être

2 **a** suis; **b** sommes; **c** avons; **d** est; **e** a; **f** ai; **g** ont; **h** a; **i** ai; **j** a; **k** ont; **l** ai; **m** est; **n** sont; **o** sommes; **p** ai

3 Students' own answers.

193

Grammar and Skills Workbook Answers

Imperfect tense
Workbook page 39

1 **a** 3 J'<u>étais</u> fan des Rolling Stones. Il y <u>avait</u> un poster sur le mur de ma chambre. **b** 4 Le soir, mes amis et moi, nous <u>écoutions</u> des disques. **c** 1 Les émissions à la télé <u>étaient</u> en noir et blanc. On n'<u>avait</u> pas la télé en couleur. **d** 2 Mon père <u>avait</u> une Renault 4, elle <u>était</u> super! On <u>allait</u> souvent à la mer.

2 **a** avais, jouais; **b** choisissais; **c** était, avions; **d** habitais, attendait **e** étais, pouvais **f** étaient

3 Students' own answers.

depuis
Workbook page 40

1 **a** 2; **b** 4; **c** 6; **d** 3; **e** 1; **f** 5

2 **(t)** **a** I've played/been playing in a football club for three years. **b** My parents have sold/been selling cars for 20 years. **c** They have worked/been working in the suburbs of Dijon for five years. **d** We've lived/been living on a boat since June. **e** For two weeks there have been problems in the town centre. **f** My (girl)friend has been ill since last night/yesterday evening.

3 Students' own answers, e.g.: **a** J'habite [ville] depuis [x ans/mois/semaines/2012]. **b** J'apprends le français depuis [un an/cinq ans/...] **c** Je [le/la] connais / Je connais [nom] depuis [x ans/mois/semaines/2012].

4 **(t)** **a** She had been waiting 30 minutes when the bus arrived. **b** How long had you been working when I phoned? **c** I had been playing online for three hours when my father asked me to stop!

quand and si
Workbook page 41

1 **a** 2; **b** 4; **c** 5; **d** 1; **e** 3

2 **a** pleut / sors (present); **b** vais / aime (present); **c** avais / jouais (imperfect); **d** était / existait (imperfect); **e** irai / regarderai (future); **f** aurai / pourrai (future)

3 **a** Quand je n'ai pas de devoirs, je suis très content. **b** Quand j'avais six ans, je voulais être pilote. **c** Quand j'aurai 18 ans, je partirai en vacances avec mes copains.

4 **a** visiterai; **b** travaillera; **c** resterai; **d** fera

Conditional
Workbook page 42

1 **(t)** **a** 3 I'd like to live on a farm in the country. **b** 6 My dream house would be a villa by the sea. **c** 4 I would buy a nice flat in the centre of Paris. **d** 8 My friends would often visit me. **e** 1 My parents would like to go round the world. **f** 7 Would you have an eco-house built? **g** 2 Yes, it would have all the new technologies. **h** 5 And what would you do?

2 Students' own answers.

Using several tenses together

Workbook page 43

1

infinitive	present	perfect	imperfect	future	conditional
travailler	je travaille	j'ai travaillé	je travaillais	je travaillerai	je travaillerais
choisir	tu choisis	tu as choisi	tu choisissais	tu choisiras	tu choisirais
vendre	il vend	il a vendu	il vendait	il vendra	il vendrait
avoir	elle a	elle a eu	elle avait	elle aura	elle aurait
être	on est	on a été	on était	on sera	on serait
faire	nous faisons	nous avons fait	nous faisions	nous ferons	nous ferions
aller	vous allez	vous êtes allé(e)s	vous alliez	vous irez	vous iriez
pouvoir	ils peuvent	ils ont pu	ils pouvaient	ils pourront	ils pourraient

As a follow-up task, students work in pairs and test each other on the meanings of each form of the verb (e.g. I work, I worked, etc.). They challenge each other to give a different part of the verb (e.g. 'they worked' – *ils ont travaillé*).

2 **a** était; **b** étais; **c** avais; **d** écoutait; **e** as fait; **f** ai travaillé; **g** ai; **h** adore; **i** voudrais; **j** finirai; **k** aurai; **l** serai

3 Students' own answers.

Unit 1: Cultural awareness strategies

Workbook page 44

1–3 Students' own answers.

Unit 1: Motivation strategies

Workbook page 45

1 No answers
2 **a** Algérie; **b** Ile Maurice; **c** Syrie; **d** Maroc
3 On parle français dans un pays francophone. Il y a plus de 150 millions de francophones dans le monde. Ils habitent dans plus de quarante pays sur les cinq continents. Le français est une langue très, très importante car …

Additional challenge: Students' own answers.

Unit 2: Reading strategies

Workbook page 46

1 a, b, c, d
2 Possible cognates include: conservé; territoires; globe; touristes; adorent; située; l'océan Pacifique; températures; humide; maritime; surface équivalente; observer; admirer; les danses; activités; aquatiques; marine; sites de surf
3 Students' own answers.
4 **a** 1888; **b** 40; **c** in the south of France; **d** beaches, flowers and colours

195

Grammar and Skills Workbook Answers

Unit 2: Writing strategies
Workbook page 47

1–6 No answers

Unit 3: Memorisation strategies
Workbook page 48

1–3 No answers
For activity 3, students will need to experiment with online word cloud creators. Try *Word It Out* or *Wordle*, which allow you to experiment with fonts and colours, retain accents on words you paste in and use non-breaking space characters (~ or _) to keep phrases together in the cloud.

Unit 3: Speaking strategies
Workbook page 49

1–3 No answers

Unit 4: Listening strategies
Workbook page 50

1 Students' own answers.

2 Past tense: a, c, d and e; **Present tense**: b. Imperfect tense verbs should be circled.

Unit 4: Cultural awareness strategies
Workbook page 51

1 a another world/a better world; **b** generous and caring/tender-hearted; **c** 1985

2–3 No answers

Unit 5: Checking written work
Workbook page 52

1 a handball – noun masc.; **b** les céréales – noun fem.; **c** peser – verb; **d** condiment à la mangue – noun masc.; **e** campagne – noun (mener une campagne or faire campagne pour ... – verb); **f** grimpeur/grimpeuse – noun masc./fem.

2 Students' own answers.

3 Salut! La semaine dernière, nous sommes allés au restaurant Dans le noir. C'était l'anniversaire de Sophie. Elle a choisi un menu surprise! Nous avons mangé du poulet avec des frites et du gâteau au chocolat. C'était délicieux mais cher, surtout les boissons. Moi, j'ai bu du coca – 5€!! Une petite bouteille d'eau minérale coûte 7€ et un grand café 4.80€. Au revoir, Marc

4 Students' own answers.

Unit 5: Evaluating your performance
Workbook page 53

1–3 Students' own answers.

Unit 6: Cultural awareness strategies
Workbook page 54

1 a formal (vous); **b** formal (Pourriez-vous); **c** informal (tes); **d** informal (Tu vas); **e** formal (Recevez)

2–3 Students' own answers.

Unit 6: Evaluating your and others' performance
Workbook page 55

1–4 Students' own answers.
The work in activity 3 should ideally be completed over two lessons to give students the opportunity to use the strategies mentioned in activity 4 when reviewing their work.

Unit 7: Grammar memorisation strategies
Workbook page 56

1 **Present**: a, b, c; **Imperfect**: f; **Perfect**: d, e

2–3 Students' own answers.

Unit 7: Transcription and identifying language patterns
Workbook page 57

1–3 No answers
4 **a** Possible words ending in -isme include: Office de Tourisme, le cyclisme, le cynisme; **b** Shop names ending in -erie include: boulangerie, pâtisserie, charcuterie, boucherie, librairie. Other words ending in -erie include: buanderie, loterie, gendarmerie

Unit 8: Personalising your work
Workbook page 58

1 **a** la banlieue de Paris; **b** l'eau courante; **c** des matériaux récupérés; **d** l'électricité; **e** je voudrais faire construire; **f** la maison de mes rêves

2–4 No answers
5 Students' own answers.

Unit 8: Translation strategies
Workbook page 59

1 **a** Benin is a country in Africa/an African country and the capital is Porto Novo. **b** In Benin they often eat pasta. **c** Specialities are maize/sweetcorn, cassava and banana balls (or balls made with …) **d** You can buy peanut cakes and spicy cheese at the market. **e** A dugout/canoe full of merchandise/goods is used as a shop.
2 Hi! I'm thirteen and my name is Djimon. I live in Benin in Africa, on the river at Ganvié, 20 kilometres from Cotonou. I've lived there for eleven years. My Dad has often told me that Benin is the Venice of Africa/Africa's Venice! Ganvié is a traditional fishing village. We eat fish nearly every day. More than 80% of the houses are built on piles/stilts. We don't have any privacy, but I am happy. Fortunately for our family, my grandparents live here and we have two dugouts/canoes. The dugout/canoe is the only means of transport in our village. The house of my dreams? If I had a well-paid job later on, I would like to buy a wooden house for my family.
3 Students' own answers.
Activity 3 asks students to create a 'freeze frame' – a tableau with their bodies – in groups. The action in their scene(s) about life in Benin should be frozen to make a still image; other groups describe in French what the image illustrates.

Unit 9: Motivation strategies
Workbook page 60

1 No answers
2 Students' own answers.

Unit 9: Speaking strategies
Workbook page 61

1–3 No answers

Grammar and Skills Workbook Answers

Transcription strategies
Workbook page 62

1–4 (t) Students' own answers.
For activity 4, students will need access to the audio file for activity 1 on page 8 of the Student Book (on famous French people). This activity could be completed in a computer room to allow students to choose when to start and stop the audio, or at home if they have access to Kerboodle or a VLE.

Translation strategies
Workbook page 63

1 **a** apparaître/disparaître; **b** heureusement/malheureusement; **c** populaire/impopulaire; **d** la patience/l'impatience

2 Nouns: d; Adjectives: c; Verbs: a; Adverbs: b

3 (t) Angélique Kidjo was born in Benin in the economic/financial capital, Cotonou, but today she lives in New York. Benin is a country in West Africa, situated between Togo and Nigeria. The capital is Porto Novo and French is the official language. Angélique speaks Fon, French, Yoruba, Mina and English fluently. She sings in these five languages. One song, *Malaika,* from the album *Logozo,* is in Swahili. Her musical influences are African pop, the music of the Caribbean, zouk, Congolese rumba, jazz, gospel and different styles of Latin music. She is famous in Africa and throughout the whole world. She is a singer but also a dynamic and devoted champion of the poor. She sang in Berlin at the G8 concert.

4 (t) **a** Quand j'aurai dix-huit ans, je voudrais voyager. **b** Pour être vétérinaire, il est très important d'aimer les animaux. **c** Ma mère est professeur. Elle travaille dans un grand collège et elle aime aider les gens.